ART APPRECIATION
AN INTRODUCTION TO THE FORMAL ELEMENTS AND MEDIUMS

FIRST EDITION

BY DAVE PLOUFFE

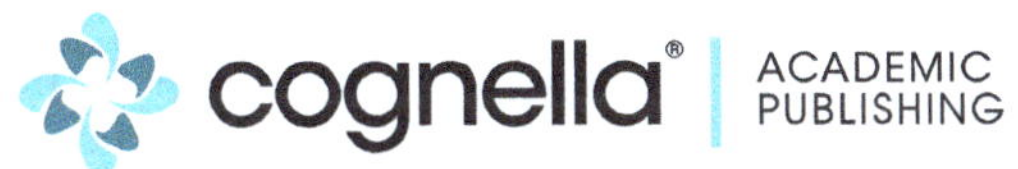

cognella® | ACADEMIC PUBLISHING

Bassim Hamadeh, CEO and Publisher
Kassie Graves, Director of Acquisitions and Sales
Jamie Giganti, Senior Managing Editor
Miguel Macias, Graphic Designer/Senior Graphic Designer
Bob Farrell, Acquisitions Editor
Gem Rabanera, Project Editor
Alexa Lucido, Licensing Specialist
Berenice Quirino, Associate Production Editor
Chris Snipes, Interior Designer

ISBN: 978-1-63487-937-8 (pbk) / 978-1-63487-938-5 (br)

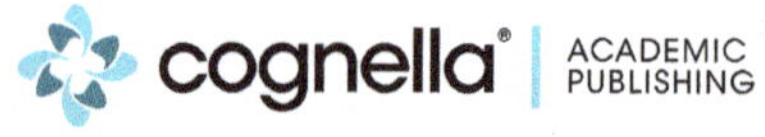

CONTENTS

INTRODUCTION

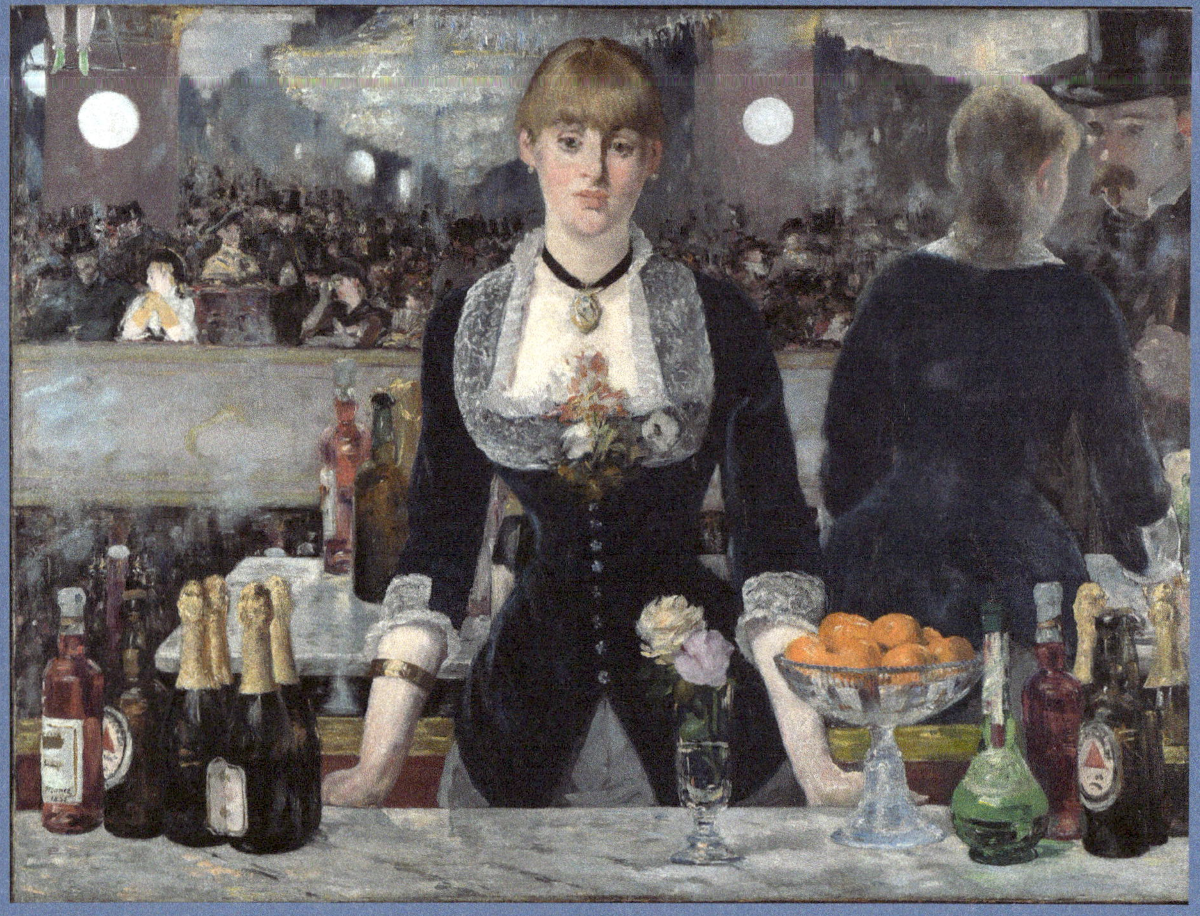

Figure 1.1: Édouard Manet, *A Bar at the Folies-Bergère*, 1881–82. Oil on Canvas, 37.8 in × 51.2 in, Courtauld Institute of Art, London.

AN INTRODUCTION TO ART

CHAPTER 1

WHAT IS ART?

WELCOME TO THE STUDY OF ART!

But, what exactly is … *art*? How does one go about defining that term? Most of us have not spent much time thinking about its definition. After all, it is only a three-letter word and somewhat difficult to misspell. It is a word we all know and use, yet it is a very deceiving word. Take a moment and think about keywords that could be used to build a definition that would explain what art is to someone who has never experienced it before. Among the first words that usually comes to mind is *expressive*. Yes, art is definitely expressive. How about *communication*? Much of the art that has been produced over the past centuries involves some sort of narrative; it tells a story. Other words quickly start coming to mind: *passion, beauty, ugliness, intellect, radical, unique, creative, confusing, religious, political, fun, symbolic, subjective, emotional, propaganda*, and the list continues from there. But when we take a look back at those 17 words, we can see how diverse they are, and that all of them can be used to define that three-letter word … *art*.

Art is a boundless term. It truly escapes definition and means different things to different people. What I consider to be art may not be what you consider to be art. Not only does the meaning vary from person to person, but also from culture to culture and from generation to generation. Each person looks at and interacts with art differently.

This is what makes the study of art so enjoyable and interesting. Art is amorphous, shapeless, and nebulous. You can think of it as a gray cloud with indistinct edges. Just when we are able to put a definition to it the cloud changes; it transforms, it develops, and it evolves into something different. Consider the art produced during the Renaissance, which includes those famous works that we all know about, such as Leonardo da Vinci's *Last Supper* (see fig 22.8) and the *Statue of David* by Michelangelo (see fig 22.7). That art is very different from the art produced during the modern era (chapter 23). This is because the definition and meaning of art changed. Art will continue to evolve. It will be different 50 or even 100 years from now. The definition you create today will most likely be altered by the end of the semester. The important thing to remember is that *you* get to decide what is or what is not art.

APPROACHING THE TEXT

This book is *not* a chronological survey of the history of art. That can be found in boundless other tomes of varying complexity. Instead, the intention of this book is to serve as a starting point for someone as they enter the study of art. It is geared for the person with little or no experience with this topic. It is meant to serve as a stepping-stone into a new and exciting world.

The first two sections of the text (chapters 2 through 11) introduces you to the formal elements of art. These include topics such as line, space, and color. They are the building blocks that artists utilize when they construct their works, as well as the terms viewers would use to dissect and talk about artworks. These chapters are heavy on vocabulary so that the learner can gain the language needed to feel more comfortable talking about the subject. It provides a basis or starting point from which to learn about the subject.

The third section of the text (chapters 12 through 20) explores the different media and processes that artists use in the creation of their art forms. Here we look at mediums such as drawing, painting, sculpture, and photography. We can see the advantages and disadvantages, even the struggles, that artists might have within a particular medium.

The last four chapters stand alone and focus on subjects of particular interest to students of art. The Italian Renaissance is a very comfortable period to study, as we are already familiar with many of the artists emerging from that era, such as Leonardo da Vinci and Michelangelo. Even today the cities of Florence and Rome remain popular destinations for the world traveler to see the incredible works of art that emerged from this 300-year time span. In the chapter on modern art we see how the avant-garde artists took art in a totally different direction, breaking from the traditions that were established during the Renaissance. The chapter on design styles makes one take notice of the stylistic influences that affected artistic output during the nineteenth and twentieth centuries.

The final chapter deals with the singular artist, Vincent van Gogh. This artist and his works, more than any other artist in this book, seem to resonate with students across their varied backgrounds. However, the average person knows little about him except for the fact that he severed his ear. His story is worthy of being told.

Each chapter contains a study guide, which could include vocabulary words as well as artistic concepts. The vocabulary words are in bold throughout the text and are defined in the glossary found at the back of the book. Although it is nice to memorize definitions, a definition becomes useless if an individual cannot apply the term to the context in which it is presented. For example, one might be able to perfectly recite a definition of symmetrical balance (chapter 9), but without being able to look at a specific artwork and explain whether that work in in symmetrical balance is paramount in terms of importance. Therefore, many examples of the terms are used throughout the book.

Many of the chapters also contain projects. The goals of these projects are to keep students engaged with the material being presented and to help them master the concepts. People can read all they want about art, but until they actually take part themselves, they cannot be fully invested in the process of learning about the subject. Creating an artwork, no matter how minor or insignificant it may be, changes the way an individual thinks about the subject.

HELPFUL HINTS

The study of art is probably new and unfamiliar to most of you reading this book. The study of art is much different than the study of math or science. In those subjects, there are strict formulas and rules to follow. They lead you along a specific pathway or through a set of instructions in order to reach a singular correct answer. Art has few formulas and rules. We occasionally see them in certain aspects of art, such as in linear perspective, which is a mathematical formula, but in art we may reach a conclusion where no answer is correct or perhaps several conclusions can be decided upon.

A couple of basic things need to be kept in mind when talking or writing about art. First, artists are referred to by either their full name or by their last name. As an example, you would refer to Pablo Picasso by his full name or as Picasso. It would be awkward to hear him referred to as Pablo.

Next, when talking about a specific art object you can refer to it either as an *artwork* (one word, not two) or you can use the term *work of art*. Never call it a *piece of art* or a *piece of work*. Think about how a piece of pie denotes a fraction or fragment; the last thing we want is a fragmented or broken artwork.

When writing about an artwork the title should always be italicized. You will notice throughout this text that anytime a painting or sculpture is mentioned the name is italicized as it is here in chapter 1 with *A Bar at the Folies-Bergère* (**fig 1.1**). The only exception to this rule is architecture: we do not italicize the titles of buildings.

One final note, when looking at the illustrations positioned throughout the chapters you will find that some of their dimensions are using English units while others are listed in metric. The reason for this is the information provided by the institutions that hold that particular work. If the work was found in an American museum then the dimensions are listed in inches or feet. Artworks held by foreign museums are listed in centimeters or meters. These units were not converted in order to maintain the best accuracy to the size of the artwork.

IMAGE CREDIT

- Fig. 1.1: Édouard Manet, "A Bar at the Folies-Bergère," https://commons.wikimedia.org/wiki/File:Edouard_Manet,_A_Bar_at_the_Folies-Bergère.jpg. Copyright in the Public Domain.

SYLLABUS ACKNOWLEDGMENT

Student name (printed legibly): ____

I have downloaded and read the course syllabus................................Initials ___________________

I understand the final exam is on ________________ at _________ am/pm….Initials ___________________

____

IN-CLASS ASSIGNMENT

Definition: Define the term *art* using keywords rather than formal sentences.

Description: Write a paragraph about *A Bar at Folies-Bergère* by Édouard Manet (fig 1.1).

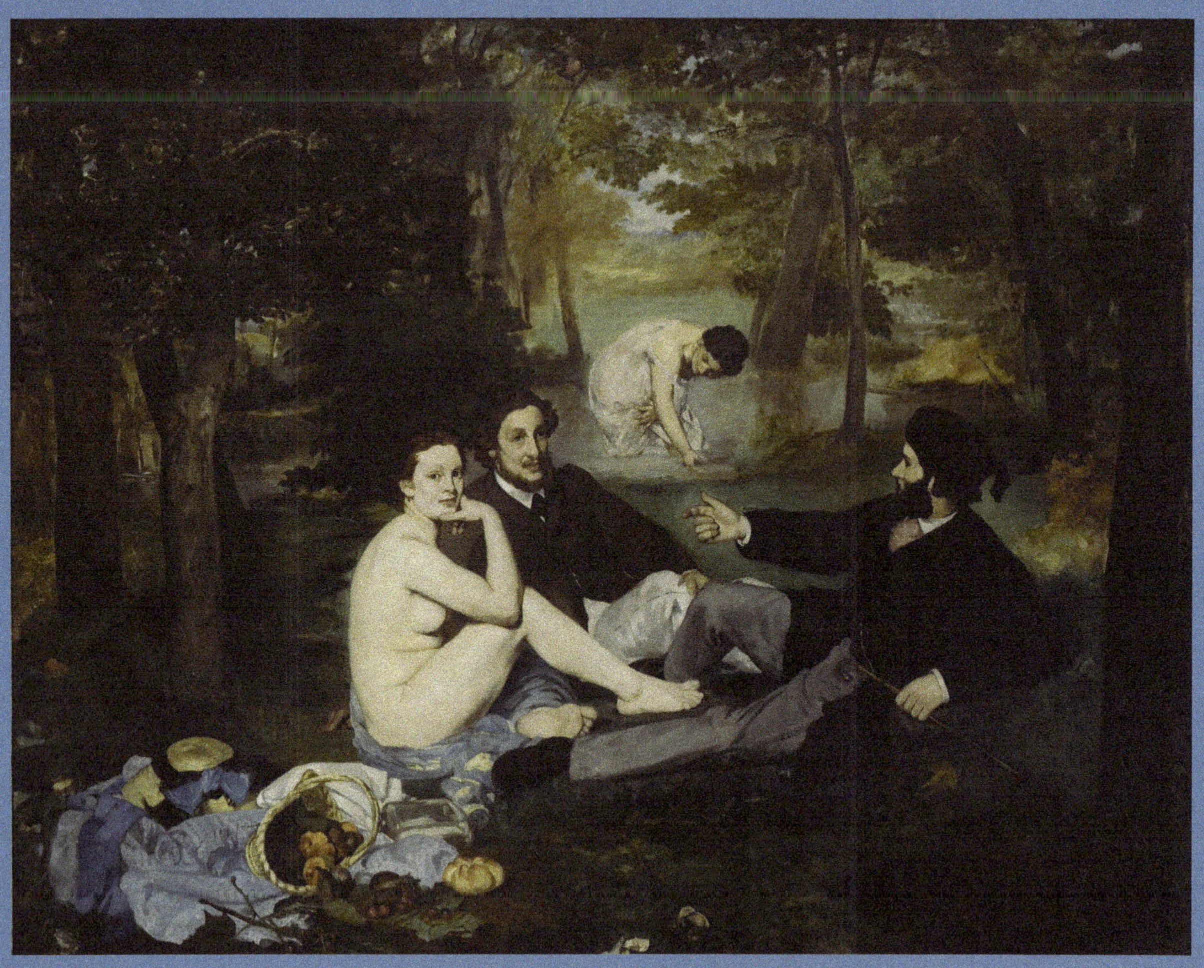

Figure 2.1: Édouard Manet, *Le Déjeuner sur l'herbe (Luncheon on the Grass)*, 1863. Oil on Canvas 81.9 in × 104.1 in, Musée d' Orsey, Paris.

ART IN THE PUBLIC SPHERE

ART IN THE PUBLIC SPHERE

The creation of art is very unique. Its genesis is personal and private, as it emerges from the artist's mind, hands, and soul. Yet it is the public that gets to serve as its judge and jury. Sometimes it even serves as its executioner.[1] Artists, especially contemporary artists, have little or no say regarding their own work when it is put out on display. When have we ever heard of an artist getting the opportunity to explain the meaning of his or her work or justify its existence? That job seems to land in the hands of the art critique or the public in general.

Art placed on public display tends to garner the harshest criticism. When has anyone said anything complimentary about an artwork placed in a public arena? Perhaps never. Although there will be no lack of people offering their opinion on the artwork, most likely it will be negative—that the work somehow purposely intruded into their lives and offended them or the artwork's aesthetic fell somewhat short of pleasing.

Public criticism of artwork is not a new issue. Debates about artworks have been around for hundreds of years, but they seem to be especially heightened since the advent of the modern era. All of a sudden people were seeing artworks that many argued had less and less artistic "talent" behind them. Subject matter was disappearing, and in its place were swatches of paint that had no meaning and that failed to communicate. To add to the public's frustration, the price tags of these works seemed incomprehensible. Why was someone paying so much for an artwork that looked like a child could create it?

ÉDOUARD MANET AND THE FRENCH SALONS

In Europe, during the eighteenth and nineteenth centuries, it was the Académie des Beaux-Arts in France that set the standards for artists to follow. Instruction took place through the École des Beaux-Arts, which, in turn, held annual exhibits called **Salons**. At the Salons the students were able to showcase their art once it met with the approval of the jury. The jury, made up of accomplished artists, made sure the artwork exhibited in the Salon adhered with their strict academic rules. Salons were very competitive, and artworks were regularly rejected.

The most notable work to be rejected from the Salon was Édouard Manet's *Le Déjeuner sur l'herbe*, more commonly known in America as *Luncheon on the Grass* (**fig 2.1**). Today, many art historians consider this painting to be the very first work of "modern art" and one of the two most important paintings of the modern era.[2] Because of this painting Édouard Manet is looked upon as the father of modern art.

By today's standards *Luncheon on the Grass* does not look shocking in the least, but when the painting was unveiled in 1863 it was considered to be scandalous! There were several reasons for this.

The first thing people usually point out is the nude female figure in the company of two dressed males. This was not the issue they were complaining about. Consider the large number of paintings of nude females throughout history, many painted under

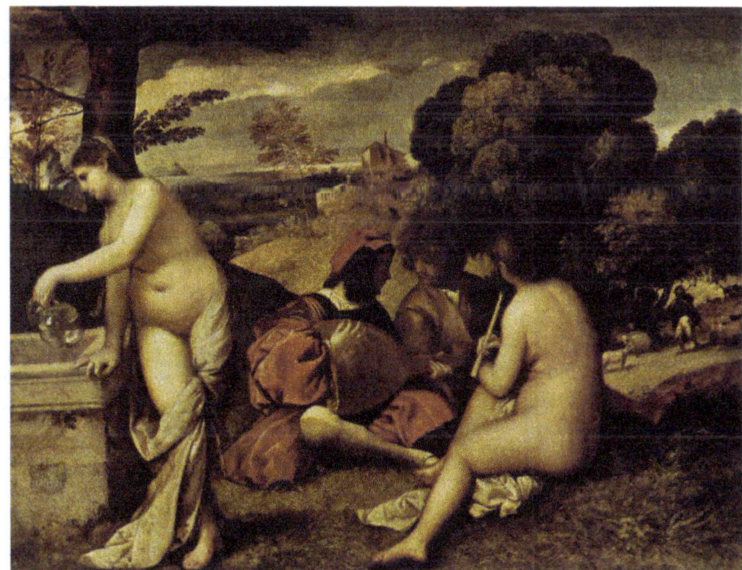

Figure 2.2: Giorgione, *Pastoral Concert*, c. 1508–09. Oil on Canvas, 43.3 in × 54.3 in, *Musée du Louvre*, Paris.

the guise of some type of goddess, such as Venus. Among the inspirations for Manet's painting was *Pastoral Concert* by Giorgione (**fig 2.2**). Giorgione's work has two nude females presented with two dressed males, some of whom are playing musical instruments. Manet would have seen this painting in the Louvre while he was a student. He also would have been familiar with Marcantonio Raimondi's engraving of the *Judgment of Paris* (**fig 2.3**), where the figures in the lower-right-hand

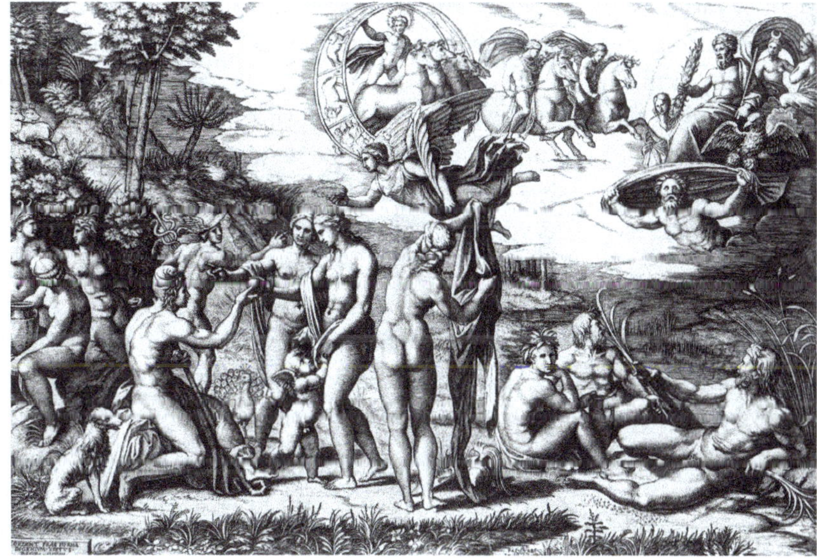

Figure 2.3: Marcantonio Raimondi (engraving after a drawing by Raphael), *Judgment of Paris*, c. 1515–16, Copper Engraving, 29.1 cm × 43.7 cm, *Staatsgalerie*, Stuttgart.

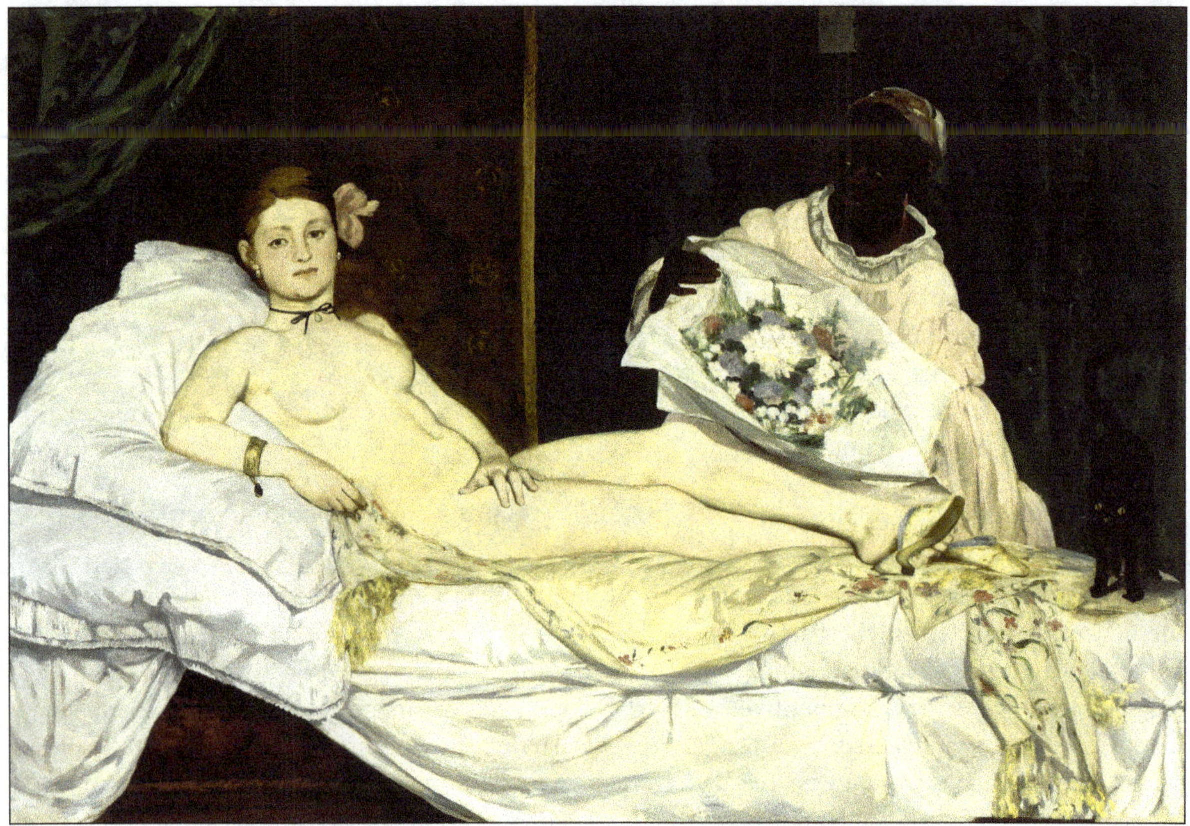

Figure 2.4: Édouard Manet, *Olympia*, 1863.
Oil on Canvas 51.2 in × 74.8 in, *Musée d'Orsey*, Paris.

corner of the image match those Manet positioned in *Luncheon on the Grass*. The real issue with the nude figure is that Manet painted her poorly, rather stark in color. The semitones are gone, making her look more two-dimensional than sculptural.[3]

Not only is the female flattened, but the entire scene seems to be presented to us in just that way. What Manet has done was to disregard the rules of linear perspective! As you will learn in chapter 5, linear perspective is the most effective way of creating a three-dimensional scene on a two-dimensional surface. When it was codified during the Middle Renaissance, it became the gold standard that artists had to learn and apply to their works in order to be considered a successful and viable artist.

There is also a disassociation between the background and the foreground. Do they belong together? Are they part of the same scene or narrative? Is the woman wading in the water part of the group we see in the foreground?

Although they are not visible in the picture presented in the text, if you were to see *Luncheon in the Grass* in person you would be able to see visible brushstrokes on the canvas. This would not have been allowed at the time. Artists would have been taught to blend the brushstrokes into one another, rendering them invisible, and giving the painting a more polished look.

Finally, the painting itself is gigantic, measuring roughly seven feet by eight feet. During the mid-1860s there were certain rules regarding the size of a painting in relation to its subject matter. The size of Manet's painting would have been held exclusively for paintings with historical or religious subject matter, but instead Manet presents us with a genre scene, a scene from everyday life.

Manet presented *Luncheon on the Grass* to the jury of the Salon of 1863, and it was swiftly rejected. However, the 1863 Salon was unique in that there were roughly 3,000 works of art that were rejected, quite a few by any standard.[4] Napoleon III was the Emperor of France during this time, and he authorized a Salon des Refusés, a Salon of the rejected or refused. Here the public could judge for itself what was good art, and what was bad. This is where *Luncheon on the Grass* was hung in May of 1863.

This was not the only time that Manet would be considered a controversial painter. Two years later in the Salon of 1865 he would exhibit his painting *Olympia* (**fig 2.4**). This time his painting would be hung in the Salon proper. The painting depicts a prostitute reclining on a daybed as her maidservant is seen delivering a bouquet of flowers to her. With this painting Manet is again referencing a classic painting. This time the image he is recycling is the *Venus of Urbino* (**fig 2.5**) by the Venetian artist Titian. Titian's painting also references a prostitute, a courtesan, but hides her true identity under the mask of a mythological goddess.[5]

The paintings make a good comparison set side by side. Not only are the figures posed similarly, but the actual sizes of the paintings are extremely similar to one another. The most striking difference between the paintings is the gaze of the female. In the *Venus of Urbino*, the viewer of the artwork is in the dominant position as he or she looks down upon the figure's body. She tries to return the viewer's gaze in a somewhat coy manner. The scene is juxtaposed in *Olympia*, where the prostitute, rather than the viewer, is placed the dominant role. She is now looking down upon us in a very direct fashion.

This painting, too, caused a flurry of public outrage; "Women became hysterical when they saw this painting and men threatened to attack it with their walking sticks."[6] A constable was posted nearby the painting in order to preserve order.[7]

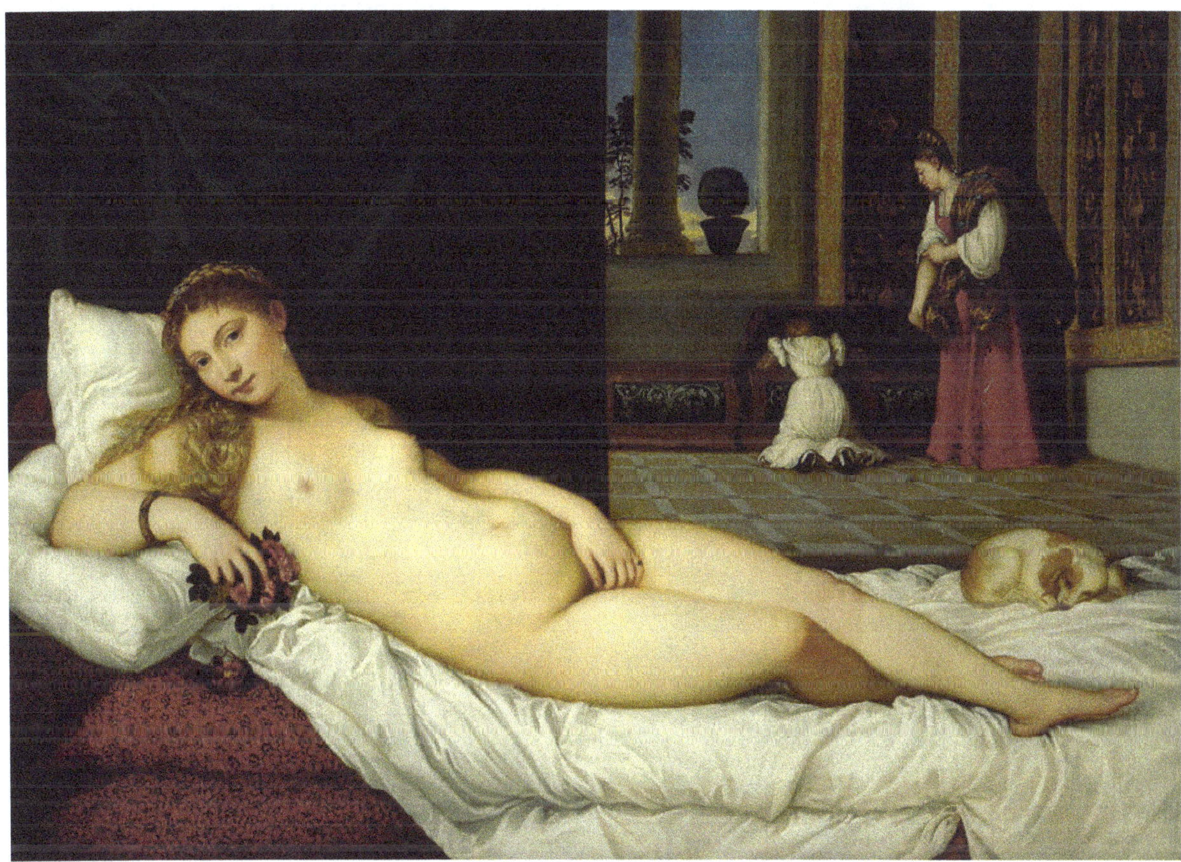

Figure 2.5: Titian, *Venus of Urbino*, 1538.
Oil on Canvas, 46.9 in × 65 in, Uffizi Gallery, Florence.

In 1913 the famous **Armory Show** was held in New York City. The official title of the exhibition was the International Exhibition of Modern Art. It was the first time American artists interfaced directly with the modern art movements of

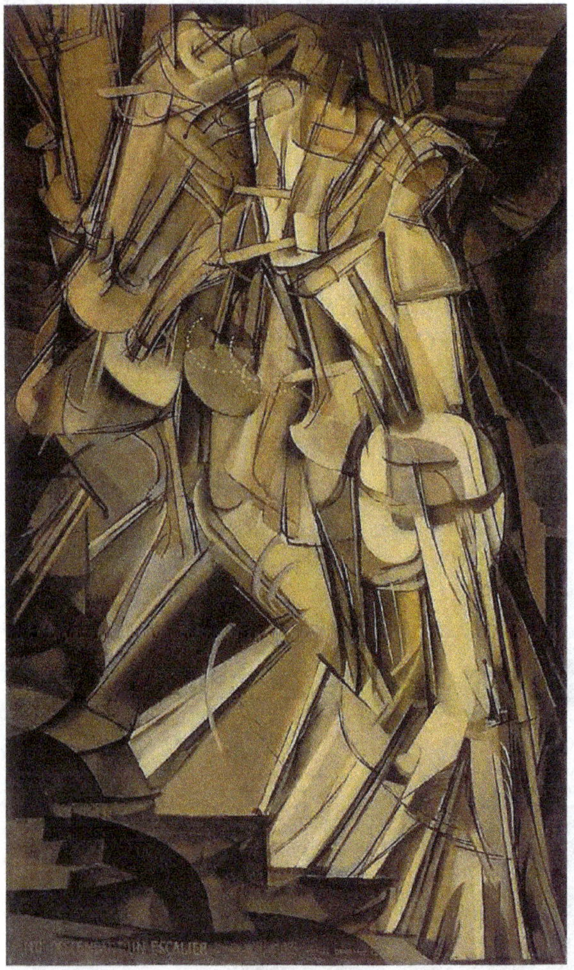

Figure 2.6: Marcel Duchamp, *Nude Descending a Staircase, No. 2*, 1912.
Oil on Canvas, 58 in × 35 in, Philadelphia Museum of Art.

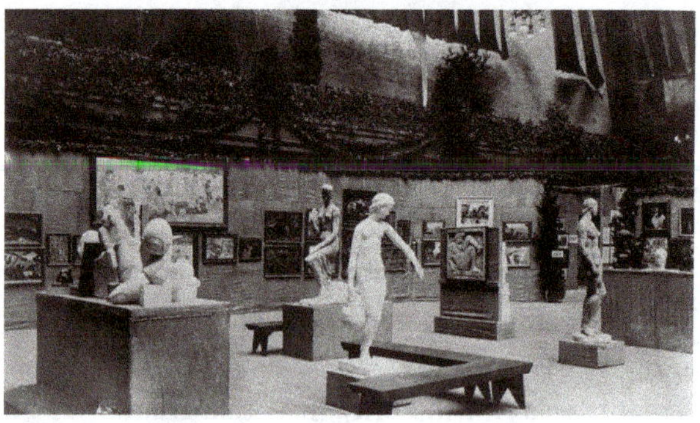

Figure 2.7: Armory Show, 1913, New York City.

Europe. While these avant-garde movements were developing in Europe, Americans were painting relatively the same way they had been for the past hundred years. When they experienced modern art, specifically abstraction, for the first time, they did not understand or know how to interpret it.

The most infamous work of the show was Marcel Duchamp's *Nude Descending a Staircase, No. 2* (**fig 2.6**). In this painting a very abstracted figure, almost to the point of not being able to ascertain the figure as human, moves diagonally from the upper left to the lower right. The figure is superimposed upon itself, giving it the illusion of movement.[8] Teddy Roosevelt saw the painting and said that "The painting reminded him of a Navajo blanket."[9] Another critique "likened [this painting] to an explosion in a shingle factory."[10] Many cartoons came out making fun of this new style of art. One depicted a child holding his father's hand in front of *Nude Descending a Staircase, No. 2* and with the other hand the child pointed toward the painting. The caption read, "Papa, buy me that puzzle."

NATIONAL ENDOWMENT FOR THE ARTS

The **National Endowment for the Arts (NEA)** was established by an act of Congress in 1965,[11] with a focus on the creation of art in public spaces. The NEA currently has three goals. The first goal is to "Support the Creation of Art that Meets the Highest Standards of Excellence." The second is to "Foster Public Engagement with Diverse and Excellent Art." And the third is to "Promote Public Knowledge and Understanding about the Contributions of the Arts."[12]

The very first work commissioned by this new program was Alexander Calder's *La Grand Vitesse* (**fig 2.8**), a 42-ton metal structure, which resembles something like the form of an insect.[13] It reaches 43 feet in height, is painted bright red, and is put together by nuts and bolts that are plainly visible. The sculpture looks unfinished and raw, as if some grand building project had been started but then abandoned.

When the plan for the sculpture was first unveiled to the public they hated it, not unlike how people despised the Eiffel Tower when it was first constructed (chapter 19). Some referred to Calder's sculpture as a "piece of junk."[14] But today, nearly 50 years after its creation, it is embraced by the city of Grand Rapids, Michigan. It is the "place to meet" at the plaza and it adorns much of the city's souvenir mugs and key chains.

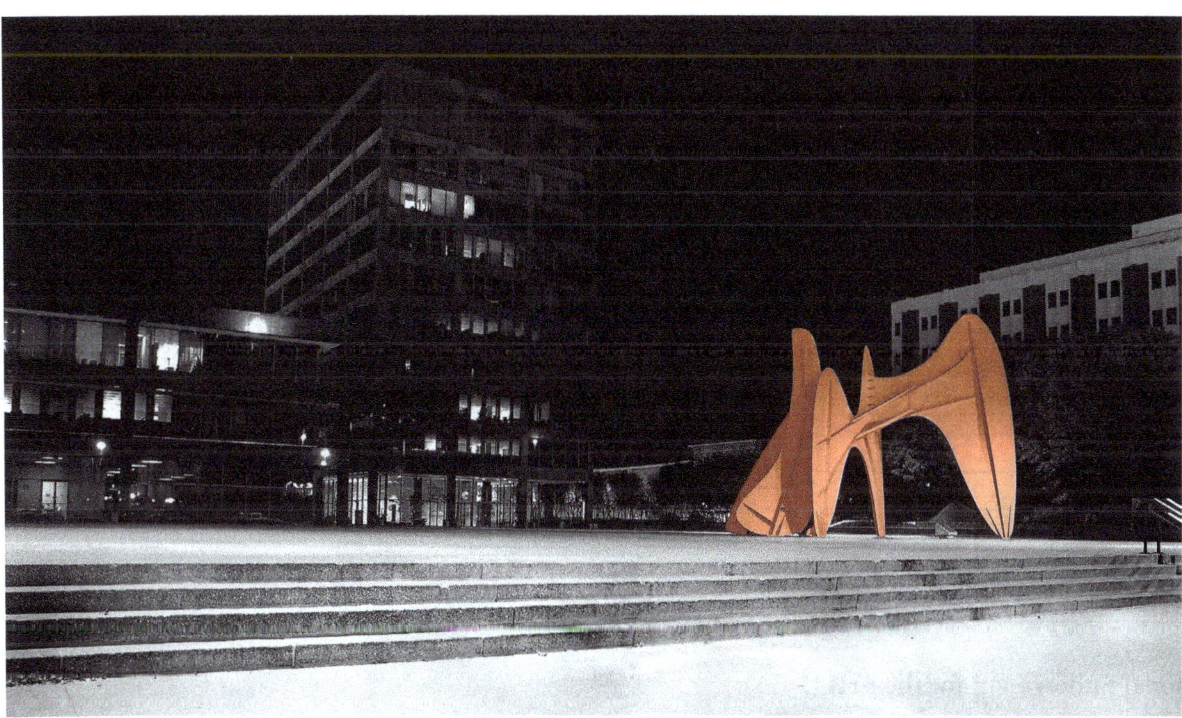

Figure 2.8: Alexander Calder, *La Grand Vitesse*, 1969.
Painted Steel, height 43 ft, Calder Plaza, Grand Rapids, Michigan.

Art in the Public Sphere:

Salon:

Armory Show:

National Endowment for the Arts (NEA):

PROJECT: STREET ART

Goal

Street art is one of the newest and most exciting segments of the contemporary art world. It is also extremely controversial, and there is much debate surrounding this form of art. This assignment will allow you to create your own street art persona.

Assignment

View the documentary film *Exit Through the Gift Shop*. The film will introduce you to several street artists, such as Shepard Fairey, Mr. Brainwash, Monsieur André, and Space Invader. Now, go and create your own street art persona!

1. Give yourself a name, such as when Thierry Guetta became "Mr. Brainwash."
2. Define your goals and intentions as a street artist. What is it you want to accomplish?
3. What message does your work contain?
4. Where is your street art going to be placed so people will see it?
5. What medium are you going to use? What size is it ideally going to be?

Develop your ideas and write an essay explaining the five points above.
Create a work of street art! ON PAPER! Attach it to your essay.

Essay Format

- Upper-left-hand corner of the paper should have (single-spaced):
    Your name
    Days and time of class
    Project number
- Skip two lines and begin your paper. *Do not* give your paper a title.
- One page (20–23 lines of text)
- Typed
- Double-spaced (Format —> Paragraph —> Spacing —> Double—> Click OK)
- 1" margins (Format —> Document —> Change Margins —> Click OK)
- Use Times or Times New Roman
- 10-point font
- Don't forget to proofread your paper! Grammar does count!

Art Format

- Complete your work on a standard 8.5" × 11" sheet of paper. Do not deviate from this.
- The medium is up to you, but pencil (or colored pencil) is preferred.
- I am sorry, but no computer-generated artwork is acceptable.
- Do the artwork on a separate piece of paper. Do not complete it on the same paper as your essay.

Packet

Essay
Attach a sample of your street art

Point value: ___________________
Due date: ___________________

ENDNOTES

1. Such was the case for Richard Serra's *Tilted Arc* (1981). The work was dismantled in 1989 and later destroyed.
2. The other painting considered extremely important to modern art is Picasso's *Les Demoiselles d'Avignon*, which is discussed in chapter 3.
3. Ross King lecturing on his book, *The Judgment of Paris*, at Cody's Bookstore in Berkeley, California, accessed November 29, 2016, http://library.fora.tv/2007/01/14/Ross_King.
4. Ingo F. Walther, ed., *Masterpieces of Western Art* (Köln, Germany: Taschen, 2002), 491.
5. Ingo F. Walther, ed., *Masterpieces of Western Art* (Köln, Germany: Taschen, 2002), 176.
6. Ross King lecturing on his book, *The Judgment of Paris*, at Cody's Bookstore in Berkeley, California, accessed November 29, 2016, http://library.fora.tv/2007/01/14/Ross_King.
7. Ross King lecturing on his book, *The Judgment of Paris*, at Cody's Bookstore in Berkeley California, accessed November 29, 2016, http://library.fora.tv/2007/01/14/Ross_King.
8. The Futurism art movement (1909–1914) frequently used superimposed figures to show movement.
9. Henry Sayre, *A World of Art*, 5th ed. (Boston: Prentice Hall, 2006), 60.
10. H. H. Arnason and Elizabeth Mansfield, *History of Modern Art*, 7th ed. (Upper Saddle River, NJ: Pearson Education, 2013), 350.
11. National Endowment for the Arts website, accessed November 27, 2016, https://www.arts.gov.
12. National Endowment for the Arts, "Strategic Plan, FY 2014–18, Feb 2014," p. 9. Available at the https://www.arts.gov.
13. Associated Press, "Michigan Sculpture Marks 25th," *Las Vegas Review (Journal)*, June 4, 1994.
14. Associated Press, "Michigan Sculpture Marks 25th," *Las Vegas Review (Journal)*, June 4, 1994.

IMAGE CREDITS

- Fig. 2.1: Édouard Manet, "Le Déjeuner sur l'herbe (Luncheon on the Grass)," https://commons.wikimedia.org/wiki/File:Edouard_Manet_-_Luncheon_on_the_Grass_-_Google_Art_Project.jpg. Copyright in the Public Domain.
- Fig. 2.2: Giorgione, "Pastoral Concert," https://commons.wikimedia.org/wiki/File:Giorgione,_Pastoral_Concert_01.jpg. Copyright in the Public Domain.
- Fig. 2.3: Marcantonio Raimondi and Raphael, "Judgment of Paris," https://commons.wikimedia.org/wiki/File:Urteil_des_Paris.jpg. Copyright in the Public Domain.
- Fig. 2.4: Édouard Manet, "Olympia," https://commons.wikimedia.org/wiki/File:Edouard_Manet_-_Olympia_-_Google_Art_Project_3.jpg. Copyright in the Public Domain.
- Fig. 2.5: Titian, "Venus of Urbino," https://commons.wikimedia.org/wiki/File:Venus_urbino.jpg. Copyright in the Public Domain.
- Fig. 2.6: Marcel Duchamp, "Nude Descending a Staircase, No. 2," https://en.wikipedia.org/wiki/File:Duchamp_-_Nude_Descending_a_Staircase.jpg. Copyright in the Public Domain.
- Fig. 2.7: Percy Rainford, "Armory Show Photograph," https://commons.wikimedia.org/wiki/File:Armory_Show_2.jpg. Copyright in the Public Domain.
- Fig. 2.8: Copyright © Alexander Calder; Photo by Brad Gillette (CC by 2.0) at https://commons.wikimedia.org/wiki/File:Alexander_Calders_"La_Grande_Vitesse".jpg.

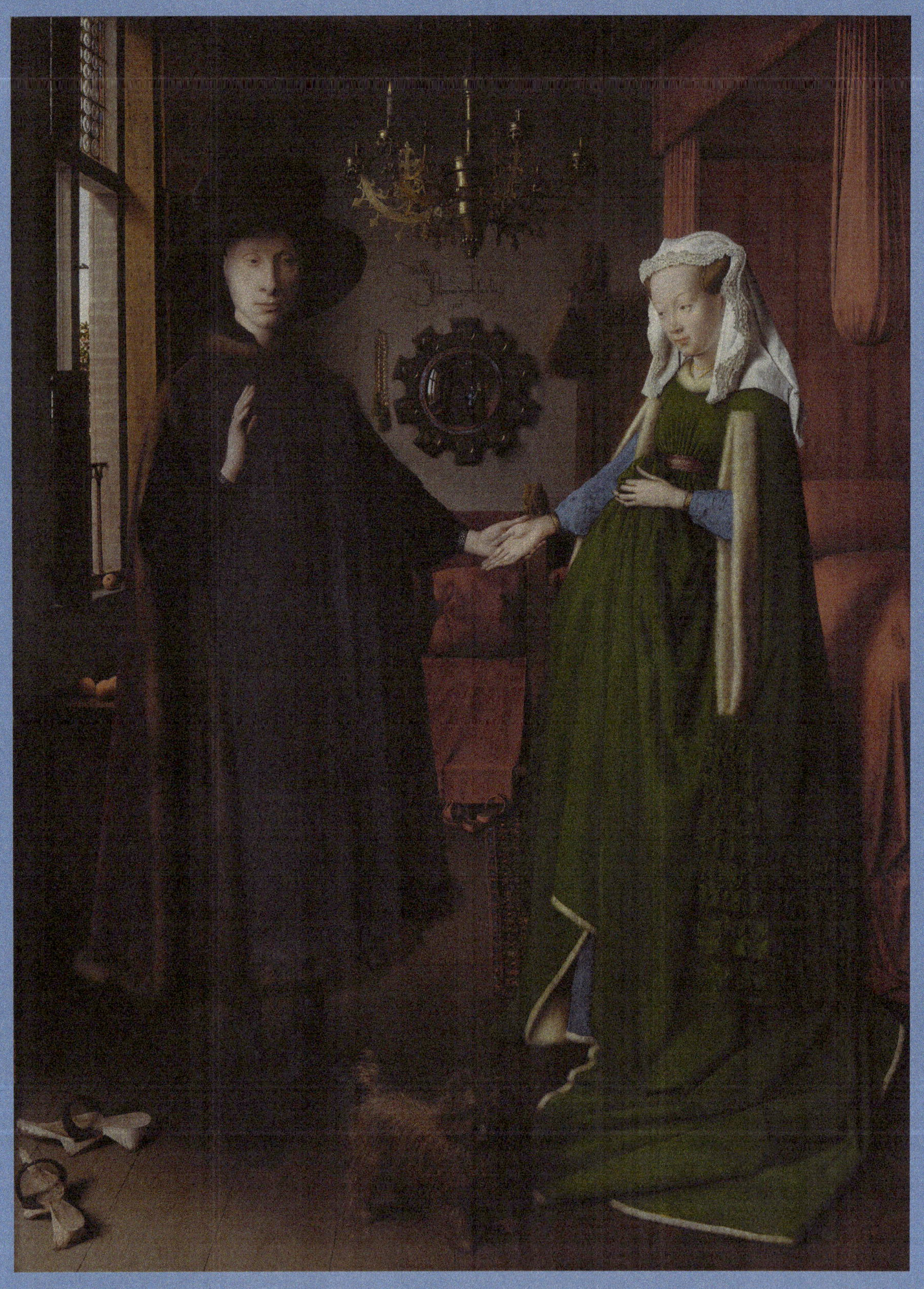

Figure 3.1: Jan van Eyck, *The Arnolfini Portrait*, 1434. Oil on canvas, 32.3 in × 23.4 in, National Gallery of Art, London.

THE LANGUAGE OF ART

CHAPTER

3

THE LANGUAGE OF ART

Throughout history art has been used as a communication tool or device. The artist, through the mediums of drawing, painting, photography, and sculpture, as well as others, seeks to transfer a message to future viewers of the artwork. As the viewer, we examine the artwork and translate its meaning. Sometimes this translation is a simple one and we can read the artwork with a simple glance, as in Giotto's *Last Judgment* (see fig 22.4). At other times the meaning is much more difficult to translate, as in Duchamp's *Fountain* (see fig 23.6). An artwork such as this could leave us perplexed or feeling inferior because we do not "understand" the work. We then criticize the work—questioning whether it is art or not—because of its poor ability to communicate.

In order to help the viewer interpret the meaning of a work of art we are going to delve into the different ways that art can be classified. Art falls into one of three categories: representational, abstract, or nonobjective.

REPRESENTATIONAL ART

Throughout most of history artists were tasked with creating **representational art**. This means that the objects within the artwork, in the case of painting and photography, or the artwork itself, as in the case of sculpture, resemble the objects as they are found in nature. Up until the invention of photography in 1839, one of most important jobs of artists was to document the world around them. Artists were creating imprints of nature. Whatever object they painted needed to appear natural in every capacity.

The Arnolfini Portrait (**fig 3.1**) by Jan van Eyck is an example of representational art. Looking at the painting one can immediately recognize the components; from the well-dressed individuals returning our gaze to the subtle details of the room, such as the wooden carving on the bedpost or the Passions of Christ depicted around the mirror on the back wall. We can even identify the breed of dog in the foreground, an Affenpinscher. Nothing in the painting looks distorted or confusing, and it appears we could step right into this scene and interact with the characters.

ABSTRACT ART

Abstract art has less of a resemblance to the real world than representational art does. We are still going to be able to recognize the objects presented to us, but they are not going to appear as they do in nature. The artist's intentions here are not to replicate the object. Instead, the focus is on creating the geometric equivalents of organic forms. For example, a person's torso might be represented as a rectangle and the face represented as a circle, oval, or square. An important point in identifying an abstract work is that "abstraction MUST be derived from something."[1]

There are also expressive aspects to consider when dealing with abstraction. An artist might use unnatural colors that will either mute or enhance the visual impact of the artwork. In many of the Cubist works created during the early twentieth century, the colors tend to be very dark and drab, even monochromatic. In contrast, in the German Expressionist works of the same time period the colors are eye-catching, such as seen in the paintings of Franz Marc.

One of the reasons that abstraction is so difficult to define, or at least the reason it is so complex, is that its application can vary widely between artists. An abstract painting by Pablo Picasso is going to have a different level or intensity than an abstract work painted by Marcel Duchamp (see fig 2.6).

Consider the definition of abstraction listed above when looking at *Les Demoiselles d'Avignon*

(**fig 3.2**) by Pablo Picasso. Completed in 1907, this remains one of the two most important works of the modern art era.[2] It was a painting unlike anyone had seen before. The title itself translates to *The Young Women of Avignon*, referring to a street in the red light district of Barcelona.[3] The women in this painting are prostitutes inviting us directly into their brothel.

The women themselves, however, do not appear to be that inviting. We can still identify them as women, but they have lost any traditional sense of beauty. No longer are they sensual or desirable. Their bodies have been transformed from organic, curvilinear shapes to ones that are rectilinear and geometric. By eliminating the three-dimensional aspects of this painting, linear perspective (chapter 5) and chiaroscuro (chapter 6), the artist emphasizes only these newly created geometric forms.

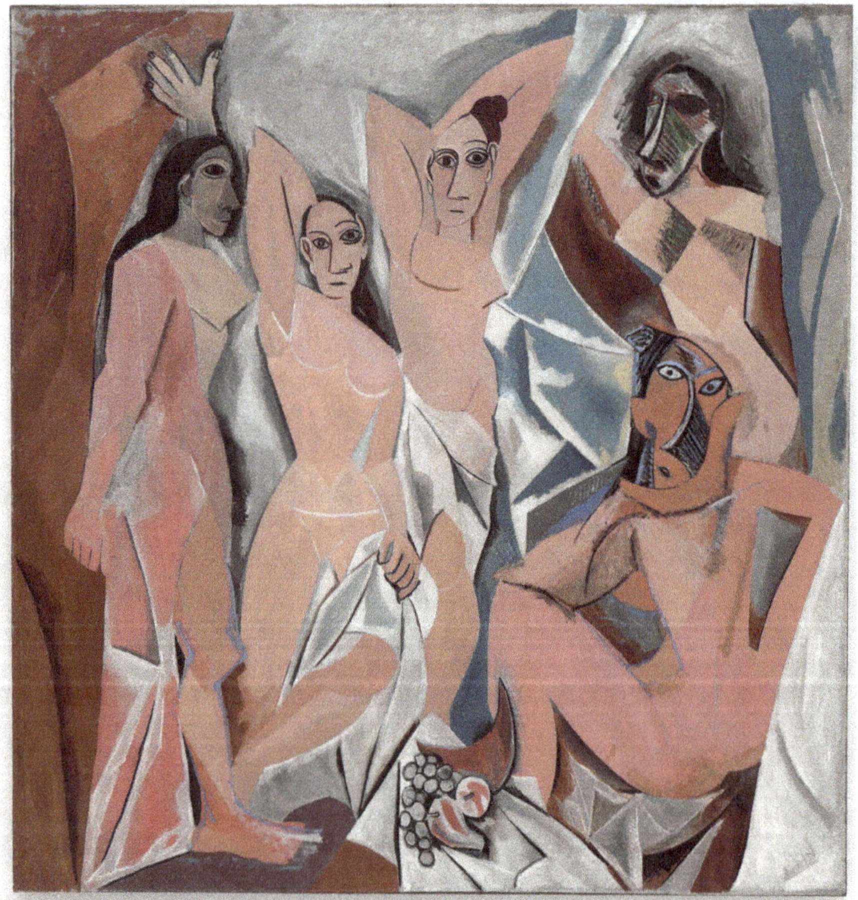

Figure 3.2: Pablo Picasso, *Les Demoiselles d'Avignon*, 1907.
Oil on Canvas, 8 ft × 7 ft 8 in, The Museum of Modern Art, New York.

NONOBJECTIVE ART

Nonobjective art is the complete opposite of representational art and therefore makes no reference to the natural world.[4] We can only talk about these artworks through the formal elements, such as line, shape, and color. We cannot look at these artworks and distinguish recognizable subject matter, such as a car, person, or tree. Jackson Pollock's "drip" paintings (see fig 7.7) would fall under this category, as would Mondrian's painting *Composition with Red, Blue, and Yellow* (see fig 4.1).

Keep in mind that nonobjective art is a recently coined terminology. We will learn later, in chapter 23, that Jackson Pollock is considered an Abstract Expressionist painter. Why then do we classify his work as nonobjective? Because back in the 1940s and 1950s when Pollock and other Abstract Expressionists were working in New York, the term *nonobjective* had not been created. Had it been, they might be known as the "Nonobjective Expressionists" today.

FORM

Form focuses on the purely visual aspects of an artwork. It is the way artists apply and use the formal elements. Note that *all artwork has form*! A work such as Mondrian's *Composition with Red, Blue, and Yellow* (see fig 4.1) is based entirely on form. It has line, shape, and color. But keep in mind that *The Arnolfini Portrait* (**fig 3.1**) has form as well. It contains line, shape, and color, just as Mondrian's work does. The forms are just different.

CONTENT

Content implies that there is subject matter or a narrative involved with the artwork. The artist is seeking to communicate something to the viewer. Whereas all artwork has form, *not all artwork has content*! Examining a work by Mondrian or Pollock may leave us unsure of the message, if one exists at all. However, in *The Arnolfini Portrait* there is a plethora of information waiting to be translated. Art historians are able to examine paintings such as these and interpret their meanings through the process of iconography. **Iconography** is defined as the study of the meaning of images.

The Arnolfini Portrait is among the most famous paintings in the world. We can use iconography to establish its meaning. On the surface it is an elaborate portrait of two wealthy individuals. We can establish this by looking at their clothing, which is elegant and lined with fur. The rest of the room shows sumptuous décor with the bed linen, chandelier, and ornate mirror. The dog is even a rare breed, an Affenpinscher. And if you look upon the windowsill and sideboard there are oranges, a southern fruit, which would have had to be imported to the northern climate of Flanders where this portrait was painted.[5]

Many people, such as art historian Marilyn Stokstad, have suggested this scene to be one of a marriage ceremony.[6] A primary indicator is the way the artist signs his name on the back wall above the mirror. It says, "*Johannes de eyck fuit hic*," which translates into "Jan van Eyck was here."[7] The way the phrase is worded suggests that the artist served as a witness to the ceremony that is taking place before us rather than a statement that he is the artist of this work. This is further proven when looking deeper into the mirror on the back wall, in which you can see the reflection of two other individuals in the room, the artist and (perhaps) a priest. The single lit candle in the expansive chandelier implies the presence of Christ, as we see this symbol more commonly in paintings of the Annunciation. The couple's shoes are kicked aside, referring to God's commandment to Moses, "put off thy shoes from thy feet, for the place where you are standing is holy ground."[8] Through iconography we can establish that this painting could serve as a marriage portrait or even a unique marriage certificate.

Representational art:

Abstract art:

Nonobjective (nonrepresentational) art:

Form:

Content:

Iconography:

ENDNOTES

1. *Pollock*, directed by Ed Harris (Hollywood: Sony Pictures Home Entertainment, 2001), DVD.
2. The other work being Édouard Manet's *Luncheon on the Grass*, which was presented in chapter 2.
3. Henry Sayre, *A World of Art*, 5th ed. (Boston: Prentice Hall, 2006), 52.
4. Nonobjective art is also called *nonrepresentational art*. This may be a good memorization tool, as nonobjective art is as far away from representational art that an artwork can get.
5. Flanders occupies a region in Northern Europe that includes parts of Belgium, France, and the Netherlands.
6. Marilyn Stokstad, *Art History*, revised ed. (New York: Harry N. Abrams, 1999), 628.
7. Ingo F. Walther, ed., *Masterpieces of Western Art* (Köln, Germany: Taschen, 2002), 123.
8. Exodus 3:5, King James Version.

IMAGE CREDITS

- Fig. 3.1: Jan van Eyck, "The Arnolfini Portrait," https://commons.wikimedia.org/wiki/File:Van_Eyck_-_Arnolfini_Portrait.jpg. Copyright in the Public Domain.
- Fig. 3.2: Pablo Picasso, "Les Demoiselles d'Avignon," https://en.wikipedia.org/wiki/File:Les_Demoiselles_d%27Avignon.jpg. Copyright in the Public Domain.

VOCABULARY OF FORMALISM

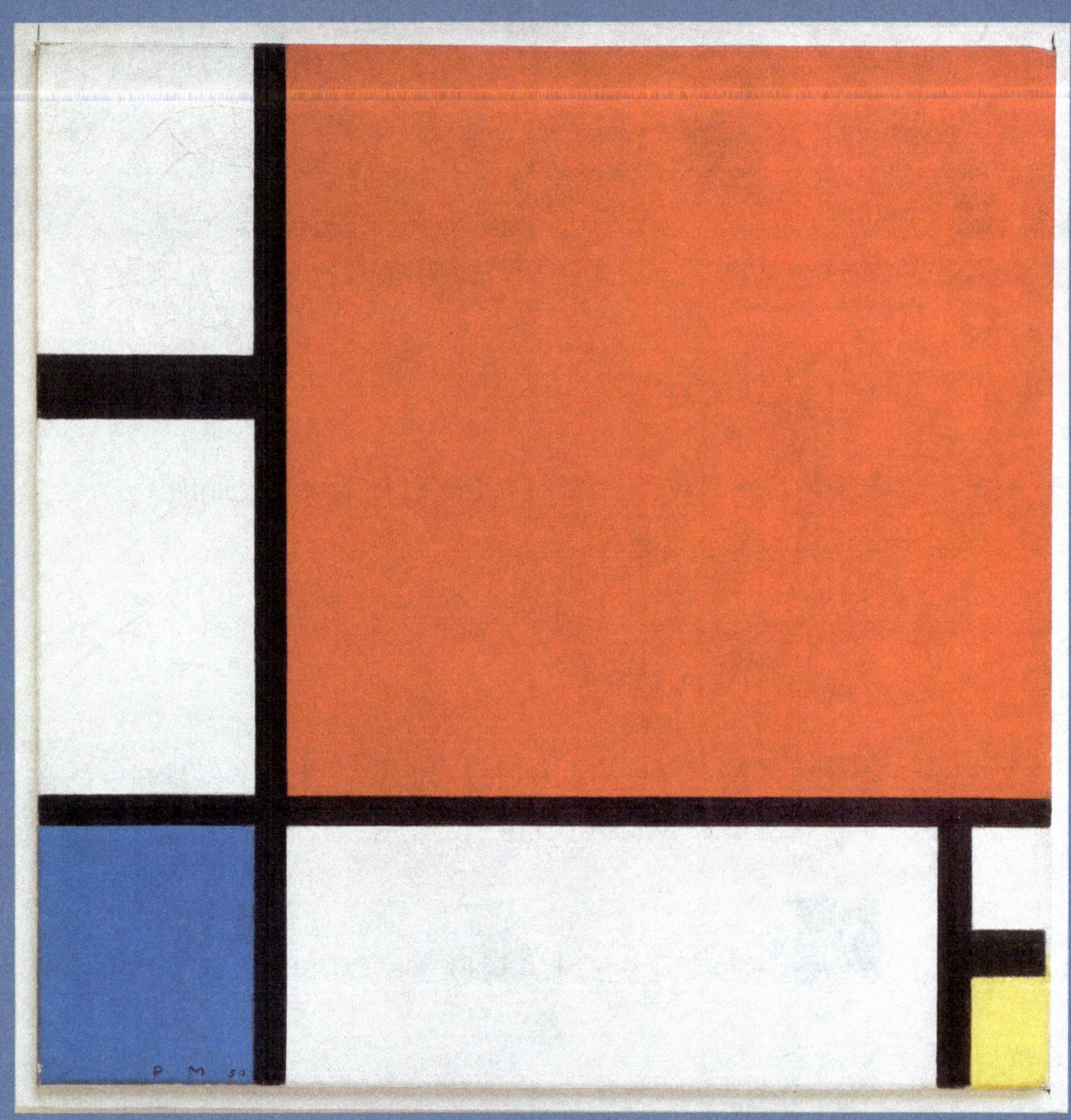

Figure 4.1: Piet Mondrian, *Composition with Red, Blue, and Yellow*, 1930. Oil on canvas, 18 in × 18 in, The Museum of Modern Art, Zürich, Switzerland.

LINE

THE POWER OF LINE

Line is a point that has been set in motion. While that definition might seem simple, line is really a much more complex device than most people realize. It offers the artist infinite variety and versatility: lines can be short, or they can be long. They can be thick or thin. Lines can be straight, curved, vertical, horizontal, or diagonal. They can appear static or dynamic, passive or aggressive. They allow us to see the edges of objects. Lines can connect objects just as readily as divide them. There are even some lines that are so powerful that they are invisible. There are no rules limiting what line can achieve.

Considering lines in their most basic arrangements (**fig 4.2**) enables us to see some of their inherent characteristics and applications in art. Artists commonly use horizontal, vertical, and diagonal lines to manipulate the viewer's interpretation of or feeling toward their work.

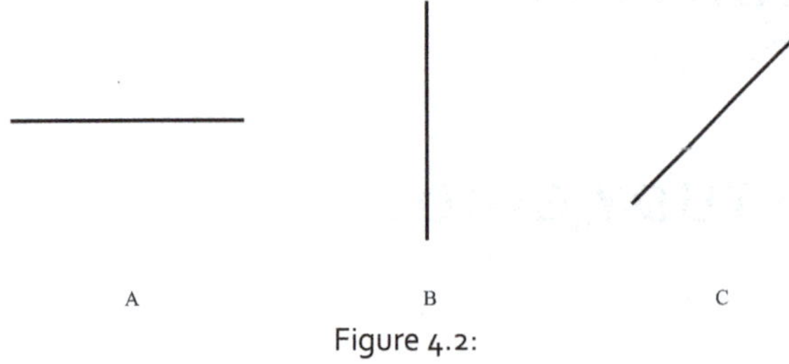

Figure 4.2:

A **horizontal line** (**fig 4.2A**) is a very static type of line with virtually no movement. Imagine that lines are representations of human figures. In this case a horizontal line is like a body lying prostrate. The body could be resting, asleep, or even deceased. Whatever the situation, the figure is going to be devoid of movement.

Fur Traders Descending the Missouri (**fig 4.3**) is an example of a painting that is dominated by horizontal lines. At first glance the painting pervades a certain sense of calm and peacefulness. We are able to sense that the canoe in which the traders are riding is just sort of drifting along. The horizontal ripples that are seen in the water support this feeling. They are layered one on top of another from the bottom of the image up to the

horizon, spanning the entire width of the canvas. Strong horizontal lines also appear in the form of the canoe, as well as in the landscape in the background. Our interpretation of this painting is based on the tremendous number of horizontal lines that are present in the work.

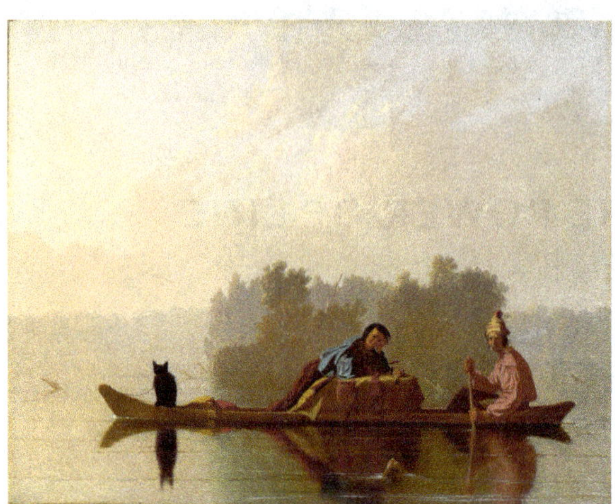

Figure 4.3: George Caleb Bingham, *Fur Traders Descending the Missouri*, 1845. Oil on Canvas, 26 in × 36.5 in, Metropolitan Museum of Art, Morris K. Jesup Fund.

Vertical lines (**fig 4.2B**) also mimic a body, but this time the figure is in a standing position. While there is definitely more potential for movement when a person is standing, there is no guarantee that this will be carried out. Therefore, a vertical line still feels restrained.

Consider the figures in Gustave Courbet's *Burial at Ornans* (**fig 4.4**). Given the large number of people present in this painting (46 to be exact), we have surprisingly very little movement. The work is static. Everyone, including the viewer, is standing around waiting for something to happen. Add in the horizontality of both the landscape behind the figures as well as the realization that the figures themselves all stand, with few exceptions, at a similar height, we see the vertical line in *Burial at Ornans*, just as the horizontal line in *Fur Traders Descending the Missouri*, projecting a work of art with very little movement.

It is **diagonal lines** (**fig 4.2C**) that makes a work dynamic and active! Have you ever tried standing at a diagonal? It doesn't work; at least not for long. Our brains recognize unstable positions, such as diagonals, and we know that change is imminent. Diagonal lines are able to create a sensation of movement, much more than horizontal and vertical lines can.

Case in point is Claude-Joseph Vernet's *A Storm on a Mediterranean Coast* (**fig 4.5**). Movement dominates this painting as Vernet utilizes diagonal lines throughout this work to provide us with an extremely dynamic scene. Working our way around the lighthouse—the stabilizing feature of the composition—we are immediately drawn to the ship at the right tipping at a 45-degree angle. Below this is a beached ship leaning the opposite way. The rocks that make up the shoreline and the cliff are also set at diagonals. Even the atmosphere is in motion as there are noticeable diagonals of clouds and rain surrounding the lighthouse.

We can examine these principles further in the following exercise: Place a three-ring binder flat on the desk with the spine facing you, creating a horizontal line. What does it do? Nothing! It just sort of lies there. It is not going to move without physical force. This is just like the horizontal lines in *Fur Traders Descending the Missouri*, which weigh the painting down and restrict its movement. Stand the folder so the spine is vertical, or perpendicular, to the desk. How has your perception of the folder changed between its horizontal and vertical positions? With the change in alignment we now have a potential for movement. Someone could brush by it or hit the desk and knock it over, but without that happening it

will stay standing, not utilizing its potential for movement. Now, place the folder at a 45-degree angle to the table. Let it go and see what happens. It will fall 100% of the time, guaranteed! We instinctively know this is going to happen before we let go of the folder. This is why when our brain sees diagonals in artworks we anticipate movement.

RECTILINEAR AND CURVILINEAR LINES

Artists can create many different varieties of line. These varieties of line are categories rather than particular positions lines are arranged in.

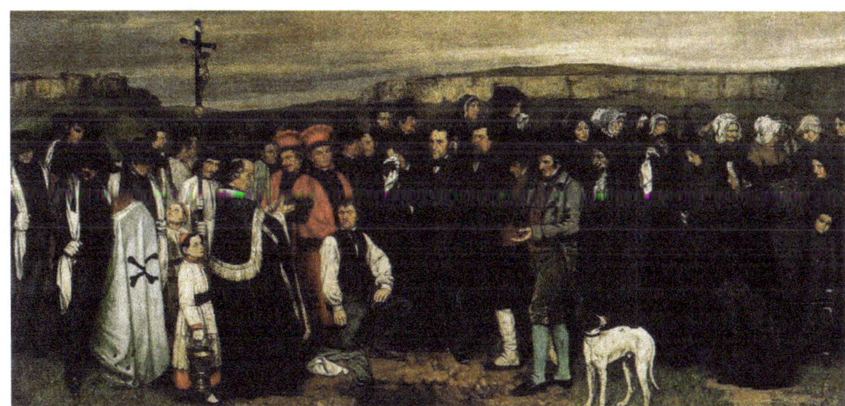

Figure 4.4: Gustave Courbet, *Funeral at Ornans*, 1849–50.
Oil on Canvas, 124 in × 263 in, Musée d'Orsay.

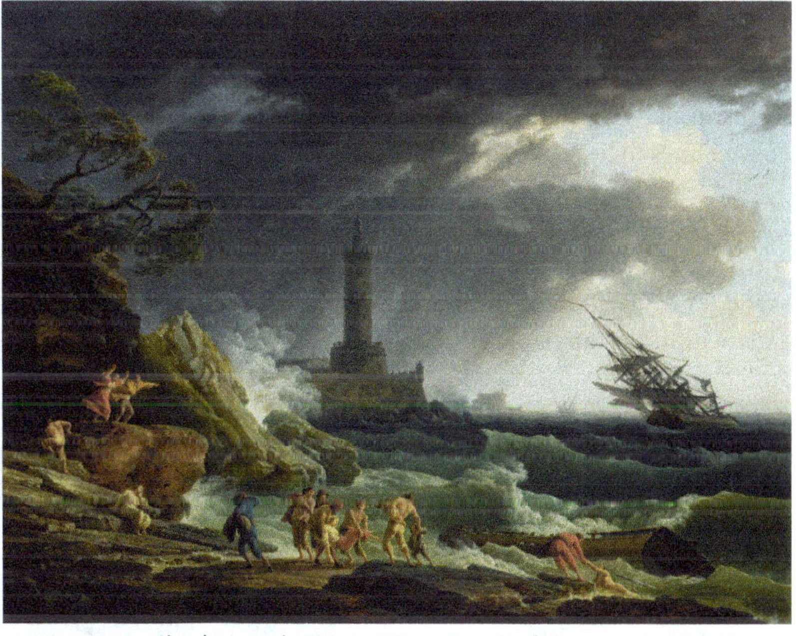

Figure 4.5: Claude-Joseph Vernet, *A Storm on a Mediterranean Coast*, 1767.
Oil on Canvas, 44.5 in × 57.4 in, The J. Paul Getty Museum at the Getty Center.

This textbook breaks line down into eight categories. The first two varieties—rectilinear and curvilinear—relate to the basic formation of the line, while the remaining six—outline, contour, implied, expressive, analytical, and classical—are more descriptive classifications.

Rectilinear line and *curvilinear line* are terms artists, art critics, and art historians use quite frequently when describing line in an artwork. These terms are finite descriptions, meaning that lines tend to fall into one category or the other.

Rectilinear lines are straight lines. They are man-made. How many times do you see a straight line in nature? Not that often, if at all. *Composition with Red, Blue, and Yellow* (**fig 4.1**) by Piet Mondrian is a perfect example of a work created with rectilinear line. Every line in this work is straight. (Please note that although many of the examples throughout this and other chapters are paintings, the formal elements can be applied to *all* forms of art, including sculpture, photography, and architecture.)

As the name suggests, **curvilinear lines** are lines that are curved. It can't get much simpler than that. If the line bends slightly or has a more justified curve, it will fall under this classification. Curvilinear lines can be described as organic, natural, and flowing. The adjectives *organic* and *natural* relate to the fact that we readily find these forms in nature. There is an abundance of curved lines to be found in the landscape.

Vincent van Gogh's *Wheatfield with Crows* (**fig 4.10**) is an example of a work with curvilinear line. This is a landscape scene, and no straight lines are going to exist within this arena. Even the pathways, which are man-made, are not straight; they curve and undulate with the topography of the land. The curved lines van Gogh uses gives us a sensation of movement as the wheat field appears to be blowing softly in the breeze.

How wonderful would it be if everything we saw were able to fit neatly into our specific classifications? However, because we are dealing with the subject of art, things will not always be black and white. In fact, many times we will come across areas of gray. This is also one of the things that makes the study of art so great! There isn't always going to be a singular correct answer. Take as an example the photograph of *Lisa Lyon* (**fig 4.6**), who was a bodybuilder in the late 1970s. The photographer, Robert Mapplethorpe, was able to capture both rectilinear and curvilinear aspects of her body simultaneously. One could address her stance as being rectilinear as we could draw a straight line from her head down through her right leg. A perpendicular line crosses from the elbow of her bent arm, across her chest, to her extended left arm. One would also have to agree that her body is still feminine and contains many curvilinear aspects. We could even take the analysis deeper by incorporating in the characteristics of line we have just covered. There is a horizontal line created by the extended arms. The figure itself

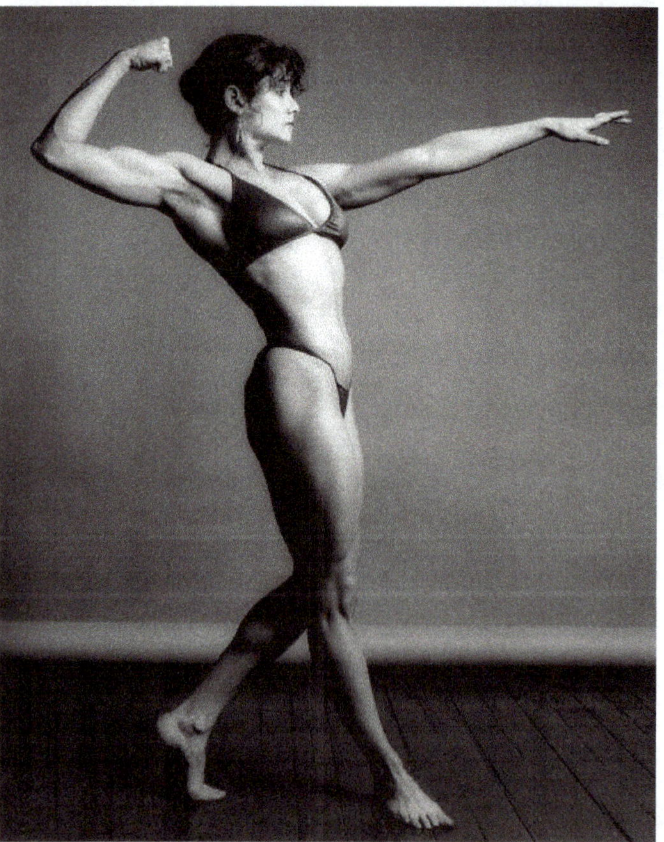

Figure 4.6: Robert Maplethorpe, *Lisa Lyon*, 1982.

creates a vertical line. The combination of these makes Lyon's stance very solid and formidable. However, both the right arm and left leg are bent to form diagonals, which give the sensation of movement. The juxta-position between recti-linear and curvilinear, masculine and feminine, stasis and motion, along with the black and white of the photograph itself showcases the talent Mapplethorpe possessed when he created this photograph.

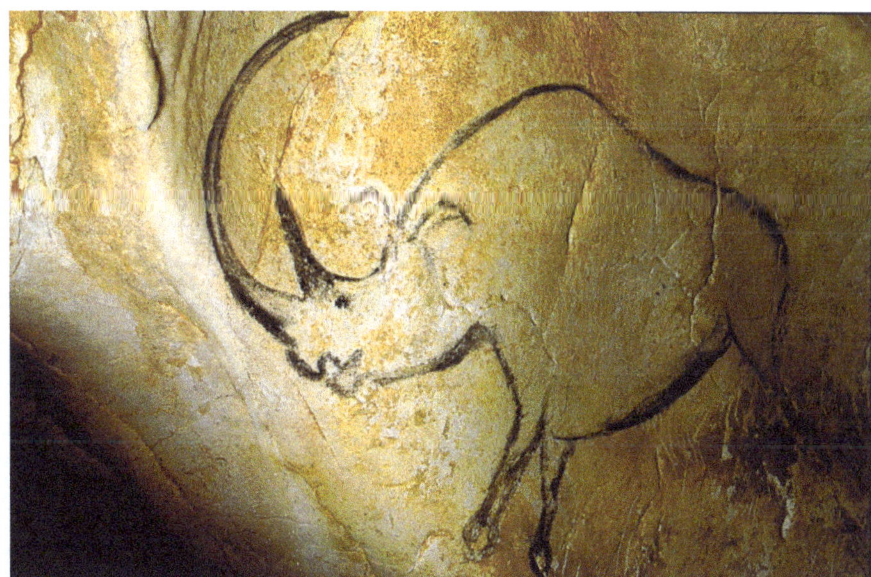

Figure 4.7: Chauvet Cave. Ardèche, France. *Rhinoceros*, c. 30,000 BCE.

OUTLINE AND CONTOUR LINE

The next pair of lines we will look at are outlines and contour lines. There are some commonalities in their definitions, but don't be fooled, as they are drastically different. **Outlines**, first and foremost, indicate the edges of a figure or object. Imagine the figures in a coloring book. They rely almost exclu-sively on outlines. Outlines are usually enhanced or very bold in appearance. Objects created with outlines tend to be two-dimensional and maintain a certain stencil-like quality about them.

The cave painting (**fig 4.7**) gives credence to the artist Paul Klee's statement that line is "the most primitive of elements."[1] This and many other cave paintings concentrate on early man's ability to create identifiable animals (in this case a rhi-noceros) solely from the application of line. But outlines are not restricted to primordial works. Children use crayons to create "masterpieces" of art that rely exclusively on outlines. Even contem-porary artists, such as Keith Haring, frequently use outlines to help establish the innate flatness in their works.

Contour lines also indicate the edges of a figure or object. But that is where their simi-larities to outlines end. The difference between outlines and contour lines is that contour lines are concerned with establishing volume, mass, and three-dimensionality. Take a look at *Walking Barefoot* (**fig 4.8**). The contour lines establish the boundaries of the foot and lower leg just as an outline does, though not nearly as bold. They also seem to curve around the leg, ankle, and bottom of the foot, supporting a more three-dimensional scene. Contour lines are curvilinear, and they help to shape the object and give it volume.

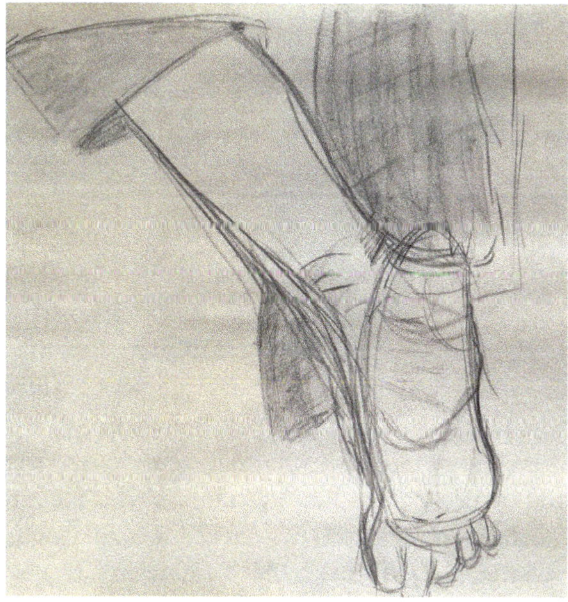

Figure 4.8: David Plouffe, *Walking Barefoot*, 2004. Graphite on Paper.

IMPLIED LINE

With **implied lines** no physical lines exist. These are "understood" lines, and they are extremely powerful! An example of an implied line in everyday life might be a stewardess on an airplane pointing toward the emergency exits. No physical line extends from her fingers to the exit doors, but we follow the direction she is pointing as if one does. Line-of-sight would be another type of implied line. If you were to walk outside and notice everyone looking up into the sky you are more than likely going to join them to try to see what they are looking at. Eye contact between two people works in the same manner.

In the *Assumption and Consecration of the Virgin* by Titian (**fig 4.9**), we see Mary being assumed into heaven to be reunited with her soul after burial. Implied line is abundant throughout the work in its various forms. The scene is separated into three distinct registers: God above swooping down out of heaven, Mary ascending on clouds to be crowned Queen of Heaven, and the apostles positioned at the base. Implied lines unite the three registers. Mary maintains eye contact with God as he looks down upon her. Some of the *putti* (the cherub-like figures supporting the cloud) are pointing toward her. The apostles below all gaze in the direction of Mary, and a few raise their hands as they witness the event. All of these implied lines help to bring the composition together and establish Mary as the focal point (focal points will be discussed in detail in a later chapter).

EXPRESSIVE LINE

Expressive line conveys the artist's mood and feelings. It is more personal and autographic than any of the other lines discussed thus far. Each artist tends to have his or her own style of expressive line, much like each of us has our own unique signature when we sign our name. A certain human element is present in these artworks that seems to resonate with their viewers. Take the work of Vincent van Gogh as an example. We looked at van Gogh's *Wheatfield with Crows* (**fig 4.10**) when we discussed curvilinear line, but we can also label this work as having expressive line. There are no rules

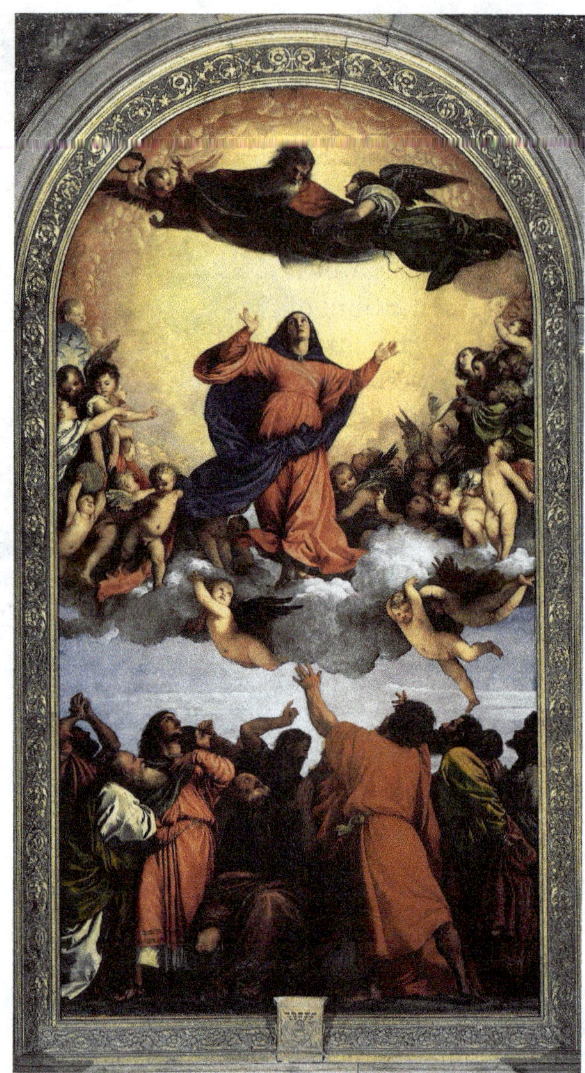

Figure 4.9: Titian, *Assumption and Consecration of the Virgin*, 1516–1518
Oil on Wood 271.7 in × 141.7 in, Basilica di Santa Maria Gloriosa dei Frari, Venice.

that artworks can't be described under two categories. What is van Gogh trying to express to us in this painting? What are the feelings that dominate this work? Happiness? Jubilation? Probably not, the painting exudes a sense of loneliness and sadness. There is an absence of people in the scene. The sky is ominous and foreboding, as if a storm is fast approaching. This is one of van Gogh's last paintings. Shortly after this work was completed he picked up a revolver and committed suicide. He wrote about this painting (along with two others) in a letter to his brother Theo: "I did not need to go out of my way to try to express sadness and extreme loneliness … I almost think that these canvases will tell you, what I cannot say in words."[2]

Jackson Pollock is another artist noted for his use of expressive line (see fig 7.7). There are a lot of conflicting opinions on Pollock's works. Some argue that a child could create them, whereas others state that they are the works of a genius. Wherever you stand on his works, they utilize expressive line. You can almost see the pathway Pollock's arm took in their creation. Pollock created paintings in a completely unorthodox way by laying the untreated (raw) canvas on the ground. He would then walk around the edges, sometimes even stepping into the canvas, in order to drip, pour, and splatter the paint.[3]

ANALYTICAL LINE

We saw earlier that outlines and contour lines share many commonalities in their definitions yet are drastically different; the same can be said for analytical and classical lines. **Analytical line** is precise, controlled, and based on mathematical principles. It can easily be reproduced. Looking back to Mondrian's *Composition with Red, Blue, and Yellow* (**fig 4.1**), it wouldn't take an artist to render this work. Most, if not all, of us could recreate this painting.

Another example of analytical line is Sol LeWitt's *Wall Drawing #681 C* (**fig 4.11**). This artwork contains four scenes (working right to left): the first two contain diagonal lines, the third horizontal lines, while the fourth has vertical lines. This work, like Mondrian's, fulfills the definition of analytical line: precise, controlled, based on mathematical principles, and easily reproducible. In fact, the

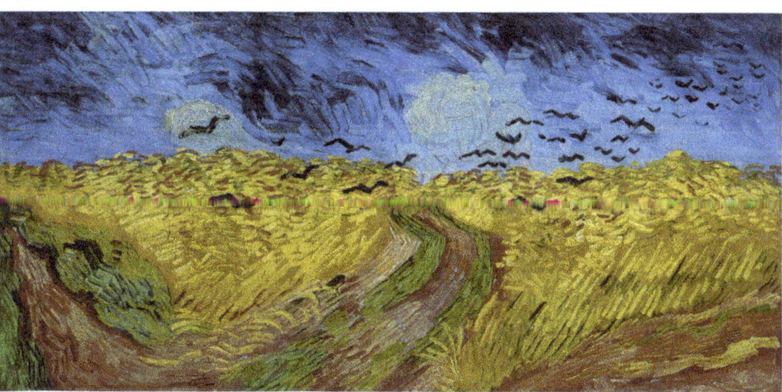
Figure 4.10: Vincent van Gogh, *Wheatfield with Crows*, 1890
Oil on Canvas, 50.5 cm × 103 cm, Rijksmuseum Vincent van Gogh, Amsterdam.

artist didn't physically create this work; the museum staff created this work according to LeWitt's set of instructions.[4]

CLASSICAL LINE

Anytime you see the word *classical* applied to art it refers back to the Greek and Roman era, which would be the classical period. The artworks of this time went on to inspire Renaissance and neoclassical artists such as Donatello and Jacques-Louis David. Classical artwork was created with an emphasis on ratio, proportion, and balance, which brings in a mathematical

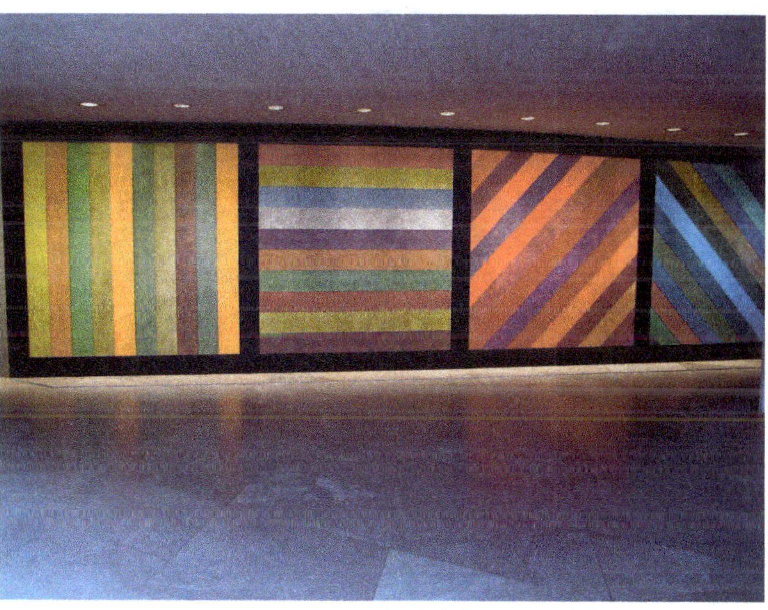
Figure 4.11: Sol LeWitt, *Wall Drawing No. 681 C*, 1993
Colored Ink Washes, 120 in × 444 in, National Gallery of Art, Dorothy and Herbert Vogel Collection 1993.

element. Whereas analytical line deals exclusively with these mathematical principles, **classical line** is based on beauty and the aesthetic. The beauty of these classical works come from the ordered process of their creation. It would be simple to discuss the beauty that resonates from a painting such as Jacques-Louis David's *Oath of the Horatii* (**fig 4.12**) that uses classical line compared to convincing someone of the aesthetic value in the works of Sol LeWitt and Mondrian that use analytical line.

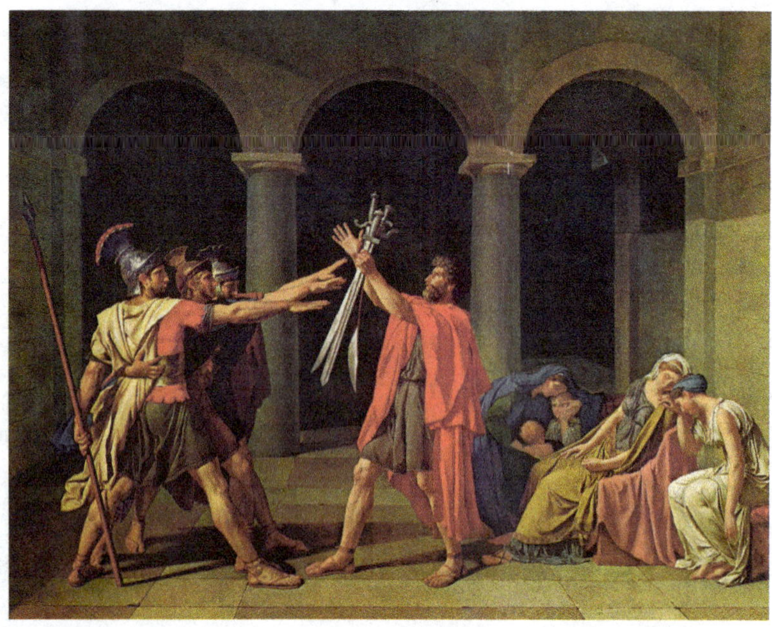

Figure 4.12: Jacques-Louis David, *The Oath of the Horatii*, 1784
Oil on Canvas, 129.9 in × 167.3 in, Musée du Louvre.

HATCHING AND CROSS-HATCHING

Artists use the techniques of hatching and cross-hatching in order to create value in a composition. Value (discussed in chapter 6) deals with variations of lightness and darkness within a work of art. **Hatching** can be defined as closely spaced parallel lines, whereas **cross-hatching** is lines that overlap one another at either regular or variable intervals. We use hatching and cross-hatching in two distinct venues. First, they are commonly employed in comic strips. Second, they are used in the printmaking processes of engraving and etching.

Both hatching and cross-hatching are used extensively in Edward Hopper's etching *House Tops* (**fig 4.14**). Hatching is used sparingly in sections of the railcar's bench as well as the box next to the figure at the right. Cross-hatching is used much more prolifically throughout the etching. We see it making up the top of the railcar as well as the figure of the woman at center. In the lower-left-hand corner we see it used to give the impression of a shadow falling across the seat.

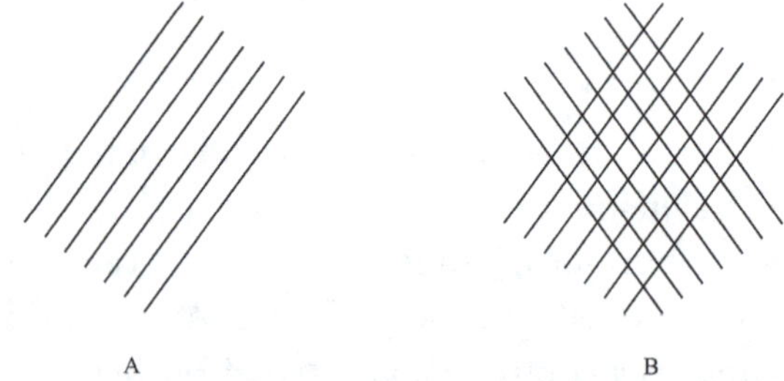

Figure 4.13: Hatching & Cross-Hatching.

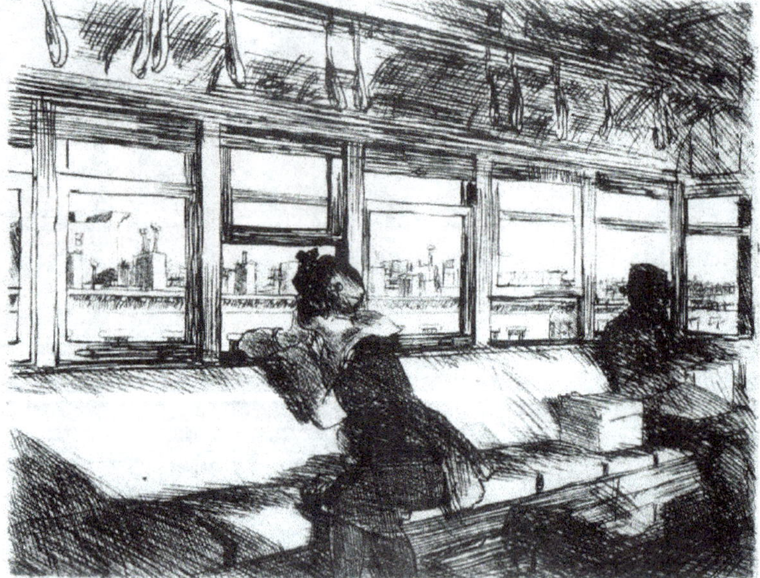

Figure 4.14: Edward Hopper, *House Tops*, 1921
Etching, 15.2 cm × 20.3 cm, Philadelphia Museum of Art; Thomas Skelton Harrion Fund.

STUDY GUIDE: LINE

Horizontal line:

Vertical line:

Diagonal line:

Rectilinear line:

Curvilinear line:

Outline:

Contour line:

Implied line:

Expressive line:

Analytical line:

Classical line:

Hatching and cross-hatching:

PROJECT: LINE

Goals

To develop an understanding of the interrelationships between line and shape as well as the use of positive and negative space within a cohesive and successful composition.

Required Media

15" × 20" illustration board
Pencils: #2 and 6B (Please do not use charcoal pencils)
Straight edge
Vinyl eraser

Assignment

This assignment gives you the opportunity to create your own work of art while putting into practice some of the principles covered in our lectures on line and space.

1. Begin with the 15" × 20" illustration board. Using the straight edge and #2 pencil, create a border 1 inch in from the edge of the illustration board. The border should be "floating," which means that no lines should extend to the edges of the illustration board. The border should be crisp and clean.
2. Once the border is complete, begin drawing curvilinear lines with the 6B pencil. The lines should originate from one border and end on another. The lines MUST begin and end on a border, not on another line. You will need a minimum of ten (10) lines. Concentrate on creating a variety of *interesting and varied shapes* within the composition.
3. Once your design is completed, shade in every other closed shape using the side edge, rather than the point, of the 6B pencil. You might want to lightly mark the shapes you plan to shade in before you begin. Shade shapes east/west and then a second time north/south. This eliminates any directional marks. Be careful not to smudge, as there will be a considerable amount of graphite on your illustration board. Clean up the empty spaces with the vinyl eraser. An example of a finished artworks is provided below. It is for reference only. *Do not copy it!*

   Note: There should be no visible lines in your completed work with the exception of the border. If there are lines, you will need to blend them in to already existing shaded areas.

4. On the *back* of the illustration board, in the *upper-left-hand corner*, write your name, the project number, and your class information (e.g., MWF 9 a.m.). *Please use a marker!*

Consider the following:

- The orientation of the drawing surface
- The size and scale of the shapes
- Open spaces versus closed spaces
- The "flow" of the composition
- Balance of the composition

Point value: ___________

Due date: ________________________ (weather permitting).

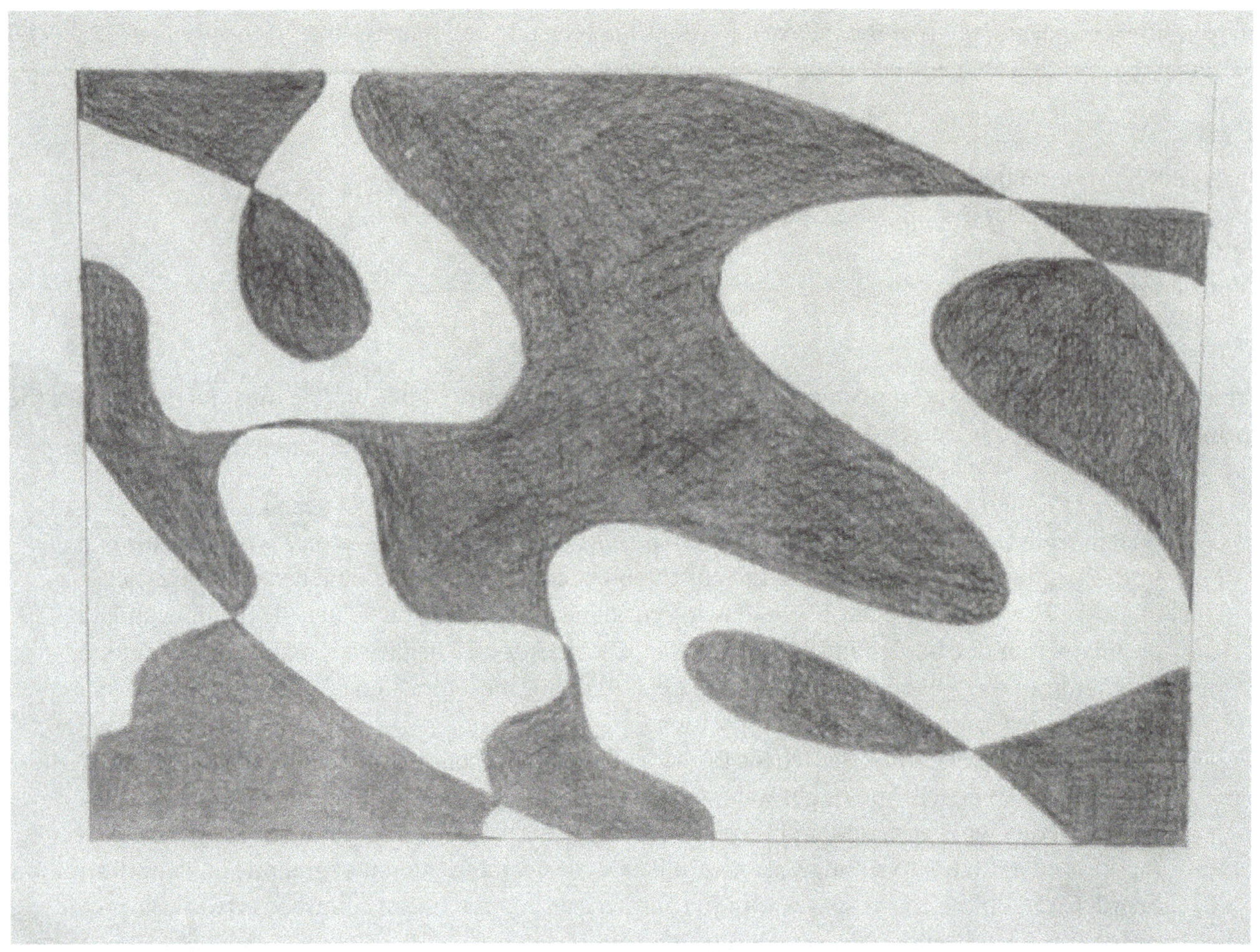

Figure 4.15: Example

ENDNOTES

1. Paul Klee and Jürg Spiller, *Paul Klee Notebooks*, vol. 1, *The Thinking Eye* (London: Lund Humphries, 1969), 103.
2. Mark Roskill, ed., *The Letters of Vincent van Gogh* (Touchstone: New York, 2008), 338.
3. Dorothy Seiberling, "Jackson Pollock: Is He the Greatest Living Painter in the United States?" *Life Magazine*, August 8, 1949, 42–45.
4. Henry Sayre, *A World of Art*, 7th ed. (Boston: Prentice Hall, 2013), 69.

IMAGE CREDITS

- Fig. 4.1: Piet Mondrian, "Composition with Red, Blue, and Yellow," https://commons.wikimedia.org/wiki/File:Piet_Mondriaan,_1930_-_Mondrian_Composition_II_in_Red,_Blue,_and_Yellow.jpg. Copyright in the Public Domain.
- Fig. 4.3: George Caleb Bingham, "Fur Traders Descending the Missouri," https://commons.wikimedia.org/wiki/File:George_Caleb_Bingham_-_Fur_Traders_Descending_the_Missouri_-_WGA2205.jpg. Copyright in the Public Domain.
- Fig. 4.4: Gustave Courbet, "Funeral at Ornans," https://commons.wikimedia.org/wiki/File:Gustave_Courbet_-_Burial_at_Ornans_-_WGA05458.jpg. Copyright in the Public Domain.
- Fig. 4.5: Claude-Joseph Vernet, "A Storm on a Mediterranean Coast," https://commons.wikimedia.org/wiki/File:Claude-Joseph_Vernet_-_A_Storm_on_a_Mediterranean_Coast_-_Google_Art_Project.jpg. Copyright in the Public Domain.
- Fig. 4.6: Robert Mapplethorpe, "Lisa Lyon." Copyright © 1982 by Robert Mapplethorpe.
- Fig. 4.7: Inocybe, "Chauvet Cave Painting," https://commons.wikimedia.org/wiki/File:Rhinocéros_grotte_Chauvet.jpg. Copyright in the Public Domain.
- Fig. 4.9: Titian, "Assumption and Consecration of the Virgin," https://commons.wikimedia.org/wiki/File:Tizian_041.jpg. Copyright in the Public Domain.
- Fig. 4.10: Vincent van Gogh, "Wheatfield with Crows," https://commons.wikimedia.org/wiki/File:Vincent_van_Gogh_-_Wheatfield_with_crows_-_Google_Art_Project.jpg. Copyright in the Public Domain.
- Fig. 4.11: Sol Lewitt, "Wall Drawing No. 681 C," http://www.nga.gov/content/ngaweb/Collection/art-object-page.82836.html.
- Fig. 4.12: Jacques-Louis David, "The Oath of the Horatii," https://commons.wikimedia.org/wiki/File:Jacques-Louis_David_020.jpg. Copyright in the Public Domain.
- Fig. 4.14: Edward Hopper, "House Tops," https://commons.wikimedia.org/wiki/File:Night_on_the_El_Train,_1918.jpg. Copyright in the Public Domain.

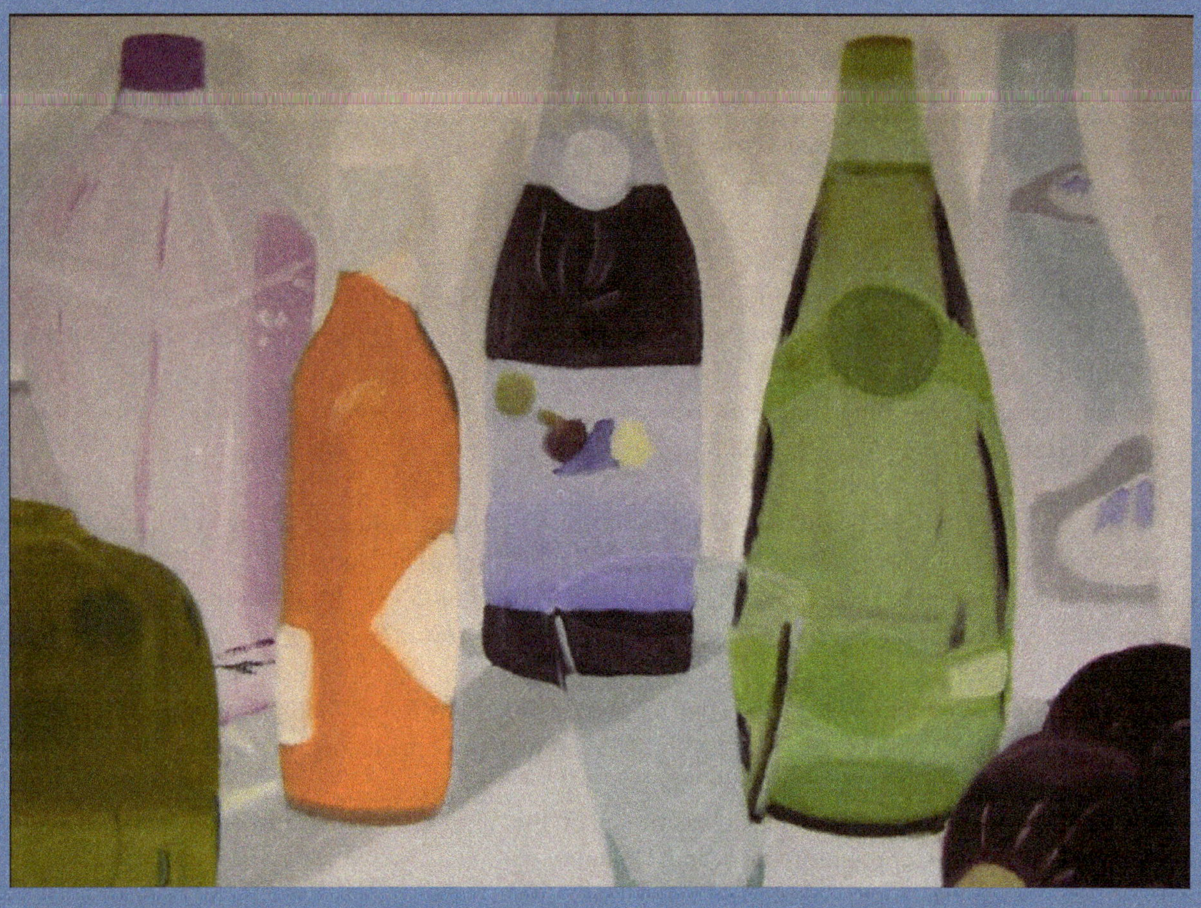

Figure 5.1: David Plouffe, *Still Life with Bottles and Spider*, 2004. Oil on canvas, 20.25 in × 15 in.

SPACE AND THE ILLUSION OF SPACE

SPACE AND THE ILLUSION OF SPACE

In this chapter we will cover the terms used to talk about space, and also explore the different ways artists can create the illusion of three-dimensional space on a two-dimensional surface.

POSITIVE AND NEGATIVE SPACE

The terms *positive space* and *negative space* are used to refer to three-dimensional art objects, such as sculpture or architecture. **Positive space** is anything you can see, feel, or touch. If we look at a chair, the seat, arms, legs, and backrest would all be considered positive space. **Negative space** is defined as empty space. This would be the space under the chair or between the backrest and seat if they were separate pieces.

The *Watts Towers* (**fig. 5.2**) by Simon Rodia contain both positive and negative space. The steel, wire, glass, and tile all help to create the positive form of the structures. However, the towers in the work are not completely solid forms, with the negative space just as prevalent as the positive. The steel circular bars placed at regular intervals around the vertical supports make the structures look like they would be incredibly fun to climb on, which Rodia did in order to build and maintain the artwork.[1]

No law says that artworks must contain both positive and negative space. Plenty of artworks can be labeled as only having positive space, especially sculptural works from early civilizations, such as Egypt.[2] There are even a few artworks that exist only in negative space, such as *Double Negative* by Michael Heizer (not pictured).

When dealing with two-dimensional artworks, such as drawings and paintings, positive and negative space still exist, but we refer to them now as **figure** and **ground**. Both positive space (the figure/form) and negative space (ground/background) are created simultaneously and hold equal importance to the artist! You participated in this process while completing the project in chapter 4.

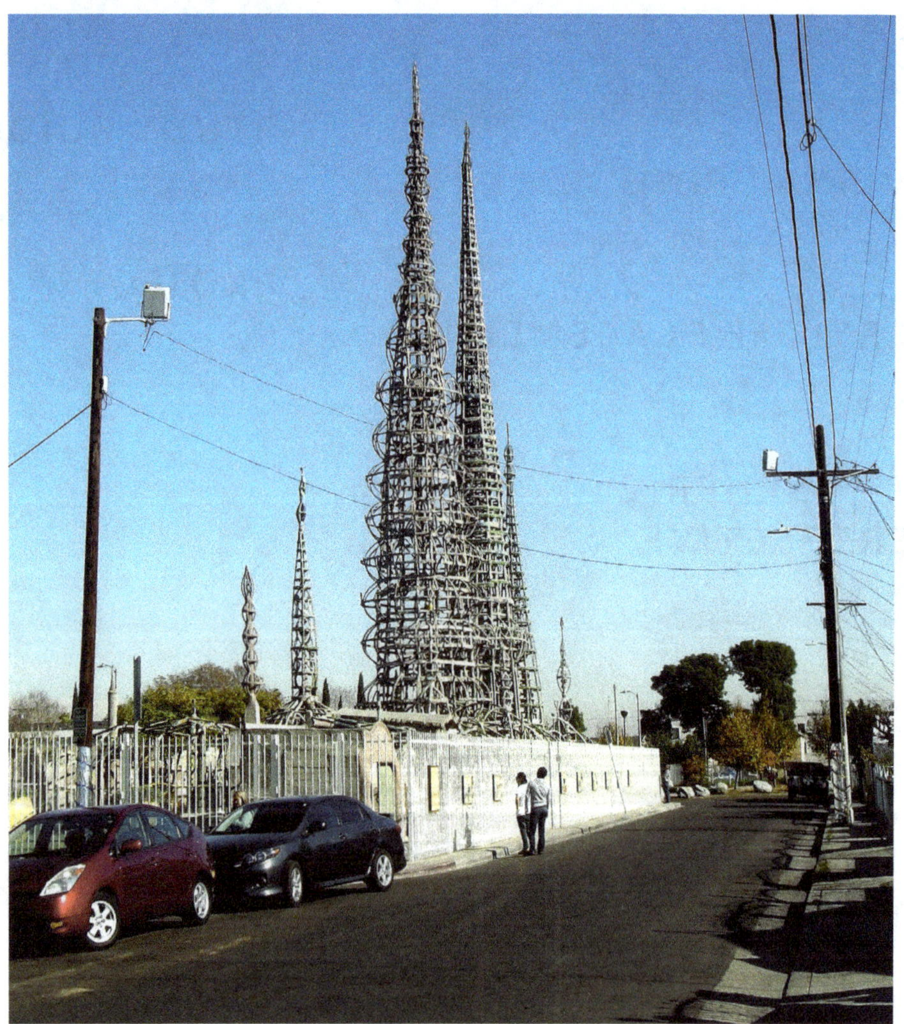

Figure 5.2: Simon Rodia, *Watts Towers*, 1921–54. Mixed Media, 30 Meters in Height (Tallest Tower), Los Angeles, California.

The first three illusionary techniques we will cover—scale, overlapping, and vertical placement—are very basic and simple to construct. With scale, the rule is that objects closer to us appear larger than those farther away. Many of us watched *Sesame Street* when we were children. In a segment called "Near and Far," Grover gives a prime example of how scale can be altered to reflect spatial relationships.[3] When the segment begins, Grover is front and center, taking up a majority of the screen. He lets us know that "this is near." Grover then turns and runs to the back of the set, where he barely takes up a fraction of the space he did before. At this point he turns back to us and yells out, "this is faaarrr!" By taking note of what happens to the scale of a person, or object, in a three-dimensional space, artists can then translate this effect onto a two-dimensional surface and create an illusion of space.

In a more artistic example, Alfred Sisley's painting *Snow on the Road, Louveciennes* (**fig 5.3**) shows how the manipulation of scale can create space on a flat surface. The tree at the far left looks as if it is within arm's length because of its size, nearly filling the entire width of the canvas. Each tree in the row then seems to diminish in height while the space between the trunks of the trees becomes tighter until they become one solid mass toward the end of the road. Our eyes literally follow the tree line back into the painting as if this was a true three-dimensional space rather than a flat canvas.

OVERLAPPING

With **overlapping**, objects that are closer to us partially cover or hide objects that are farther away. At the lower-left-hand side of *Still Life with Bottles and Spider* (see fig 9.1), there is a bottle of apple juice that overlaps part of the bottle of Fiji water. The same happens at the right-hand side of the painting where a Perrier bottle covers part of the Evian bottle. The overlapping of these bottles forces us to acknowledge the presence of space between the objects.

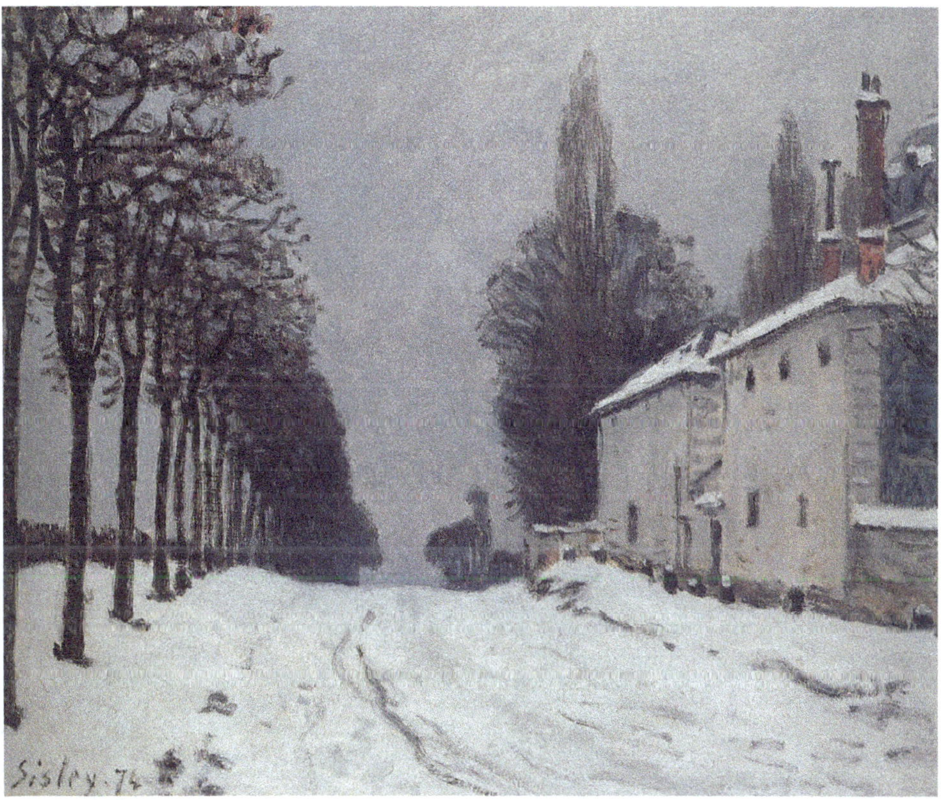

Figure 5.3: Alfred Sisley, *Snow on the Road, Louveciennes*, 1874. Oil on Canvas, 15 in × 22 in, Private Collection.

VERTICAL PLACEMENT

With **vertical placement**, the higher an object is placed in the artwork, the farther away it is from the viewer. Vertical placement was a common way that artists from Eastern cultures created space in artworks. In Ogata Korin's *Irises* (see fig 11.1), the irises are scattered at various heights. The higher the iris is placed, the farther away it is from us. Vertical placement makes the scene look realistic, as if we are looking over a field of these flowers.

Looking back at *Still Life with Bottles and Spider*, we saw that overlapping played a role in establishing space, but vertical placement does as well. The base of the apple juice container is positioned below the frame, the orange soda to its right is placed higher up, and the bottle of Martinelli's Sparkling Grape Juice is even higher. While these three bottles do not overlap one another, they are placed at different heights in the painting, and this helps to create the illusion of space that we see in this painting.

ATMOSPHERIC PERSPECTIVE

These next three illusionary techniques—atmospheric perspective, amplified perspective, and linear perspective—are more advanced and complex ways of creating space than those previously covered. **Atmospheric perspective** states that as forms recede into the distance their contours will become less distinct and the forms will begin to take on the color of the atmosphere.[4]

The photograph of Yosemite Valley (**fig 5.4**) gives us a beautiful view of the landscape, with El Capitan on the left and Bridal Veil Falls on the right. Note how crisp and clear the foreground is. The color is bright and vibrant, and you can literally see the pine needles hanging from the trees! But as we move toward the center of the photograph, where the more distant peaks are, we are not able to pick up the amazing detail that was present in the foreground. The details of the mountains have become less distinct and their color has changed from a rich, dark green to a very light blue, which is nearly the color of the surrounding sky. Is the color of the mountains in the distance really blue? No, of course not. The way our eyes work is far from perfect, and atmospheric perspective illustrates this point. But in order to create an artwork that matches what our idea of what the world looks like, artists continue representing this, and other, optical illusions that our eyes tell us are "natural."

In *Lake Lucerne* (**fig 5.5**) the artist, Albert Bierstadt, paints an image very much like our photograph of Yosemite. We have a very crisp and clear foreground where we can note the details of individual rocks strewn along the trail at the lower-left portion corner of the painting. The countryside beyond is still very concise, with individual plants and trees along with a beautiful lake in the distance. Behind the lake is a mountain range where the use of atmospheric perspective is evident. The mountain to the far right is very much the color of the foreground, but as we move

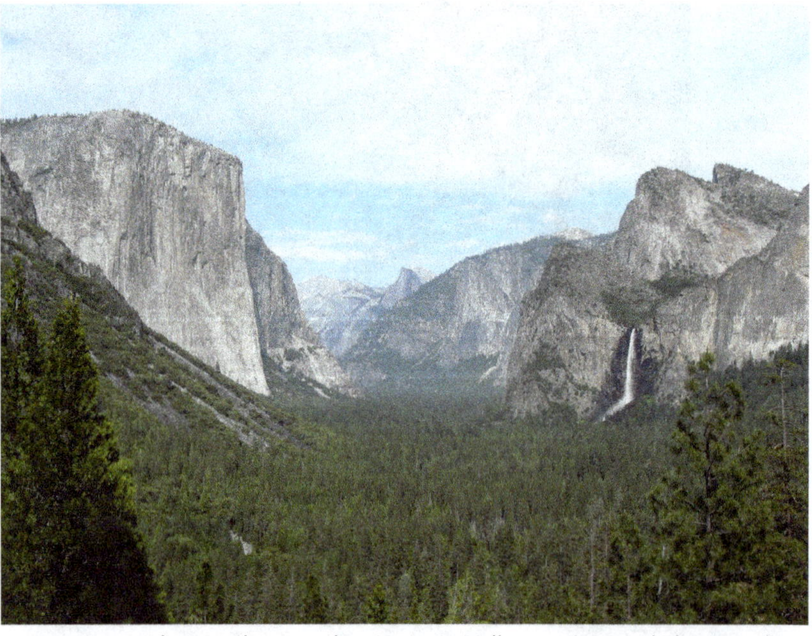

Figure 5.4: Unknown Photographer, *Yosemite Valley,* 2006. Digital Photograph.

to the left the mountains continue to lose their color to the point that the mountain at the far left is nearly the same color as the atmosphere. The amount of detail also diminishes with the color. By using the illusion of atmospheric perspective, the artist makes this scene look lifelike.

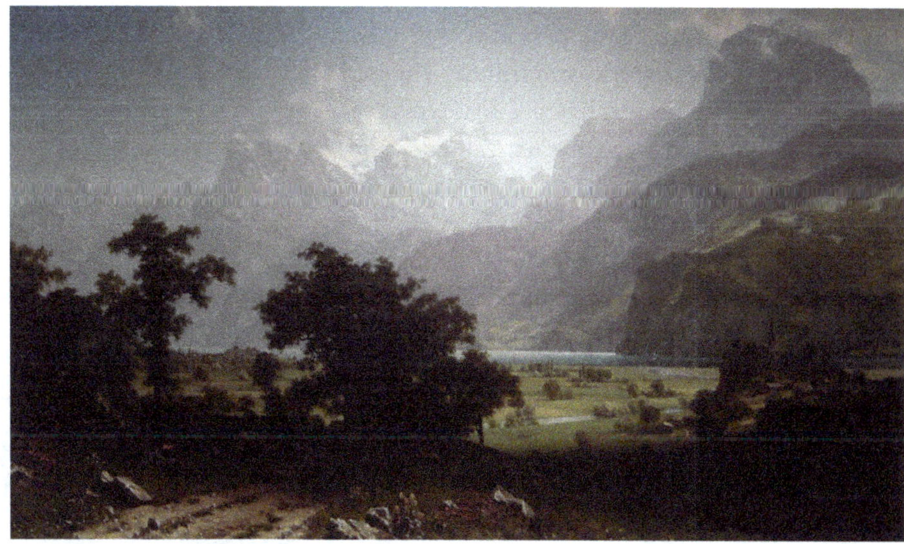

Figure 5.5: Albert Bierstadt, *Lake Lucerne*, 1858. Oil on Canvas, 72 in × 120 in, National Gallery of Art, Gift of Richard M. Scaife and Margaret R. Battle.

AMPLIFIED PERSPECTIVE

Amplified perspective is when an artist reduces or distorts parts of an object, but is still able to convey the illusion of three-dimensionality.[5] Amplified perspective is used to bring the viewer very quickly into a work of art, usually at a very unique angle. Andrea Mantegna's *The Dead Christ* (**fig 5.6**) is one of the best examples of this technique. Approaching this painting we are standing at Christ's feet as he is positioned on a marble slab following the deposition. We stand here, at a rather odd angle, and contemplate both the agony of his crucifixion as well as his sacrifice. If Mantegna were to paint the scene the way it would naturally look, the body would be difficult to view because Christ's feet would be in our way. Therefore, the artist shortens both the torso and legs and props the body up slightly so that we have a much more striking and meaningful view of the body.

LINEAR PERSPECTIVE

The most convincing way of rendering three-dimensional space onto a two-dimensional surface is through the technique of **linear perspective**. First codified during the Renaissance by Filippo Brunelleschi, it remains one of the most important artistic contributions from that time period.[6]

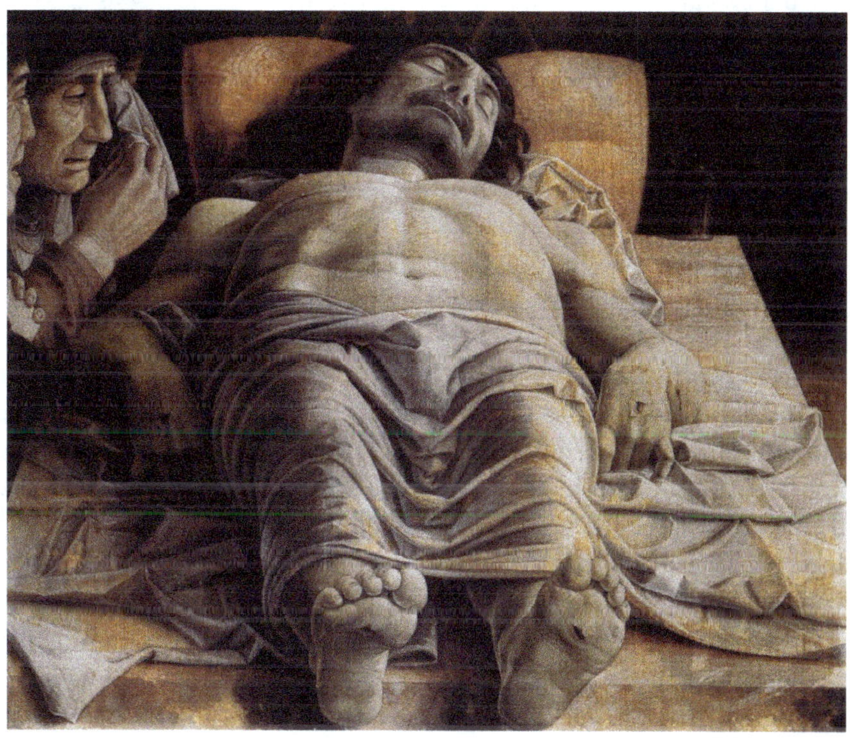

Figure 5.6: Andrea Mantegna, *The Dead Christ*, c. 1501. Oil on Canvas, 26.75 in × 31.88 in, Brera Gallery, Milan.

The good news is that linear perspective is nothing more than a mathematical formula. The bad news is that linear perspective is a mathematical formula. As with any mathematical equation, there is only one correct answer, so everything must be just done perfectly.

The easiest way to illustrate how this formula works is through the use of train tracks (**fig 5.7**). The question: Are train tracks parallel? Yes, they had better be, otherwise train derailments would be a common occurrence. However, our eyes want to give us a different story. When we look at train tracks heading toward the horizon they don't look parallel. It appears as if they are going to merge somewhere in the distance. What should we do if we are the engineer of the train headed down these tracks? Do we trust our eyes that tell us we should pull the emergency cord and stop the train? Or, do we trust our brain, which is telling us to relax, that our eyes are imperfect, and that the tracks are parallel? Of course, the latter is correct. But it also uncovers the basis of linear perspective: parallel lines appear to meet at a point in the distance. We have already seen through other illusionary techniques that our eyes are imperfect and that as artists we are trying to replicate the world that we see so it looks convincing.

To create a work in linear perspective, the first step is for the artist to establish the horizon line (**fig 5.8**). The **horizon line** is where the land and the sky meet. It is an arbitrary line that can be situated anywhere on the canvas: up high, down low, or right in the middle. The horizon line does not end at the frame, but rather extends past the frame infinitely in either direction.

The second step is for the artist to establish the vanishing point, which lives on the horizon line (**fig 5.8**). The **vanishing point** is where all the parallel lines in the artwork are going to converge. Like the horizon line, this, too, is an arbitrary point that can be placed off to the left, off to the right, or in the center. It doesn't even have to be situated on the surface of the canvas! Remember, the horizon line extends past the frame, and the only rule is that the vanishing point must rest somewhere on it.

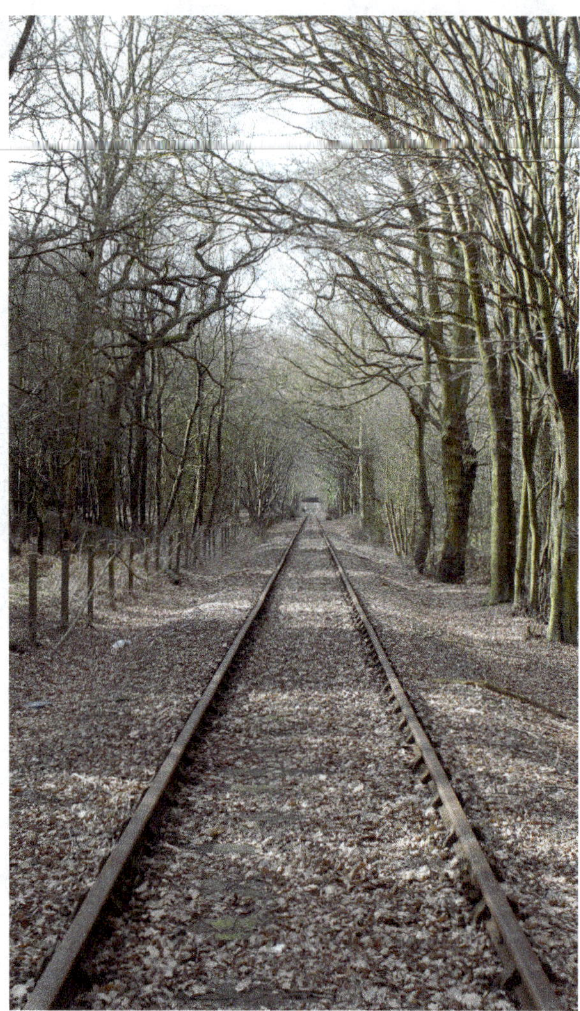

Figure 5.7: Mike Knell, *Train Tracks*, 2006. Digital Photograph, Zürich, Switzerland.

The third, and final, step is that all parallel lines must meet at the vanishing point. This step sounds pretty easy, but let me reiterate that *all* lines must meet at the vanishing point. The artist must be vigilant with this step, as missing just one line will throw the entire illusion off.

Back in 1427 Masaccio unveiled the very first work done in linear perspective, *Trinity with Mary, John the Evangelist, and Two Donors* (**fig 5.9**).[7]

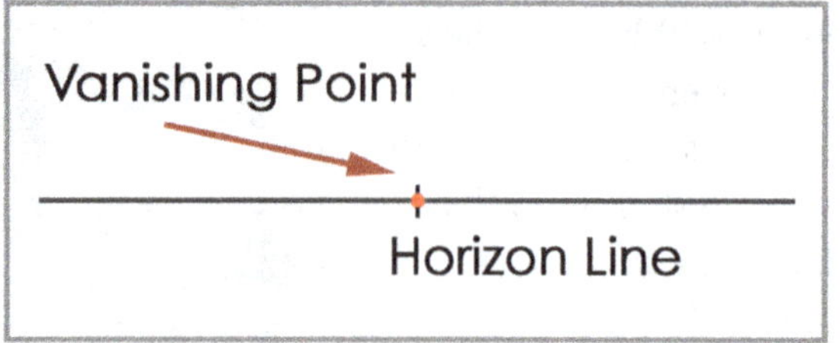

Figure 5.8:

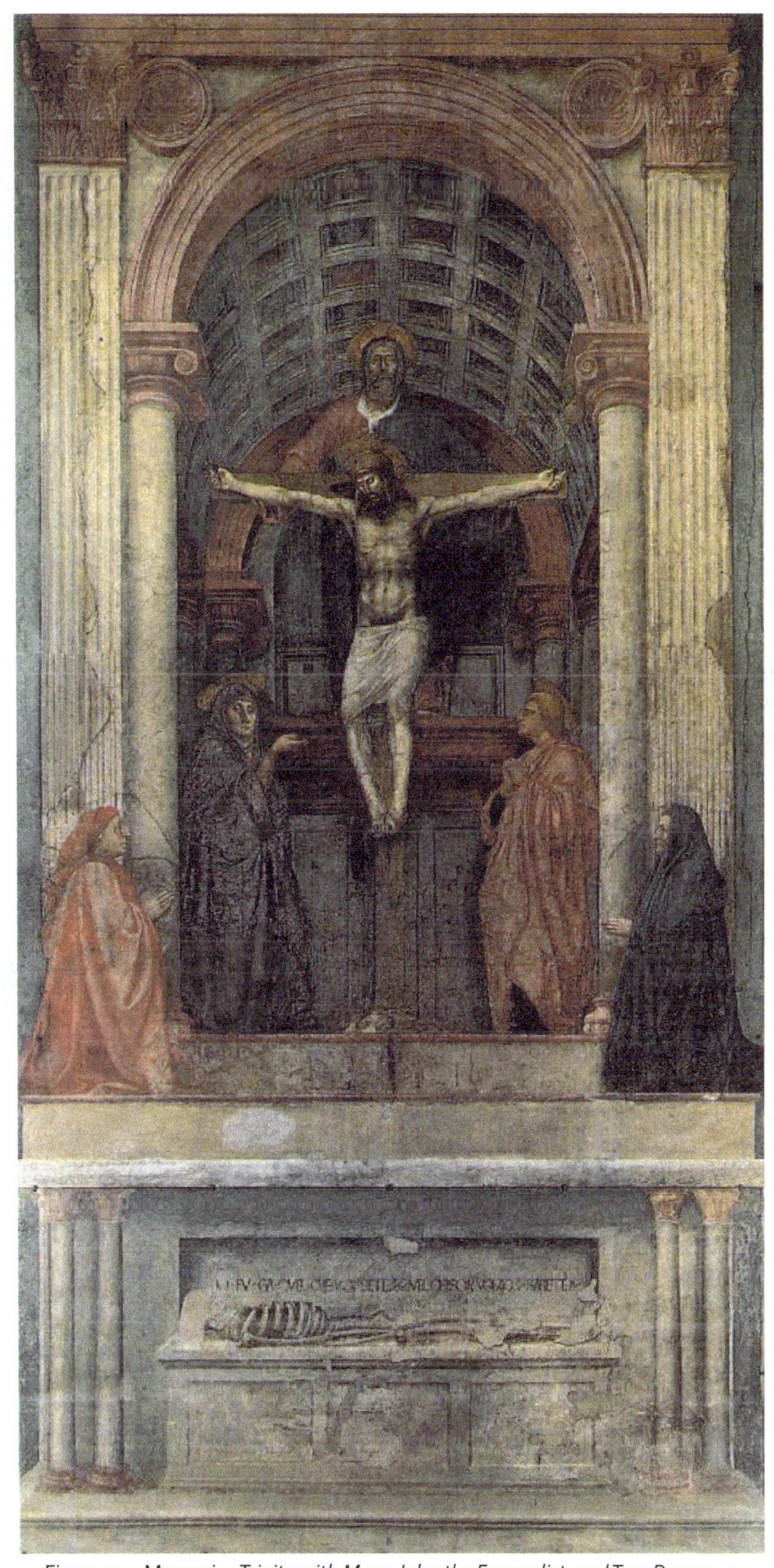

Figure 5.9: Masaccio, *Trinity with Mary, John the Evangelist, and Two Donors*, c. 1426–27. Fresco, 21 ft × 10 ft 5 in, Santa Maria Novella, Florence, Italy.

The image appears incredibly natural, as if it truly extends into the wall it is painted on. We can prove a work is in linear perspective by working in reverse order from how the artist created it. First, we extend lines from the architectural features, such as the corbeled barrel vault above or the sides of the tomb the skeleton lies on below to see if they all meet at one point (**fig 5.10**). In this case they do, and we have determined the position of the vanishing point, which is positioned directly below the base of the cross. When the vanishing point is in the center the painting, as it is here, the work is said to be in **frontal recession**. Simultaneously, we have also figured out where the horizon line is placed, as the vanishing point must be attached to this line.

Not all vanishing points are placed in the center of the artwork. In *Boston Common at Twilight* from chapter 9 (see fig 9.1), the vanishing point is slightly off-center toward the left. Anytime the vanishing point is not in the center the work it is considered to be in **diagonal recession**.[8] Once again, we can prove this by establishing that all parallel lines meet at a single point. If we begin at the architectural features of the buildings at the left and work in a counterclockwise fashion, we can see that the tops of the trolley cars, the road, the edges of the sidewalk, the park benches, and even the bases of the trees are all lined up with the vanishing point (**fig 5.11**), which is slightly off to the left. This placement also lends itself to the asymmetrical balance of the painting.

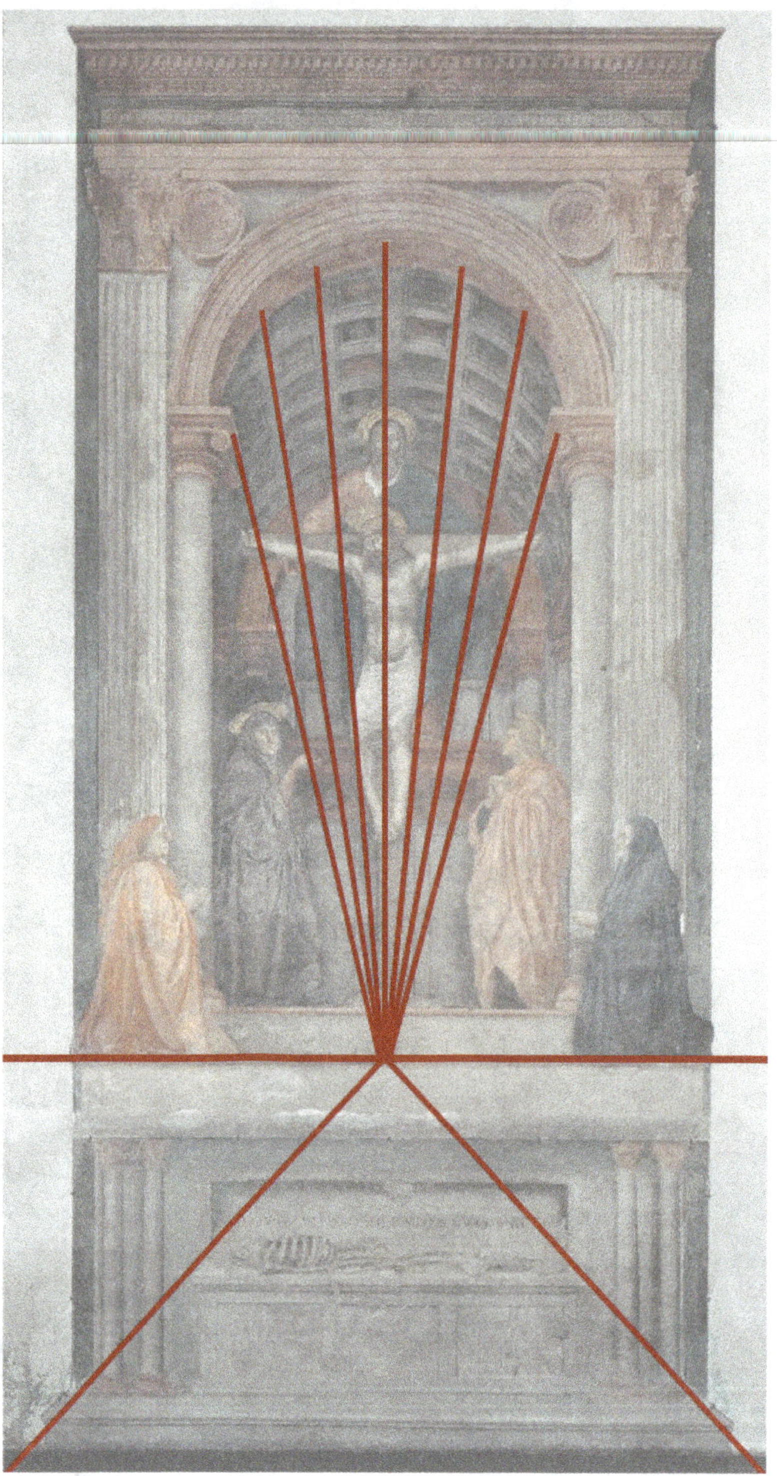

Figure 5.10:

When there is only one vanishing point, we say the work is in **one-point linear perspective**. However, artists are not limited to having just one vanishing point. When a second vanishing point is added to a work, it is considered to be in

two-point linear perspective. The advantage of the second vanishing point is that we can now turn buildings/structures at an angle and present them as they are more naturally seen. The rule remains that vanishing points must be placed on the horizon line.

Paris Street on a Rainy Day (**fig 5.12**) illustrates many of the illusions of space discussed in this chapter. It shows an altering of scale with the figures of the people walking toward us as the largest people, but as we move off to the left the next person is smaller, and the next couple continue to diminish in size, and so on. Vertical placement is also at play, as the figures walking toward us are standing below the level of the frame. The person at the left is placed higher, the couple left of that are higher yet. Overlapping plays a part with the two figures under the umbrella at the extreme left of the canvas, where the primary figure nearly obscures all but a leg and a thin section of the second person. Finally, linear perspective plays a part in the construction of the building in the background at the left of the street lamp. With the building at an angle we begin to draw lines from each of the floors and note that each line meets at points to the left and right of the building (**fig 5.13**). The vanishing points are at the same level, denoting the placement of the horizon line at the street level, which is where it should occur. Scale, overlapping, vertical placement, and two-point perspective all help to establish the naturalness of the scene.

The artist can continue to add vanishing points. After we have two vanishing points we simply say that the work is in **multipoint perspective**, and the points are no longer restricted to the horizon line. One artist who created impressive multipoint perspective work is M. C. Escher. His illusionary masterpieces leave many of us in awe as we try to unravel them and try to figure them out. With Escher being a mathematician, and linear perspective being a mathematical formula, it is no wonder he was able to create incredible works such as *Relativity* (not pictured).

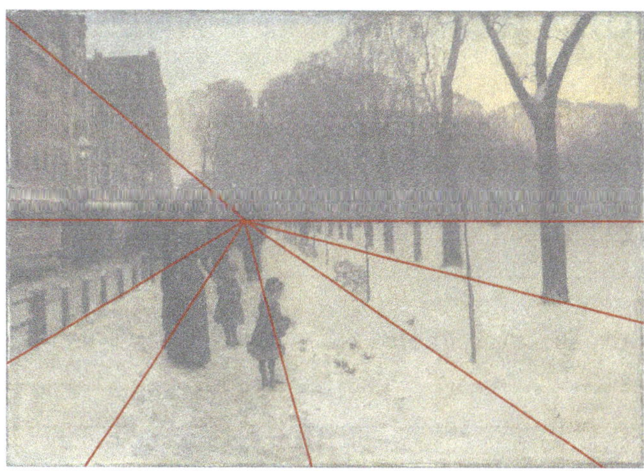

Figure 5.11:

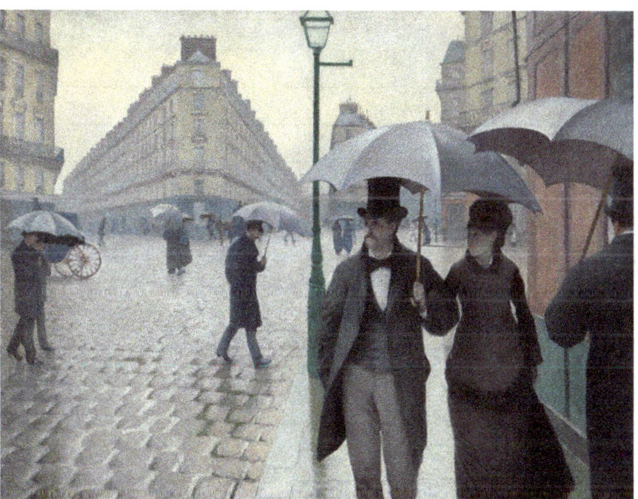

Figure 5.12: Gustave Caillebotte, *Paris Street on a Rainy Day*, 1877. Oil on Canvas, 83.25 in × 108.75 in, Art Institute of Chicago, Chicago, Illinois.

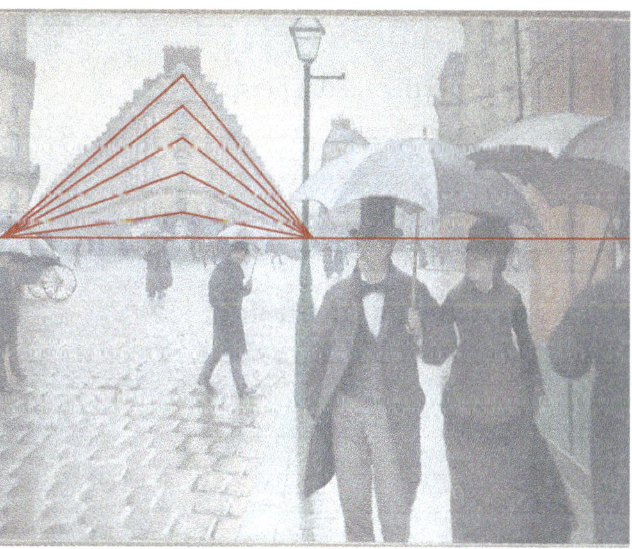

Figure 5.13:

Positive space (figure):

Negative space (ground):

Scale:

Overlapping:

Vertical location:

Atmospheric perspective (aerial perspective):

Amplified perspective (foreshortening):

Linear perspective:

Horizon line:

Vanishing point:

Frontal recession:

Diagonal recession:

One-point linear perspective:

Two-point linear perspective:

Multipoint perspective:

PROJECT: LINEAR PERSPECTIVE

Goal

Linear perspective revolutionized the world of art and was among the most significant contributions of the Italian Renaissance. This assignment gives you the opportunity to examine and apply those principles.

Required Media

15" × 20" illustration board
Pencils: #2 and #6B (Please do not use charcoal pencils)
Straight edge
Vinyl eraser

Assignment

In this assignment you will develop a composition using the principles of linear perspective.

1. Begin with the 15" × 20" illustration board. Using the straight edge and #2 pencil, create a border 1 inch in from the edges of the board. The border should be "floating," which means that no lines should extend to the edges of the board. The border should be crisp and clean.
2. Using the #2 pencil, draw a horizon line lightly across the board. You may choose where the horizon line goes, but it will be easier for you to place this line somewhere near the center of the board. You will need to erase the horizon line before you turn in your project.
3. Establish a vanishing point on the horizon line. This is an arbitrary location; however, it will be easier for you to place this line somewhere near the center of the board.
4. Use the straight edge to draw a square anywhere on the board. The square may be any size, but you might want to begin with one that measures 3" × 3".
5. Draw a light/faint line from the vanishing point to each of the four corners of the square.
6. From an arbitrary point along these light/faint lines you are going to create another square. Start by placing a point along the line leading from the upper-left-hand corner of the original square. The second point that you establish will be the upper-left-hand corner of your second (smaller) square. Use the straight edge to draw vertical and horizontal lines to create the second square. *The lines of both squares should be parallel with one another!*
7. Erase the lines that extend between the newly established second square and the vanishing point. The two-dimensional squares should now look more like a three-dimensional cube.
8. Erase any lines that would be hidden by the newly formed (solid) cube.
9. Using the #6 pencil go over the *visible* lines of the cube. Much of the score you receive on this project is derived from the structural formation of these cubes.
10. Shade the sides of the cube with the edge of the #6 pencil. Keep the shading lighter than the structural lines made in the previous instruction. The shading should be complete and fill the cube.
11. Repeat until you have seven or more of these cubes.
12. On the *back* of the illustration board, in the *upper-left-hand corner*, please write your name, the project number, and your class information (e.g., MWF 9 a.m.). *Please use a marker!*
13. Examples are below. They are for reference only. *Do not copy them!*

Point value: _______________

Due date: __________________ (weather permitting).

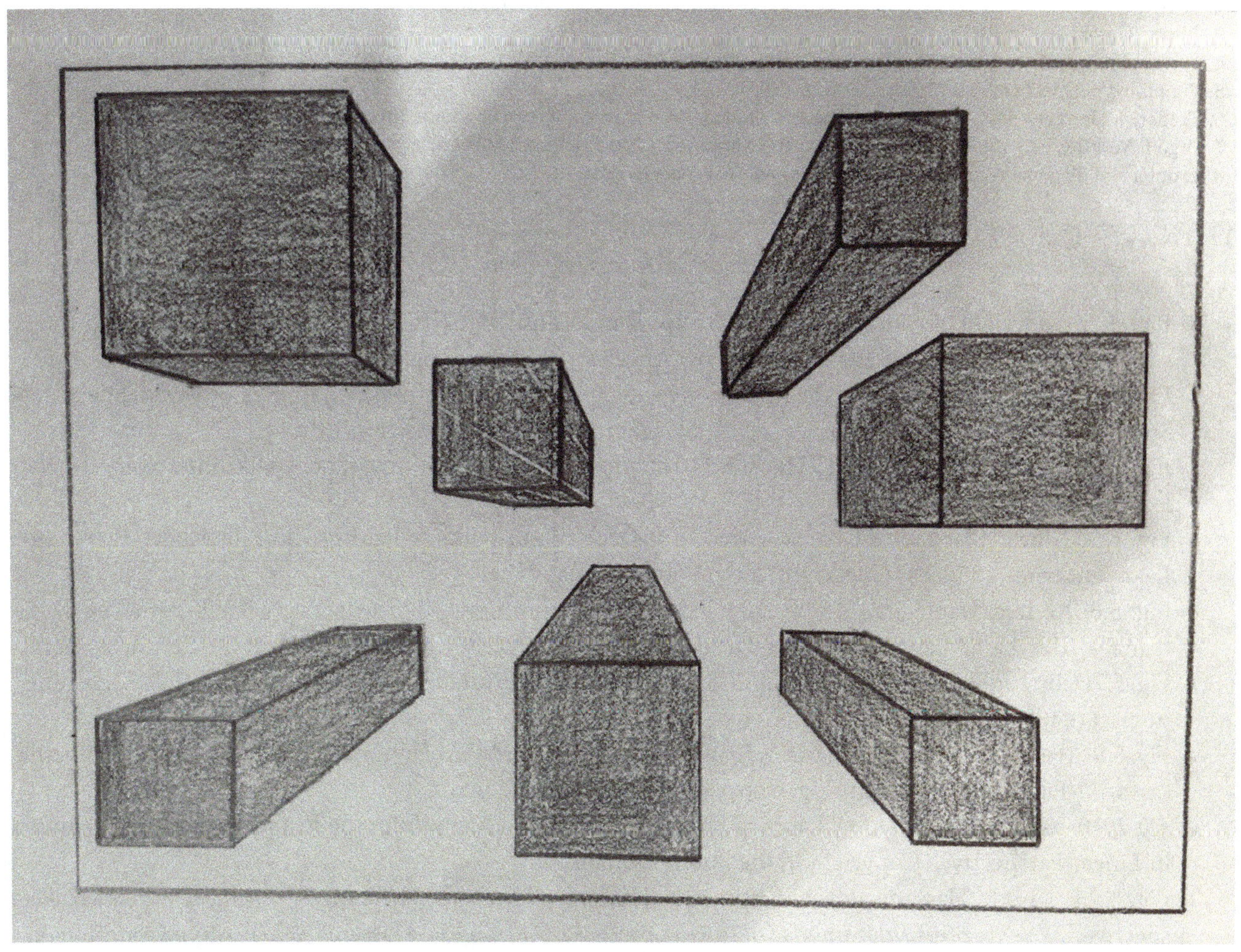

Figure 5.14: (Minimum requirement is seven cubes.)

ENDNOTES

1. According to the guided tour of the *Watts Towers*, Simon Rodia fell from one of the towers and fractured his hip. This ended his construction of the artwork.
2. Artworks such as *Khafre* or *Menkaure and His Wife* are sculptures that only contain positive space.
3. https://youtu.be/iZhEcRrMA-M.
4. Atmospheric perspective is also referred to as *aerial perspective*.
5. Amplified perspective is also referred to as *foreshortening*.
6. Frederick Hartt and David G. Wilkins, *History of Italian Renaissance Art* (Upper Saddle River, NJ: Prentice Hall, 2003), 183.
7. Ingo F. Walther, ed., *Masterpieces of Western Art* (Köln, Germany: Taschen, 2002), 93.
8. Frontal and diagonal recession are exclusive to one-point perspective.

IMAGE CREDITS

- Fig. 5.2: Copyright © Simon Rodia; Photo by DameEdithDivine (CC BY-SA 3.0) at https://commons.wikimedia.org/wiki/File:Watts_Towers,_Los_Angeles,_California.jpg.
- Fig. 5.3: Alfred Sisley, "Snow on the Road, Louveciennes," https://commons.wikimedia.org/wiki/File:Sisley-Snow_on_the_Road_Louveciennes.jpg. Copyright in the Public Domain.
- Fig. 5.4: Copyright © Boris D. (CC BY-SA 3.0) at https://commons.wikimedia.org/wiki/File:Yosemite_Valley_observation.jpg.
- Fig. 5.5: Albert Bierstadt, "Lake Lucerne," https://commons.wikimedia.org/wiki/File:Albert_Bierstadt,_Lake_Lucerne,_1858.jpg. Copyright in the Public Domain.
- Fig. 5.6: Andrea Mantegna, "The Dead Christ," https://commons.wikimedia.org/wiki/File:Andrea_Mantegna_-_The_Lamentation_over_the_Dead_Christ_-_WGA13981.jpg. Copyright in the Public Domain.
- Fig. 5.7: Copyright © Mike Knell (CC BY-SA 2.0) at https://commons.wikimedia.org/wiki/File:Vanishing_point_(104888019).jpg.
- Fig. 5.9: Masaccio, "Trinity with Mary, John the Evangelist, and Two Donors," https://commons.wikimedia.org/wiki/File:Masaccio_trinity.jpg. Copyright in the Public Domain.
- Fig. 5.10: Masaccio; adapted by Laura Hoffman, "Trinity with Mary, John the Evangelist, and Two Donors in Linear Perspective." Copyright in the Public Domain.
- Fig. 5.11: Childe Hassam; adapted by Laura Hoffman, "Boston Common at Twilight in Linear Perspective," https://commons.wikimedia.org/wiki/File:Childe_Hassam,_%27Boston_Common_at_Twilight%27,_1885%E2%80%9386.jpg. Copyright in the Public Domain.
- Fig. 5.12: Gustave Caillebotte, "Paris Street on a Rainy Day," https://commons.wikimedia.org/wiki/File:Gustave_Caillebotte_-_Paris_Street;_Rainy_Day_-_Google_Art_Project.jpg. Copyright in the Public Domain.
- Fig. 5.13: Gustave Caillebotte; adapted by Laura Hoffman, "Paris Street on a Rainy Day in Linear Perspective." Copyright in the Public Domain.

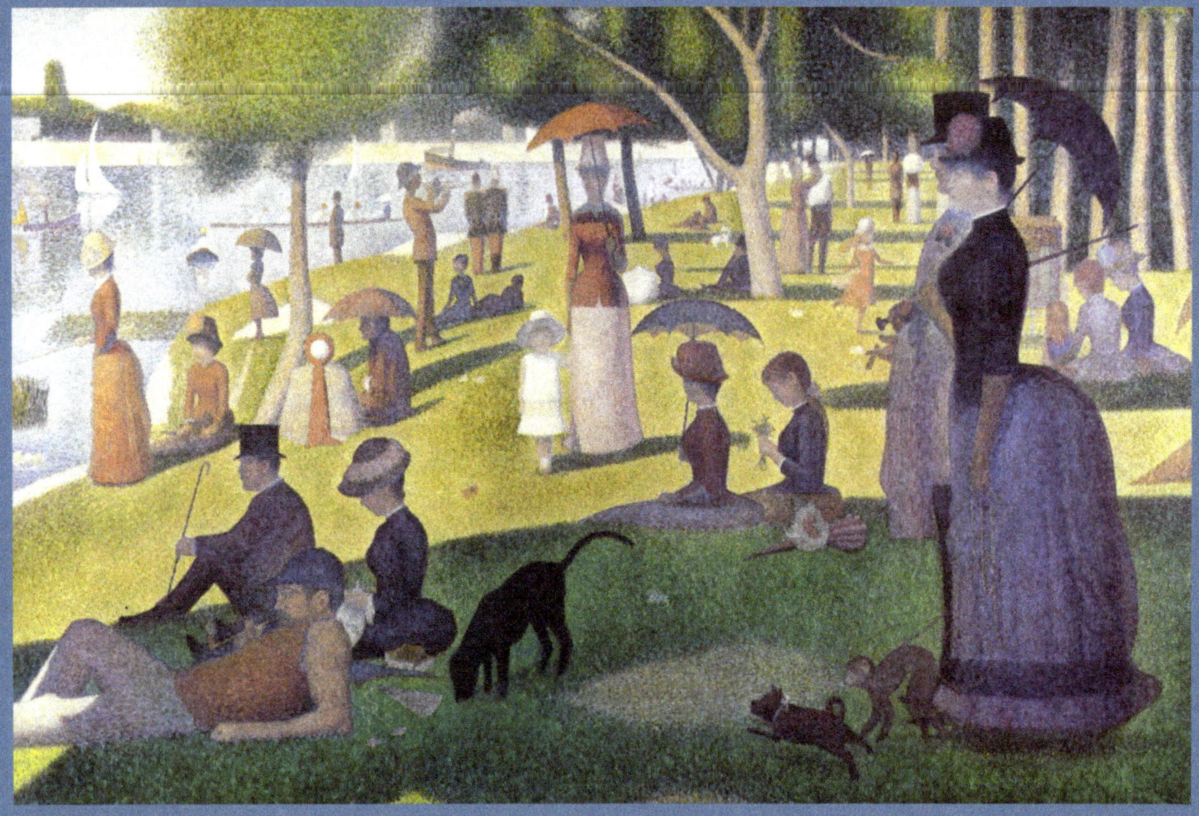

Figure 6.1: Georges Seurat, *Sunday Afternoon on the Island of La Grande Jatte*, 1884–86. Oil on canvas, 81 in × 120.4 in, Art Institute of Chicago.

COLOR

COLOR

All of us deal with color on a daily basis: What color clothes should I wear? What color am I going to paint my room? What color nail polish is going to look better? There are people who spend more time deciding on the color of their vehicle than on any other option. The bottom line is that color plays a significant role in our lives, and we deal with it on a daily basis. Just think about the role color plays in the life of an artist.

Color is the first thing people notice when they look at a work of art. It is noticed before line, space, pattern, or texture. So where does color come from? Color comes from light! That answer seems a little strange because for most of us light appears to be colorless. But in 1666 Sir Isaac Newton discovered that when light is refracted through a prism it is broken down into a spectrum of colors (known as **hues**): red, orange, yellow, green, blue, and violet (**fig 6.2**). It is from these six colors that all other colors are created.

Creating other colors from the six hues can be done a couple of different ways. The first is by altering a hue by mixing in white or black. When we add white to a hue, we are creating **tints**. When we add black to a hue, we are creating **shades**. For example, if we begin with the hue of red and mix in white we can create colors such as pink, salmon, coral, and rose. These are all tints of red. Now, if we were to mix in black to the hue of red we would create colors such as maroon, crimson, and scarlet. These are all shades of red.

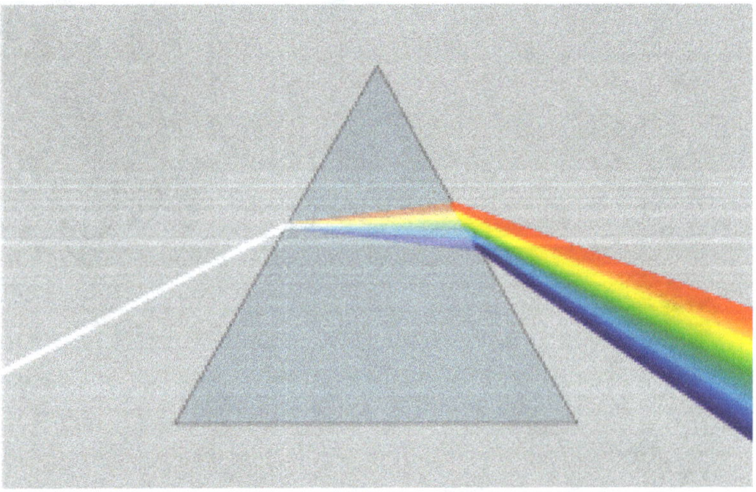

A second way of creating colors from the original six hues is by mixing two or more of the hues together. There are two processes you should be aware of: the additive process and the subtractive process. The **additive process** deals with light. This is not a process most artists come into contact with. It is usually reserved for those working in the theatre or places such as Disneyland where colored spotlights would be used. When two colored lights cross, they will create a different color. Most artists utilize the **subtractive process**, which deals not with light, but with paint and pigment. A characteristic of this process is that every time paint or pigment is mixed together the resulting color is going to be darker and duller than either of the parents. The reason for this is because paint acts as a filter. When you mix two colors of paint, you are in essence combining two filters. An analogy to this would be the way sunglasses filter out the light. If you were wearing a pair of sunglasses and then put on a second pair, the world would look darker and duller than if you only had the one pair on. Artists must be cautious not to over mix paint. It is really easy to end up with a color that looks something like mud.

THE COLOR WHEEL

Knowing how to use a color wheel is extremely important. It is a way to organize color and see the working relationships they have with one another. Color wheels date back to the 1700s, and there are many different types and formats. Among the easiest to use is what is known as the **conventional 12-section color wheel (fig 6.3)**.

Next to each name on the color wheel is a number. The number denotes whether the color is classified as a primary color, a secondary color, or a tertiary color.[1] The number one is assigned to the **primary colors**, which are red, yellow, and blue.[2] It is from these three colors

Figure 6.2: Light Being Refracted Through a Prism.

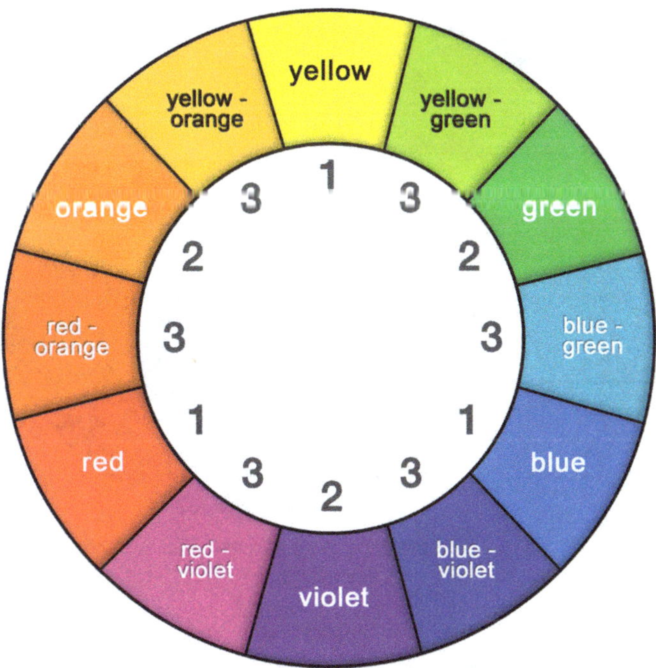

Figure 6.3: Conventional 12-Section Color Wheel.

that all of the others are created. They are the Adam and Eve of the color chart. You can also think about this in reverse, that no combination of colors mixed together can form these three colors. Therefore, they are primary.

The number two is assigned to the secondary colors. **Secondary colors** are created when two primary colors are mixed together. Mixing red and blue creates violet, mixing yellow and blue creates green, and mixing red and yellow creates orange. Note that the six hues, which emerge from white light as it is refracted through a prism, are the primary and secondary colors.

The number three is assigned to the tertiary colors. Mixing a primary color with its neighboring secondary color results in a **tertiary color**. The color's name reflects its parentage. For instance, primary red mixed with secondary violet creates the tertiary color of red-violet. There are six tertiary colors: red-violet, red-orange, yellow-orange,

yellow-green, blue-violet, and blue-green.

COLOR SCHEMES

The color chart can also be broken down into three distinctive color schemes: analogous, complementary, and triadic. Color schemes allow the artist to employ color in very specific ways that affect the viewer. The **analogous color scheme** relies on the fact that colors next to each other on the color wheel have similar characteristics (**fig 6.4**). Analogous color schemes are broken down into two subcategories: warm colors and cool colors. We can draw a line through the color wheel that creates two sides. One side features **warm colors** such as red (we say something is "red" hot) and yellow (the color of the sun). The other side features the **cool colors** such as green (the color of grass) and blue (the color of water).

Sanford Robinson Gifford uses an analogous color scheme in his painting *October in the*

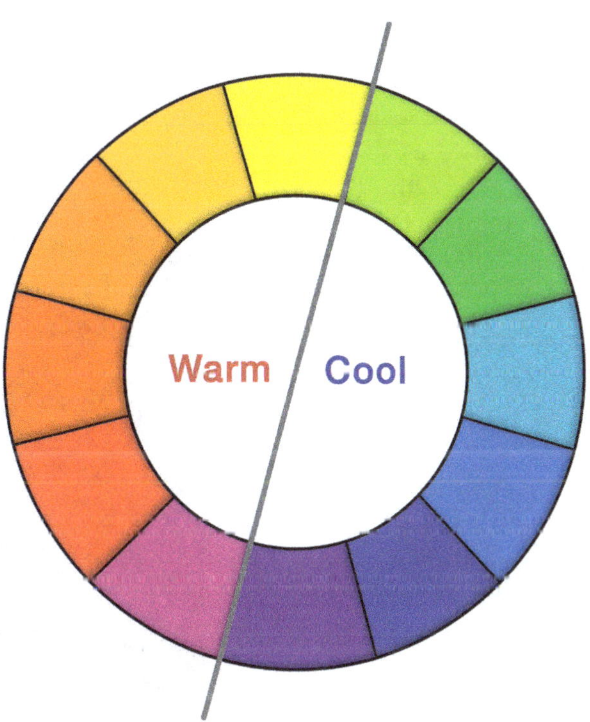

Figure 6.4: Analogous Color Scheme.

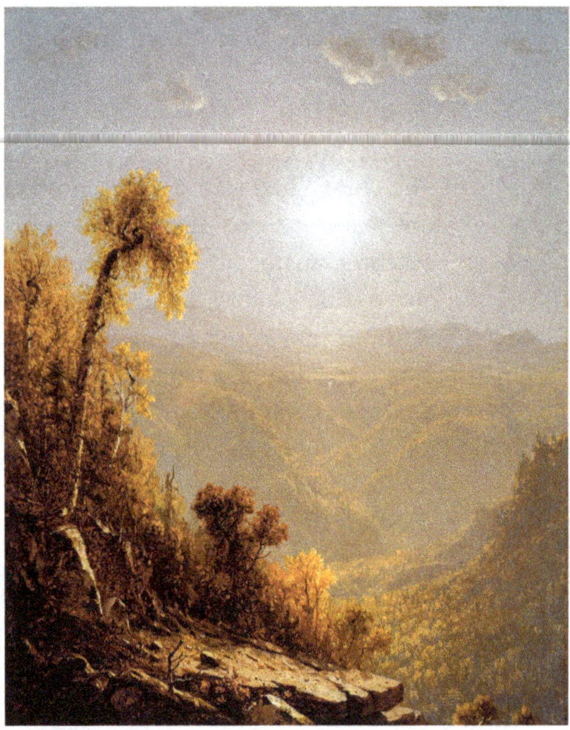

Figure 6.5: Sanford Robinson Gifford, *October in the Catskills*, 1880.
Oil on Canvas, 36 5/16 in × 29 3/16 in, Los Angeles County Museum of Art.

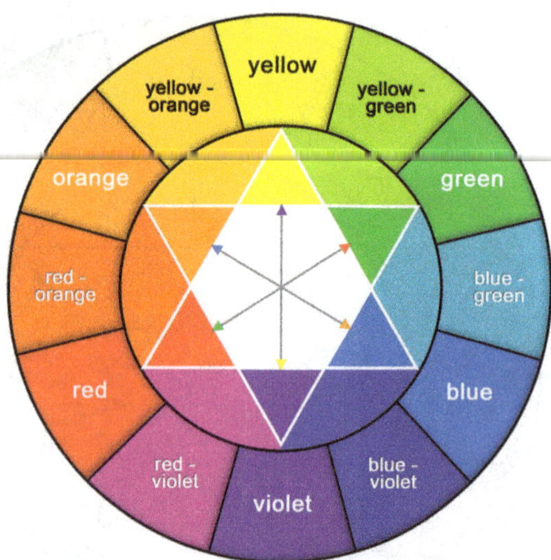

Figure 6.6: Complimentary Color Scheme.

Catskills (**fig 6.5**). The painting exudes a feeling of warmth, so much so you want to shield your eyes from its brightness and heat and go searching for a shaded spot in which to rest. Even the sky, which would normally appears blue, takes on a yellowish haze. This painting could also be used as an example of atmospheric perspective (chapter 5). The foreground is clear and very detailed, but as the forms recede into the distance their contours become less distinct and begin to take on the color of the atmosphere. Indeed, it is difficult to see where the land stops and the sky begins.

In a **complementary color scheme**, the artist uses colors that are on opposite sides of the wheel from one another (**fig 6.6**). One of the most common complementary color pairs is red and green. Placing complementary colors next to one another results in the colors intensifying one another. The reason this happens is that cool colors, such as green, appear to recede away from the viewer, whereas warm colors, such as red, look to be accelerating toward the viewer. When you have these colors next to one another it affects our optic nerve, making us feel tense and uneasy.[3]

Vincent van Gogh purposely used this type of color scheme in many of his paintings. In a letter that van Gogh writes to his brother Theo, he explains the use of complementary colors in the painting called *The Night Café* (**fig 6.7**): "I have

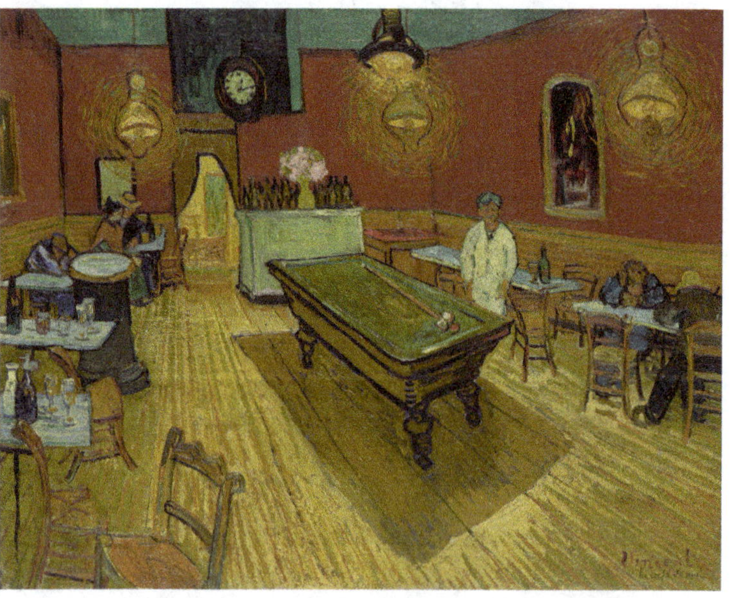

Figure 6.7: Vincent van Gogh, *The Night Café*, 1888.
Oil on Canvas, 28.5 in × 36.3 in, Yale University Art Gallery.

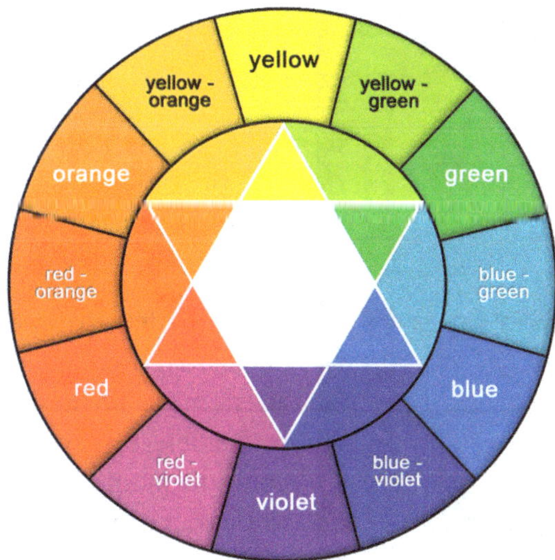

Figure 6.8: Triadic Color Scheme.

tried to express the terrible passions of humanity by means of red and green. The room is blood red and dark yellow with a green billiard table in the middle; there are four lemon-yellow lamps with a glow of orange and green. Everywhere there is a clash and contrast of the most alien reds and greens."[4]

A **triadic color scheme** utilizes three colors that are spaced evenly around the color wheel. Four triadic color schemes are possible; however, the one most frequently used contains the three primary colors. By placing an equilateral triangle within the color wheel, we can see that red, blue, and yellow are equally spaced (**fig 6.8**). Another triadic color scheme would include the secondary colors. Whereas complementary color schemes create uneasiness, triadic color schemes are considered to be balanced and harmonious.

The triadic color scheme is very subtle. It appears in the least likely of places, such as in the logo for Burger King or Superman's costume. A famous artwork that incorporates the triadic color scheme would be Vermeer's *Girl with the Pearl Earring* (**fig 6.9**). The girl's clothing is red,

while her oriental turban contains both blue and yellow.[5] Yet another work would be Mondrian's *Composition of Red, Blue, and Yellow* (see fig 4.1), which relies specifically on a triadic color scheme, as well as the extremes of value (discussed later in this chapter).

REPRESENTATIONS OF COLOR

An artist can represent color in an artwork in three ways: local, perceptual, or arbitrary. **Local color** is the color we know the object to be without us having to go and look. If someone asked you to paint a banana, you would immediately reach for the yellow paint. A fire engine would be red. Grass would be green, and so on. For most of the history of art, paintings would be rendered in local color because the artist was trying to reproduce or mimic the natural world.

In 1970 the United States Postal Service issued a stamp celebrating Maine's 150th anniversary as

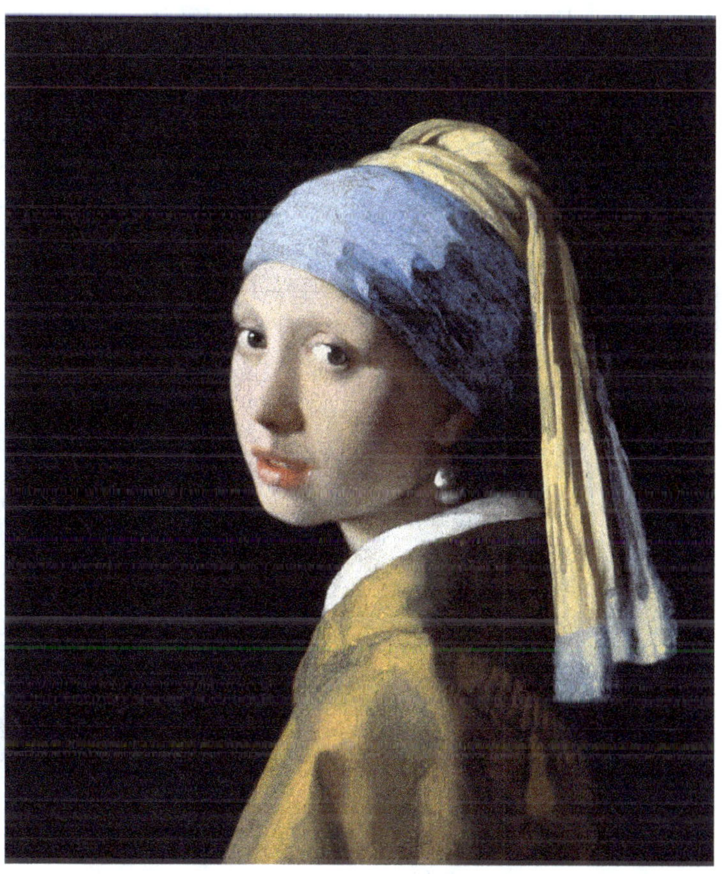

Figure 6.9: Johannes Vermeer, *The Girl with the Pearl Earring*, 1665. Oil on Canvas, 18.3 in × 15.7 in, Royal Picture Gallery, Mauritshuis.

Figure 6.10: Edward Hopper, *The Lighthouse at Two Lights*, 1929 (Stamp issued in 1970). Oil on Canvas, 29.5 in × 43.25 in, The Metropolitan Museum of Art.

a state. Featured on the stamp was a reproduction of Edward Hopper's *The Lighthouse at Two Lights* (**fig 6.10**). This painting utilizes local color because everything appears as it should: the grass and shrubbery are green, the sky is blue, and the clouds are white. None of these colors are questioned as far as their accuracy to nature is concerned.

The end of the nineteenth century brought experimentation and innovation, which resulted in a new way of representing color. **Perceptual color** is the color the object is at a particular moment in time. Aren't objects the same color all the time? No, they aren't. As we learned earlier, color is derived from light. Because light changes throughout the day, color must change as well.

Monet, the leader of the Impressionists, was among the first to experiment with this representation of color. He would paint an object in a series of paintings. For example, *Grainstack in the Morning, Snow Effect* (**fig 6.11**) is one of over 30 paintings Monet executed using a grainstack as the subject matter. In each of these paintings, the grainstack looks different. It is because Monet painted this work during different times of the day, different seasons, and in different atmospheric conditions.

In order to paint perceptual color, the artist must be in front of the object he or she is going to paint. We refer to this act as painting *en plein air*. It is a French term that translates to "in the open air." In the late nineteenth century this would have been a radical and innovative idea. No one had ever done this before. Up until this time artists would paint in a controlled environment, a studio. Granted, artists may have gone outside to sketch an object, but the painting would be rendered within the confines of their studio.

As the nineteenth century moved into the twentieth, artists continued with innovative experiments in color. **Arbitrary color** is created when the artist gets to decide on the color for a particular object. Sometimes referred to as

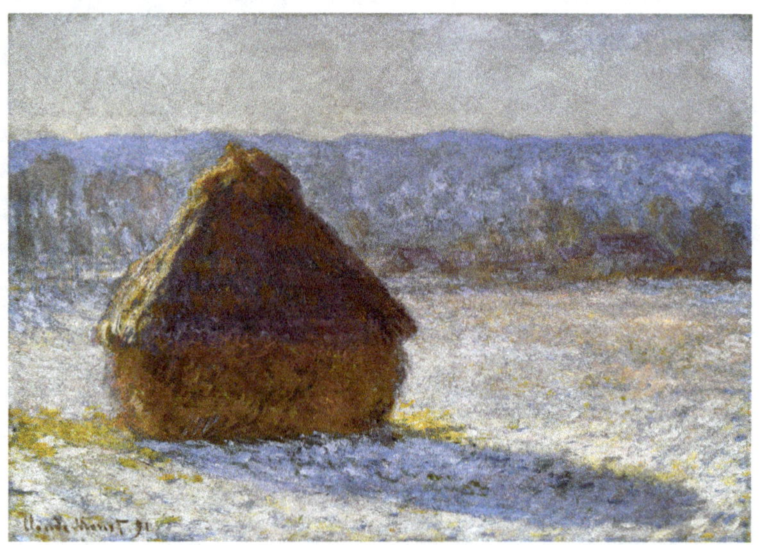

Figure 6.11: Claude Monet, *Grainstack in the Morning, Snow Effect*, 1891. Oil on Canvas, 29 in × 36.6 in, Museum of Fine Arts, Boston.

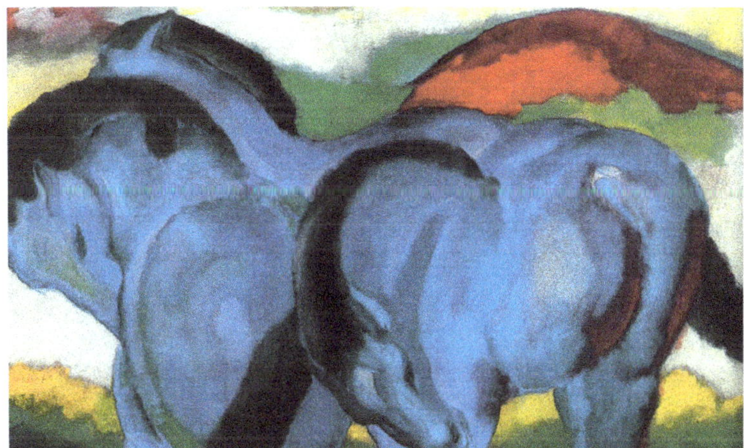
Figure 6.12: Franz Marc, *The Little Blue Horses*, 1911.
Oil on Canvas, 61.5 cm × 101 cm, Staatsgalerie Stuttgart.

subjective color, an artist might paint the sun blue or mauve. He might paint the grass red or purple. The color choice could be based on either emotive or design reasons. The Fauvists, led by Henri Matisse (discussed in chapter 23), were the first modern art movement to champion the use of arbitrary color.

The German Expressionists were another group that frequently employed arbitrary color. The title of Franz Marc's painting, *The Little Blue Horses* (**fig 6.12**), gives us a hint that we are going to be experiencing something never seen in nature. The painting contains three vibrantly painted horses with assorted colors in the background. Nothing in this artwork relates to the natural world except the form of the animals. The employment of this radical arbitrary color makes this work stimulating to look at.

POINTILLISM

As you can see with the continued experimentation with perceptual and arbitrary color toward the end of the nineteenth century, there was a growing interest in color theory. The artist Georges Seurat investigated a new way of applying paint to canvas with the technique of Pointillism. **Pointillism**, sometimes called *divisionism*, is when the artist places dots or points of pure color next to one another rather than mixing them together in the traditional fashion.

Ordinarily, if the artist wanted to create the color green he or she would mix together blue and yellow. The newly formed green would then be applied to the canvas. With Pointillism the artist would not mix the colors, but rather place a small point of blue directly onto the canvas and then add a small point of yellow adjacent to the blue. The theory is that our eyes would mix the colors for us and the viewer would see green.

Does Pointillism work? It does, to a certain extent. If you stand at a predetermined distance from a painting, such as Seurat's *Sunday Afternoon on the Island of La Grande Jatte* (**fig 6.1**), which is the most famous Pointillist painting ever produced, everything looks as it should. However, if you move closer and start to examine the painting's details, you begin to see the individual points of color, which will disrupt the image.[6] If you stand too far away, the eye brings in so much color the result is that the painting appears dull, just as if we were to over mix paint on the palette. It took Seurat an incredible amount of time to produce this image. A painting of this size might take an artist a few months to produce, but because of the Pointillist technique that was used it took him nearly two years to produce this work, along with having to create close to 60 preliminary drawings and sketches to make sure each point color was in its proper place.[7]

VALUE

Value is a measurement of how dark or light an object is. The extremes of value are black and white. When you mix these two colors together at different percentages, they form infinite shades of gray (**fig 6.13**). Value is an extremely important element in the discussion of color because it

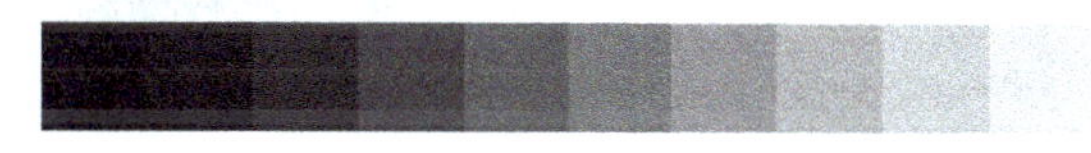
Figure 6.13: Value Scale.

helps us to see. We can define forms and objects because of the change in their value. A black-and-white photo such as *North Palisade from Windy Point* (**fig 6.14**) by Ansel Adams is created using various shades of gray. Even though there may only be five or six variations of gray, we can still identify clouds, mountains, shadows, and snow.

When two values are positioned next to one another, we look at the **value contrast** between them. Value contrast can be used to help determine and define space, as well as to create emphasis or direct the viewers to where the artist wants them to look. Sometimes the value contrast can be quite bold, such as black text on a white page. Other times it is not as noticeable, but still very important. In fact, this is how atmospheric perspective works. In *Wanderer Above the Sea of Fog* (**fig 6.15**), there is high value contrast between the dark rock outcropping and the figure in the foreground with the whiteness of the clouds. Our eye views this contrast as being close to us. In the background of the painting, the sky, clouds, and mountains share a value. We can still tell they are separate objects, but there is not as much value contrast. Our eye views this contrast as being more distant.

An artist can manipulate value so that objects look more three-dimensional. The technique of **chiaroscuro**, developed during the Renaissance, is when there are several gradual value changes to an object that give it the sensation of having depth and volume. In the case of Malevich's *Black Square* (**fig 6.16**), there is only one value

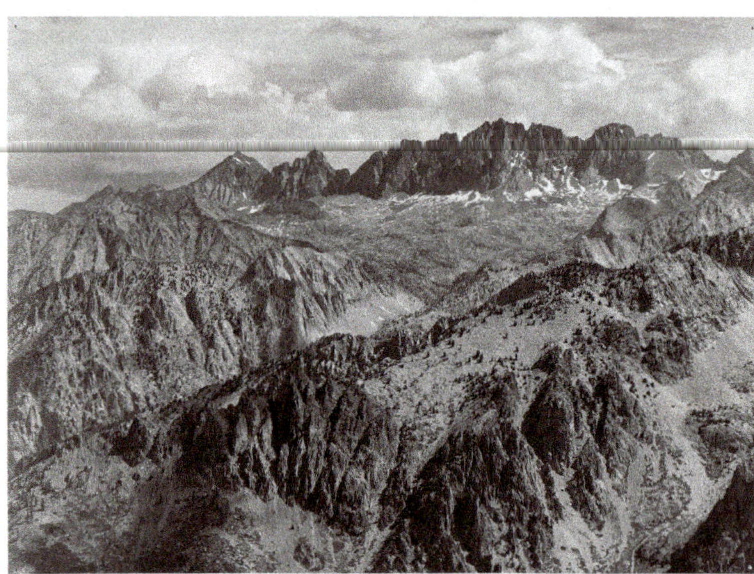

Figure 6.14: Ansel Adams, *North Palisade from Windy Point,* 1936. Photograph.

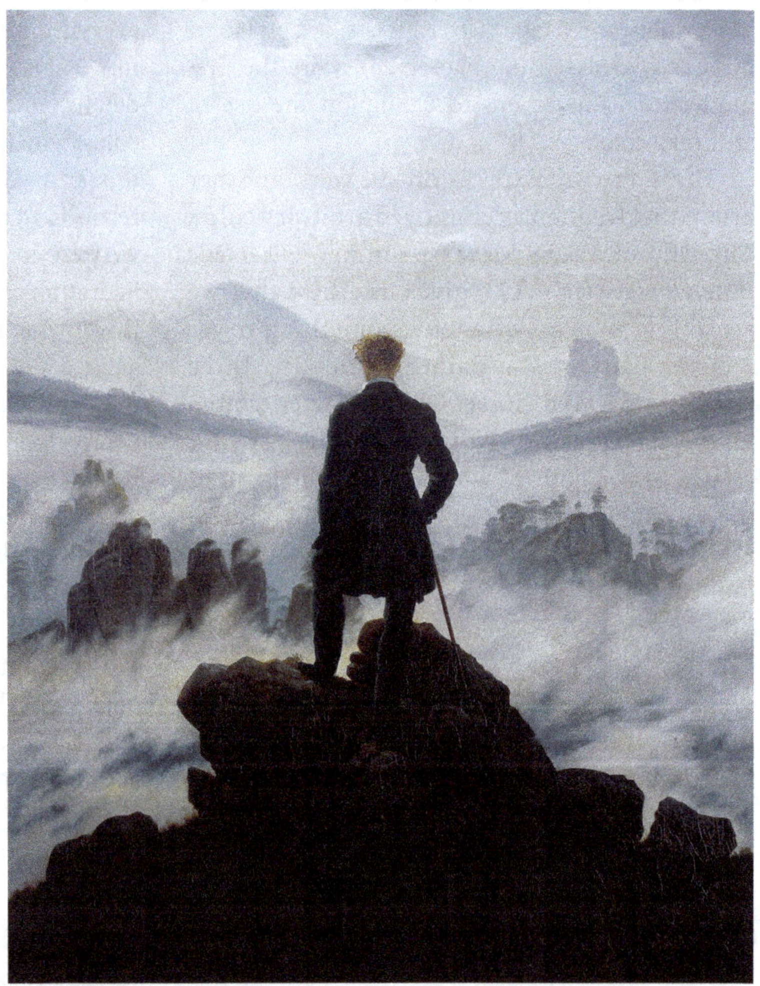

Figure 6.15: Caspar David Friedrich, *Wanderer Above the Sea of Fog*, 1818. Oil on Canvas, 38.6 in × 29.1 in, Kunsthalle, Hamburg.

Figure 6.16: Kasimir Malevich, *Black Square*, c. 1923. Oil on Canvas, 106 cm × 106 cm, State Russian Museum, St Petersburg.

the focal point, which is usually illuminated by a single candle. It gives the same effect as watching the stage in a darkened theatre and having a single spotlight shine down on a specific place, which becomes the focal point of the scene.

In Georges de la Tour's painting *The Penitent Magdalen* (**fig 6.17**), the single candle shines a luminescent glow over Mary Magdalen as she stares across into the mirror unaware of our presence. Her hands rest on a skull in her lap, which is a reference to human mortality that is a commonly addressed in religious paintings, such as this one. The technique of tenebrism adds a theatrical element to the painting. The viewer waits to see what will happen next in this quiet and solemn scene.

change—from white to black. The object is flat and two-dimensional. But when an artist uses the technique of chiaroscuro, as seen with the figures in *The Tribute Money* (**fig 22.6**), these figures stand as three-dimensional sculptural elements.

Whereas chiaroscuro is defined as a gradual shift in value, the technique of **tenebrism** is defined as a dramatic shift in value, creating dramatic illumination. Tenebrism was very popular during the 1600s and is most commonly associated with the artist Caravaggio.[8] After his death his followers, the Caravaggisti, which included Georges de la Tour, continued using this technique in their paintings. Tenebrism is a very theatrical element; most of the painting is dark except for

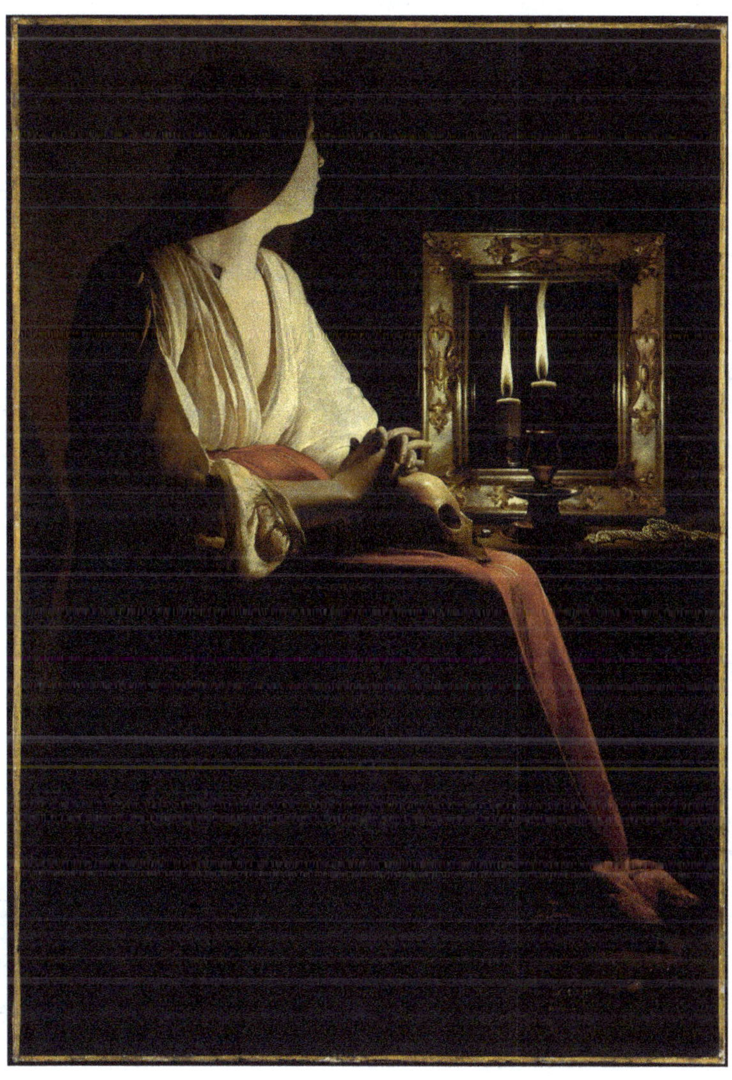

Figure 6.17: Georges de La Tour, *JThe Penitent Magdalen*, 1625-1650. Oil on Canvas, 52.5 in × 40.2 in, Metropolitan Museum of Art.

Hue:

Tint:

Shade:

Additive process:

Subtractive process:

Color wheel (conventional 12-section):

Primary colors:

Secondary colors:

Tertiary colors (intermediate colors):

Analogous color schemes:

Warm colors:

Cool colors:

Complementary color schemes:

Triadic color schemes:

Local color (objective color):

Perceptual color (optical color):

En plein air:

Arbitrary color (subjective color):

Pointillism:

Value:

Value contrast

Chiaroscuro:

Tenebrism:

PROJECT 1: THE COLOR CHART

Goal

By creating your own color chart, you will be able to visually recognize the working relationships of color.

Required Media

15" × 20" illustration board
#2 pencil
Straight edge
Paintbrush (#12 flat tip watercolor/gouache)
Cup of water
10-well plastic tray
Gouache: primary red, primary yellow, primary blue
Newspaper/cloth/paper towels
Palette knife (optional)

Assignment

1. Begin with the illustration board in a *vertical* position.
2. Using the #2 pencil, create a grid pattern that is centered on the illustration board. The grid pattern should be three boxes wide and six boxes tall, with each box being 3" square. This will leave you a 1" border on the top and bottom and a 3" border on the left and right sides of the illustration board. Note that the borders will vary if you use another size of illustration board.
3. Fill in each square with the appropriate color using gouache paint (beginning with yellow). Do not deviate from the chart below. You will be able to create all the colors by using a mixture of the primary colors: red, yellow, and blue.

Red	Yellow	Blue	**Primary Colors**
Green	Violet	Orange	**Secondary Colors**
Red/Violet	Red/Orange	Yellow/Orange	**Tertiary Colors**
Yellow/Green	Blue/Green	Blue/Violet	**Tertiary Colors**
Red/Green	Yellow/Violet	Blue/Orange	**Mixed Compliments**
R/V and Y/G	R/O and B/G	Y/O and B/V	**Mixed Compliments**

4. Each box will contain only one solid color!
5. On the *back* of the illustration board, in the *upper-left-hand corner*, please write your name and your class information (e.g., MWF 9 a.m.). *Please use a marker!* DO THIS AFTER THE PAINT HAS DRIED OR BEFORE YOU BEGIN YOUR PROJECT!!!
6. Do not turn in projects that are still wet. They should be allowed to dry overnight.
7. Only use gouache paint for this project.
8. There should be no white space between the painted squares. The colors of paint should be touching, but not overlapping. An example is shown below.

- Plan ahead as this project takes about three to four hours to complete.
- Keep a moist paper towel close by.
- Protect the area you are painting on with newspaper or drop cloth.
- Wear older/work clothes just in case.
- It's best to begin with yellow since it has the highest value.
- It's best to work with the same color families at a time; that is, yellow, green, blue/green, yellow/green, red/green. *Do not work left to right, top to bottom.*
- A little gouache goes a long way, so use it sparingly.
- Use even smaller amounts of paint when mixing two colors. You can always add more if you need to.
- When mixing paint to create another color use equal amounts.
- Sometimes it is easier to mix the gouache with your brush than with the palette knife.
- Red + yellow = orange; yellow + blue = green; red + blue = violet.

Point value: _____________________

Due date: __________________ (weather permitting).

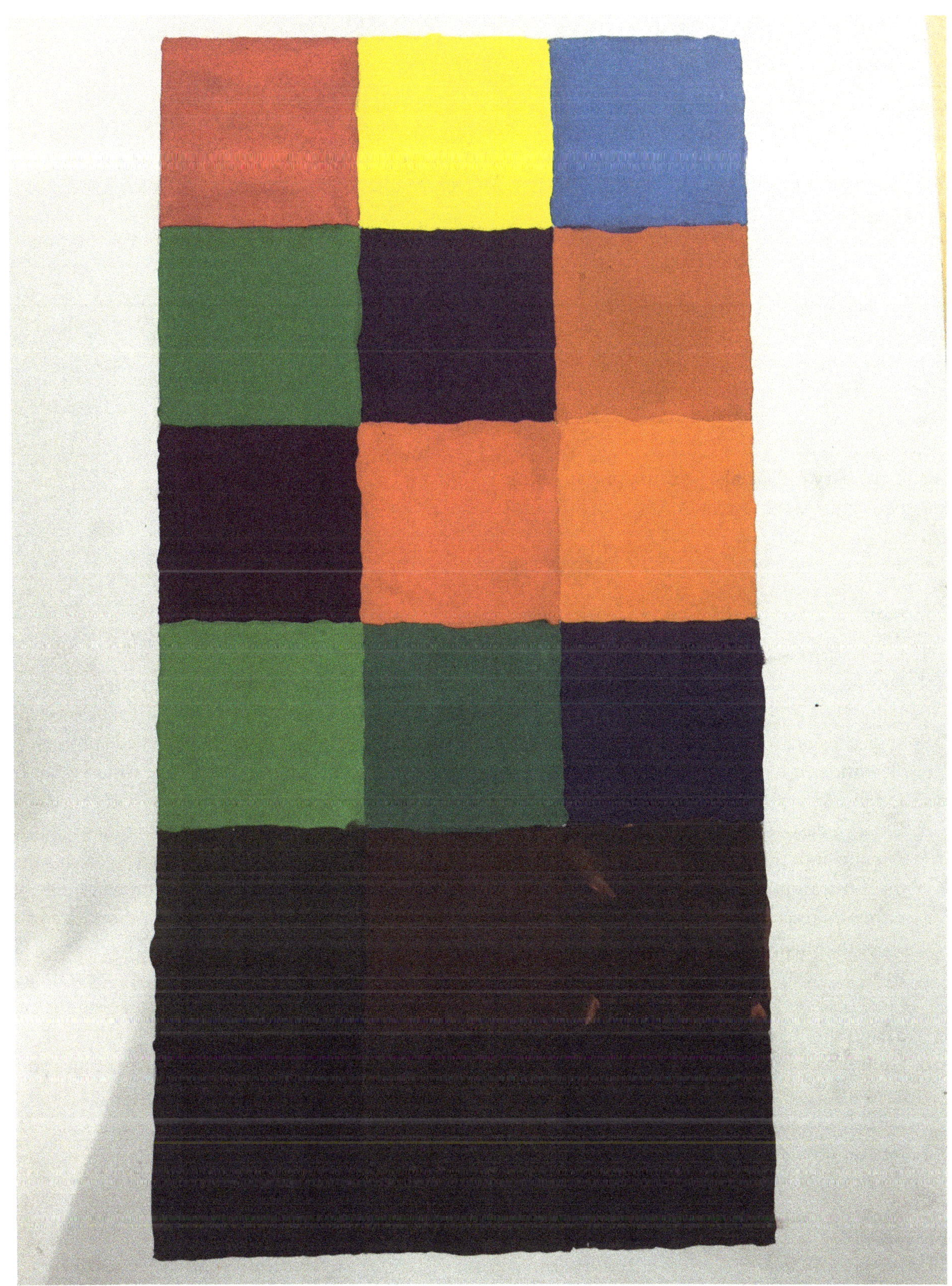

Figure 6.18: Example of a finished color chart.
(Note: Colors might differ slightly. They will not exactly match those shown in this example.)

PROJECT 2: ANALOGOUS COLOR SCHEMES

Goal

This project continues our exploration of the interrelationship of color. Your objective is to create two designs similar to the works of Piet Mondrian. The finished project should contain shapes, solid colors, and an innate sense of flatness within the pictorial plane.

Required Media

15" × 20" illustration board
#2 pencil
Straight edge
Paintbrush (#12 flat tip watercolor/gouache)
Cup of water
10-well plastic tray
Gouache: primary red, primary yellow, primary blue
Newspaper/cloth/paper towels
Palette knife (optional)
Viewfinder (optional)

Assignment

1. Begin with the illustration board in a *horizontal* position.
2. Draw a vertical line dividing the illustration board in half. Each side will be an independent design.
3. Using the viewfinder, concentrate on finding interesting abstract/nonobjective (rectilinear) lines and angles. I suggest you consider buildings (both exterior and interior) and other man-made objects. (A viewfinder is a piece of material, such as cardboard, with a window in the center. The window can be roughly 3" × 4".)
4. Create a design by drawing the *outlines* (no interior lines) from the objects found using the viewfinder directly onto the illustration board using pencil. Make sure to create a different design for each side of the illustration board. The sides do not have to correlate or match. Consider forms and relationships rather than recognizable objects (nonobjective over representational). Consider the importance of cropping shapes to build a good composition.
5. Paint in the shapes of each design using gouache paint. *Paint to the edges of the illustration board, as there is no border on this project.* The left design should be completed using warm colors, and the right design should be completed using cool colors.
6. On the *back* of the illustration board, in the *upper-left-hand* corner, please write your name and your class information (e.g., MWF 9 a.m.). *Please use a marker!* DO THIS AFTER THE PAINT HAS DRIED OR BEFORE YOU BEGIN YOUR PROJECT!!!
7. Do not turn in projects that are still wet. They should be allowed to dry overnight.
8. An example of a finished artwork is below. It is for reference only. *Please do not copy it!*

Point value: ______________________

Due date: ____________________ (weather permitting).

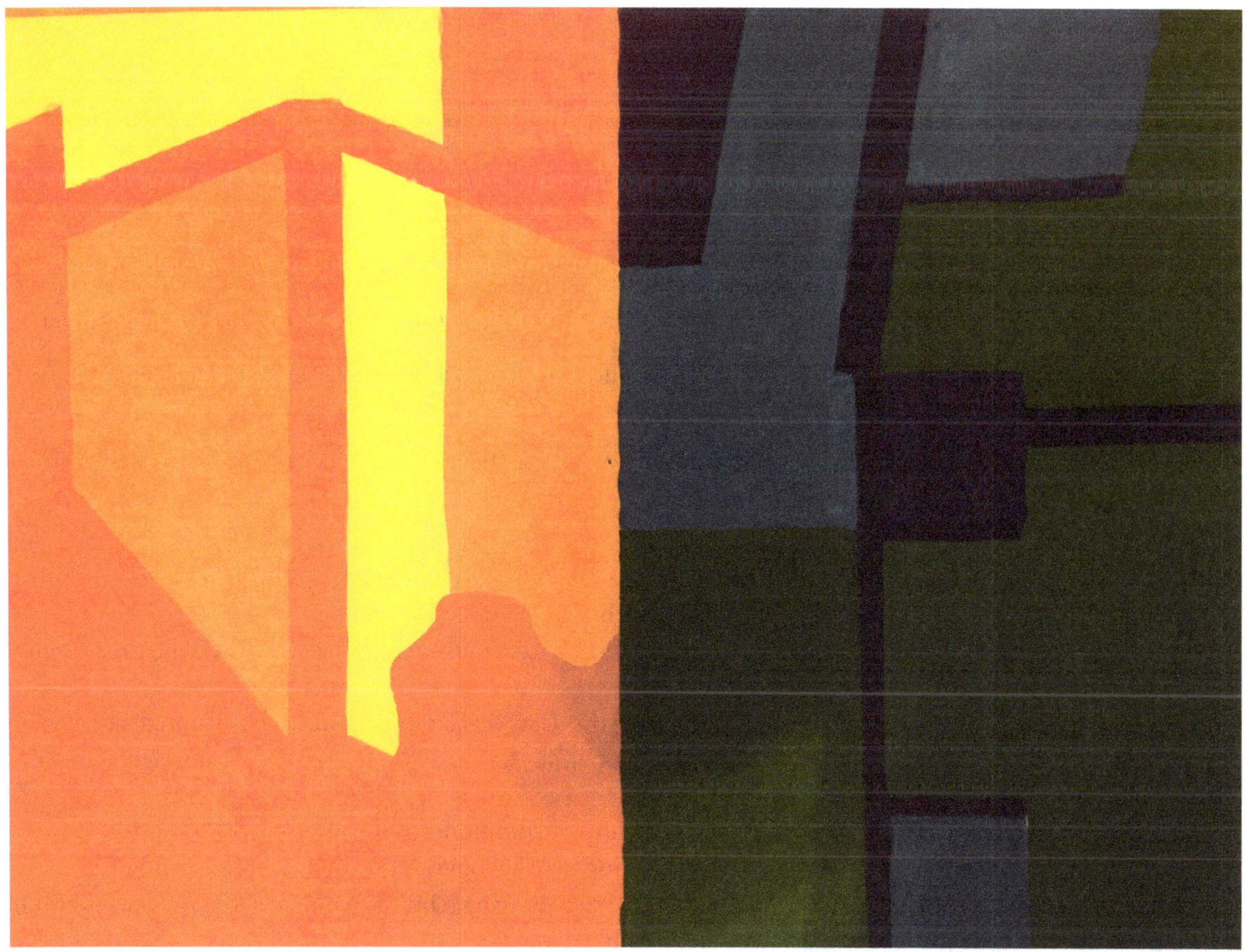

Figure 6.19a: Analogous—Warm   Figure 6.19b: Analogous—cool

ENDNOTES

1. Tertiary colors are sometimes referred to as *intermediate colors*.
2. The primary colors of red, yellow, and blue relate specifically to the subtractive process of paint and pigment. The additive process of light has a completely different set of primary colors.
3. The use of complementary colors is inherent in horror movies. Case in point is the *Nightmare on Elm Street* series where Freddie Kruger dresses in red and green.
4. Mark Roskill, ed. *The Letters of Vincent van Gogh* (New York: Touchstone, 2008), 288.
5. The Mauritshuis Museum website, accessed March 30, 2016, http://www.mauritshuis.nl/en/discover/mauritshuis/masterpieces-from-the-mauritshuis/girl-with-a-pearl-earring-670.
6. A close-up of this painting showing the individual dots of color can be seen in the movie *Ferris Bueller's Day Off*, https://youtu.be/p89gBjHB2Gs.
7. H. H. Arnason and Elizabeth Mansfield, *History of Modern Art*, 7th ed. (Upper Saddle River, NJ: Pearson Education, 2013), 44.
8. Rudolf Wittkower, Joseph Connors, and Jennifer Montagu, *Art and Architecture in Italy 1600–1750* (New Haven, CT: Yale University Press, 1999), 19.

IMAGE CREDITS

- Fig. 6.1: Georges Seurat, "Sunday Afternoon on the Island of La Grande Jatte," https://commons.wikimedia.org/wiki/File:Georges_Seurat_031.jpg. Copyright in the Public Domain.
- Fig. 6.2: Copyright © Joanjoc (CC BY-SA 3.0) at https://commons.wikimedia.org/wiki/File:Prism_rainbow_schema.png.
- Fig. 6.5: Sanford Robinson Gifford, "October in the Catskills," https://commons.wikimedia.org/wiki/File:WLA_lacma_Sanford_Robinson_Gifford_October_in_the_Catskills_1880.jpg. Copyright in the Public Domain.
- Fig. 6.7: Vincent van Gogh, "The Night Café," https://commons.wikimedia.org/wiki/File:Le_café_de_nuit_%28The_Night_Café%29_by_Vincent_van_Gogh.jpeg. Copyright in the Public Domain.
- Fig. 6.9: Johannes Vermeer, "The Girl with the Pearl Earring," https://commons.wikimedia.org/wiki/File:Meisje_met_de_parel.jpg. Copyright in the Public Domain.
- Fig. 6.10: Edward Hopper, "Stamp of Edward Hopper's The Lighthouse at Two Lights," https://commons.wikimedia.org/wiki/File:Maine_statehood_1970_U.S._stamp.jpg. Copyright in the Public Domain.
- Fig. 6.11: Claude Monet, "Grainstack in the Morning, Snow Effect," https://commons.wikimedia.org/wiki/File:Monet_grainstack-in-the-morning-snow-effect-1891_W1280.jpg. Copyright in the Public Domain.
- Fig. 6.12: Franz Marc, "The Little Blue Horses," https://commons.wikimedia.org/wiki/File:Marc-little_blue_horses.jpg. Copyright in the Public Domain.
- Fig. 6.13: Oliver Harrison, "Value Scale," https://commons.wikimedia.org/wiki/File:ART_VALUE_SCALE.png. Copyright in the Public Domain.
- Fig. 6.14: Ansel Adams, "North Palisade from Windy Point," https://commons.wikimedia.org/wiki/File:North_Palisade_from_Windy_Point.jpg. Copyright in the Public Domain.
- Fig. 6.15: Caspar David Friedrich, "Wanderer Above the Sea of Fog," https://commons.wikimedia.org/wiki/File:Caspar_David_Friedrich_-_Wanderer_above_the_sea_of_fog.jpg. Copyright in the Public Domain.
- Fig. 6.16: Kasimir Malevich, "Black Square," https://commons.wikimedia.org/wiki/File:Malevich.black-square.jpg. Copyright in the Public Domain.
- Fig. 6.17: Georges de La Tour, "The Penitent Magdalen," https://commons.wikimedia.org/wiki/File:Georges_de_La_Tour_009.jpg. Copyright in the Public Domain.

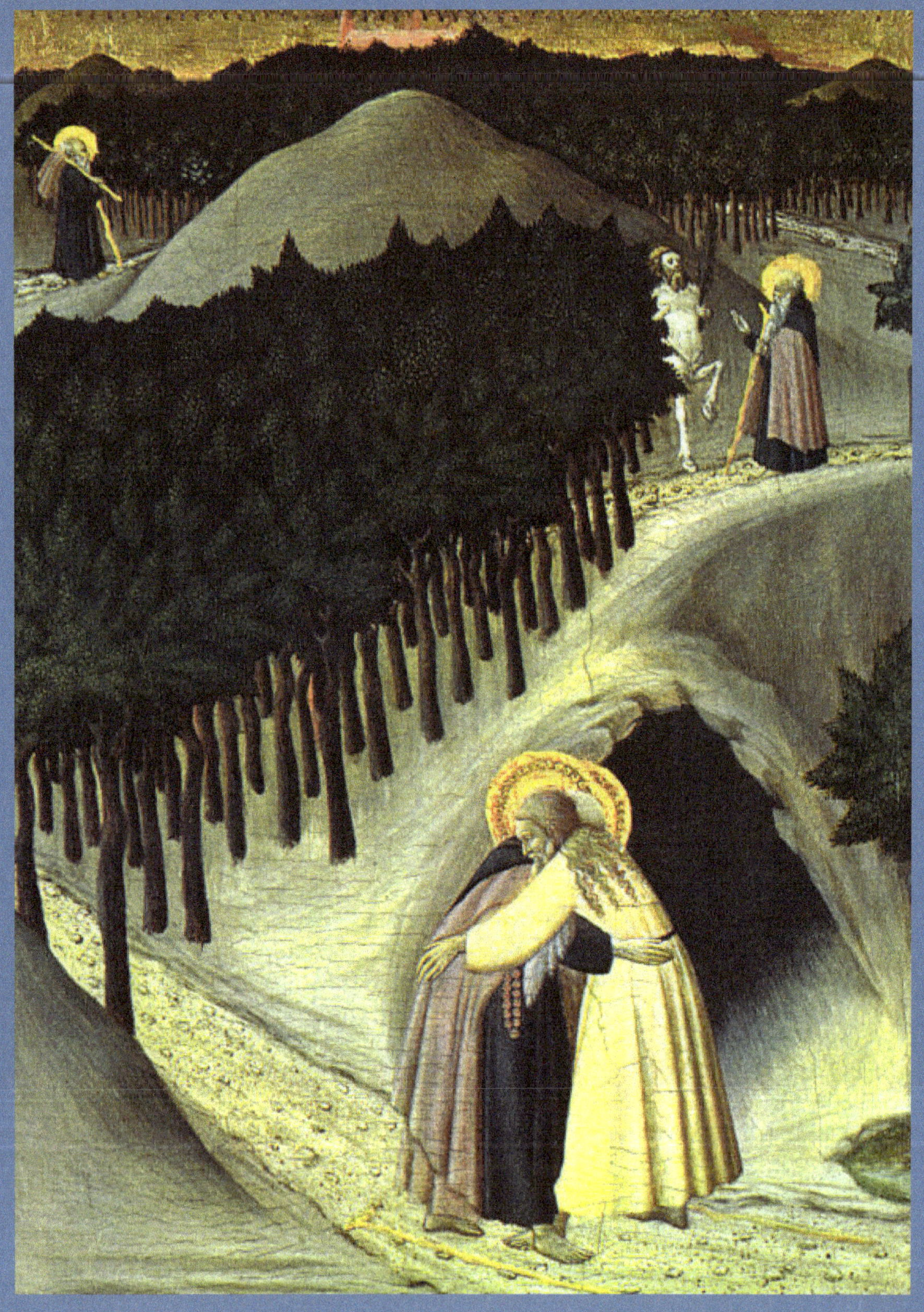

Figure 7.1: Sassetta, *The Meeting of St. Anthony and St. Paul*, c. 1440. Tempera on panel, 18.25 in × 13.25 in, National Gallery of Art.

MOTION AND THE ILLUSION OF MOTION

Being an artist is not as easy as it seems. We have already seen how artists are called upon to recreate images of our three-dimensional world and place them onto two-dimensional surfaces (chapter 5). Now we are going to see how they are able to create the sensation of motion using static mediums. Once again the artist is tasked with mirroring the world around us, a world constantly in motion. An artist might be called upon to paint milk being poured or asked to capture some sort of action in an unfolding drama. In order to accomplish this, the artist must resort to illusion to trick our eyes and our brain into making the static object dynamic.

KINETIC ART

Illusion is not needed for all artworks. Sometimes the artist will create a work that actually moves, such as Duchamp's *Rotary Glass Plates* (**fig. 7.2**).

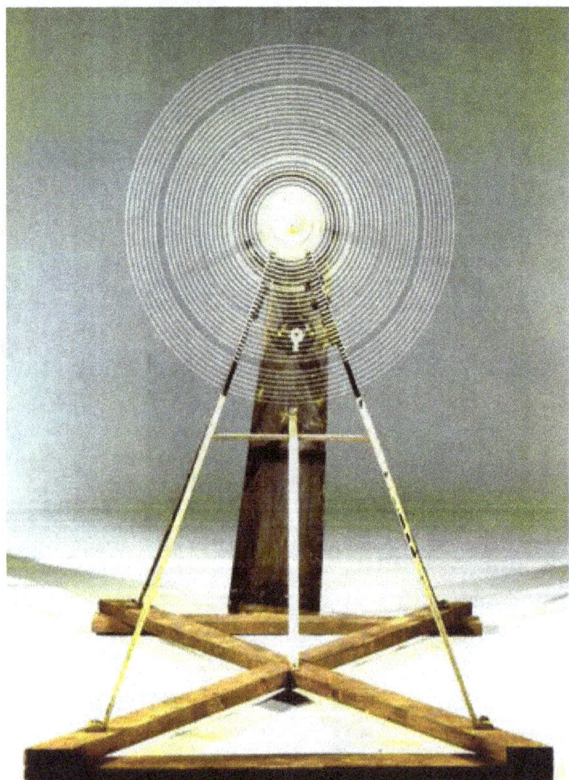

Figure 7.2: Marcel Duchamp, *Rotary Glass Plates*, 1920. Mixed Media.

The artwork is a series of five rectangular glass plates that are connected by a belt to a small engine. The plates are spaced one in front of the other and have markings toward their edges so that when they spin they create what looks like a series of concentric circles.

Art that is designed to move is labeled as **kinetic art**. The word *kinetic* is derived from the Greek word *kinesis*, meaning "movement." Kinetic art is a fairly new development in the history of art. Marcel Duchamp created one of the earliest examples with *Bicycle Wheel* (not pictured) in 1913. Today, there are many noted artists recognized for their work in the kinetic art realm, such as Alexander Calder, who creates gigantic mobiles of abstract shapes that turn slowly with the air movement, the most prominent of which hangs inside the National Gallery of Art in Washington, D.C.

REPEATED FIGURE

In the overall scheme of things, artwork that physically moves is pretty rare, not to mention the hundreds of years of artistic tradition prior to the invention of kinetic art where artists had to find other ways to illustrate movement. So what did artists do? Among the earliest devices artists used to present an illusion of movement in painting was repeating a figure.

Much of the artwork we come into contact with before the modern era attempts tell a story or relate some type of narrative. However, artworks are frozen moments of time where we have only a partial glimpse of what is happening. Using repeated figures in a work lets us see the linear progression of events.

In *The Meeting of Saint Anthony and Saint Paul* (**fig. 7.1**), completed around 1440, we see Saint Anthony at three different points/situations of his journey. At the top-left Saint Anthony first comes into view as he approaches the wilderness. Next, we see him encountering the centaur at the middle-right. And finally, he emerges into the clearing in the foreground and meets Saint Paul. Notice how the figure and scenery increase in scale the closer we get to the

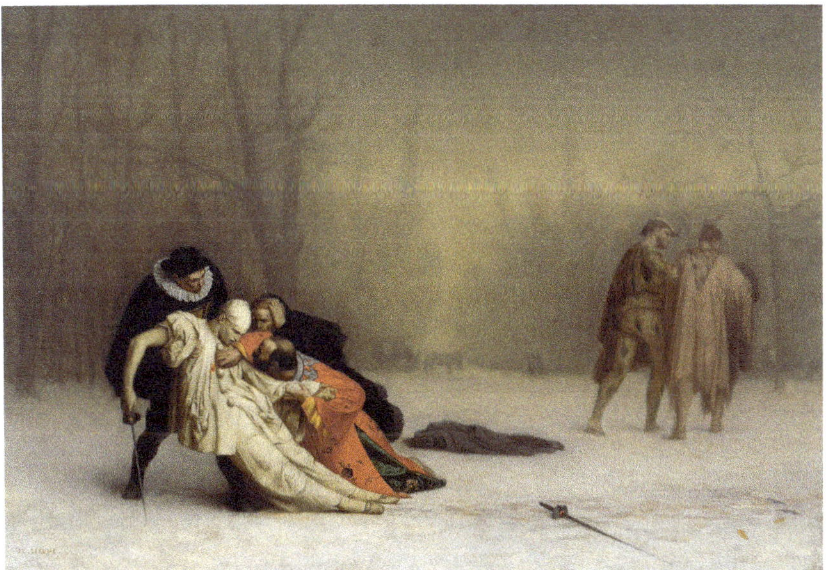

Figure 7.3: Jean Léon Gérôme, *The Duel After the Masquerade*, 1857–59. Oil on Canvas, 15 3/8 in × 22 3/16 in, Walters Art Museum.

lower portion of the painting (the most current time).[1]

ANTICIPATED MOVEMENT

Chapter 4 discussed the importance of the inherent characteristics found in line. Whereas horizontal and vertical lines tend to make artworks feel static and restrained, it is diagonal lines that made them appear more dynamic. Our brain recognizes that objects in a diagonal position don't stay that way for long. In Jean-Léon Gérôme's *The Duel after the Masquerade* (**fig 7.3**), we can see the figure of Pierrot slumping at a diagonal at the bottom-left corner of the painting.[2] We instinctively know he is falling to the ground, dying. The sword that lays to the right of Pierrot's, which mirrors his form, reinforces the diagonal. Even the figures trying to assist Pierrot are themselves leaning at a diagonal.

The same rule applies to sculpture. Compare the iconic statue of *David* by Michelangelo (see fig 22.7) and a later version by Gian Lorenzo Bernini (**fig 7.4**). There is a massive difference in the interpretation of these two sculptures. Michelangelo's *David* stands upright, like a vertical line, gazing into the distance waiting for something to happen. This is in direct contrast to Bernini's *David*, whose body appears fully wound, muscles pulled to extremes, and ready to release the stone in his slingshot. At this position the figure of David is leaning back and forms a solid diagonal from the top of his head, down his torso, and through his left leg. This makes the sculpture appear active. If we encountered this sculpture straight on, we would immediately move out of the way.

BLURRED FIGURE

It is common for us to identify a blurred figure as one that is in motion. It begins when we are young watching Saturday morning cartoons. When the Roadrunner takes off from Wile E. Coyote or

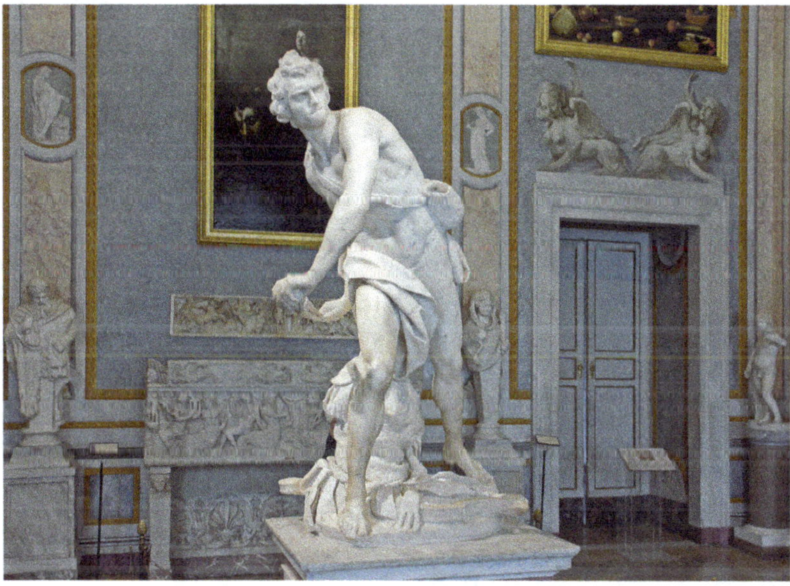

Figure 7.4: Gian Lorenzo Bernini, *David*, 1623. Marble, height 5 ft 7 in, Galleria Borghese, Rome.

when we see the Tasmanian Devil spinning, all we see is a blurred figure. While this is an aspect commonly associated with illustration and photography, it occasionally makes its way into other mediums, such as painting. Gerhard Richter's painting *Woman Descending the Staircase* (1965; not pictured) is an image of a blurred woman on a set of stairs. We instinctively know the woman is in motion, rather than just standing on the stairs, because her form is blurred.

CROPPED FIGURE

When part of a figure has been "cut-off" by the frame we refer to it as being *cropped*. Most of the time this is unintentional. Think of all the photos that have had to be retaken because someone wasn't fully in the picture. But other times an artist will intentionally crop a figure to call our attention to some other element, such as motion. Sports photographers commonly crop figures as they are reaching for a pass, going up for a basket, or stealing a base.

It is especially exciting to see cropped figures used in painting. Prior to the modern era the entire scene would have been centered within the confines of the frame, not unlike watching a play or performance on a stage. However, after the invention of photography we get a much different approach by artists such as Edgar Degas. In *Three Dancers in a Practice Room* (**fig 7.5**), Degas creates something more like an image captured with a camera lens than a painting. By having the ballerina at the left cropped, we know we are only looking at a partial image of reality, that the scene continues outside the frame as well. Why isn't she centered or at least fully in view? Perhaps she is in motion and wouldn't stay still long enough for the artist to capture her.

The cropping of her figure lends itself to the mobility of the ballerina.

OPTICAL ART (OP ART)

Back in the twelfth century the Chinese figured out a way to introduce graphic elements, such as the tapering and undulating of line and space, to an artwork that would create a visual sensation of movement.[3] We see this manipulation of line and space once again in the mid-1960s in New York. The movement is called **Optical Art**, or *Op Art* for short.

One of the most recognized Op Artists was Bridget Riley, who would make paintings similar in form to the background seen in Heini Scheffler's cartoon (**fig. 7.6**). Op Art could be either black and white or brilliantly colored. Riley's work became so popular that fashion designers designed clothing based on her paintings.[4]

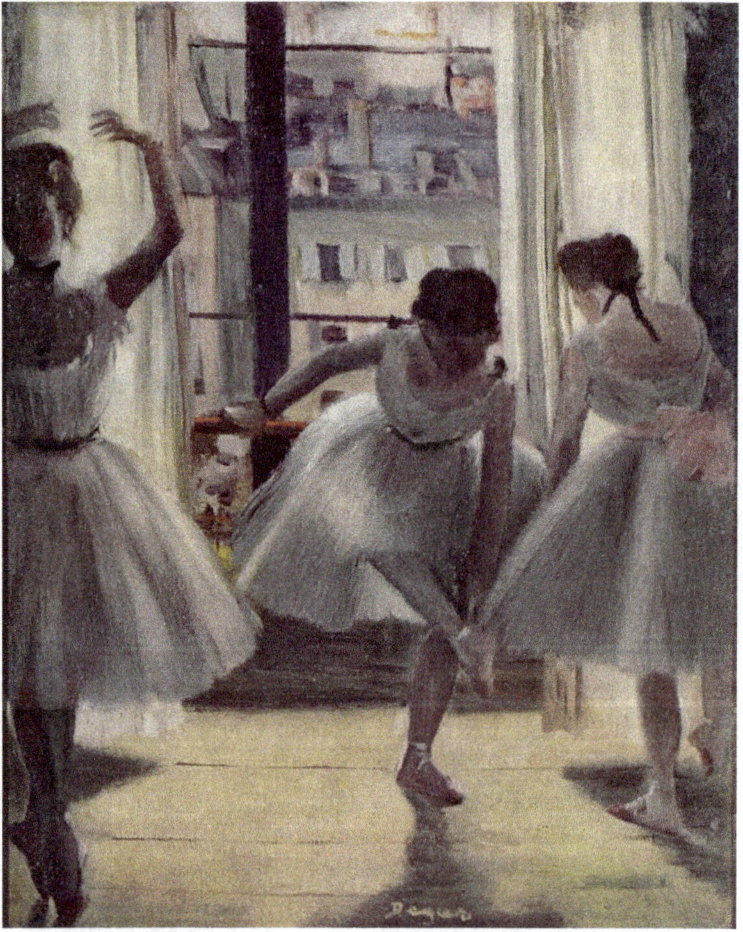

Figure 7.5: Edgar Degas, *Three Dancers in a Practice Room*, 1873. Oil on Canvas, 10.6 in × 8.7 in, Sammlung H. de Ganay, Paris.

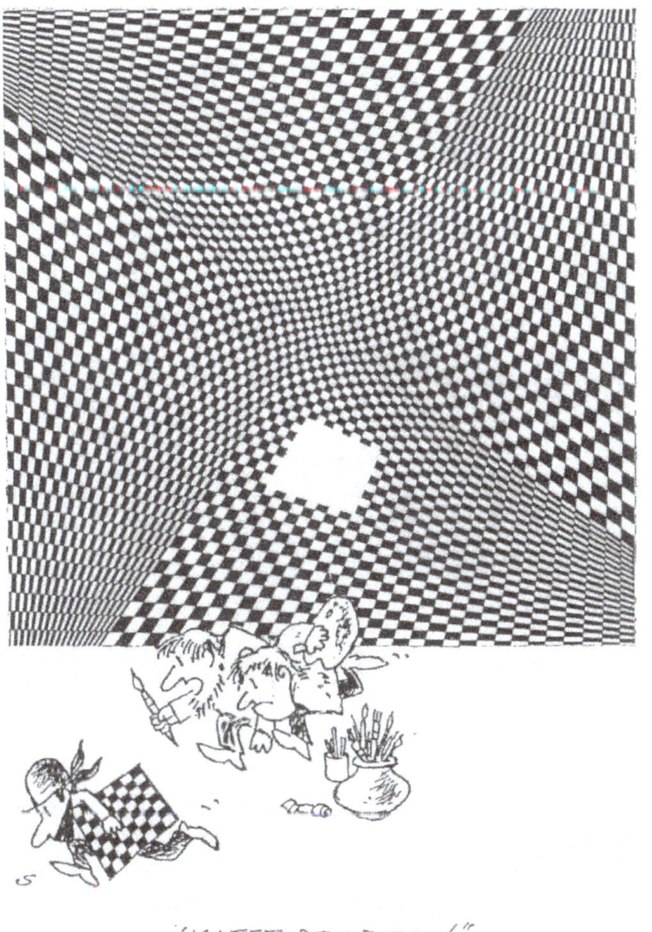

Figure 7.6: Heini Scheffler, *Chessboard Thief*.

ACTION PAINTING

In 1952 the art critic Harold Rosenberg wrote, "At a certain moment the canvas began to appear to one American Painter after another as an arena in which to act—rather than as a space in which to reproduce, redesign, analyze, or 'express' an object, actual or imagined. What was to go on the canvas was not a picture but an event."[5] Rosenberg was describing a new way of painting, **action painting**. The Abstract Expressionist artist Jackson Pollock had invented a new way of painting. Pollock would lay the canvas on the ground and then drip, splatter, and pour paint onto its surface as he moved around the perimeter, sometimes even stepping onto the canvas. Looking closely at *One* (**fig. 7.7**), you can trace the gestural movement Pollock's arms took in the painting's creation. Pollock's paintings can become mesmerizing to viewers as they trace each of the splatter patterns. There is nowhere for the eye to rest, no beginning, no end, and no focal point to these "drip paintings." The paint and the artist were active participants in the creation of these paintings.

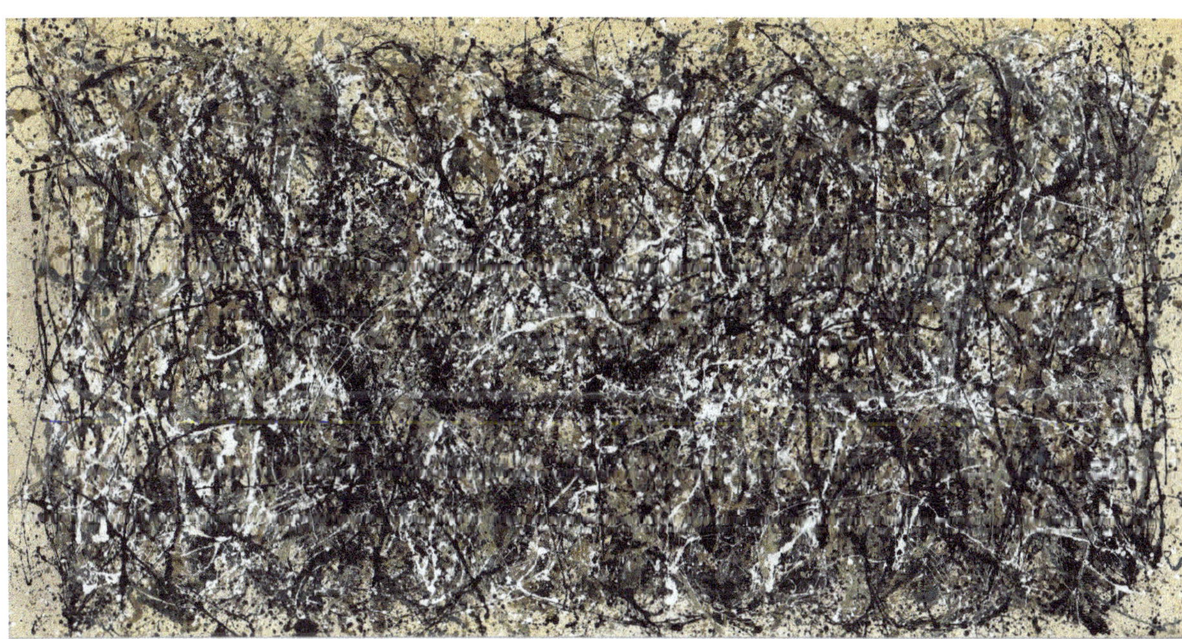

Figure 7.7: Jackson Pollock, *One: Number 31, 1950*, 1950. Oil and Enamel Paint on Canvas, 8 ft 10 in × 17 ft 5 5/8 in, Museum of Modern Art, New York, Sydney and Harriet Janis Collection Fund.

Kinetic art:

Repeated figure:

Anticipated movement:

Blurred figure:

Cropped figure:

Optical Art (Op Art):

Action painting:

ENDNOTES

1. The use of vertical placement can also be associated with this image. Objects closer to us (in time) appear at the bottom of the artwork, whereas those that are farther away appear at the top of the artwork.
2. David A. Lauer and Stephen Pentak, *Design Basics*, 8th ed. (Boston, MA: Wadsworth, Cengage Learning, 2012), 230.
3. The particular work of art referred to here is called *A Wave Under the Moon*, ink on silk scroll, twelfth century.
4. H. H. Arnason and Elizabeth Mansfield, *History of Modern Art*, 7th ed. (Upper Saddle River, NJ: Pearson Education, 2013), 505.
5. Harold Rosenberg, "The American Action Painters," *Art News*, December 1952, 22.

IMAGE CREDITS

- Fig. 7.1: Sassetta, "The Meeting of St. Anthony and St. Paul," https://commons.wikimedia.org/wiki/File:Sassetta_-_The_Meeting_of_St._Anthony_and_St._Paul_-_WGA20868.jpg. Copyright in the Public Domain.
- Fig. 7.2: Marcel Duchamp, "Rotary Glass Plates," https://commons.wikimedia.org/wiki/File:Rotary_Glass_Plates.jpg. Copyright in the Public Domain.
- Fig. 7.3: Jean-Léon Gérôme, "The Duel After the Masquerade," https://commons.wikimedia.org/wiki/File:Jean-L%C3%A9on_G%C3%A9r%C3%B4me_-_The_Duel_After_the_Masquerade_-_Google_Art_Project.jpg. Copyright in the Public Domain.
- Fig. 7.4: Gian Lorenzo Bernini; Photo by Jk1677, "David," https://commons.wikimedia.org/wiki/File:David_by_Bernini,_1623-1624,_Villa_Borghese,_Rome.jpg. Copyright in the Public Domain.
- Fig. 7.5: Edgar Degas, "Three Dancers in a Practice Room," https://commons.wikimedia.org/wiki/File:Edgar_Germain_Hilaire_Degas_024.jpg. Copyright in the Public Domain.
- Fig. 7.6: Copyright © Heini Scheffler (CC BY-SA 3.0) at https://commons.wikimedia.org/wiki/File:SchachBrettDieb.jpg.
- Fig. 7.7: Jackson Pollock, "One: Number 31, 1950," http://www.moma.org/collection/works/78386?locale=en. Copyright © 1950 by Pollock-Krasner Foundation/Artists Rights Society (ARS).

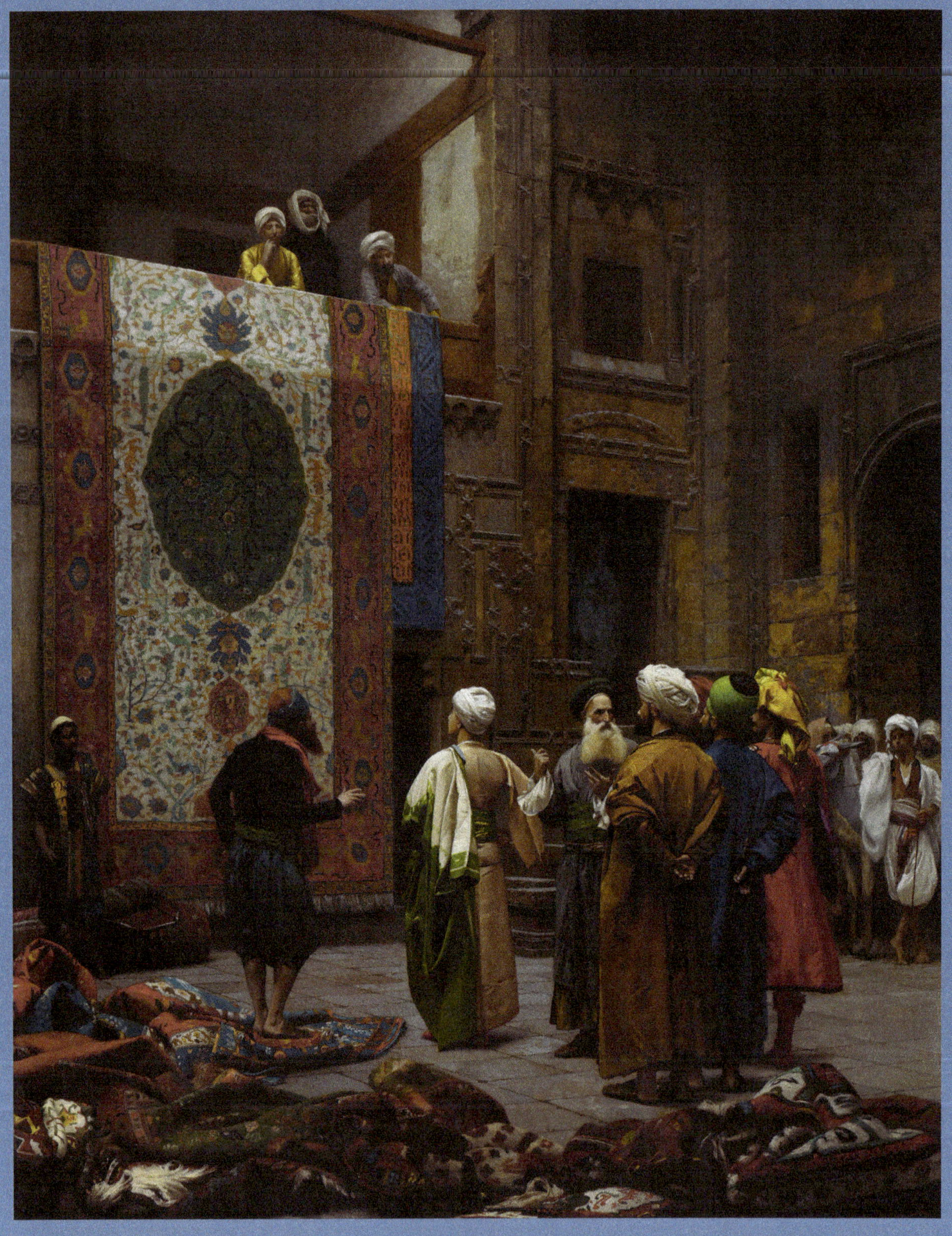

Figure 8.1: Jean Léon Gérôme, *The Carpet Merchant*, c. 1887. Oil on Canvas, 32 7/8 in × 25 1/2 in, The Minneapolis Institute of Arts.

PATTERN AND TEXTURE

PATTERN

The formal elements we have covered so far—line, shape, and color—can be arranged in such a way that they form recognizable patterns. Think of a **pattern** as a template or design motif. It is the repetition of a visual element in a regular or anticipated sequence. Patterns can behold infinite variation. This makes them important decorative tools for artists.

Consider the pattern around the top of the ceramic *Jar* by Maria Montoya Martinez (see fig 20.1). The pattern changes this work from a standard utilitarian object into a work of art. It raises both its intrinsic and cultural value. For many of us the pattern is the deciding element when purchasing objects such as rugs, wallpaper, or any other form of textile. William Morris, the leader of the Arts and Crafts movement, was a master

at creating intricately patterned textiles (see fig 21.1). His works are proudly displayed in many museums today. During the Middle Ages, monks, working in scriptoriums, would produce heavily patterned pages of religious text called *illuminated manuscripts* (**fig 8.2**). In some cases we become so overwhelmed by the pattern that we might overlook the subject matter of the page, which in this instance are the Greek letters XPI (chi-rho-iota).

Artists frequently incorporate patterns into paintings. Consider the pattern in the floor tiles found in *A Woman with a Child in a Pantry* (**fig 8.3**). The floor tiles assume a fairly dominant role in this image by not only adding color, but also by linking the two rooms together with the similarity of their pattern. These floor tiles are the perfect illustration of our definition of pattern—the repetition of a visual element in a regular or anticipated sequence. The square pattern originating in the floor tiles is also repeated in the window frames along the back wall.

Patterns can be the focal point of the entire painting, such as in Jean Léon Gérôme's *The Carpet Merchant* (**fig 8.1**). They can also play a smaller, more subtle role, as seen in his earlier painting, from the last chapter, *The Duel After the Masquerade* (see fig 7.3). In this painting the pattern is nearly indistinguishable unless we look closely at the detail of the figures walking briskly away at the far right. The left-most figure is dressed as a harlequin, a circus performer, identified by the diamond patterns on his clothing.

One of the most striking uses of pattern can be found in the painting called *The Women of Algiers* by Eugène Delacroix (**fig 8.4**). The painting is a showcase of exotic patterns and vibrant colors. The scene depicts a harem where three women are gathered along with a servant. Every possible surface has been filled with some sort of pattern or arabesque: the tiles along the back walls, the frame around the mirror hanging on the wall, the women's clothing, the rugs and pillows, even the tapestry pulled back to the right still exposes a pattern on its surface.

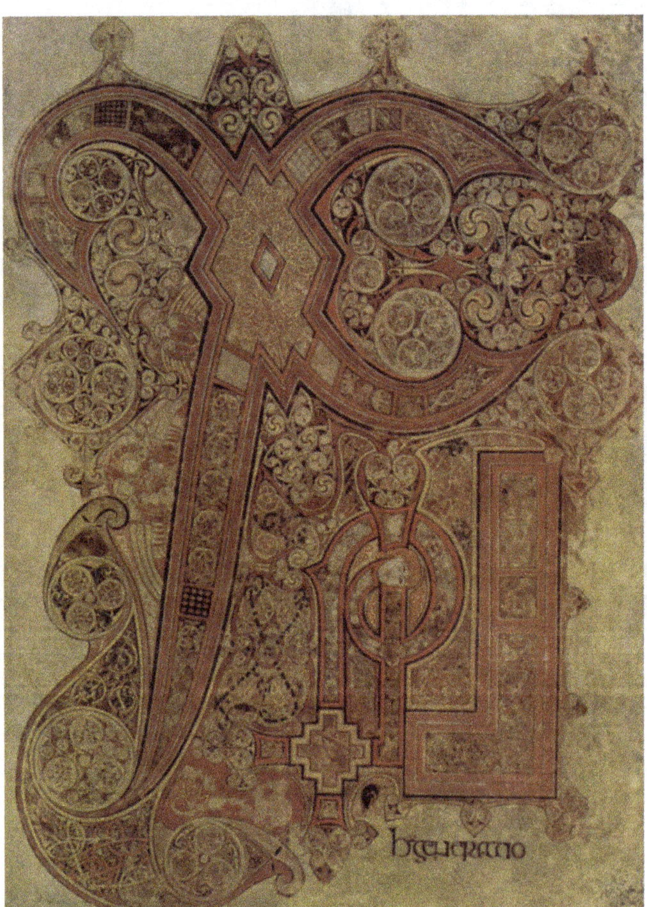

Figure 8.2: Chi-rho-iota (XPI) page, folio 34 recto of the *Book of Kells*, c. 700. 12.7 in × 9.5 in, Trinity College Library.

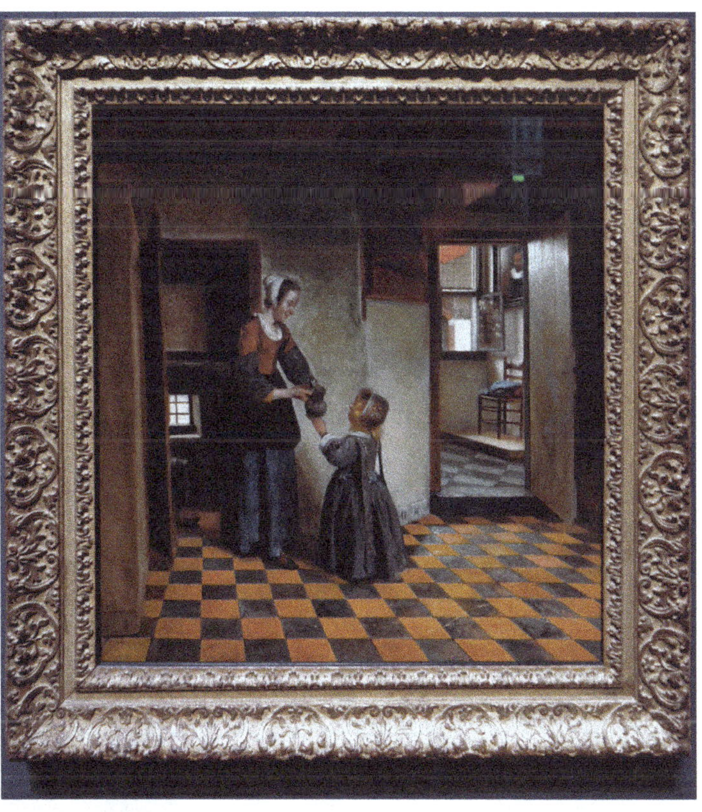

Figure 8.3: Pieter de Hooch, *A Woman with a Child in a Pantry*, 1656–1660. Oil on Canvas, 65 cm × 60.5 cm, Rijksmuseum, Amsterdam.

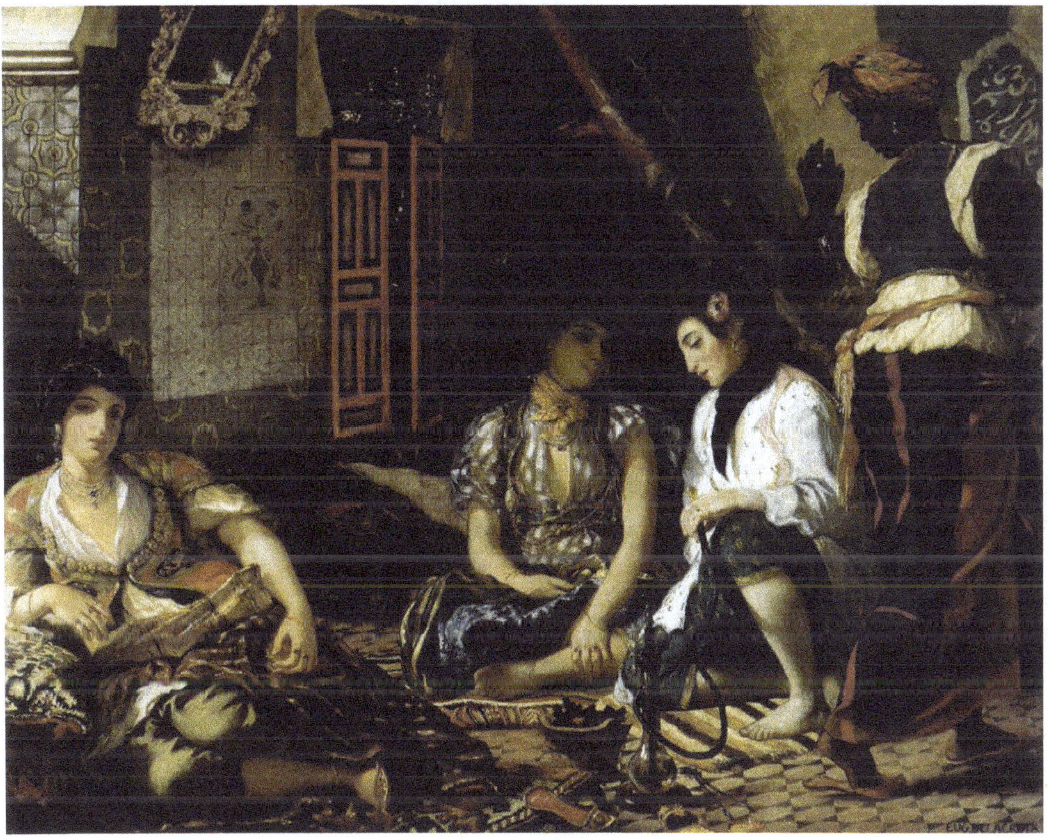

Figure 8.4: Eugène Delacroix, *The Women of Algiers*, 1834. Oil on Canvas, 180 cm × 229 cm, Louvre Museum.

TEXTURE

Texture refers to the surface quality of a work of art. Texture is based on our sense of touch. Many times the art object seemingly invites us to reach out and touch and experience its tactile quality. However, this is not something that would be met with acceptance by any museum, gallery, or art owner. Museums are covered with signs reminding us not to touch the artworks. Guards, alarms, rope banners, and Plexiglas cases are there to prevent people from coming into contact with most artworks.

ACTUAL TEXTURE (TACTILE TEXTURE)

We are concerned with three different types of texture when it comes to art: actual texture, visual texture, and subversive texture. **Actual texture** (oftentimes referred to as *tactile texture*) can be felt and physically experienced. This type of texture is mostly attributed to three-dimensional artworks such as architecture, ceramics, glassware, jewelry, and especially sculpture. Marble is a medium that demands our attention. People often wonder how it is that artists are able create such lifelike figures out of stone.

We are all familiar with the sculpture of *David* by Michelangelo, but we are going to focus on an incomplete work of his entitled *Atlas Slave* (**fig 8.5**). Pope Julius II originally commissioned this work to adorn the tomb that Michelangelo was creating for him. It was going to be an incredible tomb rising three levels high and filled with sculptures. Funds for the project ended up being diverted to the rebuilding of St Peter's Cathedral and the original tomb never reached completion. While a more modest tomb did get completed we are left with several sculptures from the original design that were left "in-progress," which allows us witness the true textural quality of marble. It is amazing how Michelangelo is able to transform this rough stone into a seemingly malleable material.

Actual texture can also be found in paintings, though this was not always the case. Vincent van Gogh employed the use of **impasto** in many of his paintings during the late 1880s. Impasto can be defined as thickly applied paint. Van Gogh would take undiluted paint and apply it in layers to his canvases. If you were to take your fingers and run them across the surface of *The Starry Night* (**fig 8.6**), you would be able to tell your friends and family about the ridges and furrows that make up the surface of this painting. Impasto is nearly impossible to detect through a glossy picture in a book or an image projected onto a screen. This is a technique you have to see in person in order to get the full impact.

VISUAL TEXTURE

Prior to the use of impasto, paintings would have been created exclusively through the use of **visual texture**. With visual texture there is an impression

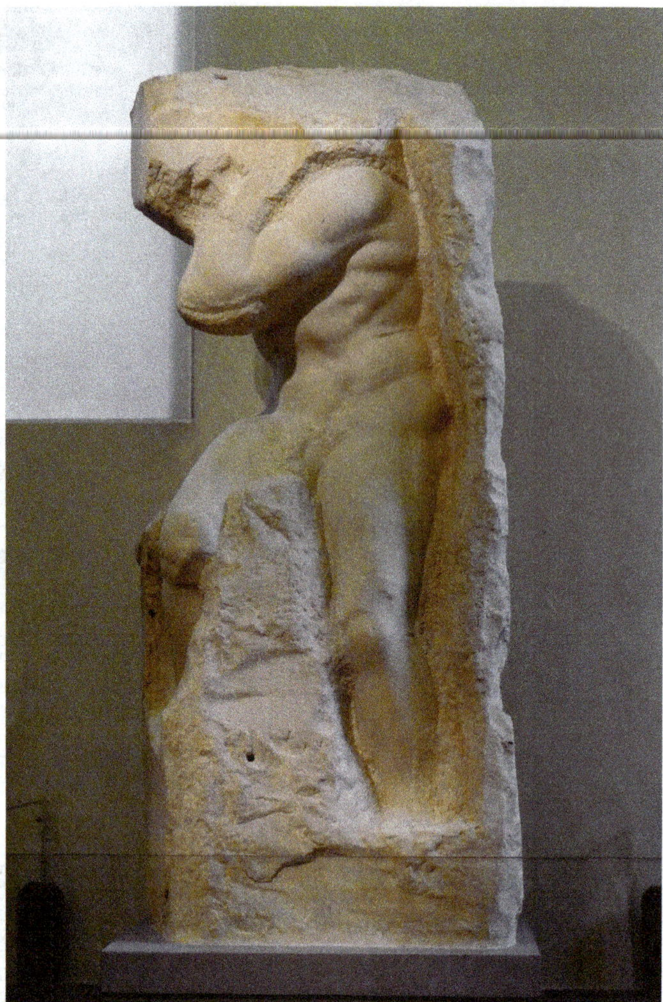

Figure 8.5: Michelangelo *Atlas Slave*, 1520-23. Marble, height 109 in, Galleria dell'Accademia, Florence.

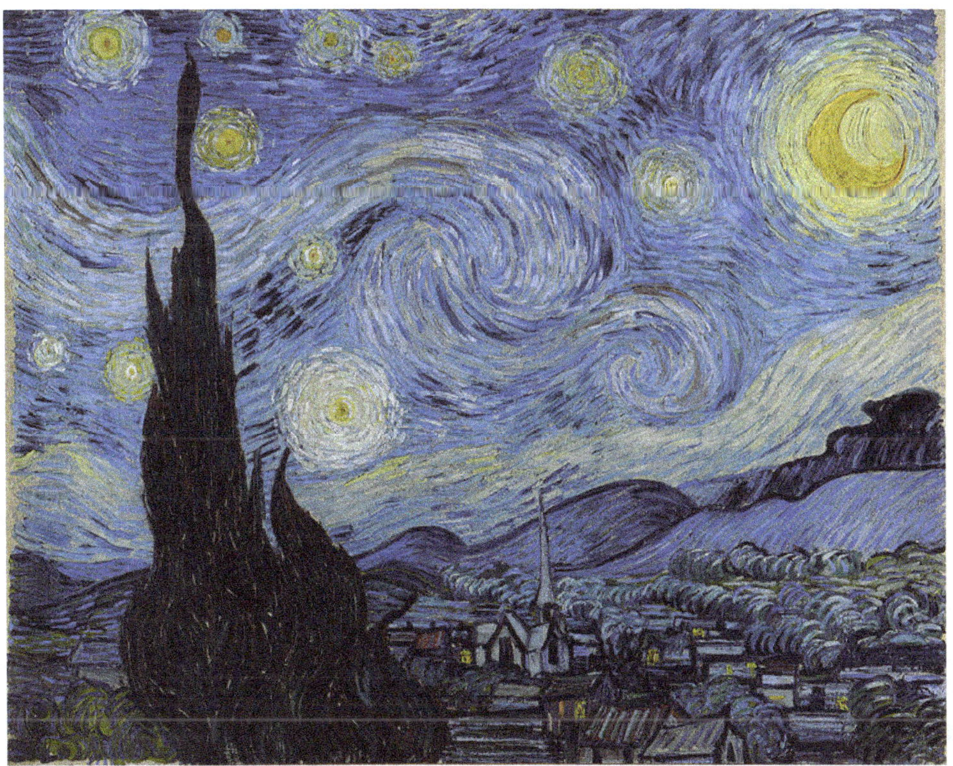

Figure 8.6: Vincent van Gogh, *The Starry Night*, 1889 Oil on Canvas, 29 in × 36 1/4 in, The Museum of Modern Art, New York, Acquired through the Lillie P. Bliss Bequest.

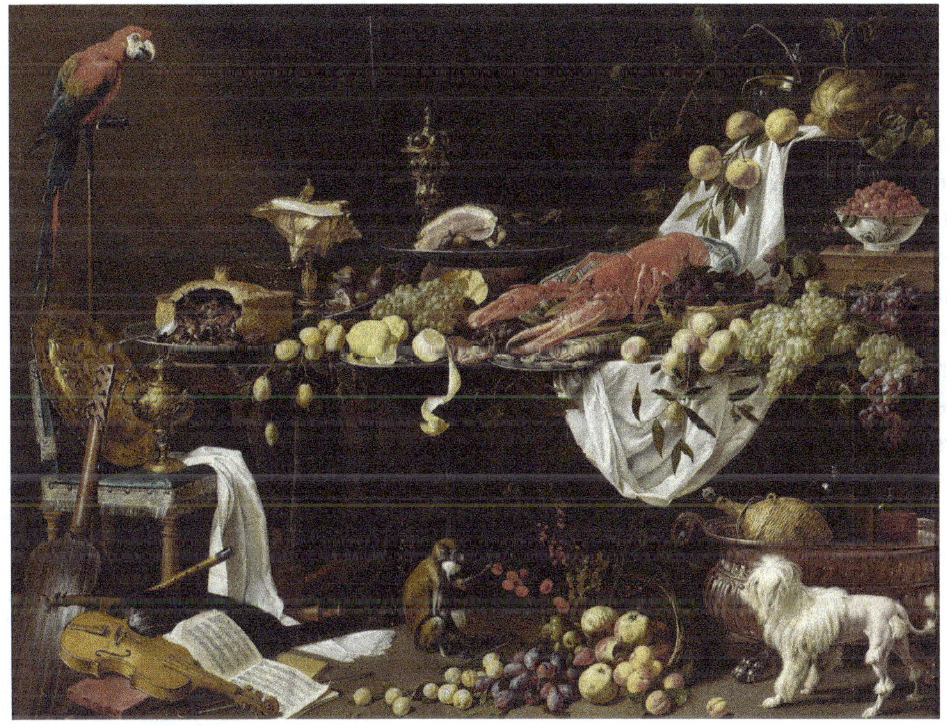

Figure 8.7: Adriaen van Utrecht, *Banquet Still Life*, 1644. Oil on Canvas, 185 cm × 242.5 cm, Rijksmuseum, Amsterdam.

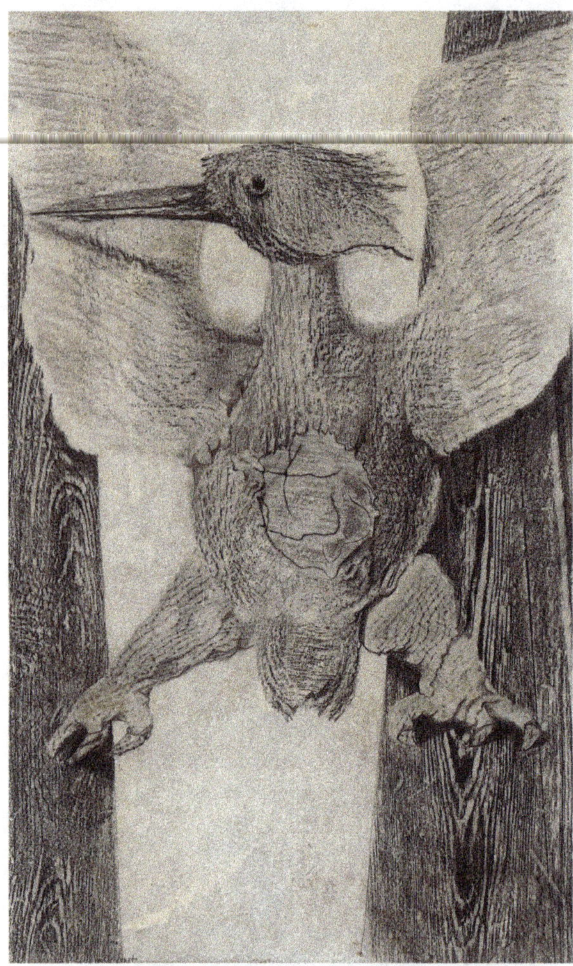
Figure 8.8: Max Ernst, *The Origin of the Pendulum*, 1925. Frottage from 'Histoire Naturelle'.

or suggestion of texture, but none truly exists. It is nothing more than an illusion. The painting *Banquet Still Life* (**fig 8.7**) contains an abundance of visual textures. The musical instruments, grapes, fruit, lobster, silver plates, tablecloth, baskets, wooden boxes, glass bottles, and animals collectively account for an incredibly vast array of textures the artist is able to capture. However, if you were to run your fingers over this work you would note that this painting is smooth and glasslike.

One way of creating visual texture is through the technique of *frottage*. Using this technique, artists would be able to recreate a texture by rubbing charcoal or graphite on a sheet of paper that had been placed over the textured surface. The Surrealist artist Max Ernst used this technique in many of his artworks throughout the 1920s and 1940s. Much of the visual texture in *Origin of the Pendulum*

(**fig 8.8**) was created when the artist placed sheets of paper over a wooden floor and rubbed graphite over their surface.[1] Many different objects can be used to create *frottage*, such as corrugated cardboard, screen, fabric, leaves, bark, and sandpaper.

The term **trompe l'oeil** is also employed when discussing visual texture. In French, the term literally means "to fool the eye." This term is applied to works of art that are rendered in incredible detail. The detail that is generally emphasized the most is that of spatial qualities. We have all received emails showing incredible sidewalk drawings done in chalk. These images show sidewalks that all of a sudden give way to limitless gulfs of space. Those drawings would definitely fall under this classification.

Trompe l'oeil is not a new technique by any means. It was used frequently during the Renaissance. An example of this is Andrea Mantegna's ceiling fresco at the *Palazzo Ducale* in Mantua, Italy (**fig 8.9**). This room, referred to as a *camera picta* (painted chamber), sports an unexpected surprise when the viewer looks up at the ceiling.[2] Looking back down through an oculus are people, putti, and animals. While their presence is a little awkward at first, the viewer also begins to worry about the planted barrel, which looks as if it could fall at any moment. The entire scene is produced through the technique of trompe l'oeil.

SUBVERSIVE TEXTURE

It is **subversive texture** that undermines or subverts our ideas about the object itself. It can attract us and repel us at the same time. The best example of this type of texture is a work simply called *Object* (**fig 8.10**). It is by the female Surrealist artist Meret Oppenheim. The cup, saucer, and spoon are each covered in the fur of a Chinese gazelle.[3] Viewers immediately react to the softness of the fur and want to reach out to "pet" it, but they stop short when they are reminded that this is a teacup. Who would pet a teacup? Teacups are for drinking out of, aren't they? Just the thought of drinking out of this cup would repel most of us. This artwork has its way with us pulling us closer and then pushing us away.

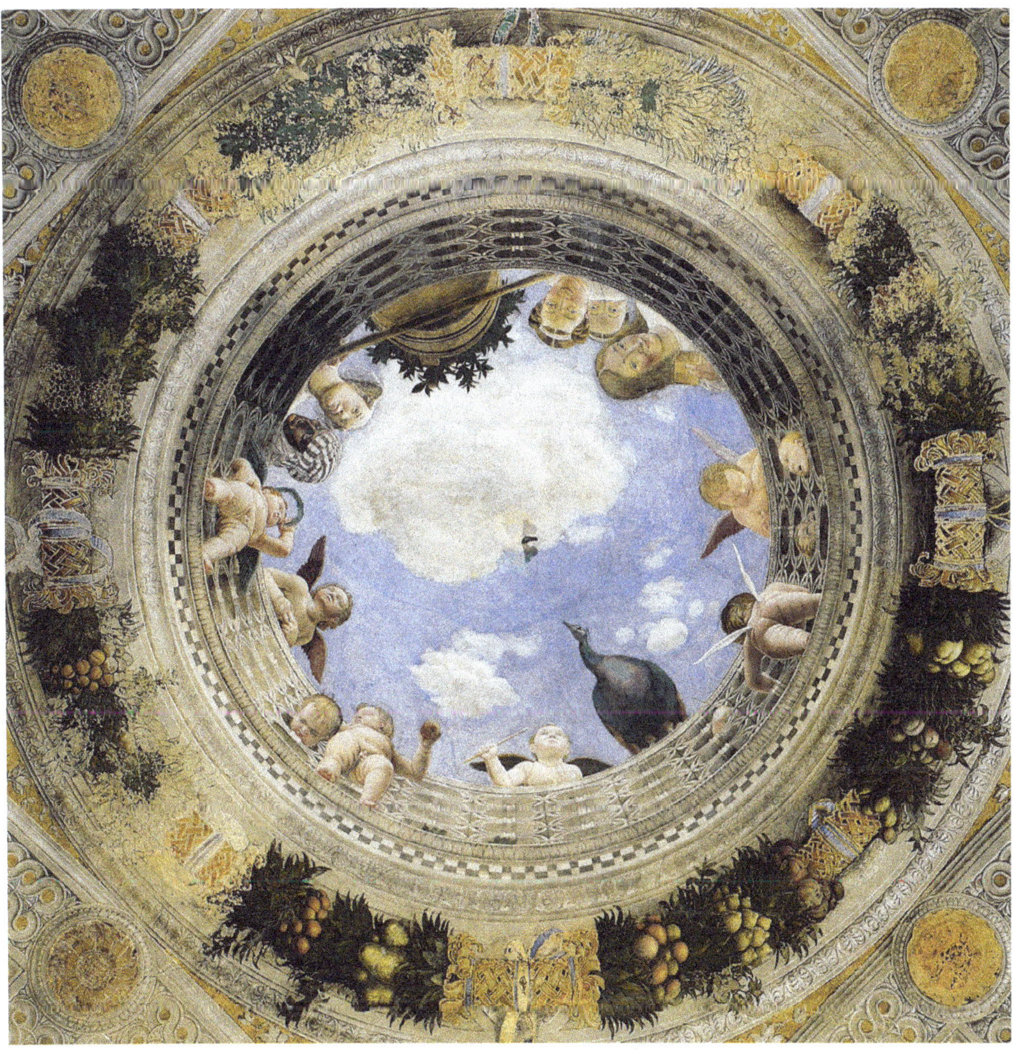

Figure 8.9: Andrea Mantegna *Ceiling Fresco*, 1465–1474, Fresco, Diameter 8 ft 9 in, Camera picta, Palazzo Ducale, Mantua.

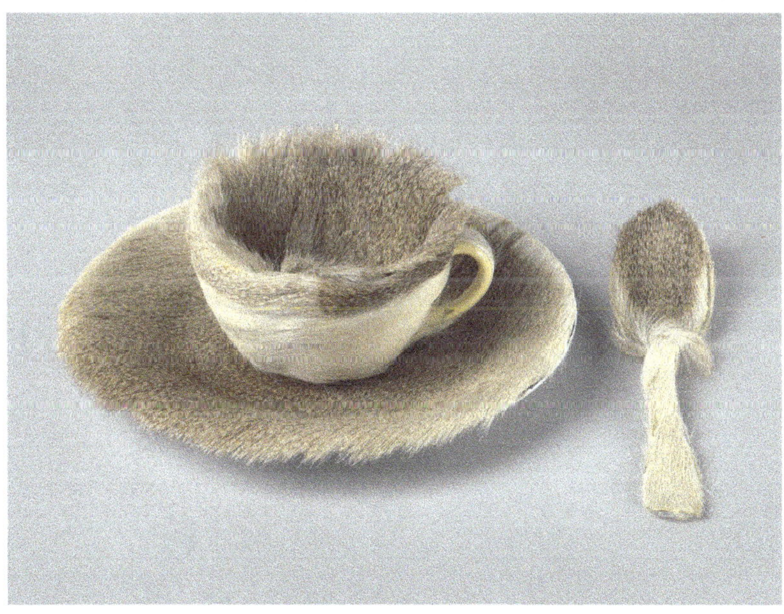

Figure 8.10: Meret Oppenheim, *Object*, 1936 Fur-covered cup, saucer, and spoon, The Museum of Modern Art; New York.

STUDY GUIDE: PATTERN AND TEXTURE

Pattern:

Actual texture (tactile texture):

Impasto:

Visual texture:

Frottage:

Trompe l'oeil:

Subversive texture:

PROJECT: PATTERN AND TEXTURE

Goal

Texture can be created in art in several different ways. For this project, you'll utilize the technique of frottage to create textures from several different sources.

Required Media

Four 8.5" × 11" sheets of standard blank paper
6B pencil (Please do not use charcoal pencils!)

Assignment

1. Turn the four pieces of paper horizontally.
2. Fold each sheet of paper in half so when they are opened back up there is a vertical crease in the center. Each side of the paper will be for a different textured image.
3. Find eight textured surfaces or objects.
4. Place your paper on top of the textured surface and, using the edge of the 6B pencil, begin to lightly rub across the surface of the paper.
5. Continue to repeat this step until you have eight unique textures.
6. Each image should be labeled on the back of the page as to the object used.
7. Staple the sheets together.
8. On the *back* of the last sheet of paper in the *upper-left-hand* corner, please write your name, the project name, and your class information (e.g., MWF 9 a.m.).

Suggested Textures

Tree bark	Leaves
Screen	Fabric
Wood	Walls
Brick/rock	Sandpaper
Lace	Coins/medals

Point value: ________________________

Due date: ________________________

1. Tate Museum website, accessed November 2, 2015, http://www.tate.org.uk/learn/online-resources/glossary/f/frottage.

2. Frederick Hartt and David G. Wilkins, *History of Italian Renaissance Art* (Upper Saddle River, NJ: Prentice Hall, 2003), 441.

3. H. H. Arnason and Elizabeth Mansfield, *History of Modern Art*, 7th ed. (Upper Saddle River, NJ: Pearson Education, 2013), 318.

IMAGE CREDITS

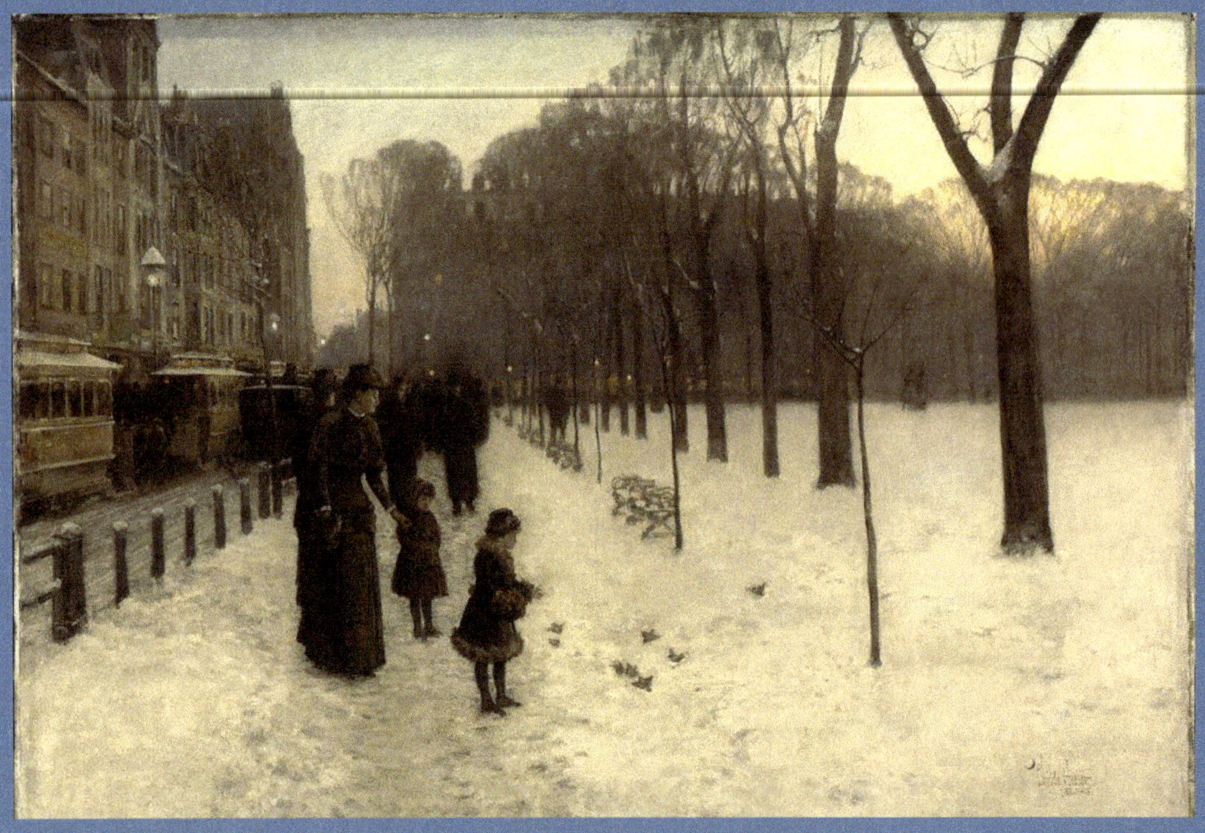

Figure 9.1: Childe Hassam, *Boston Common at Twilight*, 1885–86. Oil on canvas, 42 in × 60 in, Museum of Fine Arts, Boston.

BALANCE

As individuals, we try to obtain a certain balance in our lives. We try to balance our time between work, school, friends, family, and fun. Each person does it differently. The same can be said for artists. They also strive to attain a certain balance within their compositions. Balance is the way that weight is distributed in an artwork. In three-dimensional art, such as sculpture, architecture, and ceramics, we are dealing with actual (physical) weight. In two-dimensional artworks we are considering visual weight (the lightness or heaviness of shapes and forms) and the visual interest it creates.

Four types of balance can be used in a composition: symmetrical, asymmetrical, radial, and crystallographic. We will, on occasion, come across a work that is not balanced. In this instance we say that the work is *imbalanced*.

SYMMETRICAL BALANCE

Symmetrical balance means that there is a precise correspondence of like elements on either side of a central axis. In other words, the left side looks an awful lot like the right side. Take a look at Ghirlandaio's *Last Supper* (**fig 9.2**). Mentally place a vertical line at the center of the painting. We can see that both sides have very similar qualities. Two arches extend outward from the center, creating two landscape scenes containing citron trees, cypresses, falcons, and pheasants.[1] The walls on either side of these arches contain a window. Below the arches is the table, which is perfectly centered in the composition. The apostle John resides at the center of the composition and is flanked by six apostles on either side.[2] From looking at the way the elements are arranged in this composition, we would label it as being in symmetrical balance.

Symmetrical balance can be broken down into two subcategories: bilateral symmetry and absolute symmetry. **Bilateral symmetry** is what we see in Ghirlandaio's *Last Supper*. Although the sides of the composition correspond to one another, there are some subtle differences, such as the variance in arrangement of the birds and plant material underneath the arches or the fact that there are two different birds represented in the windows at the far sides of the arches. The apostles themselves are different. What matters is that they are equally balanced with a similar form on the opposite side of the painting.

With **absolute symmetry** both sides of the composition are mirror images of one another. It would be rare to come across this type of balance in painting and sculpture. It is more prominently

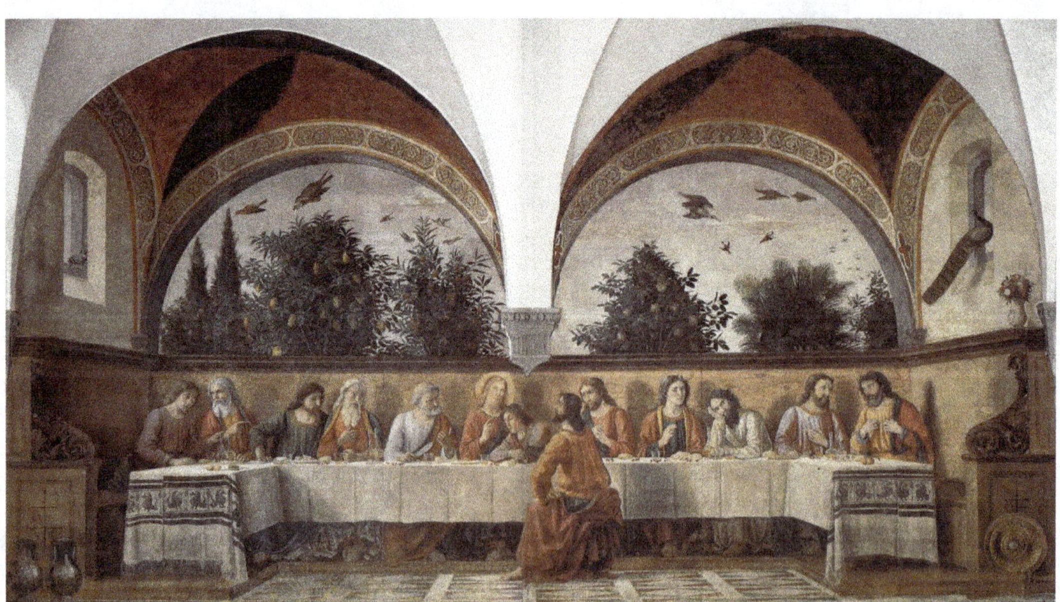

Figure 9.2: Domenico del Ghirlandaio, *Last Supper*, 1480. Fresco, 13 ft × 26.5 ft, Refectory, Ognissanti, Florence.

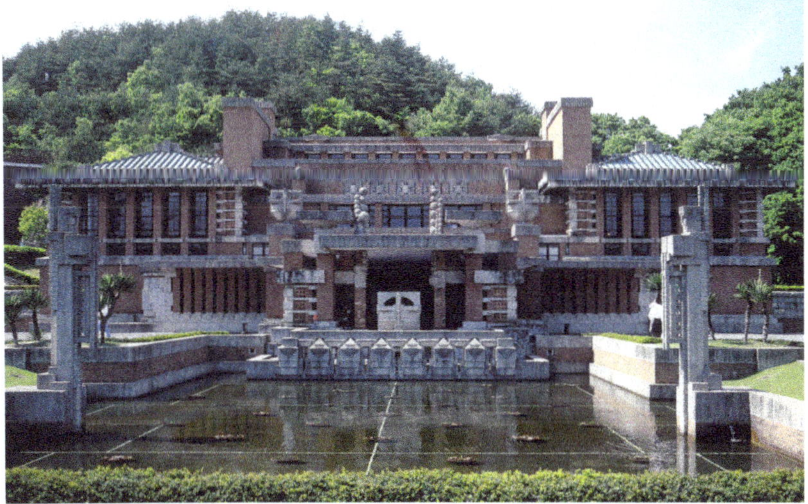
Figure 9.3: Frank Lloyd Wright, *Imperial Hotel*, 1923. Meiji-Mura Museum, Inuyama, Japan.

seen in architecture. Take for example the entrance courtyard of Frank Lloyd Wright's Imperial Hotel (**fig 9.3**). Standing at the center of this stunning architectural façade will show you just how perfectly symmetrical this work is. Whatever occurs on the left side of the building occurs on the right side as well. It brings to mind images of a Rorschach test that you would see in psychology.

ASYMMETRICAL BALANCE

Symmetrically balanced art can be classified as being ordered and calculable, perhaps even static and boring. But there is a certain strength and stability present with this form of balance. Artists can create a less formal type of artwork by using **asymmetrical balance**. In this instance, using dissimilar objects on either side of a central axis attains balance. The objects must have equal visual weight or eye appeal.

If you were to run a vertical line down the center of *Boston Common at Twilight* (**fig 9.1**), you would be greeted with two very diverse scenes. The scene at the left is one of a bustling cityscape complete with buildings, trolleys, and individuals dressed in Victorian-era clothing. The scene to the right is the exact opposite. It is one of nature populated with deciduous trees, open space, and park benches. The scene to the right exudes a sense of peaceful calm and is more relaxing than what is happening just off to the left. The scene at the right also takes up more of the canvas. The work is in diagonal recession (chapter 5), with the vanishing point slightly off-center to the left. In this instance the smaller, more densely packed cityscape asymmetrically balances out the broader, more open, park-like setting. This is just one of many ways to attain asymmetrical balance.

RADIAL BALANCE

One of the easiest types of balance to recognize is **radial balance**. Here, the artwork radiates outward from a central point, just as the sun would emanate rays. This type of balance is commonly seen in nature, but you will run across it in art as well. Examples of radial balance would be ceramics, basketry, jewelry, and interiors of domes. Standing underneath the dome of St. Peter's Basilica (**fig 9.4**) we can see how it seems to emerge from a single point and radiate downward

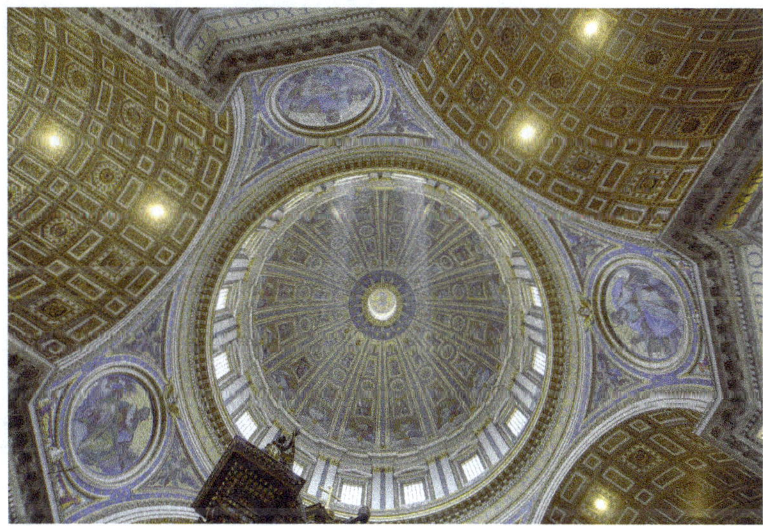
Figure 9.4: Michelangelo Buonarroti, *Interior of the dome at St Peter's Basilica*, Vatican, Rome.

to where is comes to rest on top of the pendentives, which support the dome.

CRYSTALLOGRAPHIC BALANCE

Crystallographic balance—sometimes referred to as *all-over pattern*—is when there is a repetition of the same element everywhere on the surface of an artwork. This sounds very similar to our definition of pattern from the last chapter—the repetition of a visual element in a regular or anticipated sequence. This is apparent in the *Quilt* (**fig. 9.5**) as the pattern immediately calls our attention. In terms of balance we would categorize this as crystallographic balance, because it continues throughout the entire work and there is little to no emphasis given to one particular point of the design or pattern.

IMBALANCE

There is no rule that states that an artwork must be balanced. Occasionally, we will come across a work of art that is **imbalanced**, meaning that it was created out-of-balance. Many times when an artwork is imbalanced it was done on purpose. It is meant to make the viewer feel uneasy. It is like going to have a picnic under a tree. If the tree you choose to eat under is leaning precipitously in your direction, you are going to feel uneasy and not be able to relax. Compare that to a tree that is evenly balanced. Here, the thought of the tree falling over on you wouldn't even enter your mind. A good example of imbalance is the photograph titled *Death of a Loyalist Soldier* by Robert Capa (not pictured) from 1936. This photograph was taken during the Spanish Civil War. The image is of a soldier just as he is being shot and killed. He is falling at a diagonal on the far-left-hand side of the photograph. The imbalance of the image increases the drama of the moment. It makes the viewer feel uneasy with not only the scene set before them, but also our instinctual need to center the image.[3]

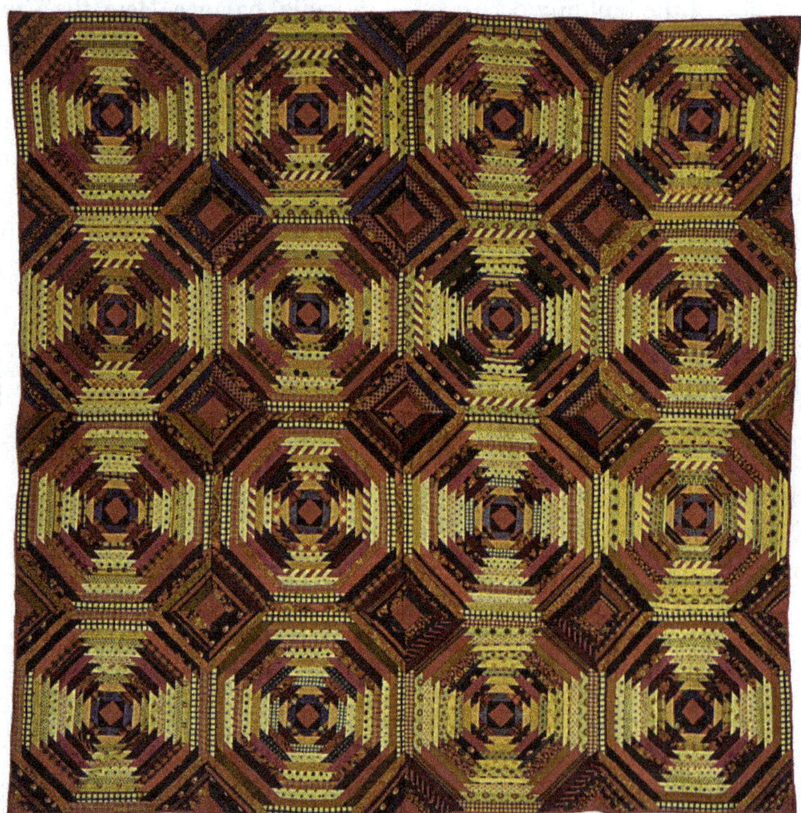

Figure 9.5: *Quilt*, 'Log Cabin' Pattern, 'Pineapple' variation. Pieced wool and cotton, 88 in × 88 in, Gift of the Betty Horton Collection. Los Angeles County Museum of Art (M.86.134.18).

Symmetrical balance:

Bilateral symmetry:

Absolute symmetry:

Asymmetrical balance:

Radial balance:

Crystallographic balance (all-over pattern):

Imbalance:

ENDNOTES

1. Frederick Hartt and David G. Wilkins, *History of Italian Renaissance Art* (Upper Saddle River, NJ: Prentice Hall, 2003), 391.
2. Ross King, *Leonardo and the Last Supper* (New York: Walker Publishing Company, 2012), ix.
3. Imbalance is also seen regularly in horror movies. A great example is the dialogue seen in Alfred Hitchcock's *Psycho* between Norman Bates and Marion Crane just subsequent to the famous shower scene. Marion Crane is shown at the far left with nothing balancing her to the right. The next scene shows Norman Bates at the far right with nothing balancing him to the left. The imbalance of the characters adds to the uneasiness and tenseness of the dialogue.

IMAGE CREDITS

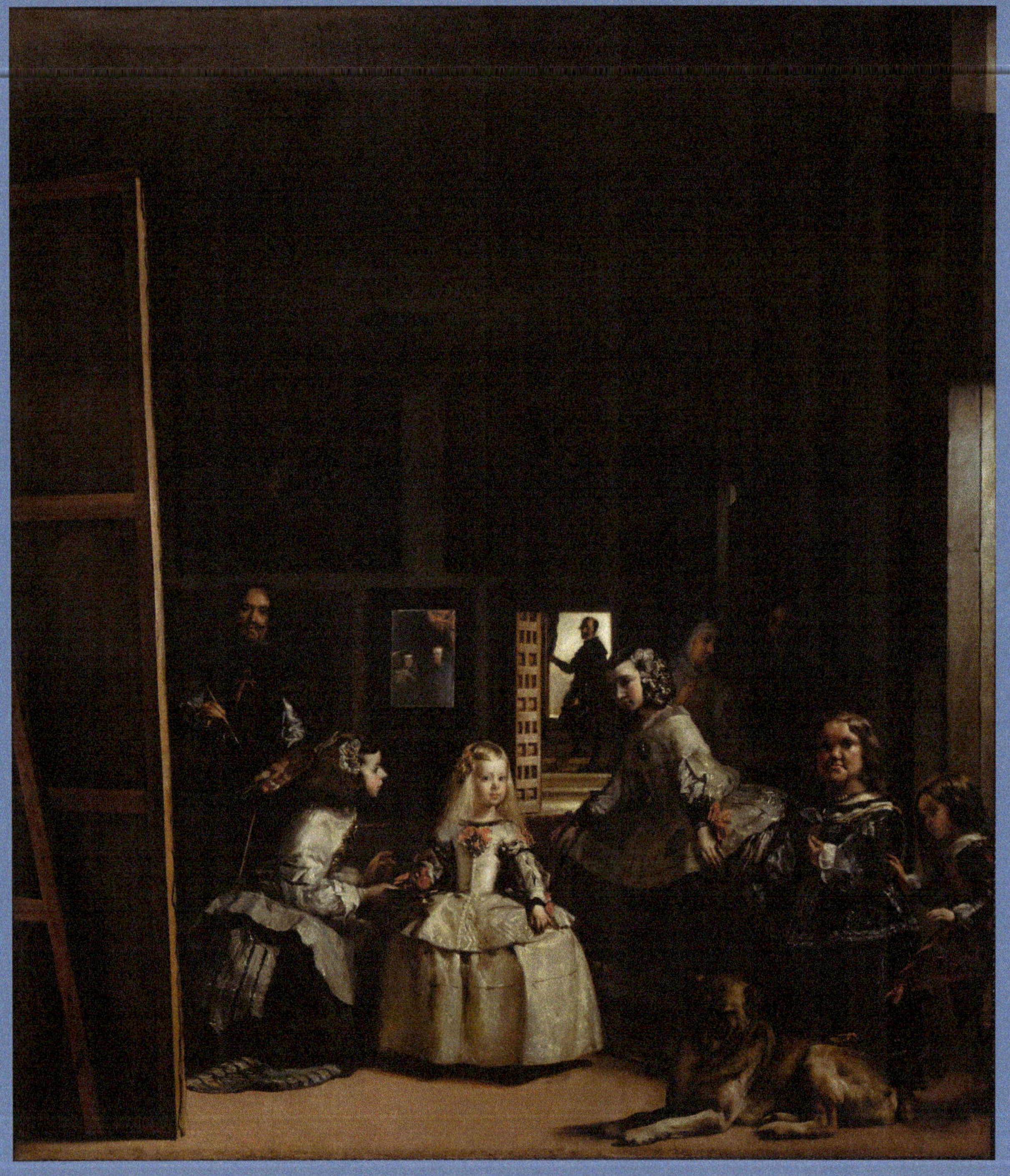

Figure 10.1: Diego Velázquez, *Las Meninas*, 1656. Oil on canvas, 125.2 in × 108.7 in, Museo del Prado, Madrid.

EMPHASIS AND FOCAL POINT

CHAPTER 10

EMPHASIS AND FOCAL POINT

Life would be simpler if reading an artwork was similar to reading a book. We could begin by looking in the upper-left-hand corner and then work our way down the canvas moving left to right. Sadly, this is not the case. Art is much more complex than that and does not have an established set of rules that we all know and follow. Furthermore, artists are at a disadvantage because they can't use arrows in their artwork or include words like "look here" to help guide their viewers.

Artists must create emphasis in order to attract the viewer's attention to a specific area of the composition called the **focal point**. This chapter discusses five types of emphasis: emphasis by contrast, emphasis by isolation, emphasis by scale, emphasis by placement, and line-of-sight. The artist might include several of these within the same work or only use one. If a work does not have a focal point, we refer to that work as being *afocal*.

EMPHASIS BY CONTRAST

Emphasis by contrast is created when one element differs drastically from another. As an example, an artist might juxtapose (in a painting) the brightness of a candle while keeping the rest of the scene in relative darkness. This is what we see done with the technique of tenebrism (chapter 6). Emphasis by contrast grabs the viewer's attention because of the major difference in the application of the formal elements: line, shape, or color. Take a look at the painting entitled *Zebra* (**fig 10.2**). The painting is a woodland scene with various shades of green blending into one another, yet right in the middle we have this striking black-and-white pattern that catches our attention and makes us stop and focus on the zebra. This bold black-and-white pattern interrupts the overall pattern of the forest.

EMPHASIS BY ISOLATION

Emphasis by isolation occurs when we take a like element and set it off by itself. In the case of *The Agnew Clinic* (**fig 10.3**), we could easily make the argument that the operation scene is the focal point. The operation is taking place at the lower portion of the painting closest to the viewer (placement). Light seems to flood the area compared to the darker background where the audience is assembled (contrast). Finally, all the individuals in the background have their eyes focused on the operation (line-of-sight). But one of the surgeons, Dr. Agnew himself, is set off to the left apart from the main group. Because of this the doctor would garner the most attention and would become the true focal point of this painting.

EMPHASIS BY SCALE

We have already discussed scale as a way to establish space (chapter 5). By varying the scale of objects we can make them appear closer to us or farther away. Now we are going to consider how scale can determine the focal point. **Emphasis**

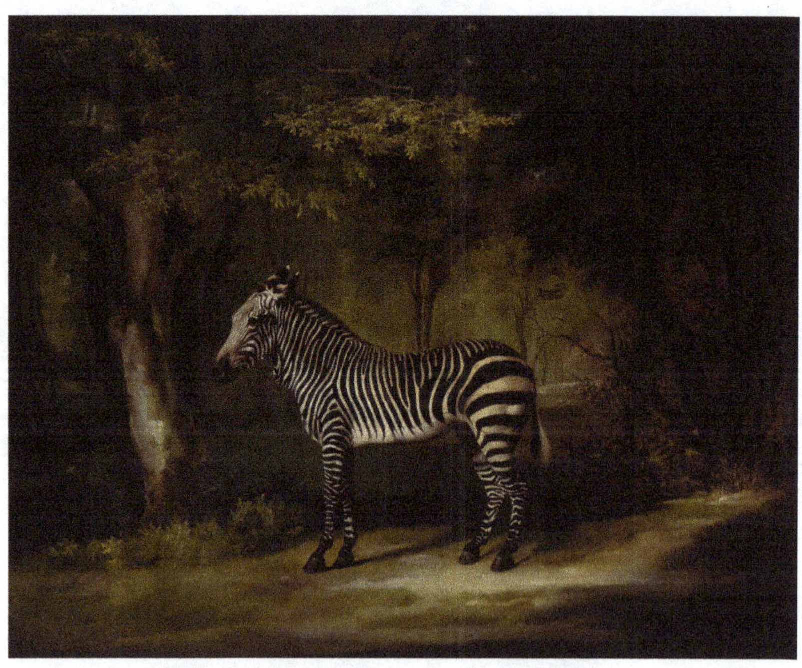

Figure 10.2: George Stubbs, *Zebra*, 1763. Oil on Canvas, 40.51 in × 50.24 in Yale Center for British Art.

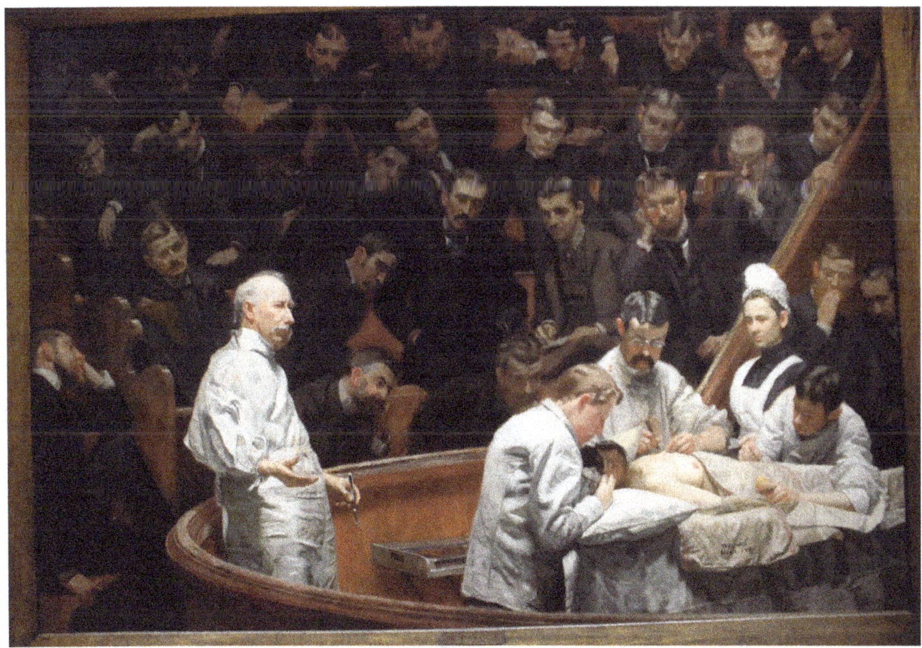

Figure 10.3: Thomas Eakins, *The Agnew Clinic*, 1889. Oil on Canvas, 84.3 in × 118.1 in, Philadelphia Museum of Art.

the other individuals in the painting, she becomes the focal point of the work.[1]

EMPHASIS BY PLACEMENT

Many times artists place the focal point at the center of the composition. Portraits would be a good example of **emphasis by placement**. While this might seem a very simple and mundane way for an artist to create a focal point, it is nonetheless effective and common. Think about the many versions of The Last Supper that have been created. Christ is always seated at the center of the scene with apostles on either side of him. Paolo Veronese's *Feast in the House of Levi* (**fig 10.4**) is no different. This painting was originally commissioned as a Last Supper painting.[2] It has Christ sitting

by scale is also referred to as *hieratic scale*. By increasing the scale of the individual, we increase his or her importance. Take a look at Giotto's *Enthroned Madonna and Saints* (see fig 22.1); even sitting down the Madonna is nearly twice the size of the angels on either side of the throne. Because of the Madonna's size in comparison to

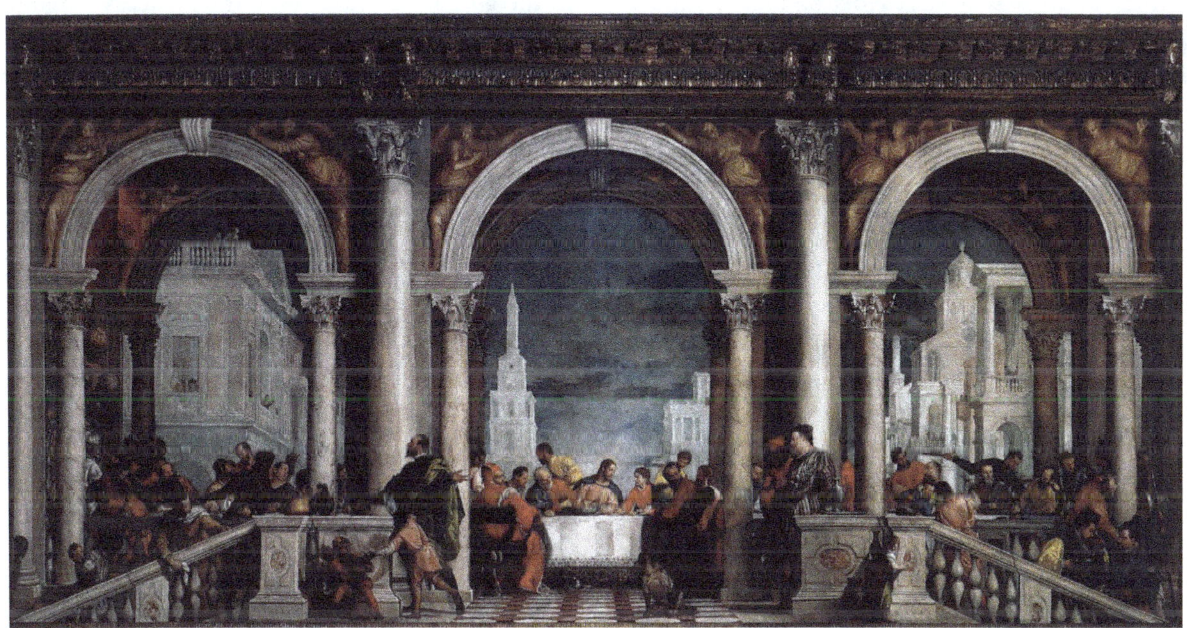

Figure 10.4: Paolo Veronese, *Feast in the House of Levi*, 1573. Oil on Canvas, 218.5 in × 503.9 in, Galleria dell'Accademia, Venice.

in the center of the work with what looks like a raucous party carrying on around him. It was because of this party (mostly the individuals in attendance) that Veronese was brought before the Inquisition. He was told to change the work, but this painting is large, roughly 18 feet by 42 feet, and it would have been an enormous task to repaint portions of the painting. Although he did not comply with the order to alter the work, he did change its title.[3]

LINE-OF-SIGHT

During the discussion of line (chapter 4), it was mentioned that implied line is one of the most powerful types of line. **Line-of-sight** is a form of implied line, and it directs us to where we are supposed to be looking in a composition—the focal point. We witnessed this in the previously mentioned painting of *The Agnew Clinic* where the figures in the background were all concentrating on the operation. In *The Assumption and Consecration of the Virgin* (see fig 4.9), God was looking down toward Mary and the apostles were looking up at Mary, thereby establishing her as the focal point of the painting.

AFOCAL

Works of art may have competing focal points or none at all. The term *focal* refers to a specific point of interest. If a work of art lacks a focal point it should be labeled as **afocal**. Think about the drip paintings of Jackson Pollock (see fig 7.7). No one section of the canvas garners or catches our attention more than any other. They are devoid of any focal point. Our eyes never seem to stop moving, continually traveling throughout the painting from one splash of paint to the next.

Las Meninas (**fig 10.1**) is a great example of a painting that has competing focal points, and therefore considered to be afocal. The artist, Diego Velázquez, was the court painter for Philip IV of Spain. This painting serves as a family portrait that shows not only the family, but their staff as well. We could make justifiable arguments to label nearly all of these individuals as the focal point of the work. At first glance we see that everyone seems to be encircling the Princess Margarita, who stands near the center of the composition (placement). Her dress shows lighter tones than the rest of the painting and her skin is the fairest. We might also consider the focus to be the gentleman climbing the stairs just beyond the open doorway as the light outlines his form and calls attention to his dark attire (contrast). There is a reflective image of the king and queen in the background, which might make them the focal point because they are the most important people in the painting.[4] The painting's title, *Las Meninas*, translates to "The Maids of Honor," which refers to the girls on either side of the princess. Finally, we can observe that everyone is looking out toward us, meaning that the focal point might not even exist within the confines of the painting (line-of-sight).

Focal point:

____
____
____
____

Emphasis by contrast:

____
____
____
____

Emphasis by isolation:

____
____
____
____

Emphasis by scale (hieratic scale):

____
____
____
____

Emphasis by placement:

____
____
____

Line-of-sight:

____
____
____

Afocal:

____
____
____
____
____

ENDNOTES

1. Besides being seen in early Renaissance art, we also see hieratic scale used in Egyptian art, such as in *The Palette of King Narmer*.
2. Frederick Hartt and David G. Wilkins, *History of Italian Renaissance Art* (Upper Saddle River, NJ: Prentice Hall, 2003), 675.
3. Robert Klein and Henri Zerner, *Italian Art 1500–1600: Sources and Documents* (Evanston, IL: Northwestern University Press, 1994), 129.
4. There are scholarly arguments as to whether it is a mirror in the background reflecting the king and queen, who would then occupy space with the viewer, or if it is a portrait of them.

IMAGE CREDITS

- Fig. 10.1: Diego Velázquez, "Las Meninas," https://commons.wikimedia.org/wiki/File:Las_Meninas,_by_ Diego_Vel%C3%A1zquez,_from_Prado_in_Google_Earth.jpg. Copyright in the Public Domain.
- Fig. 10.2: George Stubbs, "Zebra," https://commons.wikimedia.org/wiki/File:George_Stubbs_-_Zebra_-_ Google_Art_Project.jpg. Copyright in the Public Domain.
- Fig. 10.3: Thomas Eakins, "The Agnew Clinic," https://commons.wikimedia.org/wiki/File:Agnew_Phila-delphia.JPG. Copyright in the Public Domain.
- Fig. 10.4: Paolo Veronese, "Feast in the House of Levi," https://commons.wikimedia.org/wiki/File:Paolo_ Veronese_-_Feast_in_the_House_of_Levi_-_WGA24877.jpg. Copyright in the Public Domain.

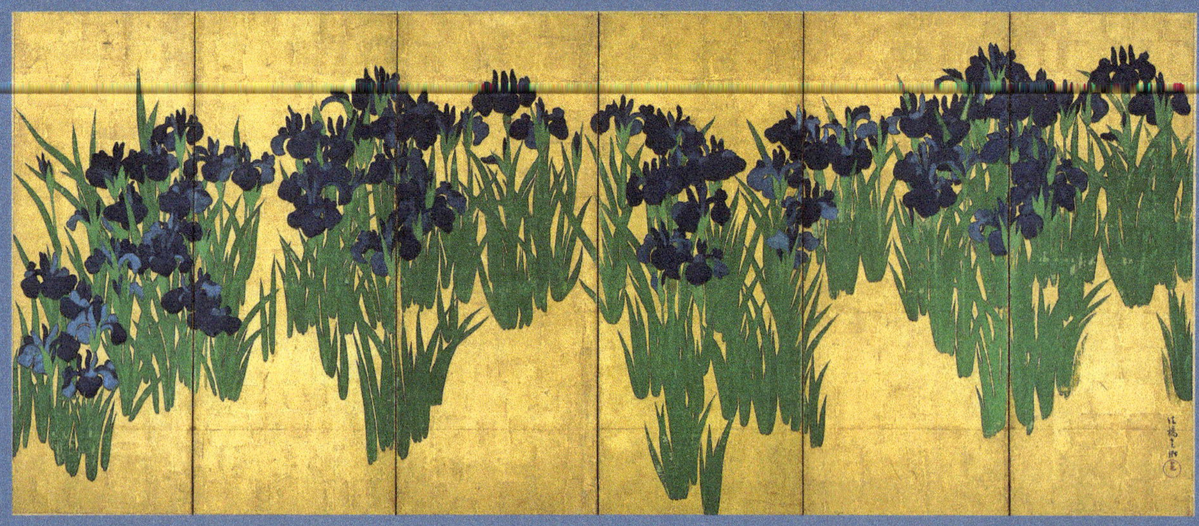

Figure 11.1: Ogata Korin, *Irises*, c. 1705. Screen (one of a pair), 150.9 cm × 338.8 cm, Nezu Art Museum, Tokyo.

SCALE, REPETITION, AND UNITY

CHAPTER

11

SCALE, REPETITION, AND UNITY

In this chapter we will wrap up our discussion of the formal elements. We are going to take another look at the use of scale and also learn about the elements of repetition and unity.

SCALE

We have talked about scale several times over the past few chapters. In chapter 5 we learned how scale is used to help create the illusion of three-dimensional space. We know that objects closer to us appear larger than those farther away. In chapter 10 we learned how scale is used to determine the focal point. The largest figure in an artwork garners more attention than smaller figures. This is commonly seen in the renderings of many of the Madonna and Child altarpieces (see fig 22.1) that were created during the Renaissance.

This chapter deals with scale in a different way. We are now considering **scale** in regards to proportion. In other words, we are considering the relative sizes of the elements/objects placed within the artwork. In *The Daughters of Edward Darley Boit* (**fig 11.2**), we are greeted with a scene of four young girls standing in a room. The girls, daughters of a

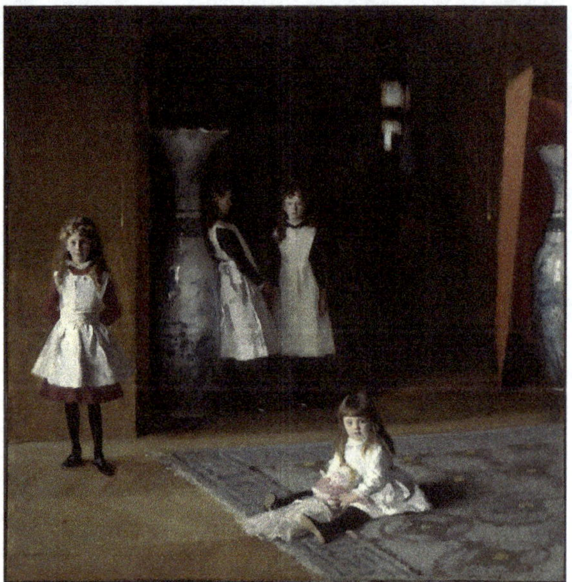

Figure 11.2: John Singer Sargent, *The Daughters of Edward Darley Boit*, 1882. Oil on Canvas, 221.9 cm × 222.6 cm, Museum of Fine Arts, Boston.

famous Boston artist, definitely look to be sisters and are dressed similarly in matching pinafores.[1] Three of the girls look forward and engage the viewer, but the fourth girl appears in profile leaning up against what appears to be a gigantic Japanese vase. When we think of vases we might think of a vessel that stands one foot in height or slightly taller, but in this painting they appear to be four feet tall! Our brain tries to process this information and asks us to make a decision in regards to the scale of these objects. Are these truly gigantic vases standing on the floor or have the girls shrunk, like Alice did in *Alice in Wonderland*?

We can also look at the proportion of the artwork itself. Neither the images in this book nor from a projector can substitute for viewing artwork firsthand. How these artworks look when you are standing in front of them helps in the interpretation of the work and with placing them in context. If we stood in front of the painting *Las Meninas* (see fig 10.1), we would be impressed by its size as it stands over 10 feet high and 9 feet wide. There is a certain feeling of importance and monumentality you get standing in its presence. The figures are life-size and look as if they might step down from the painting onto the floor of the Prado.[2] If we place Gerrit Dou's *Astronomer by Candlelight* (**fig 11.3**) next to *Las Meninas*, we might not even take notice of Dou's painting. When we view these paintings in the textbook there isn't much difference in the size of these images, but in real life they are worlds apart, as Dou's painting is less than the size of a piece of paper. Even though the two paintings were created within a few years of one another, we would naturally approach the works differently. With *Las Meninas* we stand back from the painting and interact with the figures as if they are real people, giving them space and trying to catch their gaze as they look out toward us. In Dou's painting we move in closer and marvel at the minute details of the painting, as well as noting the artist's use of tenebrism (chapter 7), as the astronomer works by the illumination of a single candle.

Modern art movements, such as Surrealism and Pop Art, deal a lot with scale and proportion

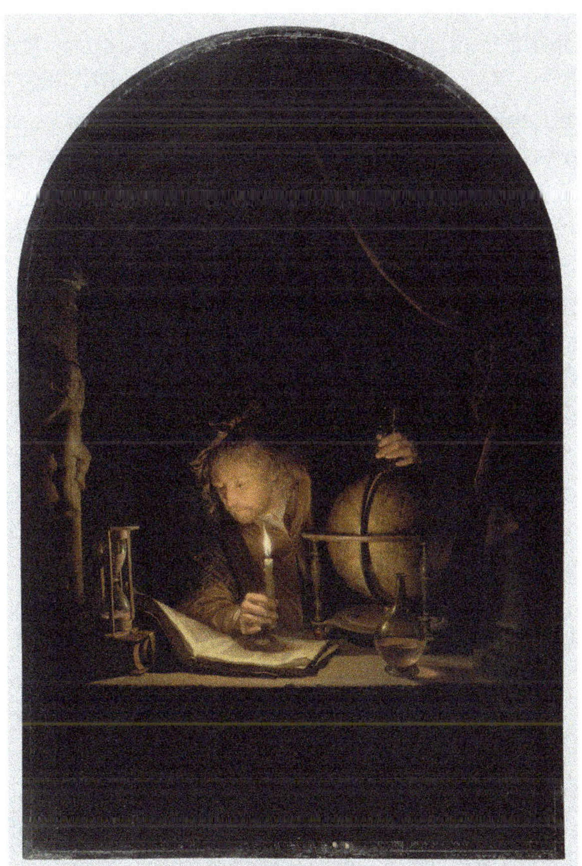

Figure 11.3: Gerrit Dou, *Astronomer by Candlelight*, c. 1665. Oil on Canvas, 12 5/8 in × 8 3/8 in, Getty Museum.

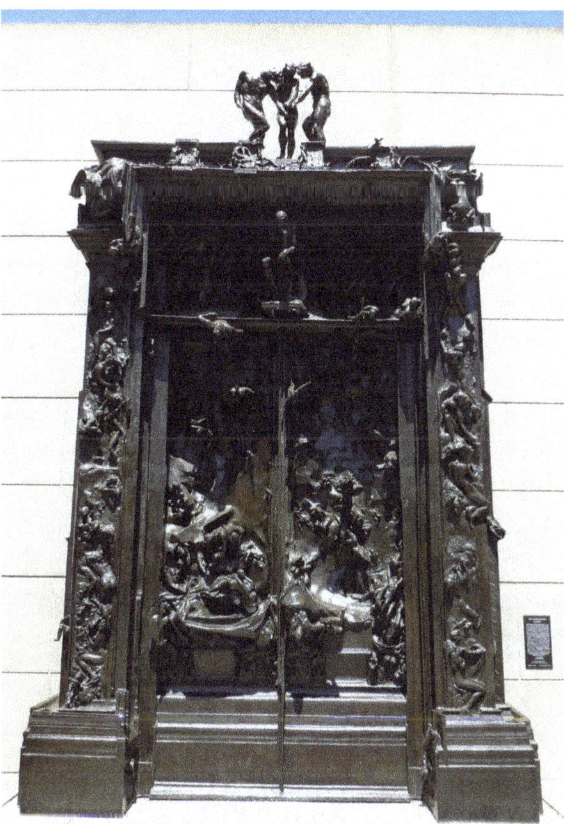

Figure 11.4: Auguste Rodin, *The Gates of Hell*, 1880–1917. Bronze, Height 6.4 m, Musee Rodin, Paris.

to make the viewers question what they are seeing. René Magritte would often manipulate the size of the objects he painted to call out attention to them. In *Personal Values* (not pictured) we see a room with oversized objects: a comb, glass, matchstick, pill, and makeup brush. Why are these objects so large? Or, are we looking at a room in a dollhouse where the objects themselves are normal-sized and the room they happen to be in is diminished in size?

REPETITION

Repetition is frequently seen in art. Repetition helps to lead or guide the viewer through the artwork, whether it is a figure like we see in *The Meeting of St. Anthony and St. Paul* (see fig 7.1) or whether it is a repetition of a pattern, such as the flooring tiles in *A Woman with a Child in a Pantry* (see fig 8.3). Repetition is everywhere, and sometimes we don't even take notice of it. Looking above *The Gates of Hell* (**fig 11.4**) by the

sculptor August Rodin, we see a sculptural group called *The Three Shades* (**fig 11.5**). While this set of figures looks like three individuals leaning over and placing their arms close together, it is in fact the same sculpture turned in three different positions. Repetition can bring unity to an artwork.

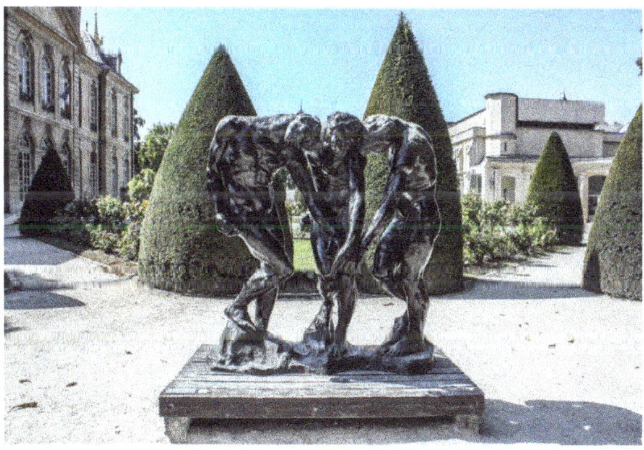

Figure 11.5: Auguste Rodin, *The Three Shades*, sculptural group from *The Gates of Hell*, 1881–86. Bronze, 97 cm × 92.2 cm × 49.5 cm, Musee Rodin, Paris.

Unity is important because it is the glue that holds all the elements within the artwork together and makes them look as if they belong. When we first look at a work of art, we take in the entire image at once rather than analyzing the individual parts. As an analogy, think about a person's garage or storage unit. Rarely do we find unity here. When the person opens up the door, there are different elements of their life scattered about: a car, lawnmower, box of books, and Christmas decorations all within a few feet of one another. But when we go into that person's home and walk into the living room, we have unity with the style and variety of furniture, vases of flowers, and pictures on the wall. It is much more inviting and harmonious because the objects belong together. Artists need to link objects within their artwork, and they do so through unity.

The unifying element in Ogata Korin's *Irises* (**fig 11.1**) is the irises themselves. They are spaced throughout the entire work and lead you from side to side as they cover the entire screen. Unity and variety go hand in hand. In fact, many times we refer to this element as *unity with variety*. Consider how the irises are created in a variety of different ways so that no two look exactly the same. Some of the flowers are painted with different colors while the plants themselves are placed on different horizon lines creating an illusion of space (as described in chapter 5).

If an artwork has unity but lacks variety, then it appears cold, boring, and calculable. We begin to imagine images of assembly lines, box stores, and institutions where everything is all the same. If an artwork has variety but lacks unity, then we have an artwork that appears extremely chaotic. There are just too many elements for our brain to process. Therefore, the goal of the artist is to create an artwork that has unity with variety.

Another example of unity with variety is Andy Warhol's *210 Coca-Cola Bottles* (not pictured). The artist has lined up seven rows of Coca-Cola bottles, one on top of another. The bottles are the unifying element in the work. But Warhol has twisted each of the bottles in a slightly different way, and each contains a different amount of Coca-Cola. By having unity with variety an artwork that could be incredible repetitious and dull instead becomes a much more intriguing scene to view and admire.

Scale:

Repetition:

Unity:

PROJECT: UNITY WITH VARIETY

Goal

To develop a design showing your mastery of the elements of unity with variety.

Required Media

15" × 20" illustration board
Black Sharpie marker or black India ink
Your choice of object(s)

Assignment

1. Select an everyday object (or objects) to use as your subject matter.
2. Create an integrated image/design with the object(s) you have chosen. An integrated image is one where the objects look as if they belong together, that there is some unifying element among them.
3. Remember to include variety! Variety creates an interesting image, but note that too much variety can create clutter and confusion.

Consider the following:

- Placement
- Presentation
- Format
- Congruity
- Proximity

Point value: _________________

Due date: __________________ (weather permitting).

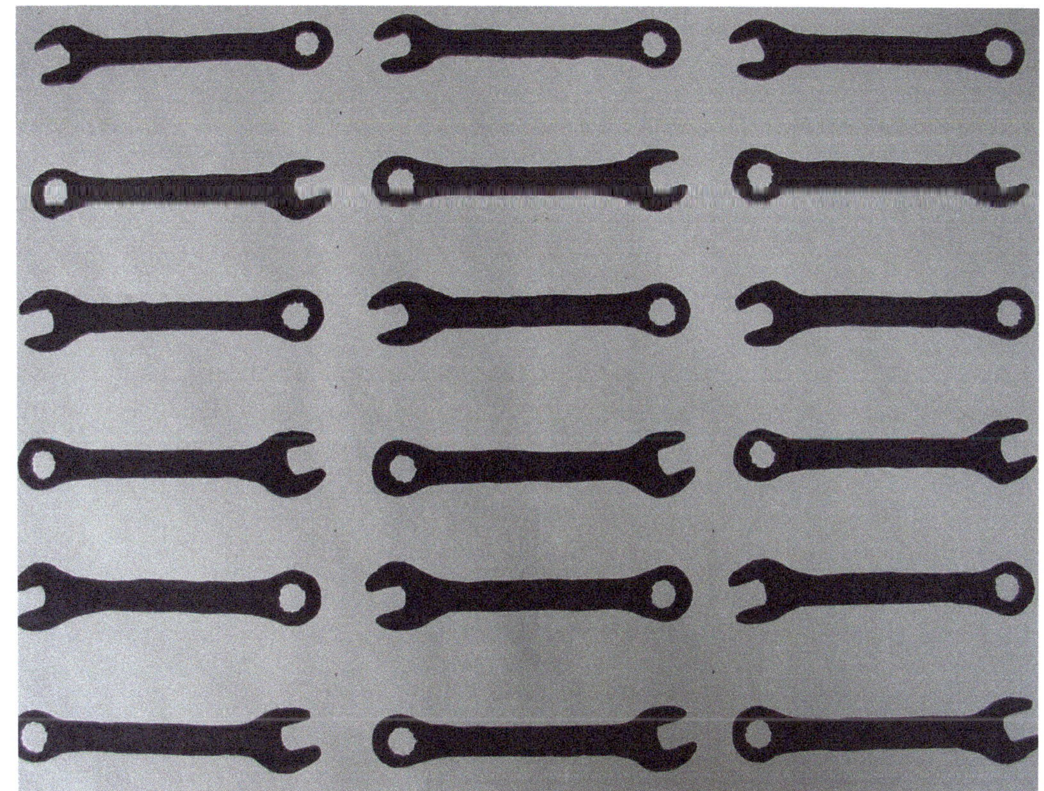

Figure 11.6: (Example #1)

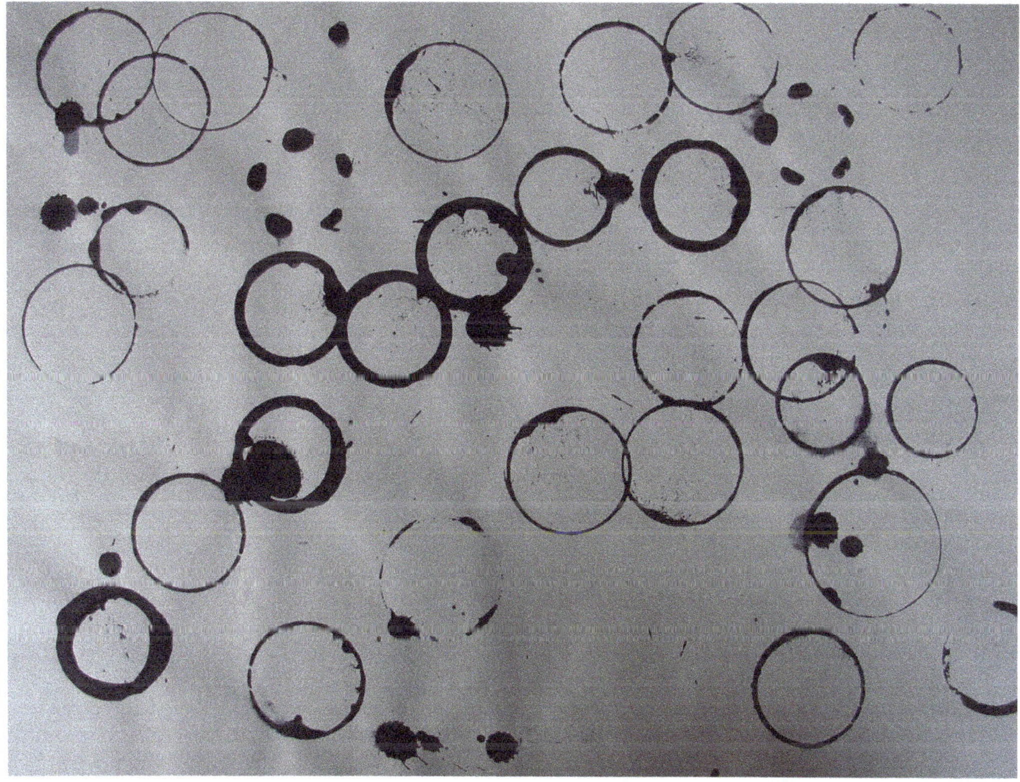

Figure 11.7: (Example #2)

1. *Masterpiece Paintings from the Museum of Fine Arts, Boston* (New York: Harry N. Abrams, 1986), 121.
2. *Las Meninas* hangs in the Prado Museum in Madrid, Spain.

IMAGE CREDITS

MEDIUMS

SECTION

III

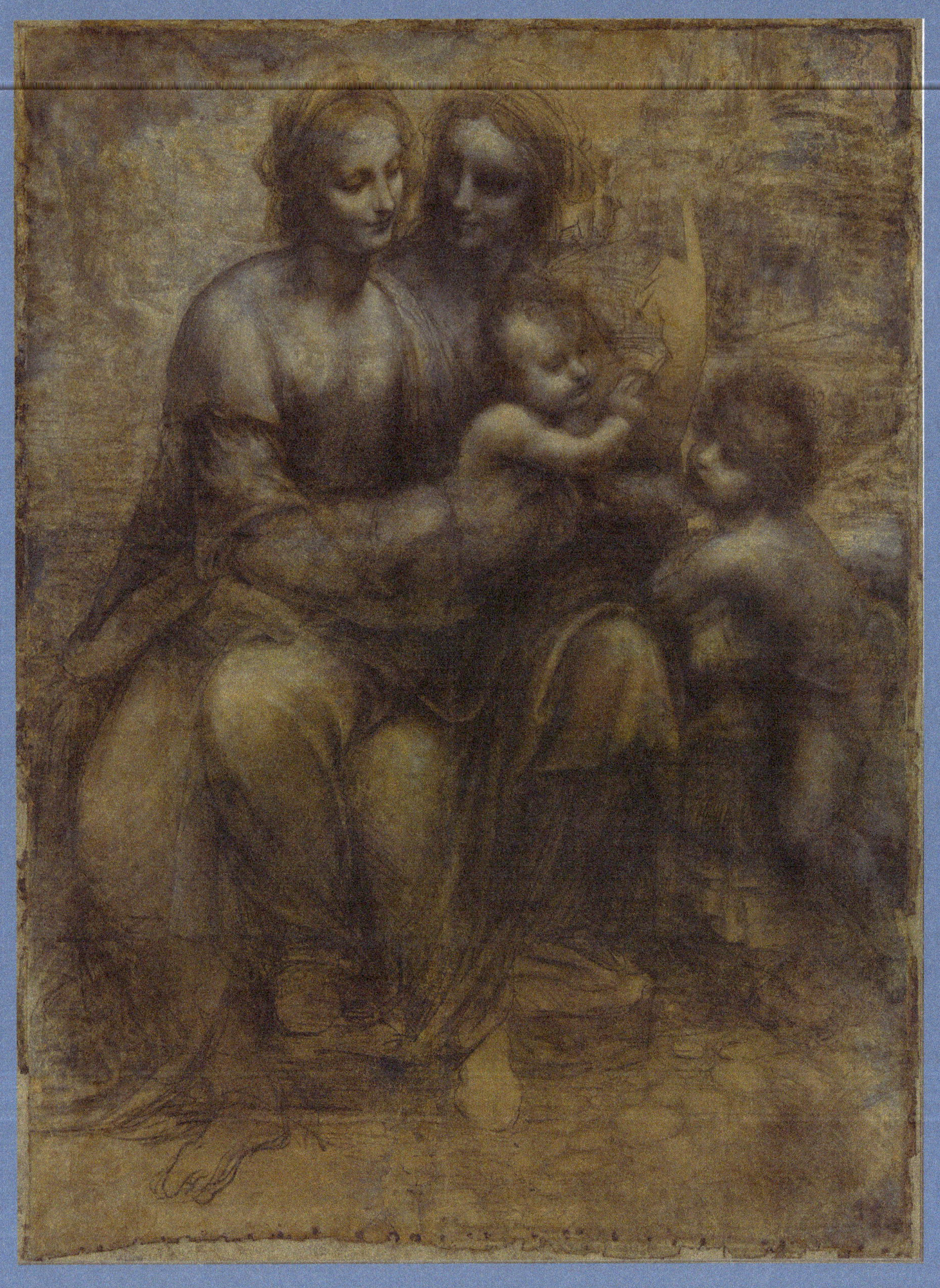

Figure 12.1: Leonardo da Vinci, *Madonna and Child with St. Anne and St. John the Baptist*, c. 1505–07. Drawing on paper, 141.5 cm × 104.6. cm, National Gallery, London.

DRAWING

CHAPTER
12

DRAWING

Over the next few chapters we will begin to examine the various mediums and processes used to create art. The very first medium that should be talked about is drawing. Drawing has been referred to as the "foundation of art." Why is drawing so important? Not only is it considered a fine art in and of itself, but it is also utilized as a preliminary step toward the completion of artworks in many other mediums, such as painting and architecture. As an example, a building could not be constructed without first consulting a blueprint.

Painters frequently use **preliminary drawings** because it gives them a chance to experiment before putting their ideas down in a permanent medium. An early form of preliminary drawing was the *cartoon*. These full-sized drawings were used during the Renaissance to transfer a drawing onto a wall/ceiling, which would then be painted. (Fresco painting will be discussed in detail in chapter 15.) During the Renaissance drawing was not looked upon as highly as it is today. It was simply thought of as a step along the way to a work of art done in a superior medium.

Cartoons were part of a process. The intention was once they were used they had served their purpose and would be discarded. One of the few cartoons still in existence today is Leonardo da Vinci's *Madonna and Child with St. Anne and Infant St. John the Baptist* (**fig 12.1**). This drawing is significant because it is considered a masterpiece in its own right. It is an important stepping-stone in the consideration of drawing as a fine art. Giorgio Vasari mentions this specific drawing in his book *The Lives of Artists*.[1] In this book Vasari states, "Finally he [Leonardo] did a cartoon showing Our Lady and Saint Anne with the figure of Christ, which not only amazed all the artisans, but once completed and set up in a room, brought men, women, young and old to see it for two days as if they were going to a solemn festival."[2]

METALPOINT/SILVERPOINT

Several different mediums can be used for drawing. Among the most commonly used tools for drawing during the Late/High Renaissance was *metalpoint*, also referred to as *silverpoint*. The artist would use a stylus made of some type of metal—silver, copper, or even gold. The paper to be drawn on would be treated with a ground, such as powdered bone and gum water.[3] When the metal touches the ground a chemical reaction occurs, resulting in a line.

Again we will look at an example by Leonardo da Vinci. His drawing of *Head of a Warrior* (**fig 12.2**) was created using metalpoint. This medium tends to be best suited for creating contour lines. Even with 500 years of oxidation taking place the drawing still appears very faint. Given the cost of the metal, along with the time it took to prepare the paper, it is easy to see how metalpoint quickly fell out of favor for easier-to-use drawing mediums, such as chalk and charcoal.

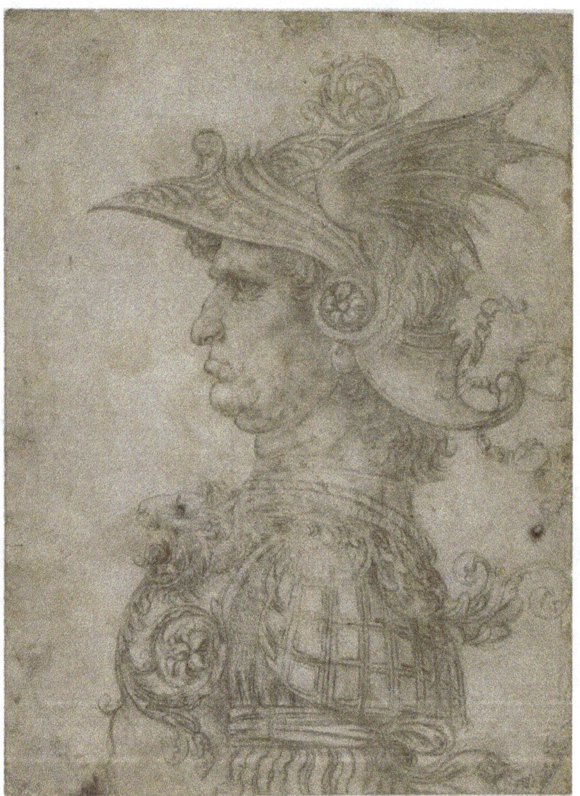

Figure 12.2: Leonardo da Vinci, *Head of a Warrior*, c. 1475–80. Metalpoint on Prepared Paper, 28.7 cm × 21.1 cm, British Museum.

CHALK

We normally think of chalk as being exclusively white, but with the inclusion of pigments it comes in a variety of colors. An advantage of both this medium and charcoal is that they can be sanded to a fine point for highly detailed work or they can be turned on their sides to create bold gestural lines. Both of these variations are present in Winslow Homer's *Schooner at Anchor* (**fig 12.3**). The figures, boats, and ripples in the water are finely detailed, yet the sails and shadowed areas of the water are broadly filled in with chalk. Chalk and charcoal allow for a more three-dimensional image through the use of chiaroscuro, effects that metalpoint would not have been able to achieve.

CHARCOAL

A wide range of charcoal products can be purchased from art supply stores. They come in pencil form as well as raw sticks. Charcoal is created from burnt wood, and the density of this medium varies from a lightweight vine charcoal to compressed charcoal. Vine charcoal creates a soft line and would be used primarily to create an under/preliminary drawing on a canvas, which would then be painted over. Compressed charcoal is available in either pencil or stick form. Charcoal sticks are typically broken down into smaller pieces, which make them easier to use. They can create a wonderful array of line with the different angles of the sticks. Charcoal pencils are used in the same way as graphite pencils and are commonly

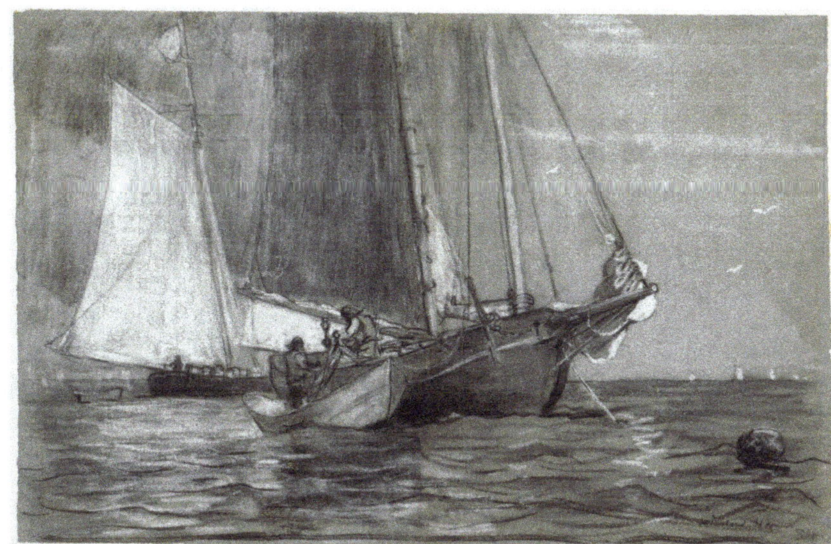

Figure 12.3: Winslow Homer, *Schooner at Anchor*, 1884. Chalk on gray-green laid paper, 40.7 cm × 63.6 cm, Clark Art Institute.

available in values such as HB, 2B, 4B, and 6B. *A Series of Twelve Plant Studies* (**fig 12.4**) was created using a 4B charcoal pencil.

Charcoal is a wonderful medium to work with because it is so delicate. It can be easily smudged, so extra care and precaution must be taken during the creation of the work as well as afterward. A sheet of glassine should be used to protect the drawing once it is completed.

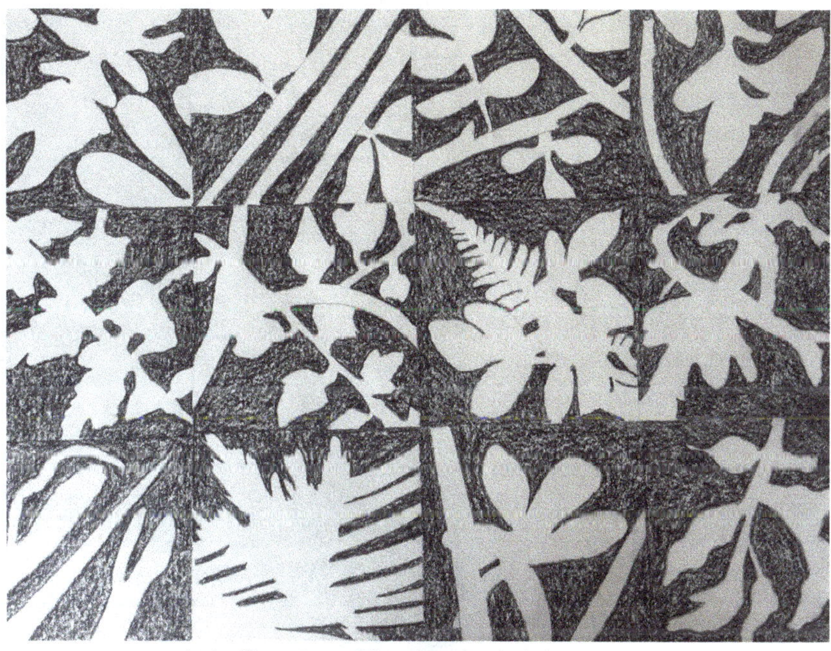

Figure 12.4: David Plouffe, *A Series of Twelve Plant Studies*, 2004. Charcoal on Paper, 18 in × 24 in.

The most common drawing material is graphite/pencil. We have all used this medium at one time in our lives or another, whether it was writing notes, taking an exam, or doodling in the margins. Like charcoal, it comes in a variety of values, ranging from a very light 8H to a very dark 8B, with a range of at least 10 recognized values in between. The artist Prisca Langlais used pencils ranging from 2H to 6B to create her drawing *Nathalie* (**fig 12.5**).[4] This drawing took the artist over 300 hours to complete, using both a live model and images.[5]

In the 1970s artists began using graphite to create photorealist drawings. **Photorealism**, as the name suggests, is the reproduction of photographs through incredibly realistic renderings. Each detail of the photograph is painstakingly reproduced by the artist, usually with the aid of a magnifier. As one can imagine, these drawings (or paintings if the case may be) take a tremendously long time to produce. Artists such as Vija Celmins and Richard Estes are especially known for their photorealist artworks.

PASTEL

Pastels, like chalk, come in a wide variety of colors (**fig 12.6**). The medium itself is created from pigment and a binding agent. Because there is very little binding agent present, pastels are a very delicate and fragile medium to work with. Paper for use specifically with pastels is available that has a textured finish to help the medium adhere to the page. Fixative sprays can also be applied once the work has been completed. Pastels should be protected from bright light, because the colors can fade. Museums, such as the Getty Museum in Los Angeles, have special rooms where they display their pastel drawings that use lower amounts of light compared to their other galleries.

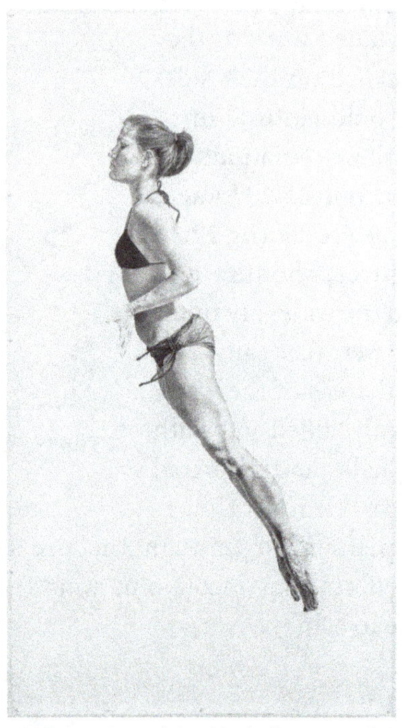

Figure 12.5: Prisca Langlais, *Nathalie*, 2015. Graphite on Paper, 94 in × 51 in.

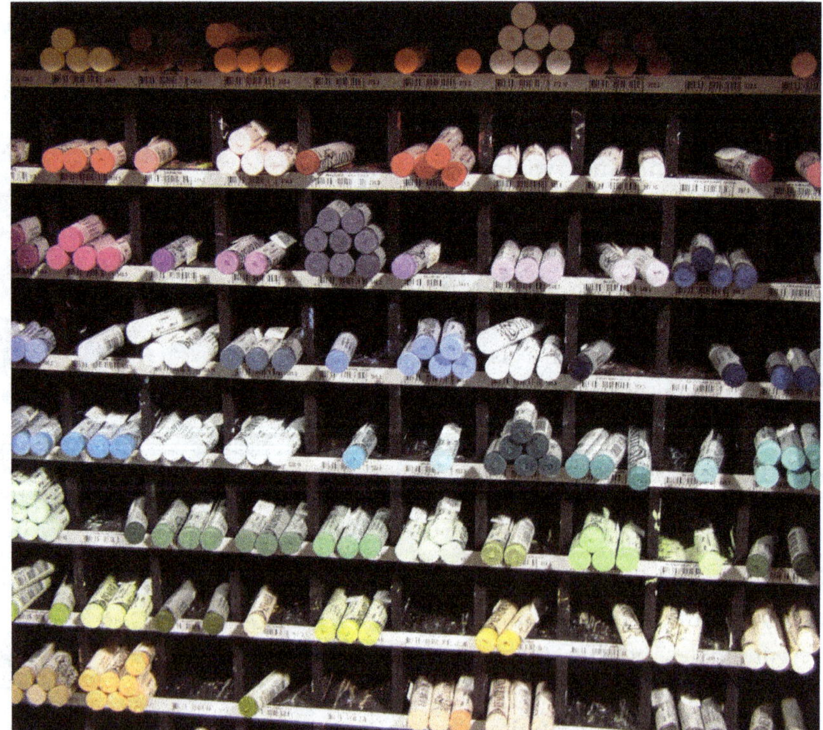

Figure 12.6: Display of Pastels.

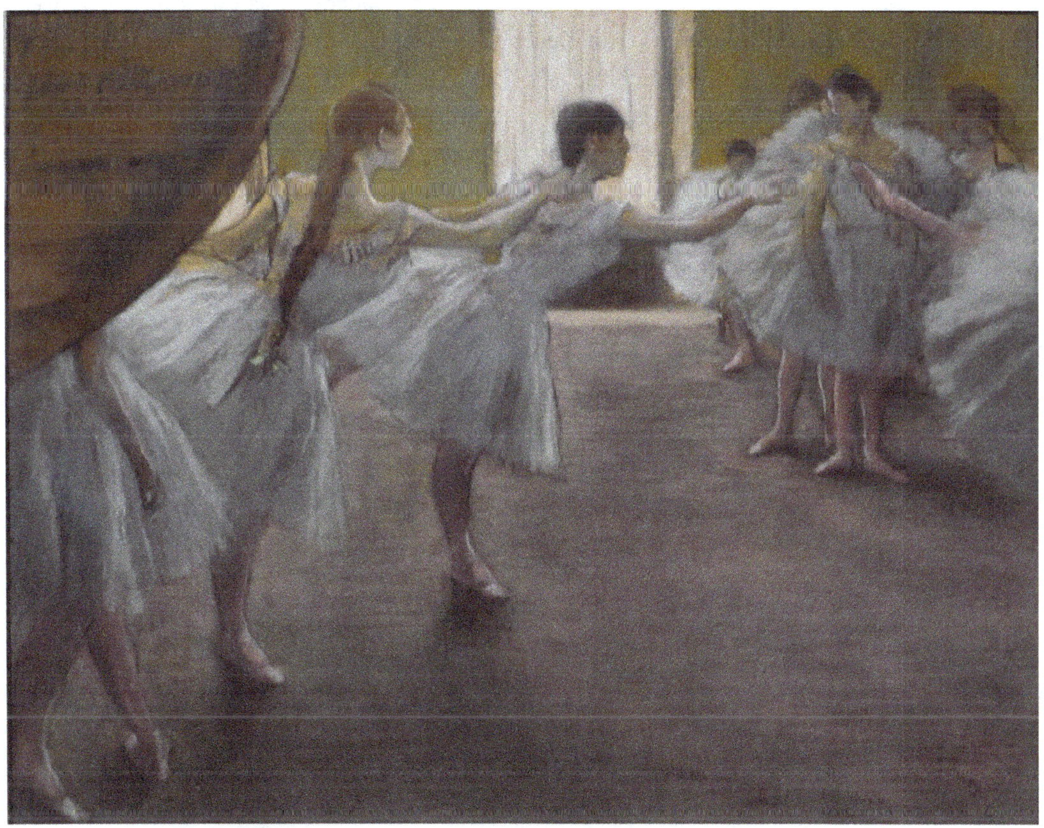

Figure 12.7: Edgar Degas, *Ballet Rehearsal,* 1875–77. Pastel on Cardboard, 50 cm × 63 cm, The Pushkin State Museum of Fine Arts, Moscow.

Among the most talented of artists who worked in pastels is Edgar Degas. This is evident in his drawing of the *Ballet Rehearsal* (**fig 12.7**). One of the attributes of using pastels is that the completed work looks like a sketch. Degas, along with the other Impressionists, were nicknamed "the sketchers," as their artworks looked unfinished, compared to the "finishers" who created art within the academic tradition and rules.

OIL STICK

Oil sticks are the newest drawing medium. Oil sticks are essentially oil paint mixed with wax and rolled like a crayon. They are ready-to-use, which is of huge benefit to the artist. If you were to paint with traditional oil paints, you would need to assemble a palette, paint tubes, brushes, palette knives, and chemical solvents and find a well-ventilated area to paint in. With oil sticks there is no preparation time nor lengthy clean up. You are immediately ready to create an artwork. The biggest downfall is the cost; as with anything that is ready-to-use, you are paying for convenience. Oil sticks have the same advantages and disadvantages as oil paints, which will be discussed in chapter 15.

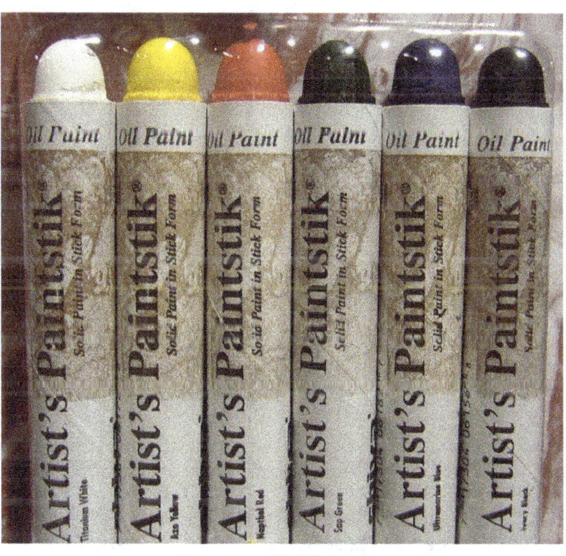

Figure 12.8: Oil Sticks.

Ink comes in a multitude of colors and can be applied with either pen or brush. When ink is diluted with water it creates a **wash**. In Tiepolo's *Three Studies of the God Bacchus* (**fig 12.9**) a wash is applied over an ink and chalk drawing. The wash helps to establish a three-dimensional scene by creating areas of light and shadow. The figure of Bacchus has parts of his figure, such as the lower half of his arm or leg, darkened with the wash. This indicates that there is a light source shining down on him at a particular angle from above. The addition of the wash assists in making the drawing more realistic than if it was left as a simple line drawing.

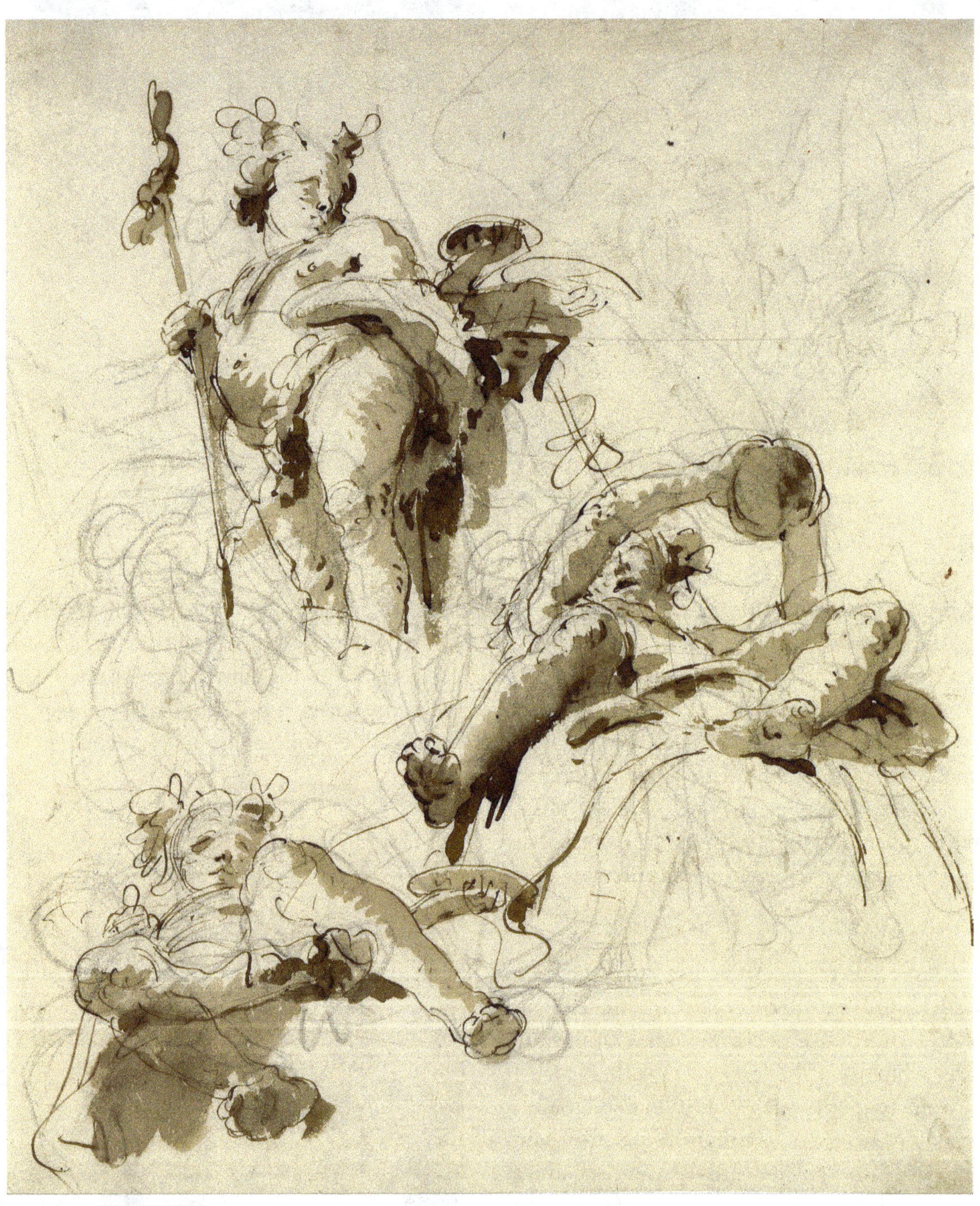

Figure 12.9: Giovanni Battista Tiepolo, *Three Studies of the God Bacchus*, c.1700-1770. Black chalk, pen and brown ink, with brown wash 27.5 cm × 33.3 cm, Morgan Library & Museum, New York City.

Preliminary drawing/preliminary study:

Metalpoint/silverpoint:

Chalk:

Charcoal:

Graphite/pencil:

Photorealism:

Pastel:

Oil stick:

Ink (pen/brush):

Wash:

Innovative drawing materials:

PROJECT: ELECTRONIC DATABASES

Goal

To become more research savvy by utilizing academic-level online tools available to you through the library's website.

Assignment

1. Find a recent article—published within the past 12 months—on a subject in art that interests you. You will do this by utilizing one of the library databases, such as *Academic Search Premier* or *ProQuest Newsstand*. Consider focusing your search on your favorite artist, artwork, or style of art. You might even try tying in art with your academic major. Keep the following in mind regarding your topic and search:
   - Do not use the general search bar on the library's website to search for an article. You must use one of the databases.
   - Internet sites or blogs cannot be used as sources.
   - Please stay away from articles about music, dance, cosmetics, cars, etc. Focus on areas of art we touch on in this class. If you have any questions about a possible topic, just ask. Articles on animation, graphic design, and illustration are acceptable
2. Once you find an interesting article, print it out. *The article must be at least 400 words in length, but fewer than 2000 words.*
3. Write a one-page essay structured as follows:

Paragraph 1. Basic information (do not list these as bullet points)
   a. What is the title of the article?
   b. Who wrote it? (If unknown, tell me it is "unknown" or "anonymous writer.")
   c. What magazine/journal/periodical was the article published in?
   d. Provide the date of publication
   e. Which of the databases did you use?
   f. What keyword did you search for?

Paragraph 2. Briefly *summarize* the article.
   Tell me what the article is about. Use general rather than specific information. Do not "lift" passages from the article! That would be plagiarizing, not summarizing.

Paragraph 3. What interested you about this article?
   Tell me why you chose the article. This is the most important paragraph in the entire essay and should be of equal length to paragraph 2.

Essay Format

   - *Upper-left-hand corner of the paper should have (single-spaced):*
      Your name
      Days and time of class
      Database project
   - Skip two lines and begin your paper. Do not give your paper a title.
   - One page (20–23 lines of text)

- Typed
- Double-spaced (Format —> Paragraph —> Spacing —> Double —> Click OK)
- 1" margins (Format —> Document —> Change Margins —> Click OK)
- Use Times or Times New Roman
- 10-point font
- Do not forget to proofread your paper! Grammar does count!
- Do not use slang in academic writing (the word is *legitimate*, not *legit*).
- Make sure to *italicize* titles of artworks if you use them.
- *Artwork* is one word, not two.
- The term is *work of art* not *piece of art* or *piece of work*.

Essay
Behind the essay please staple a printout of the article you wrote on.
(Note: There is no stapler in the classroom.)

Point value: _____________________

Due date: _____________________

ENDNOTES

1. Giorgio Vasari is considered the very first art historian, and his book *The Lives of Artists* the very first biographical account of the Italian Renaissance.
2. Giorgio Vasari, *The Lives of the Artists*, trans. Julia Conaway Bondanella and Peter Bondanella (Oxford: Oxford University Press, 1998), 293.
3. Henry Sayre, *A World of Art*, 7th ed. (Boston: Prentice Hall, 2013), 181.
4. More about Prisca Langlais and her artwork can be found on her website: priscalanglais.weebly.com.
5. Interview with Prisca Langlais, April 18, 2016.

IMAGE CREDITS

- Fig. 12.1: Leonardo da Vinci, "Madonna and Child with St. Anne and St. John the Baptist," https://commons.wikimedia.org/wiki/File:Leonardo_da_Vinci_-_Virgin_and_Child_with_Ss_Anne_and_John_the_Baptist.jpg. Copyright in the Public Domain.
- Fig. 12.2: Leonardo da Vinci, "Head of a Warrior," https://commons.wikimedia.org/wiki/File:Head_of_a_Warrior_-_Da_Vinci_1.jpg. Copyright in the Public Domain.
- Fig. 12.3: Winslow Homer, "Schooner at Anchor," https://commons.wikimedia.org/wiki/File:Winslow_Homer_-_Schooner_at_Anchor_%281884%29.jpg. Copyright in the Public Domain.
- Fig. 12.5: Prisca Langlais, "Nathalie." Copyright © by Prisca Langlais. Reprinted with permission.
- Fig. 12.7: Edgar Degas, "Ballet Rehearsal," https://commons.wikimedia.org/wiki/File:'Ballet_Rehearsal'_by_Edgar_Degas,_pastel,_Pushkin_Museum.JPG. Copyright in the Public Domain.
- Fig. 12.9: Giovanni Battista Tiepolo, "Three Studies of the God Bacchus," https://commons.wikimedia.org/wiki/File:Giovanni_Battista_Tiepolo_-_Three_Studies_of_the_God_Bacchus_-_Google_Art_Project.jpg. Copyright in the Public Domain.

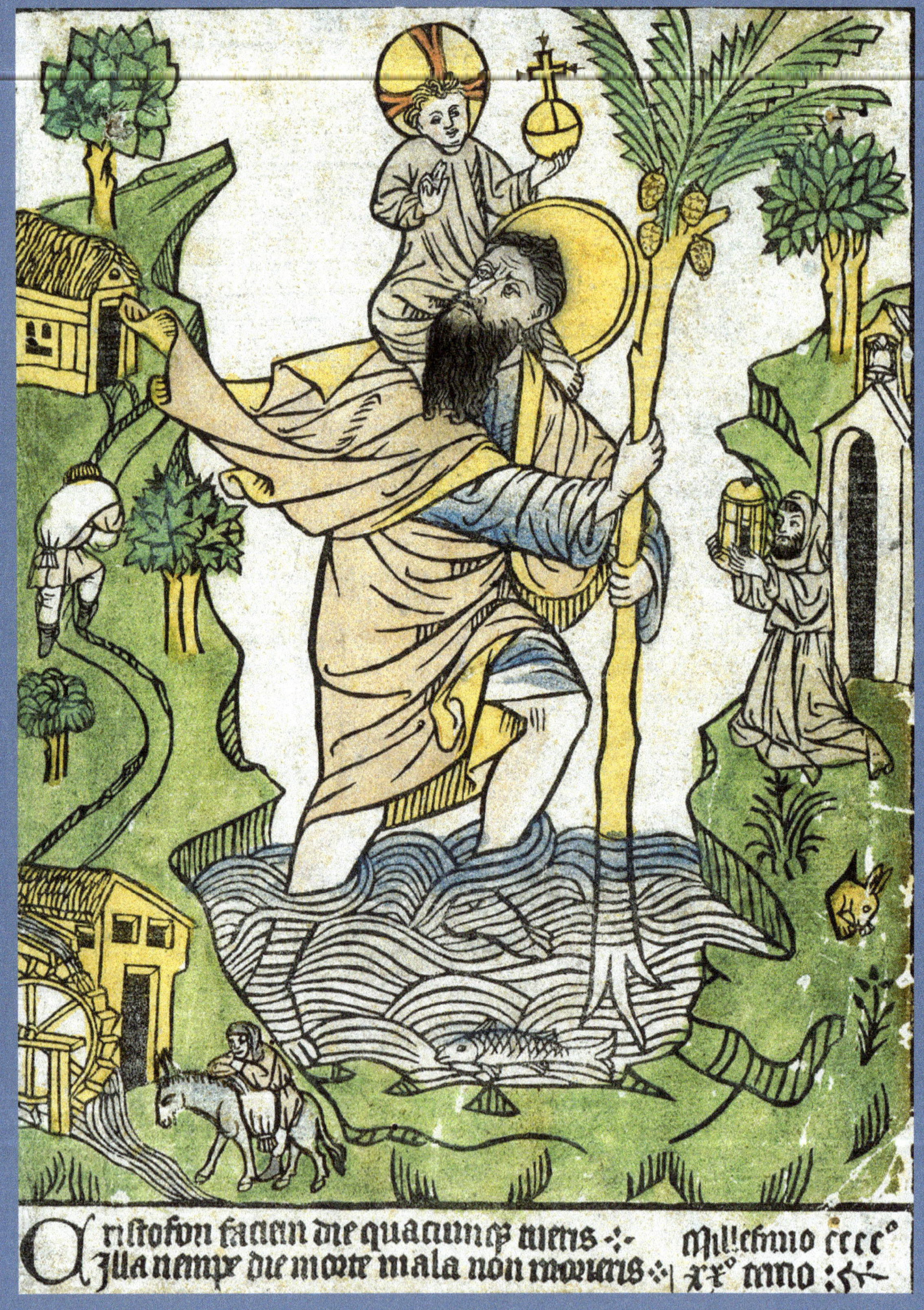

Figure 13.1: *The Buxheim of St. Christopher*, 1423. Hand-colored woodcut, 11 3/8 in × 8 1/8 in, John Rylands Library, Manchester.

PRINTMAKING

PRINTMAKING

Drawing, painting, and sculpting can all be used to create unique, one-of-a-kind works of art. There is only one *Mona Lisa*, one *Statue of David*, and one *Ghent Altarpiece*. The exciting thing about printmaking is that this medium allows for multiple works of art to be created. Printmaking allows for art to be consumed by larger audiences. We might not be able to afford an original painting by our favorite artist, but most of us could afford a print, because they are generally less expensive than an original work. Economically speaking, printmaking makes art affordable to everyone.

This chapter covers the five most common printmaking processes. A brief overview of each process is provided, but note that there is not room enough in these pages to conduct an in-depth analysis of the specific types of techniques, chemicals, inks, or presses that would be used in these processes.

RELIEF

If you have ever used a rubber stamp to mark the date on some paperwork or to note that a bill has been "paid," you have used the relief process. In relief printing we print from the positive image. What you see raised from the surface of the stamp is what will be printed. This raised area collects the ink, which is then transferred to the paper. It is a relatively easy process that, along with intaglio, was introduced during the Renaissance. The relief process has three variations: woodcut, wood engraving, and linocut.

Woodcuts are the most popular of the relief processes. Here, the artist begins with a block of wood. The design is then drawn on the wood. Negative areas—areas where the artist doesn't want ink to accumulate—are chipped and gouged out. The block is then inked and sent through the press face up with the paper resting on top. Once the image is transferred the artist usually signs, titles, and numbers each print, such as 1/60 or 7/30. Numbering is important, because the artist is working in a series rather than creating one unique work.

All three relief processes are created in a similar manner with only slight differences between them. The difference between woodcut and wood engraving is the way the lumber is milled. Standard woodcuts utilize the plank side of the wood, where you can prominently see the grain pattern. The grain can even be incorporated into the finished work, such as seen in the print *Prophet* by Emil Nolde (not pictured). With wood engraving, the artist uses a wood block that is cut perpendicular to the grain. The result of using this cut of wood is that a more photograph-like image can be created.

With linocuts, the wood block is replaced with a block of linoleum. The advantage of linoleum is that it is soft, much softer than wood, and therefore easier to carve. However, the disadvantage of linoleum is the same as its advantage. Because of the material's softness, the image is easily and quickly distorted when it is placed through the press, so only short print runs can be made.

While many relief prints are created in black and white, they can also be created in color through the techniques of registration and reduction. Prints can also be colored in by hand, as shown in *The Buxheim of St. Christopher* (**fig 13.1**). Pilgrims throughout Europe would have carried a print similar to this one because St. Christopher is the patron saint of travelers.

INTAGLIO

Intaglio printing works the exact opposite of relief. Here, the print is created from the negative space rather than the positive as the ink fills recessed grooves. Instead of using wood blocks or linoleum, intaglio printing utilizes metal plates, such as zinc and copper.[1] Like relief printing, the intaglio process also has three subcategories: engraving, etching, and drypoint. The difference between them is how the image is created on the plate; the inking and printing process remains the same.

Engravings are made using a tool called a *burin*, which is a diamond-shaped metal rod. As the burin is pushed across the plate it removes a sliver of metal. A scrapper is then used to remove any burrs from the engraved line. Once the image has been created, ink is applied to its surface with either a dense, wide, flat-head paintbrush or a piece of thick (in comparison to printer paper), but flexible, paper. The idea is to push the ink into the grooves without leaving any air pockets. The excess ink is then cleaned off from the nonprinting surface. The plate is set onto the press with a damp sheet of paper on top of the plate. The reason the paper is damp is that it needs to be malleable in order for it to be pushed down into the grooves to pick up the ink. When the plate and paper go through the press they go through at such intense pressure that the paper will be left dented with the form of the plate. This is a really important aspect to note if you ever go out and buy an intaglio print, which are sought after by collectors. You always want to check for the indentation of the paper. If there is not an indent, you don't have an intaglio print!

Saint Anthony Tormented by Demons (**fig 13.2**) is an example of an engraving. The scene is one of pure horror where Saint Anthony is being accosted by demons who are: "beating, scratching, poking, tugging, and no doubt shrieking at the stoical saint."[2] Engravings were also used to reproduce works of art and illustrate books prior to the invention of photography.[3]

Etchings are made with the help of acid. Instead of pushing a burin to create the grooves, acid eats into the plate to create them. First, the plate must be completely covered with an acid-resistant ground. Next, the image is scratched through the ground, exposing the metal plate beneath. When the image is complete, the plate is then submerged into a container of acid. How long it is left in the acid will determine the width and depth of the lines. Once removed from the acid, the remaining ground is cleaned off and the plate is ready to be inked.

House Tops by Edward Hopper (see fig 4.14) was discussed back in chapter 4 in regards to hatching and cross-hatching. This is how shading and value can be created in an etching. Etching lines tend to be softer and not as rigid as those found in engravings.

Drypoints such as *Boats in Port* (**fig 13.3**) by Auguste Brouet, are created in a very similar manner as engravings. A drypoint needle is used to draw the image directly onto the metal plate. The sliver of metal that would have been removed

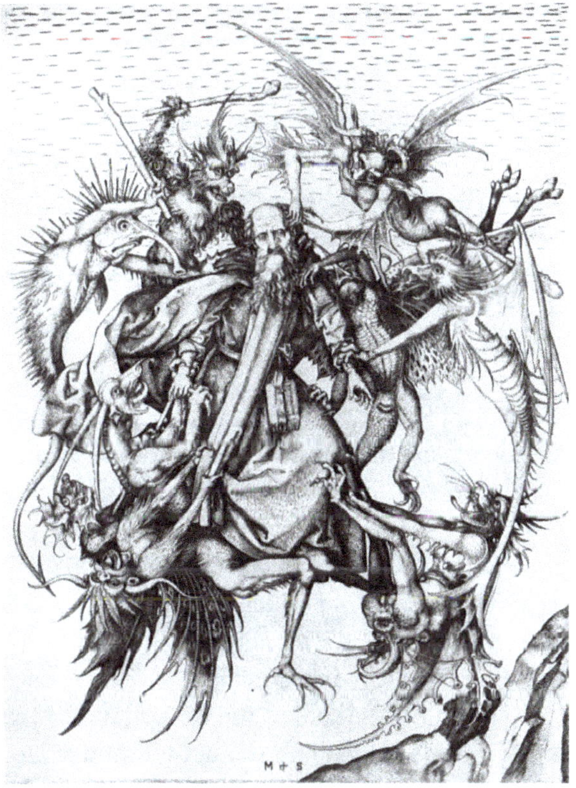

Figure 13.2: Martin Schongauer, *Saint Anthony Tormented by Demons*, c. 1480–90. Engraving, 11¹³/₁₆ in × 8⁹/₁₆ in, The Metropolitan Museum of Art, New York.

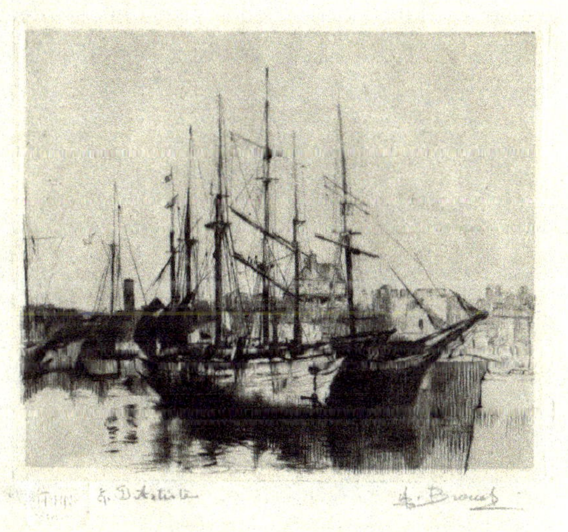

Figure 13.3: Auguste Brouet, *Boats in Port*, c 1925 .Drypoint, 4 7/8 in × 5 11/16 in, The Annex Galleries.

in the engraving process gathers on either side of the groove, creating a small ridge. The issue with drypoints, and why they are not seen very often, is that they have a very short print run. Each time the plate goes through the press the ridge is pushed back into the plate, which distorts the image.

LITHOGRAPHY

Lithography is a wonderful medium for the everyday artist to use. It doesn't require the chipping out of pieces of wood or the removal of slivers of metal. The artist, in this situation, draws directly onto a flat piece of limestone with a lithographic crayon or lithographic pencil. After the image is fixed with the help of chemicals, the ink is applied to the surface of the stone. The ink is attracted to the greasiness of the drawing medium rather than the negative, unmarked, areas. One of the advantages of this process is that you have a nearly unlimited print run as there are no distortions due to the wearing of raised or recessed surfaces. Also, once the desired number of prints has been achieved the lithographic stone can be cleaned and reused.

Among the most noted lithographers was Honoré Daumier. His famous print *Rue Transnonain, April 15, 1834* (**fig 13.4**) illustrates a scene that took place during the republican revolt of 1834.[4] On this date, a policeman had been killed by a sniper's bullet, which was thought to have originated from the address: 12 *rue Transnonain*. The policeman's colleagues sought revenge and killed those inside.[5] The father lies dead in the center of the image, crushing his small child beneath him, while his wife is seen off in the shadows

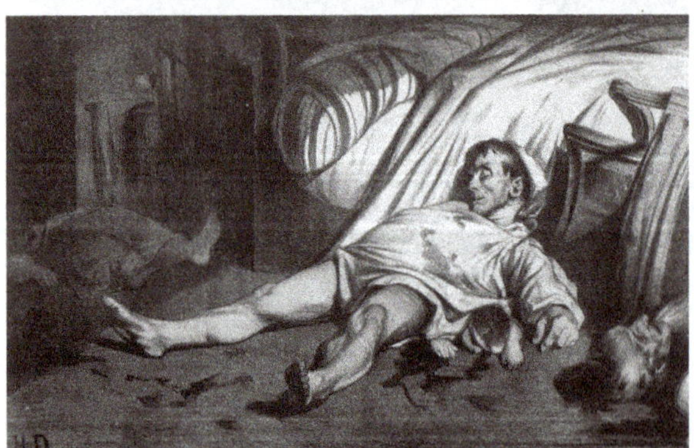

Figure 13.4: Honoré Daumier, *Rue Transnonain, April 15, 1834*, 1834. Lithograph, 28.5 cm × 44.1 cm, National Gallery of Art.

to the left while one of their parents lies immediately to the right.

SILKSCREEN

One of the newer forms of printmaking is silkscreen, also referred to as a *serigraph*. Andy Warhol and other Pop Artists brought the silkscreen technique to prominence in the 1960s and 1970s. The process is easy to learn and is based on a concept that is similar to pushing ink through a stencil. Instead of using a paper stencil, the artist is pushing ink through unobstructed areas of a screen.

To begin, a wooden frame with hinges is constructed so that the frame can be raised and lowered. Drop sticks are attached to the edges of the frame so the frame can be locked in an elevated position. Next, a screen of nylon or polyester is tightly stretched over the frame.[6] The screen holds the image of what is going to be created. Ink is applied to the screen while the screen in the raised position. The printer uses a squeegee to distribute the ink. This first stroke is called the flood stroke, and it covers the screen in ink.[7] Paper is placed under the screen, the screen is lowered, and with one pull of the squeegee the ink is pushed through the screen onto the paper. The frame is raised and the paper immediately taken out to dry and replaced with another, and the process repeated. The prints need space to dry, and this should be taken into consideration in advance of printing. Drying racks are sold specifically for this purpose, or paper can be hung up to dry similar to pinning clothes to a clothesline.

MONOTYPE

Monotypes are the rarest of the five forms of printmaking covered in this chapter. Some would even argue that this isn't printmaking because monotypes produce unique prints (*mono-* meaning "one"). It seems to stand in opposition to the reason artists make prints. Using the monotype process, the artist creates the design, in ink, on a metal plate. The image is created in reverse so that the foreground of the image is created first and the background is created last. It is run through a press, and the image is transferred onto the paper.

Relief printing:

Woodcut:

Wood engraving:

Linocut:

Intaglio printing:

Engraving:

Etching:

Drypoint:

Lithography:

Silkscreen (serigraphy):

Monotype:

ENDNOTES

1. The rough edges of these plates are filed down before use to prevent injury.
2. Marilyn Stokstad, *Art History*, revised ed. (New York: Harry N. Abrams, 1999), 675.
3. Donald Saff, *Printmaking: History and Process* (Orlando: Holt, Rinehart and Winston, 1978), 120.
4. H. H. Arnason and Elizabeth Mansfield, *History of Modern Art*, 7th ed. (Upper Saddle River, NJ: Pearson Education, 2013), 20.
5. Henry Sayre, *A World of Art*, 7th ed. (Boston: Prentice Hall, 2013), 218.
6. Originally, a screen of silk was used, hence the name *silkscreen*.
7. Donald Saff, *Printmaking: History and Process* (Orlando: Holt, Rinehart and Winston, 1978), 338.

IMAGE CREDITS

- Fig. 13.1: "The Buxheim of St. Christopher," https://commons.wikimedia.org/wiki/File:St-christopher-buxheim-1423.jpg. Copyright in the Public Domain.
- Fig. 13.2: Martin Schongauer, "Saint Anthony Tormented by Demons," https://commons.wikimedia.org/wiki/File:Schongauer_St._Antonius.jpeg. Copyright in the Public Domain.
- Fig. 13.3: Auguste Brouet, "Boats in Port," https://commons.wikimedia.org/wiki/File:Boats_in_port_by_Auguste_Brouet.jpg. Copyright in the Public Domain.
- Fig. 13.4: Honoré Daumier, "Rue Transnonain, April 15, 1834," https://commons.wikimedia.org/wiki/File:Honor%C3%A9_Daumier_-_Rue_Transnonain,_April_15,_1834_-_WGA5966.jpg. Copyright in the Public Domain.

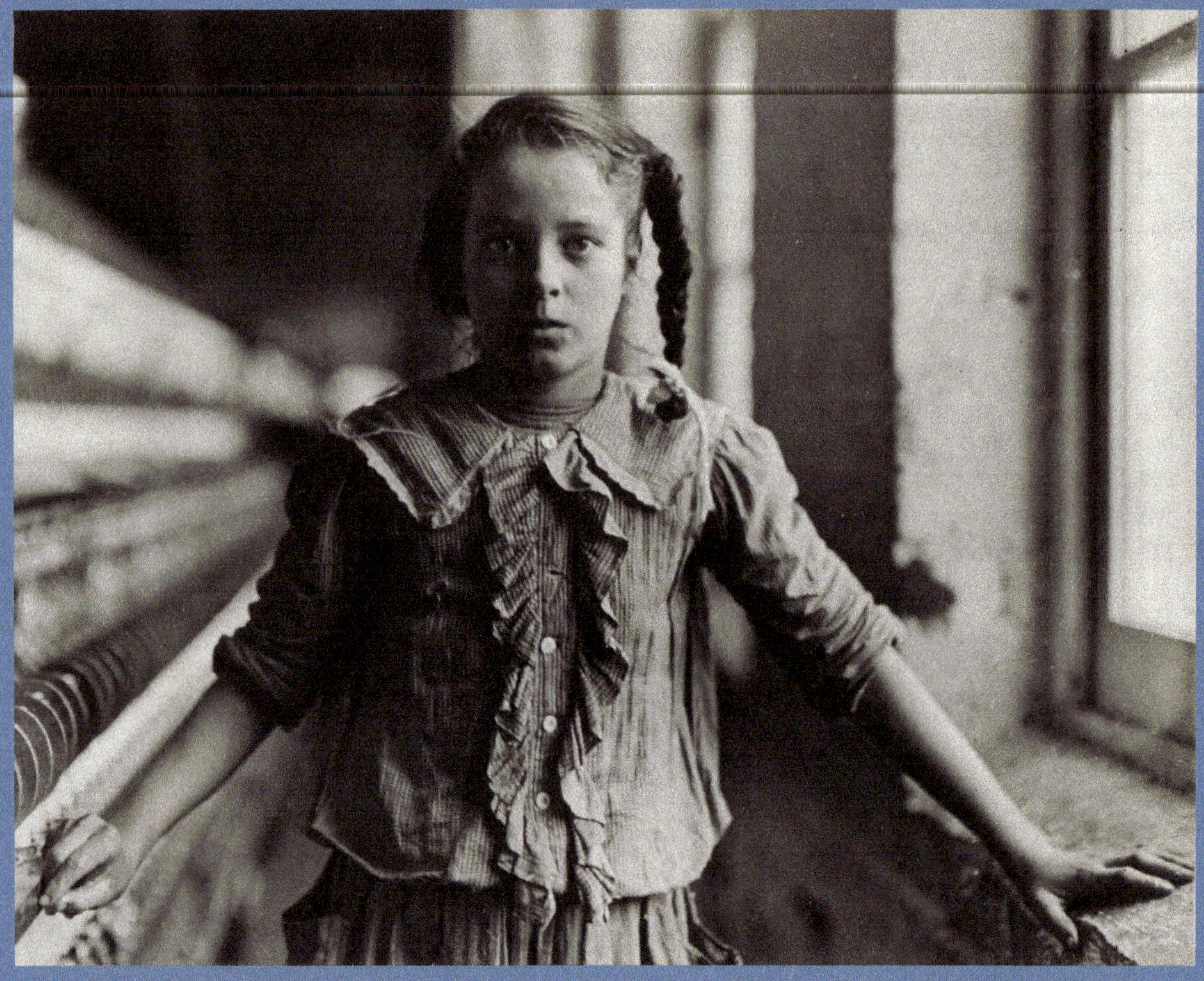

Figure 14.1: Lewis Hine, *Adolescent Girl in a Carolina Cotton Mill*, 1908. Gelatin silver print, Princeton Art Museum.

PHOTOGRAPHY

CHAPTER 14

PHOTOGRAPHY

Photography is one of the more diverse and exciting of all the artistic mediums covered in this textbook. Its diversity ranges amongst fields and topics, including science, social reform, politics, and feminism. It is an exciting medium because *everyone* can take part; all you need is a camera. While it is common to hear people saying that they "can't draw," no one has yet to say that they "can't photograph."

Photography, unlike other artistic mediums, has a birthday. It was on August 19, 1839, that Louis Jacque Mandé Daguerre introduced photography, in Paris, to the Academy of Fine Arts and Academy of Science.[1] The world, and definitely the world of art, would never be the same. Photography, while not even 200 years old, has proven to be one of man's most significant inventions.

PRECURSORS TO THE CAMERA

The silhouette machine (**fig 14.2**) was used throughout the eighteenth and nineteenth centuries. The model would sit in a chair with a candle to one side, which would cast the model's shadow onto a sheet of paper. The artist standing behind paper would trace the model's profile and later fill it in with ink or cut it from black paper.[2]

The term *camera obscura* translates to "dark room." These were originally room-sized chambers that would be set out in the landscape. A small hole would serve as a lens or aperture projecting an inverted image of the outside world onto an inside wall of paper. The artist standing in this room would trace the image. Over time the camera obscura became smaller and portable (**fig 14.3**). They were fitted with true lenses and mirrors in order to correct the inverted image, making it easier for the artist to trace it. But the problem remained that neither the silhouette machine nor the camera obscura was able to produce a fixed image.

INVENTORS OF PHOTOGRAPHY

Who invented photography? While the question might seem simple and straightforward, it

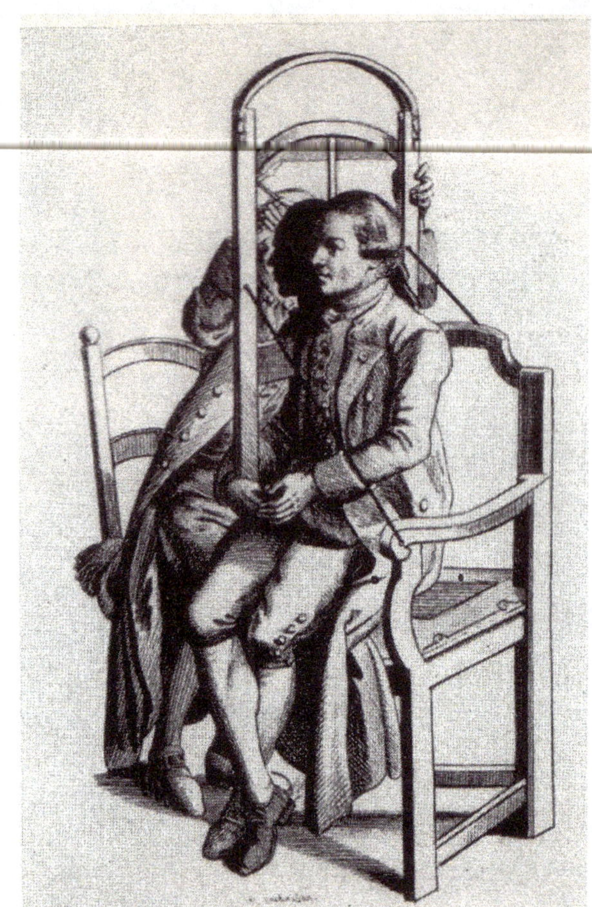

Figure 14.2: Silhouette Machine, 1778.

isn't. It would be similar to asking the question of who invented the Internet. The answer is, lots of people did! When we look back at the development of photography (no pun intended), we cannot overlook the contributions of people

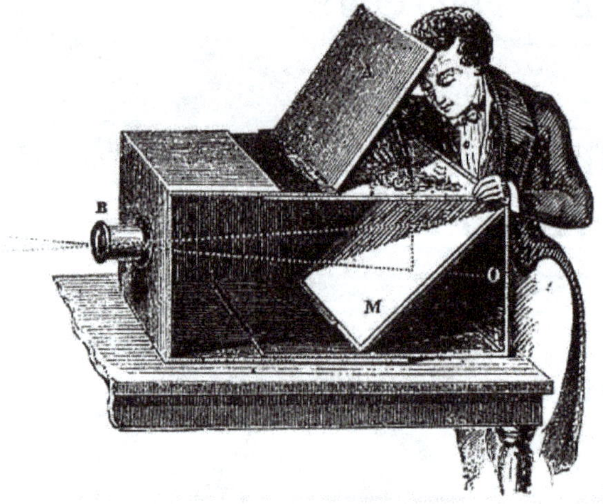

Figure 14.3: Artist using a *Camera Obscura*, c. 1850.

such as Joseph Nicéphore Niépce, the inventor of heliography, which is discussed later in this chapter; William Henry Fox Talbot, the inventor of photogenic drawing, which is the basis for the negative; Hippolyte Bayard; and John Herschel. However, the name most associated with—and the one who generally receives the credit for—the invention of photography is Louis Jacque Mandé Daguerre (**fig 14.4**). He was the one who publicly demonstrated photography to the Academy of Fine Arts and Academy of Science, on August 19, 1839, which earned him a pension from the French government.[3]

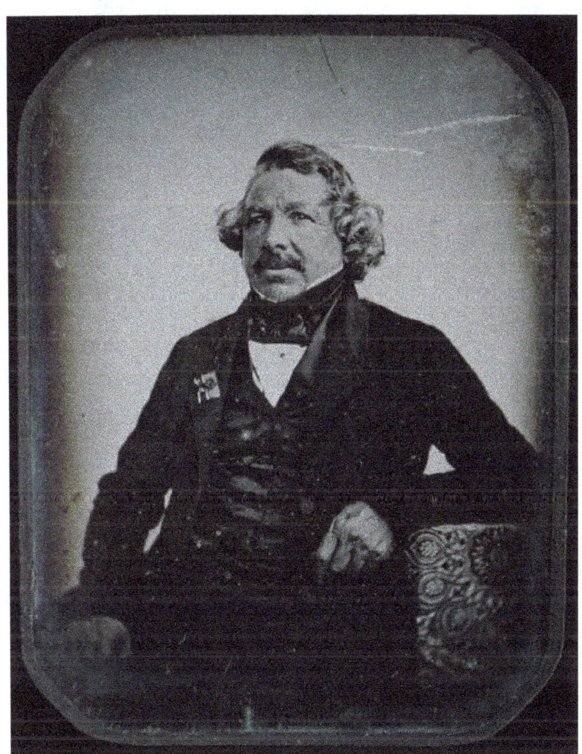

Figure 14.4: Jean Baptiste Sabatier-Blot, *Portrait of Louis Jacque Mandé Daguerre*, 1844. Daguerreotype, International Museum of Photography at George Eastman House, Rochester, N.Y.

EARLY PHOTOGRAPHY

In 1826, Joseph Nicéphore Niépce invented the process of heliography, which produced for all intents and purposes the very first photograph, titled *View from the Window at Gras* (**fig 14.5**). The scene itself is not very impressive, a view of rooftops seen from a window. What is impressive is that this is the first time a permanent direct

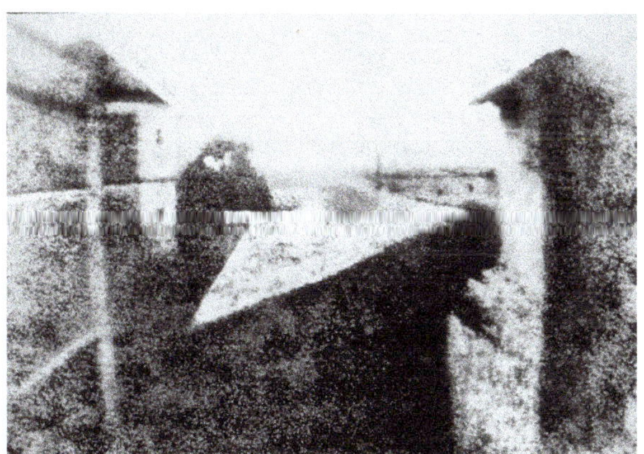

Figure 14.5: Joseph Nicéphore Niépce, *View from the Window at Gras*, c. 1826. Heliograph, Gernsheim Collection, Harry Ransom Humanities Research Center, University of Texas at Austin.

positive image had been produced using a camera obscura. Niépce took a pewter plate, covered with bitumen of Judea, which is an asphalt compound, and placed it in a camera obscura pointing out the window. The exposure time for this image was roughly eight hours. The plate was rinsed and exposed to iodine fumes, which gave the image greater contrast.[4]

Niépce and Daguerre meet one another in 1830 and begin to collaborate on refining the process of heliography. Most notably, the pewter plates are replaced with highly polished silver-faced copper plates, and mercury vapor is used at the end of the development process to help bring out the latent image.[5] However, in 1833 Niépce dies. This leaves Daguerre to continue their research, to introduce photography to the public, and to name the first photography process after himself, the *daguerreotype*.

Daguerreotypes became a mania! Everyone was rushing to get their pictures taken at one of the newly emerging photography studios. While the popularity of daguerreotypes was extremely high, there were still some issues to contend with. For example, the process is very time intensive for both the photographer and the sitter.[6] The process was notorious for long exposure times, so much so that specially produced metal head clamps were produced to keep the sitter's head from moving while the photograph was being taken.[7] Another disadvantage of the early photographic processes

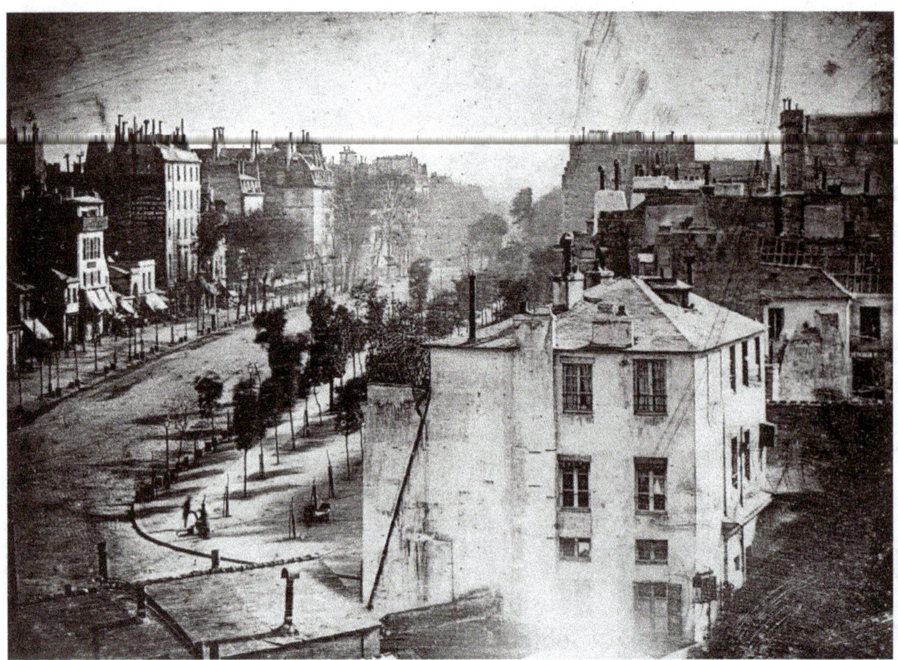

Figure 14.6: Jacques Louis Mandé Daguerre, *Boulevard du Temple, Paris*, c. 1839. Daguerreotype, Bayerisches Nationalmuseum, Munich, Germany.

inventor of photogenic drawing. The book "was the first … to explain and illustrate the scientific and practical applications of photography," such as keeping an inventory of household items.[8]

How the Other Half Lives was first published in 1890 and is still in print today. Its author, Jacob Riis, will be discussed later in the "Photography and Social Reform" section. Riis is considered by some to be the first photojournalist. The book brought to the forefront the living conditions the poor had to endure in New York City.

Finally, *Life Magazine* is extremely important to the study of photography in the United States. First published in 1936, *Life Magazine* would serve as the primary outlet for American photographers for the next 30 years.

was that these were direct positive images, so that if you wanted a duplicate image you had to take a second photograph. Finally, the mercury vapor used during the development process was extremely poisonous.

Among the earliest (and most famous) daguerreotypes is *Boulevard du Temple, Paris* (**fig 14.6**) taken by Daguerre himself. It looks like the scene is of an abandoned street in Paris, but this is due to the long exposure time of the daguerreotype. This is actually a bustling boulevard where people would be walking on the sidewalks and horse-drawn carriages filling the street. However, all these subjects were in motion, so none of them were captured. If you look in the bottom left-hand corner of the photograph, you'll notice a somewhat solid form of an individual. This person is the only person captured in this image because he stopped long enough to have his boots shined.

PHOTOGRAPHY PUBLICATIONS

There are three photographic publications you want be aware of. The first is *The Pencil of Nature*. This is the first book of photographs ever published. Its author was William Henry Fox Talbot, who was mentioned earlier in this chapter as the

PHOTOGRAPHY AND ENTERTAINMENT

Photography is an extremely broad subject that can be approached many different ways. This text chooses to break down the study of photography into seven very general topics rather than pursue a chronological history of the subject. This is not to say that there are not other topics, nor does it mean that the photographic examples used are limited to the topic in which they are placed.

When we look at photography as an entertainment medium, we must consider the fact that most people enjoy photography because of nostalgia. Photographs remind us of the past, of the people, places, and events that have impacted our lives and made us who we are. Photographs tend to be taken at happy moments in our lives, such as births, birthdays, weddings, graduations, and vacations.

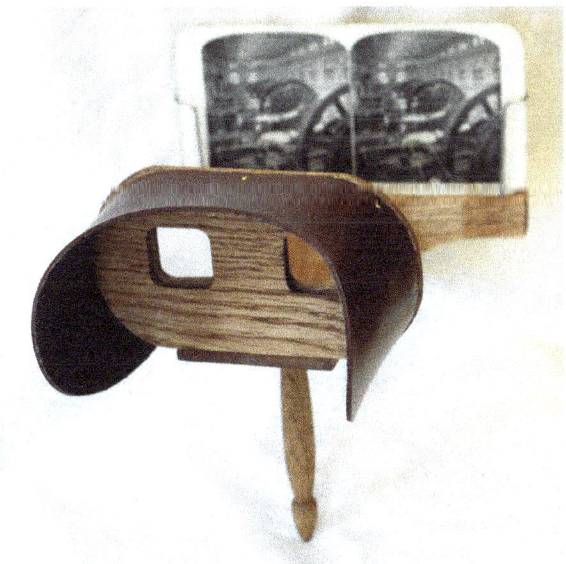

Figure 14.7: Stereoscope.

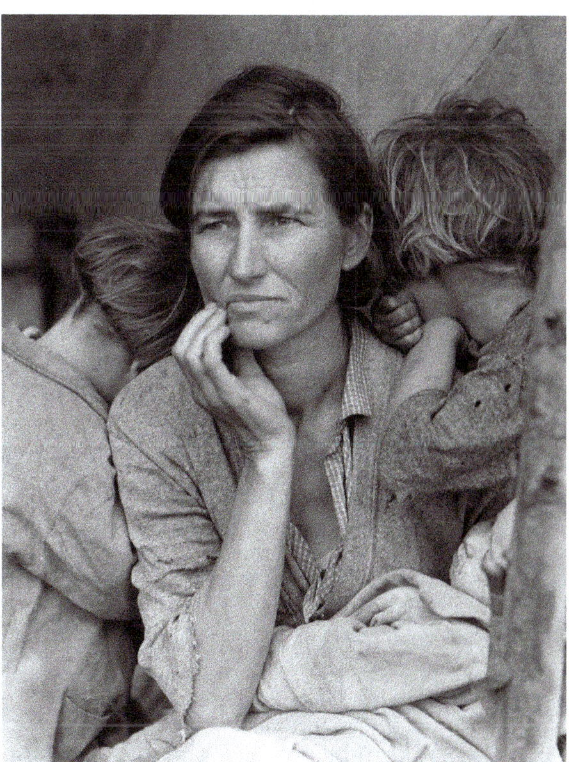

Figure 14.8: Dorothea Lange, *Migrant Mother, Nipomo, California*, 1936. Gelatin silver print, Library of Congress, Washington, D.C.

An early entertaining way to view pictures was with the use of a stereoscope (**fig 14.7**). These handheld devices were first introduced in the mid-nineteenth century and are still in production today.[9] The stereoscope holds a stereo card, which has two identical photographs. The photographs are of the same subject matter but are taken at slightly different angles. The result when you look through the lens is a three-dimensional scene that almost makes you feel as if you are standing there. The subject matter for these cards might be of far off lands, religious scenes, soldiers, important structures, or events, such as the World's Fair of 1851.

PHOTOGRAPHY AND SCIENCE

Biology, microbiology, botany, and astronomy all benefited from the invention of photography. William Henry Fox Talbot's early experimentation with photogenic drawing dealt mostly with plant specimens. By 1845, the scientist Léon Foucault was creating daguerreotypes of microorganisms.[10] A set of daguerreotypes from 1854 was able to document an eclipse of the sun.

PHOTOGRAPHY AND DOCUMENTATION

One of the broadest categories of photography is documentation. Once photography was introduced, cameras became standard equipment taken on expeditions around the globe. People began to see images of places they had only read or heard about. Early photography captured the Greek and Roman temples, the continent of Antarctica, people from far-off lands, and wars.

Dorothea Lange was one of the photographers who documented the Great Depression, and more specifically the plight of the agricultural workers who had been displaced because of the Dust Bowl.[11] Her most famous picture, *Migrant Mother, Nipomo, California* (**fig 14.8**), illustrates how Lange was able to humanize the Great Depression. Through this image we are able to put ourselves into the situation of the mother with her children huddled around her looking for comfort, while the mother herself stares off into the distance, not knowing what their future will hold. In 1960, Lange recalled the encounter in *Popular Photography* magazine:

> I saw and approached the hungry and desperate mother as if drawn by a magnet. I do not remember how I

explained my presence or my camera to her, but I do remember she asked me no questions. I made five exposures, working closer and closer from the same direction. I did not ask her name or her history. She told me her age, that she was thirty-two. She said that they had been living on frozen vegetables from the surrounding fields, and birds that the children killed. She had just sold the tires from her car to buy food. There she sat in that lean-to tent with her children huddled around her, and seemed to know that my pictures might help her. There was a sort of equality about it.[12]

PHOTOGRAPHY AND POLITICS

Art in general can be political; photography is no different. Political photography can be extremely powerful and leave us with lasting memories. We have all seen the photograph of Truman holding up an edition of the *Chicago Daily Tribune* stating that "Dewey Defeats Truman." Images of the Kennedy assassination run through our minds at the very mention of the event. John Filo won a Pulitzer Prize for his photograph of the Kent State massacre where in 1970 members of the Ohio National Guard opened fire on unarmed college students, killing four.

Among the earliest examples of political photography is Abraham Lincoln's photograph taken by Mathew Brady (**fig 14.9**). Brady was an accomplished photographer and would go on to achieve fame with his images of the Civil War. At the time Lincoln was a senator from Illinois running for president, but rumors circulated that he was ugly and malformed. Brady posed the future president, shined a bright light in his face, and made him curl his attenuated fingers of his right hand under so that they appeared normal.[13] The photograph was circulated in newspapers and magazines. Later Lincoln stated that "Brady and the Cooper Institute made me President."[14]

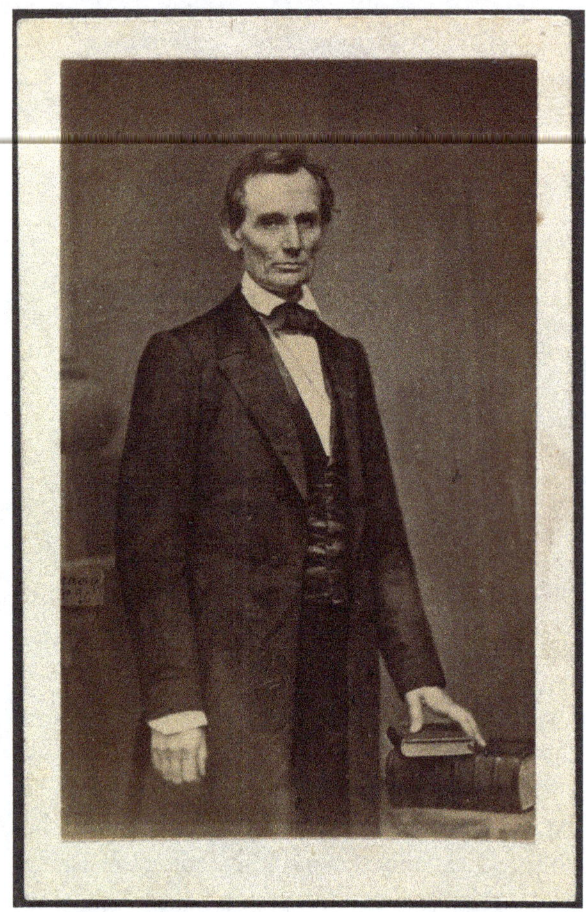

Figure 14.9: Mathew Brady, *Abraham Lincoln*, 1860. Salted paper print, Library of Congress, Washington, D.C.

PHOTOGRAPHY AND SOCIAL REFORM

Two major photographers used photography as a tool to create social reform. The first is Jacob Riis, who was a police reporter who covered Manhattan's Lower East Side. He would go out at night with a group of friends and take pictures of the living conditions of the poor. *Bandits' Roost, New York* (**fig 14.10**) is one of Riis's images. The photograph looks overexposed near the top, but that is due to the use of flash powder. The scene shows tenement houses on either side of an alleyway with clotheslines stretched across and with nearly a dozen people standing around or poking their heads out of the windows. These images were shown in lectures and published in newspapers and magazines, as well as in his book, *How The Other Half Lives*, which called for social reform.[15]

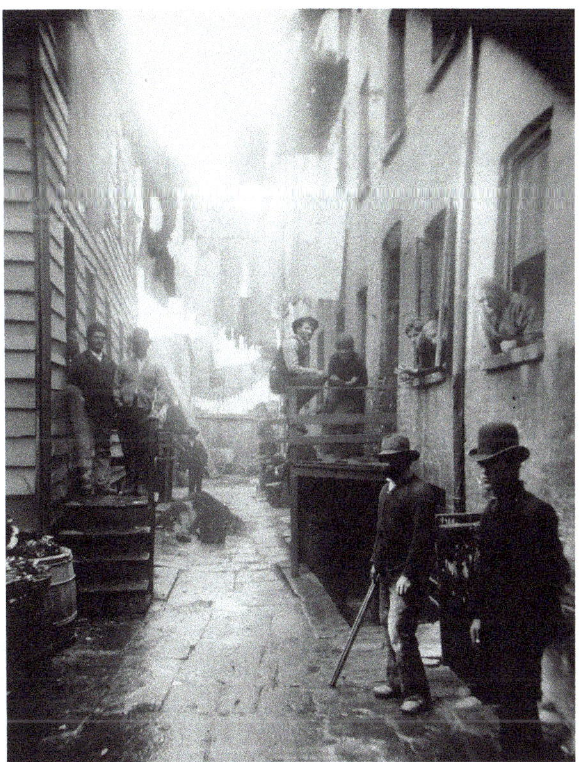

Figure 14.10: Jacob Riis, *Bandits' Roost, New York City*, 1888. Gelatin silver print, Museum of the City of New York, New York.

The second photographer who used photography to influence social reform is Lewis Hine. Hine's celebrity today stems from his "worker" photographs of the 1930s. These images showed the American worker—diligent, skillful, and hardworking—reshaping the American skyline. Earlier in his career Hine worked for the National Child Labor Committee. He would disguise himself, taking on false identities and getting hired on at mills, mines, and factories. He would sneak his camera in and take pictures of children at work. *Adolescent Girl in a Carolina Cotton Mill* (**fig 14.1**), while not showing a child being actively abused, highlighted that these companies were exploiting very young children to work long hours in dangerous conditions. Hine exposed the unfair practice of child labor and helped to institute child labor laws, which are still in effect today.

PHOTOGRAPHY AND FEMINISM

During the 1970s and 1980s, many feminist artists utilized photography as a way of communication. One of the most successful of these artists was Cindy Sherman, who is still active in photography today. From 1977 to 1980 she produced her *Untitled Film Still* series that showed ways women had been depicted in film, which would influence the identity of many young women.[16] Sherman transforms herself in each of these photographs as she places herself in the starring role. In *Untitled Film Still #21* (not pictured), we see Sherman surrounded by tall skyscrapers as she arrives in the big city looking for work. In other images from this series, she steps into the roles of secretary, seductress, runaway, housewife, librarian, and many others.

PHOTOGRAPHY AND ART

As the final topic, we cannot overlook the aesthetic aspects of photography. As mentioned at the beginning of this chapter, photography is a medium that we can all take part in because it involves mechanical skill. All of us can utilize photography as an artistic outlet. Even *The Pencil of Nature* illustrates that this is one of photography's primary uses. We can all appreciate the aesthetic value of Timothy O'Sullivan's photograph *Shoshone Falls, Snake River, Idaho* (**fig 14.11**) as we look over the tops of the waterfall to the landscape beyond.

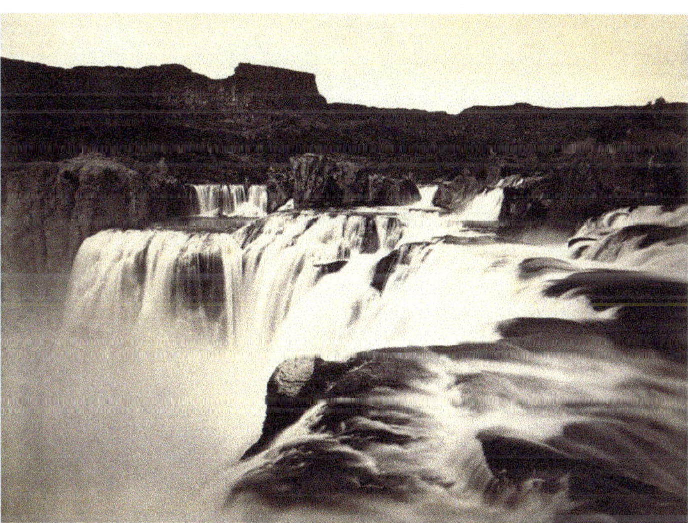

Figure 14.11: Timothy O'Sullivan, *Shoshone Falls, Sanke River, Idaho*, 1874. Albumen print, Library of Congress, Washington, D.C.

Precursors of the camera:

Inventor(s) of photography:

Early photography:

Photography publications:

Photography and entertainment:

Photography and science:

Photography and documentation:

Photography and politics:

Photography and social reform:

Photography and feminism:

Photography and art:

PROJECT: PHOTOGRAPHY

Goal

To express yourself through the medium of photography.

Assignment

You are to take a series of five photographs, each having specific subject matter. In the chapter on photography, you were introduced to many famous and groundbreaking photographers, such as Dorothea Lange, Mathew Brady, and Lewis Hine. Consider their work when you plan this project: What made them stand out as photographers? What made their work so expressive and meaningful?

Photograph 1: Still Life

A still life is a collection of inanimate objects. The classic still life is a bowl of fruit; however, *your still life will be constructed of objects that represent who you are as a person.* The objects might be something you use on a daily basis, such as makeup or electronic devices, or they might be objects that have particular significance to you, such as car keys and awards.

Please note that you may not take pictures of naturally occurring scenes, such as your desk, computer setup, bookshelves, or displays in storefront windows. This is a gathering of objects that you construct just for this photo. You must use multiple objects (minimum of five) and explain why you chose them! Each object must be different. They cannot all be makeup or all awards. No photos of food! These can be used in a later photograph.

Photograph 2: Self-Portrait

This is a photo of *you* taken by *you*! How do you choose to represent yourself? There are many ways to go about taking this picture. You can take a regular "selfie" if you wish, but don't discount the timer feature on your camera. Are you going to be just like everyone else, or are you going to stage an awesome scene like Cindy Sherman would?

Photograph 3: Landscape

This picture shows an expanse of scenery. This can be naturally occurring, such as a scene with trees, shrubs, and waterfalls, or a man-made one with buildings, cars, and streets.

Photograph 4: Nonobjective

Take a photograph that concentrates on the formal elements that we learned about earlier in the textbook: line, shape, color, pattern, and texture. These elements construct the world around us! Consider parts of an object rather than the entire object. *When in doubt, zoom in!*

Note that the viewer should not be able to identify the object being photographed. That would make it representational rather than nonobjective!

Photograph 5: Personal Choice

Here you can photograph anything you wish. This image can be of food, houses, street art, friends, children, parents, pets, cars, or something that holds meaning to you.

Instructions

- Photographs should all be the same size.
- Photographs can be in either portrait or landscape orientation, but the entire portfolio must be all the same format.
- Photographs can be either color or black and white; however, the entire portfolio must be all the same. Color tends to work best.
- Photographs must be printed on standard 8½" × 11" paper. *Do not use glossy photo paper.*
- Any camera, including smartphone cameras, can be used.
- Avoid scrapbooking! Do not adorn the photo with markers, ribbon, lace, or glitter.
- Avoid folders! Just one staple in the upper-left-hand corner is perfect.
- You should have personally taken all of the photographs.
- The photographs should be taken from today's date forward.

Format

Provide one photograph (along with its information) per page. Do not run the information to a second page!

Under each photo you must supply the following (typed):

Title: Give your photograph a title or caption.

Category: Still Life, Self-Portrait, Landscape, Nonobjective, or Personal Choice

Date taken: October 8, 20__

Camera used: iPhone 6

Description: Briefly talk about the photo. What is the viewer seeing? Why did you choose this to be your subject matter? This information should be 5 to 7 lines in length, double-spaced. Use Times or Times New Roman font at 12 points, and set the margins to 1 inch.

Packet

Place a cover sheet on top which includes:

    Your name

    Days and time of class

    Project number

Five pages in the order they are listed above:

    Still Life

    Self-Portrait

    Landscape

    Nonobjective

    Personal Choice

Point value: _______________________

Due date: _______________________

ENDNOTES

1. Mary Warner Marien, *Photography: A Cultural History* (New York: Harry N. Abrams, 2002), 1.
2. Naomi Rosenblum, *A World History of Photography* (New York: Abbeville Press, 1984), 40.
3. Mary Warner Marien, *Photography: A Cultural History* (New York: Harry N. Abrams, 2002), 20.
4. Mary Warner Marien, *Photography: A Cultural History* (New York: Harry N. Abrams, 2002), 10.
5. Mary Warner Marien, *Photography: A Cultural History* (New York: Harry N. Abrams, 2002), 12.
6. The Getty Museum has produced a video that walks viewers through the daguerreotype process. It can be found at https://youtu.be/N0Ambe4FwQk.
7. Exposure times for daguerreotypes ranged from 30 seconds to a couple of minutes. This was not nearly as bad as the eight hours needed for the *View from the Window at Gras.*
8. Naomi Rosenblum, *A World History of Photography* (New York: Abbeville Press, 1984), 31.
9. Today, stereoscopes are produced by View-Master and are marketed as a children's toy.
10. Mary Warner Marien, *Photography: A Cultural History* (New York: Harry N. Abrams, 2002), 34.
11. Dorothea Lange, "The Assignment I'll Never Forget," *Popular Photography*, February 1960, 263–265.
12. Dorothea Lange, "The Assignment I'll Never Forget," *Popular Photography*, February 1960, 263–265.
13. Mary Warner Marien, *Photography: A Cultural History* (New York: Harry N. Abrams, 2002), 95.
14. George Alfred Townsend, "Brady, The Grand Old Man of American Photography," *The World (New York)*, April 12, 1891, 26.
15. Mary Warner Marien, *Photography: A Cultural History* (New York: Harry N. Abrams, 2002), 205–207.
16. Amanda Cruz, Elizabeth A. T. Smith, and Amelia Jones, *Cindy Sherman: Retrospective* (London: Thames & Hudson, Inc., 1997), 2.

IMAGE CREDITS

- Fig. 14.1: Lewis W. Hine, "Adolescent Girl in a Carolina Cotton Mill," https://commons.wikimedia.org/wiki/File:Hine,_Lewis,_Adolescent_Girl,_a_Spinner,_in_a_Carolina_Cotton_Mill,_1908.jpg. Copyright in the Public Domain.
- Fig. 14.2: "Sihouette Machine," https://commons.wikimedia.org/wiki/File:Silhouettenstuhl.JPG. Copyright in the Public Domain.
- Fig. 14.3: "Camera Obscura," https://commons.wikimedia.org/wiki/File:Camera_Obscura_box18thCentury.jpg. Copyright in the Public Domain.
- Fig. 14.4: Jean Baptiste Sabatier-Blot, "Portrait of Louis Jacque Mandé Daguerre," https://commons.wikimedia.org/wiki/File:Louis_Daguerre_1844.JPG. Copyright in the Public Domain.
- Fig. 14.5: Joseph Nicéphore Niépce, "View from the Window at Gras," https://commons.wikimedia.org/wiki/File:View_from_the_Window_at_Le_Gras,_Joseph_Nic%C3%A9phore_Ni%C3%A9pce,_uncompressed_UMN_source.png. Copyright in the Public Domain.
- Fig. 14.6: Louis Jacques Mandé Daguerre, "Boulevard du Temple, Paris," https://commons.wikimedia.org/wiki/File:Boulevard_du_Temple_by_Daguerre.jpg. Copyright in the Public Domain.
- Fig. 14.7: Davepape, "Stereoscope," https://commons.wikimedia.org/wiki/File:Holmes_stereoscope.jpg. Copyright in the Public Domain.
- Fig. 14.8: Dorothea Lange, "Migrant Mother, Nipomo, California," https://commons.wikimedia.org/wiki/File:Lange-MigrantMother02.jpg. Copyright in the Public Domain.
- Fig. 14.9: Mathew Brady, "Abraham Lincoln," https://commons.wikimedia.org/wiki/File:Abraham_Lincoln_by_Brady.jpg. Copyright in the Public Domain.
- Fig. 14.10: Jacob Riis, "Bandits' Roost, New York," https://commons.wikimedia.org/wiki/File:Bandit%27s_Roost_by_Jacob_Riis.jpeg. Copyright in the Public Domain.
- Fig. 14.11: Timothy O'Sullivan, "Shoshone Falls, Snake River, Idaho," https://commons.wikimedia.org/wiki/File:Flickr_-_…trialsanderrors_-_Timothy_O%27Sullivan,_Shoshone_Falls,_Snake_River,_Idaho,_1874.jpg. Copyright in the Public Domain.

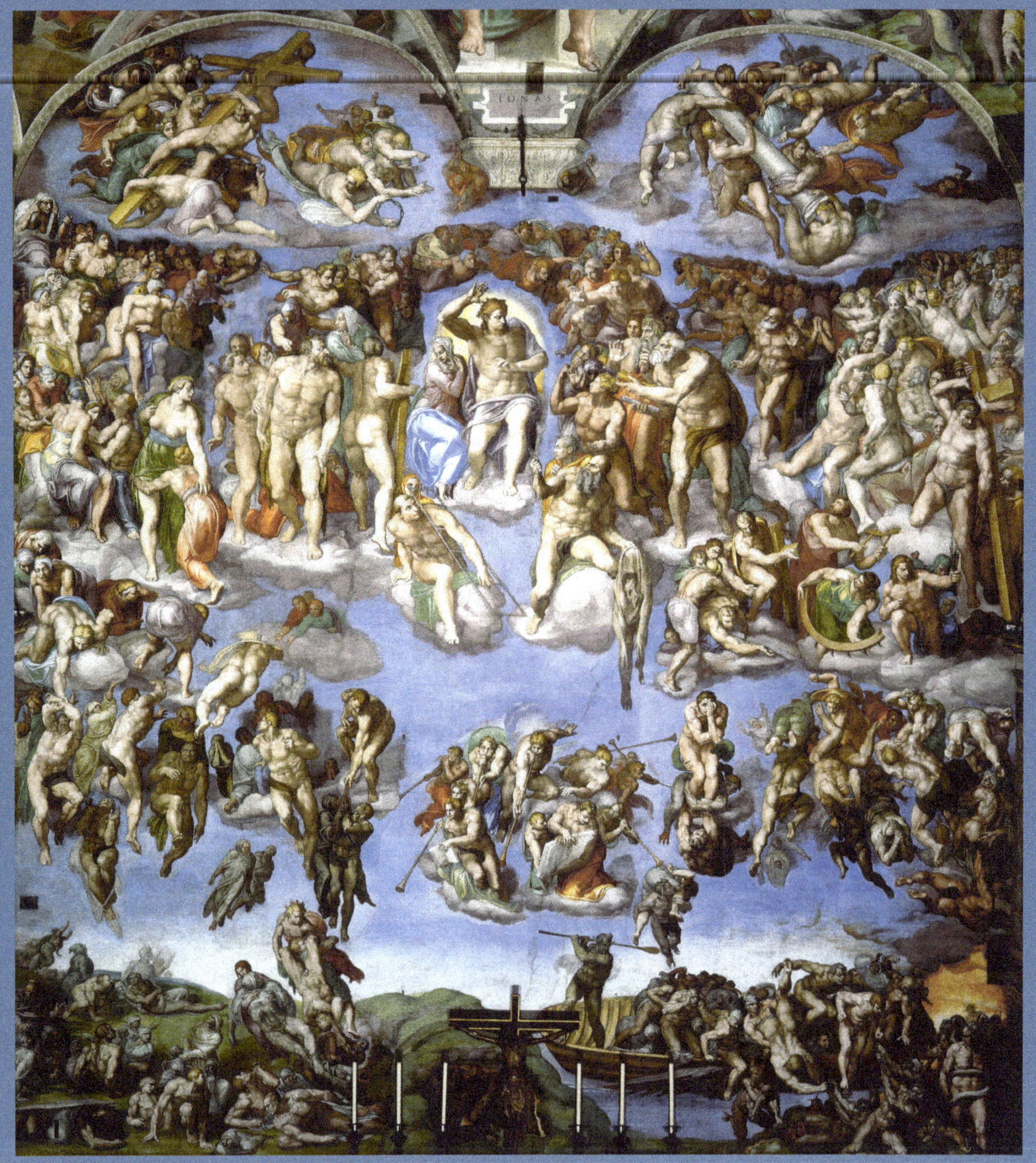

Figure 15.1: Michelangelo Buonarroti, *Last Judgment*, 1534–41. Fresco, 14.6 m × 13.41 m, Sistine Chapel, Vatican.

PAINTING

CHAPTER
15

PAINTING

Whereas photography is among the newest of the artistic mediums, painting is among the oldest. Cave paintings dating as far back as 30,000 BCE have been found in regions of France.[1] When we go to a museum or a gallery, we expect to see paintings on the wall. When you meet someone who is an artist, you would naturally assume that that person has painted.

ENCAUSTIC

The first three painting mediums we will discuss—encaustic, fresco, and tempera—are similar in many respects. All three were used before the dawn of the Renaissance, and encaustic and fresco since Greek and Roman times, and all three have fallen out of mainstream popularity. Painting mediums are very much like technology: they can become outdated and then replaced with better, more efficient tools. This is not to say these mediums have been wiped off the face of the Earth, but it is just a very rare occurrence to come across someone who has worked with them.

Encaustic is created when pigment is suspended in hot wax. As you can imagine, the artist has to work quickly, before the wax cools. Many of the early surviving encaustic works are in the form of mummy portraits (**fig 15.2**) that were found in the Egyptian city of Faiyum. These artworks span a broad base of cultures. Their use is unmistakably Egyptian, being that these boards were placed in the outer wrappings of a mummy, but the style of this artwork is far from Egyptian. These naturalistic images appear to be Greek. When these works were created, in the second century CE, Egypt was part of the Roman Empire, and the Romans promoted the Greek style of art.

Encaustic can be found at well-stocked art supply stores or through online sources. It comes in cakes that are melted in small tins. Today, artists have the advantage of keeping the encaustic in a liquid state by using heating devices. In the mid-1950s artist Jasper Johns utilized this medium in his series of *Flag* paintings as well as *Target with Four Faces* (neither pictured).

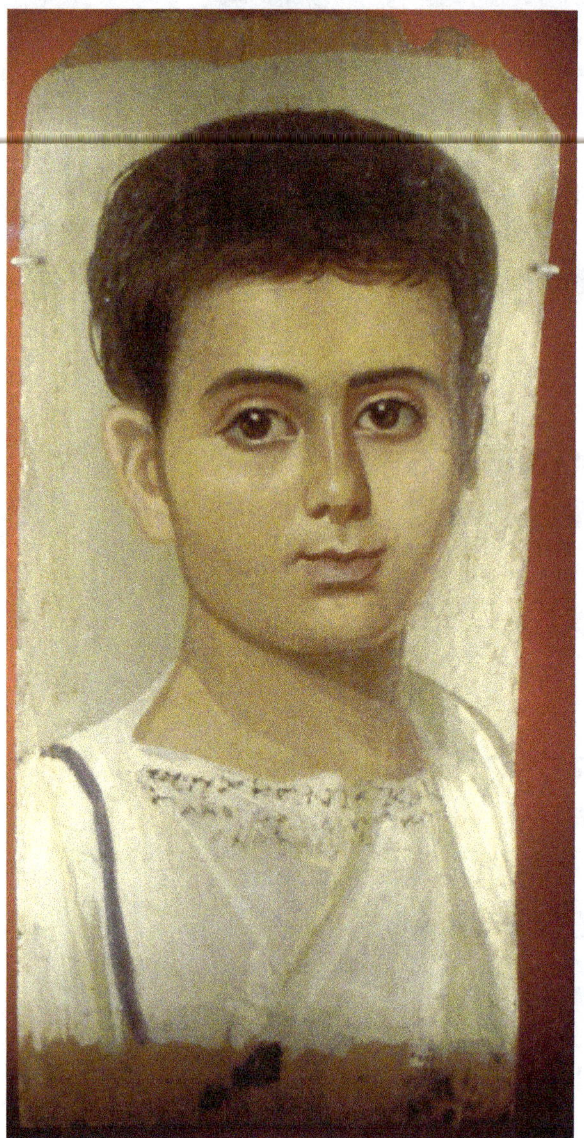

Figure 15.2: Egyptian, Roman Period, *Portrait of a Young Boy*, 2nd century C.E. Encaustic on Wood, 39 cm × 19 cm, Metropolitan Museum of Art.

FRESCO

While fresco painting is something we chiefly associate with the Italian Renaissance, its beginnings are much earlier.[2] Fresco paintings dating back to 1500 BCE, such as the *Toreador Fresco* (not pictured), have been found on the island of Crete. The reason fresco paintings are able to last so long is that the paint becomes part of the wall or ceiling rather than resting on its surface. Such paintings will last as long as the surface lasts.

Fresco is the Italian word for "fresh." This refers to the fresh layer of plaster, called *intonaco*, which is applied to a wall being prepared for painting.[3] Fresco painting involves several stages, but the basic premise is that pigment is suspended in water and applied to the wet plaster. As the plaster hardens, the paint becomes part of the wall or ceiling. Because fresco painting had to be done during warm weather, artists had to work quickly before the plaster dried.[4] The artist would paint the fresco from the top down to avoid dripping on already finished sections. A disadvantage of this technique was that not all colors were water-soluble, giving the artist a limited color palette.[5]

The Sistine Chapel contains some of the most famous paintings done in fresco. Michelangelo painted the ceiling from 1508 to 1512 at the behest of Pope Julius II. It depicts scenes from the book of Genesis, such as the *Creation of the Sun, Moon, and Planets*, *Creation of Adam*, and *Deluge*. Pope Paul III would have Michelangelo return to the chapel 24 years later to render the *Last Judgment* (**fig 15.1**) on the altar wall. The fresco covers more than 2,100 square feet of surface area. "Chaos" is the only word to describe this painting, with Christ narrating the events at the center of the work. Surrounding him are the dead rising from their graves, some figures ascending to the heavens, and others being pulled down by demons.

The term *fresco secco* refers to painting being done on dried plaster. Obviously, this type of painting would not last nearly as long as traditional fresco would, and it was sometimes used to cover up mistakes done in true fresco. *The Last Supper* by Leonardo da Vinci (see fig 22.8) is a work done in fresco secco. It was completed at roughly the same time as the works in the Sistine Chapel, but with the paint peeling and flaking off only a quarter of the original work remains.[6] Compare this to the images in the Sistine Chapel where Michelangelo's paintings look nearly brand new.

The popularity of fresco painting declined after the Baroque period. The medium saw a resurgence in the 1920s and 1930s brought about by the Mexican muralist painters David Alfaro Siqueiros, José Clemente Orozco, and Diego Rivera. They were commissioned by the government of Mexico to create large-scale murals on public buildings illustrating Mexico's revolutionary past.

TEMPERA

The term *tempera* is a little misleading. The tempera paint you would find in an art supply store or classroom today is a water-soluble, nontoxic paint used primarily by children for their arts and crafts projects. These are sometimes referred to as "poster paints." The tempera paint discussed in this section refers to "egg tempera," as egg yolk is used as the binding agent for the pigment.

Tempera was employed extensively during the Middle Ages and through much of the Renaissance until the invention of oil paint rendered it nearly obsolete. Tempera is traditionally painted on a wood panel that is first treated with a priming agent called *gesso*.[7] Several layers of gesso are applied to the panel; each layer is sanded after it has dried. Gesso provides the artist with a smooth and luminescent painting surface. It also seals the wooden board, making it nonabsorbent. Tempera paint naturally has a matte finish when dry, and the gesso helps bring out the brightness of the colors.

The *Annunciation* (**fig 15.3**) by Filippo Lippi was created using tempera. The rendering is

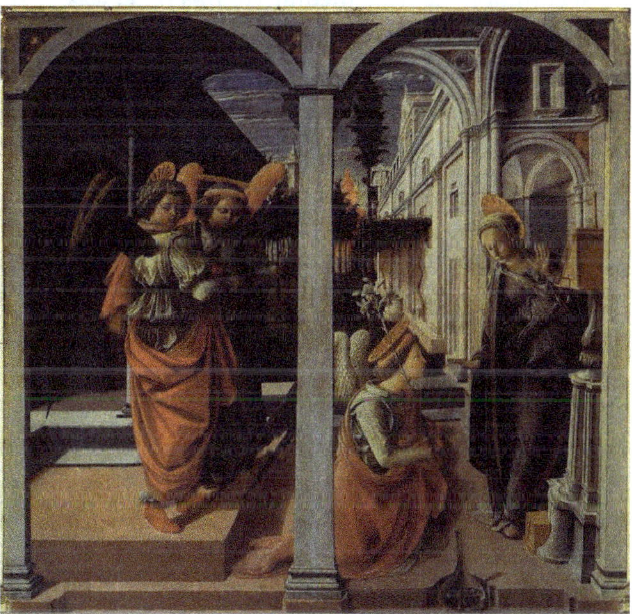

Figure 15.3: Filippo Lippi, *Annunciation*, c. 1445. Tempera on Panel, 175 cm × 183 cm, Basilica of Saint Lawrence, Florence.

unique as the artist divided the scene into two spaces. The space at the right gives us the traditional scene of the angel Gabriel kneeling down in front of Mary telling her that she will bear the Christ Child. The scene at the left balances the composition with two other angelic figures. One of the angels seems to be paying attention to the scene unfolding before him, while the other angel engages the audience and seemingly points over to the other side of the painting, as if to tell us not to look at them but to the scene at the right. The buildings in the background utilize one-point linear perspective, and trompe l'oeil is used to create the vase and niche at the lower right.

OIL PAINT

When oil paints were invented they revolutionized painting. Oil paints were first introduced in the early 1400s, and there is a reason why they are still incredibly popular more than 600 years later. Oil paints were invented in the area of Flanders in Northern Europe.[8] The use of oil paints then spread slowly throughout Europe, and we begin to see them being used by artists in Italy by the end of the fifteenth century. Once artists began to utilize this medium, tempera, which had been the most common painting medium to this time, was swiftly cast aside.

Oil paints offer tremendous advantages. For instance, oil paints can be applied with a tremendous amount of gestural freedom. Look back at Vincent van Gogh's *The Starry Night* (see fig 8.6); you can literally see the pathway the brush took across the canvas to form the night sky. Oil paints can also be applied thickly, such as in the technique of impasto. Again, van Gogh's *The Starry Night* work would serve as an example. Oil paints can be blended to create a continuous scale of colors. But the most important advantage of oil paints is that they are slow to dry. Before the development of oil paints, artists had to work swiftly and diligently while their mediums dried. With oil painting the paint can be left out on the palette overnight! Paintings can be reworked for days, weeks, or even months.

While oil paints have many advantages, one disadvantage needs to be considered. Oil paints need to be applied with the help of a spreading agent. This vehicle usually consists of one-third each of paint thinner, linseed oil, and turpentine. These chemicals need to be treated carefully, used in a well-ventilated area, and disposed of properly. Oil painting should not be done in a closed up or restricted area. The artist must work in an area with plenty of air flow and ventilation.

Among the first paintings ever completed in oil paint is the *Arnolfini Portrait* (see fig 3.1). The artist, Jan van Eyck, helped develop the medium, especially in terms of glazing.[9] In some accounts he is credited with inventing oil paints, but this accolade is not true.[10] In this painting you can see the richness of color and the incredible attention to detail.

WATERCOLOR

Watercolor is an ancient painting medium that is still utilized today. Most of us used watercolors as children. The paint would come in a narrow white tray with eight or nine circular discs of color in the row. All that needed to be done was to dip the brush in water and swirl it around inside the color disc to pick up the paint and create the picture. It was just that easy.

Professional grade watercolors come in small tubes, just as oil paint does. With watercolor the pigment is suspended in a solution of water and gum arabic. The paint is applied to rag paper, which absorbs and transfers the paint through its fibers, making it a very gestural medium. Because of its fluidity some consider watercolor more along the lines of sketching. Among the advantages of watercolor is the range of density that is available to the artist. Watercolor can be treated like a wash, because it is naturally translucent. Therefore, it is a great medium to paint objects such as the sky or water. If desired, the artist can build up areas of color through staining to make them more opaque.

In Winslow Homer's *A Basket of Clams* (**fig 15.4**), we can see a broad range of densities the artist was able to achieve. Areas lightly touched with paint include the sand in the foreground, the sky, and the rooftops of the buildings behind the sailboat. Areas where the color is built up include the sides of the buildings and the hull of the sailboat.

GOUACHE

Gouache is extremely easy to use and is a great medium for the beginning painter. It is essentially watercolor with the addition of a chalk called *blanc fixe*.[11] The addition of chalk makes the medium opaque, as well as making it the only medium that can be rewet. Just like watercolor, gouache comes in small tubes and is spreadable with water. Many brands of gouache are available on the market. As with anything in life, you get what you pay for; less expensive brands tend to have less pigment. Gouache can be applied to paper or board.

Gouache is best used for painting areas of solid color where one color ends and the next begins, similar in look to a painting by Mondrian. It is not effective when trying to blend one form into another, though the paint itself can be readily blended on the palette to create a color or a tint/shade. Gouache can be layered once the initial layer has dried and as long as the new layer is applied directly and forcefully. Care must be taken not to apply the paint too thickly, as it will have a tendency to crack due to the amount of chalk in the mixture. Gouache will also lighten in color as it dries.

Consider an example (**fig 15.5**) that was inspired by the textile production of William Morris, who will be discussed in more detail in chapter 20. It is composed of several layers, including a background of dark red, gold lines that are intermixed with black circles, and flower splotches done in yellow ochre.

ACRYLIC

Commercially introduced in the 1950s, acrylics are the newest painting medium.[12] The pigment is suspended in an acrylic emulsion and is spreadable by water. A good range of density can be attained by using acrylics, from watercolor-like washes to thick, heavy, impasto-like oil paint. The

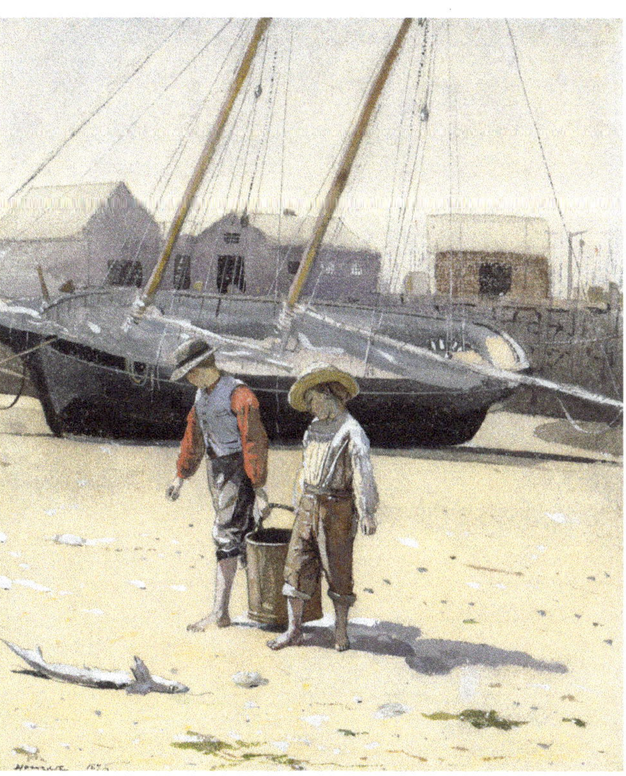

Figure 15.4: Winslow Homer, *A Basket of Clams*, 1873. Watercolor on Wove Paper, 29.2 cm × 24.8 cm, Metropolitan Museum of Art.

medium is flexible and will not crack. Acrylics have many of the same attributes as oil paints. For instance, they can be blended to form a continuous array of color, they can be layered, and there is a certain gestural freedom allowed to the artist when applying the paint. What differentiates acrylics the most from oil paints is that they dry rapidly, in minutes to hours, depending on the thickness of their application.

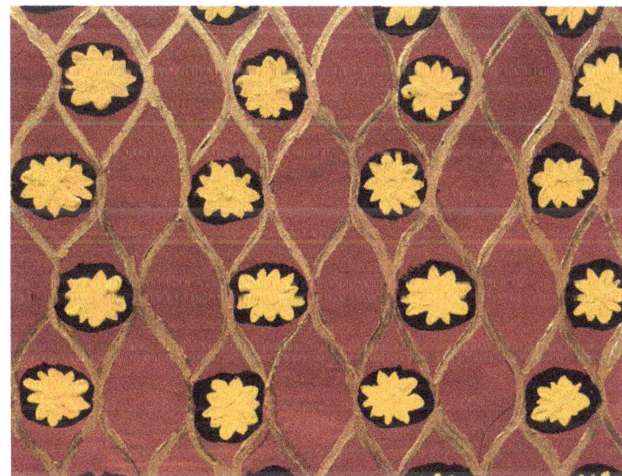

Figure 15.5: David Plouffe, *Untitled*, 2003. Gouache on Illustration Board, 11 in × 6 in.

Encaustic:

Fresco (*buon fresco*):

Fresco secco (*fresco a secco*):

Tempera:

Gesso:

Oil paint:

Watercolor:

Gouache:

Acrylic:

PROJECT: MUSEUM VISIT

Goal

Neither the images from a textbook nor presentations can substitute for viewing artwork firsthand. This project gives you the opportunity to personally visit—on your own time—one of the several major art museums we have in Southern California and see works of art in person.

Assignment

From the list below you need to choose one museum to visit. Plan your visit carefully, as museums have variable days and hours of admission. Consider travel time and the price of admission, as well as for parking. Once at the museum your job is to spend a minimum of one hour walking around and engaging with the works of art. Write an essay about your experience.

In this instance I am not looking for the traditional/formal essay. Write the essay in a conversational tone, as if you are having coffee with me telling me about your visit. Yes, spelling and grammar are still taken into consideration. You may write openly and candidly about your experience. Consider the following questions to help guide the formation of your essay, but do not answer them exclusively:

- Which museum did you visit?
- What was your reaction upon entering the museum?
- Were there any artists or artworks you recognized?
- Was there a particular artist, artwork, genre of art, or exhibition that attracted you?
- What did you like the most/least about your visit?
- Were you able to apply anything you learned over the semester during your visit?
- What predispositions/stereotypes of museums did you have prior to your visit? Did this project alter or reinforce them?

Helpful Hints

- Think of this project as more of an event rather than an assignment. Take your family and friends. What did they think of the art they saw?
- Eat elsewhere!!! Food prices at museums are equivalent to those of sporting events.
- Dress appropriately! A museum is neither a club nor a campground; dress somewhere in between. You never know who you are going to run into.
- Beat the traffic! Sunday morning is a great time to visit these museums, especially the Getty, which will park you 30 minutes prior to opening!
- Do not touch ANY of the artwork.
- Stay at least one foot away from the art unless you want the guards to come talk to you. Never point pens or pencils at the art!
- Museums can be kind of fussy about taking pictures. First off, *never* use a flash, because it will discolor paint and pastel, not to mention disturb the people around you. You may not take pictures of art in exhibitions nor art that is on loan. If you ever have a question as to whether you can take a picture of an artwork, ask the security guard.
- Do not talk on cell phones in the galleries.

The information below is derived from the museum websites, dating June 2016.
The days, times, and prices listed are subject to change.

The Los Angeles County Museum of Art (LACMA): www.lacma.org

5905 Wilshire Blvd
Los Angeles, CA 90036
(323) 857-6000

- Located between Fairfax and La Brea in the Miracle Mile District of Los Angeles.
- Open 11 am to 5 pm weekdays, Fridays later (closed Wednesdays), weekends 10 am to 7 pm.
- Admission is $15 (students with ID $10); certain ticketed exhibitions are extra.
- Parking is $12 (enter the parking structure from 6th street). Do not park on Wilshire Blvd!

This is my number one choice of where you should go. LACMA offers the widest variety of art possible. If you aren't sure what you really like or have a very eclectic taste when it comes to art, then this is the place to go. The collection covers artworks from early civilizations to modern and contemporary art. It has art from a multitude of cultures, including American, European, Korean, African, Chinese, and Japanese. The museum is made up of several multistory buildings. Friday nights there is live music in the Atrium. Impress your Facebook friends with a picture in front of Chris Burden's *Urban Lights*!

The Getty Center: www.getty.edu

1200 Getty Center Drive
Los Angeles, CA 90049
(310) 440-7300

- For GPS use N. Sepulveda Blvd and Getty Center Dr., Los Angeles (just off the 405 Fwy).
- Open 10:00 am to 5:30 pm every day, Saturdays until 9 pm!!! (Closed Mondays.)
- Admission is FREE!!!
- Parking is $15.

The museum specializes in European paintings and sculpture from the fifteenth to the nineteenth centuries, along with photography exhibits. It contains a limited amount of modern works by such artists as Monet and Renoir. The highlight of the collection is Vincent van Gogh's *Irises*! The Getty's buildings and gardens are as exquisite as their artwork. Make sure to leave time to enjoy them.

The Norton-Simon Museum: www.nortonsimon.org

411 W. Colorado Boulevard
Pasadena, CA 91105
(626) 449-6840

- Located on the famous corner of Colorado Blvd. and Orange Grove.
- Open noon to 5 pm every day, Friday and Saturday until 8 pm!!! (Closed Tuesdays.)
- Admission is $12 (FREE with Student ID!!!).
- Parking is FREE!!!

The Norton-Simon is student-friendly, offering free parking and admission to students. Keep in mind that this is a much smaller museum than the other two, but is very much worth the trip. It is privately owned, and the museum reflects the interests of its owner, who happens to enjoy modern artists, such as van Gogh, Picasso, and Degas. The top floor contains a nice sampling of works from the fourteenth through the twentieth centuries. The lower floor contains mostly Eastern sculptural works. There is also a small sculpture garden around the pond.

Essay Format

- *Upper-left-hand corner* of the paper should have (*single-spaced*):
  - Your name
  - Days and time of class
  - Museum Project
- Skip two lines and begin your paper. Do *not* give your paper a title.
- One-page (20–23 lines of text)
- Typed
- Double-spaced (Format —> Paragraph —> Spacing —> Double —> Click OK)
- 1" Margins (Format —> Document —> Change Margins —> Click OK)
- Use Times or Times New Roman
- 10-point font
- Do not forget to proofread your paper! Grammar does count!
- Do not use slang in academic writing (the word is *legitimate*, not *legit*)
- Make sure to *italicize* the titles of all artworks.
- *Artwork* is one word, not two.
- The term is *work of art*, not *piece of art* or *piece of work*.

Packet

Essay
Stapled behind the essay you must attach a picture of yourself at the museum.
Note: This is not a close-up of your face, but you at a recognizable area of the museum.

Point value: _____________________

Due date: _____________________

ENDNOTES

1. The paintings in the Chauvet Cave have been dated to between 32,000 and 30,000 BCE.
2. Fresco is sometimes referred to as *buon fresco*.
3. Frederick Hartt and David G. Wilkins, *History of Italian Renaissance Art* (Upper Saddle River, NJ: Prentice Hall, 2003), 50.
4. Frederick Hartt and David G. Wilkins, *History of Italian Renaissance Art* (Upper Saddle River, NJ: Prentice Hall, 2003), 51.
5. Frederick Hartt and David G. Wilkins, *History of Italian Renaissance Art* (Upper Saddle River, NJ: Prentice Hall, 2003), 51.
6. Personal interview with author Ross King, author of *Leonardo and The Last Supper* (New York: Walker Publishing, 2012), on November 7, 2012.
7. Gesso is a combination of plaster and glue.
8. Flanders encompasses areas of France, Belgium, Luxemburg, and the Netherlands.
9. Glazing is a transparent layer of paint laid on top of a layer of colored paint. The glazing helps to reflect light.
10. Marilyn Stokstad, *Art History*, revised ed. (New York: Harry N. Abrams, 1999), 625–626.
11. Ian Sidaway, *Mastering the Art of Oils, Acrylics, and Gouache* (London: Anness Publishing, 2004), 15.
12. Ian Sidaway, *Mastering the Art of Oils, Acrylics, and Gouache* (London: Anness Publishing, 2004), 12.

IMAGE CREDITS

- Fig. 15.1: Michelangelo Buonarroti, "Last Judgment," https://commons.wikimedia.org/wiki/File:Last_Judgement_by_Michelangelo.jpg. Copyright in the Public Domain.
- Fig. 15.2: "Portrait of a Young Boy," https://commons.wikimedia.org/wiki/File:PortraitOfAYoungBoy_MetropolitanMuseumOfArt.png. Copyright in the Public Domain.
- Fig. 15.3: Filippo Lippi, "Annunciation," https://commons.wikimedia.org/wiki/File:Fra_Filippo_Lippi_-_Annunciation_-_WGA13219.jpg. Copyright in the Public Domain.
- Fig. 15.4: Winslow Homer, "A Basket of Clams," https://commons.wikimedia.org/wiki/File:Winslow_Homer_-_A_Basket_of_Clams.jpg. Copyright in the Public Domain.

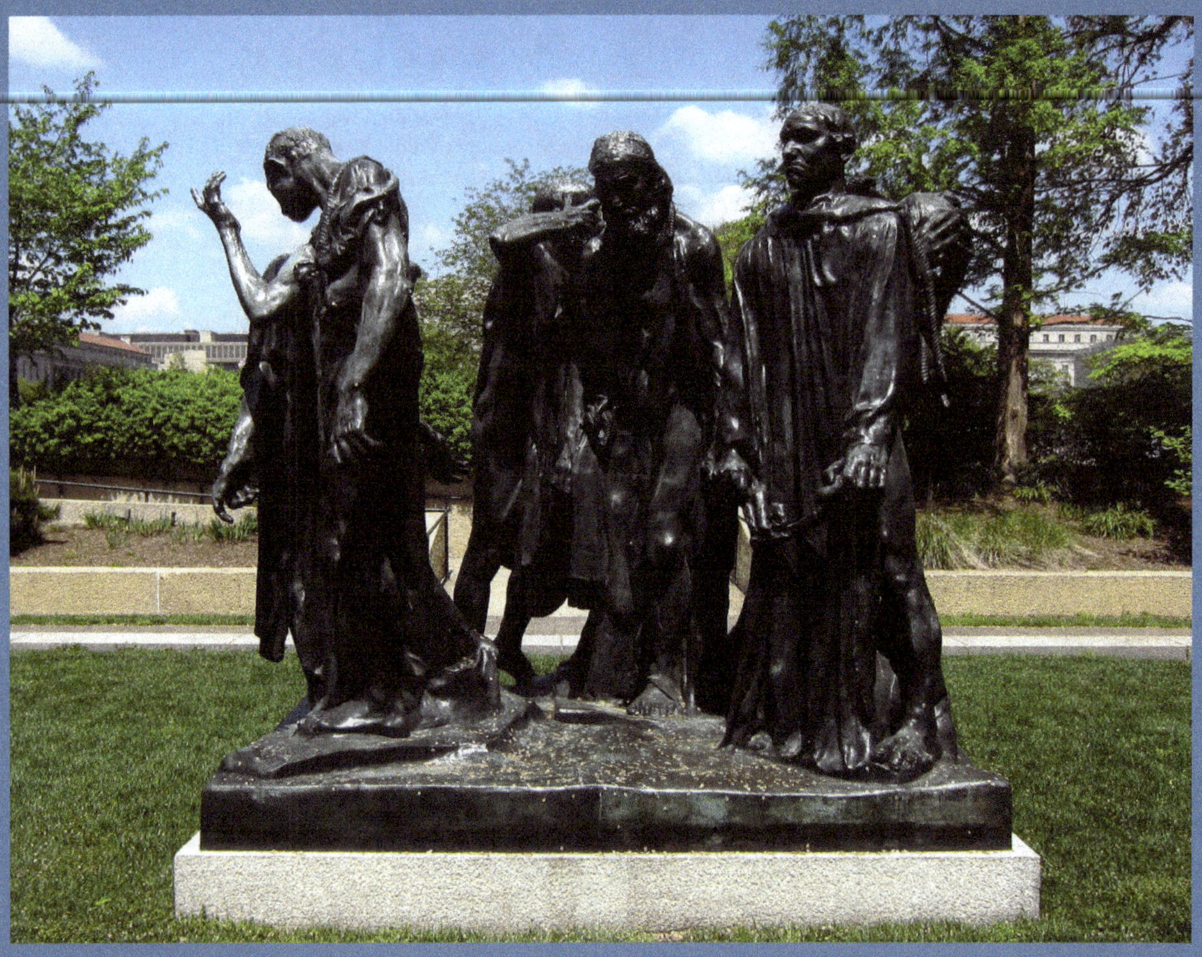

Figure 16.1: Auguste Rodin, *The Burghers of Calais*, 1886. Bronze, 6 ft, 10.5 in × 7 ft, 11 in × 6 ft, 6 in, Hirshhorn Museum and Sculpture Garden, Smithsonian Institution, Washington, D.C.

SCULPTURE

CHAPTER
16

SCULPTURE

Sculpture, along with painting and architecture, emerged from the Paleolithic era, with examples such as *Lion-Human* (**fig 16.2**) dating back to c. 30,000 BCE. *Lion-Human* stands out among early sculpture because of its uniqueness in both size and subject matter. It measures nearly a foot in length, whereas most sculptures from the Stone Age measure a couple of inches at most.[1] The subject matter itself is intriguing and lends itself to the intellectual development of early man. An individual who was able to carve a figure—half human and half animal—had to possess the power of imagination.

CARVING

Sculpture can be created in two ways, by using either the additive process or the subtractive process. We will look at the subtractive process first, because it is the older method. With the subtractive process, the artist takes a block of material, such as marble or wood, and then chips, gouges, and hammers away until the desired form is achieved. The subtractive process has only one subcategory—carving. It is the way man first began creating sculpture, as with *Lion-Human* above, and the process has been used continually since then, including during the contemporary era by artists such as Barbara Hepworth.

The sculpture of the Greek gods *Hermes and Dionysus* (**fig 16.3**) was created using the subtractive process.[2] Hermes is shown holding the child Dionysus. The figures both have their arms extended, and, although the sculpture is damaged, it is believed that Hermes was holding a cluster of grapes, which is why Dionysus, the god of wine, would be shown reaching for them. An important aspect of this sculpture is the way Hermes is positioned with his hips and legs in a different position than his shoulders and arms. The term to describe this technique, first seen in the High Classical era of the Greek civilization, is called **contrapposto**. This counter-balance or weight shift makes the sculpture appear more natural than anything that had been created previously.

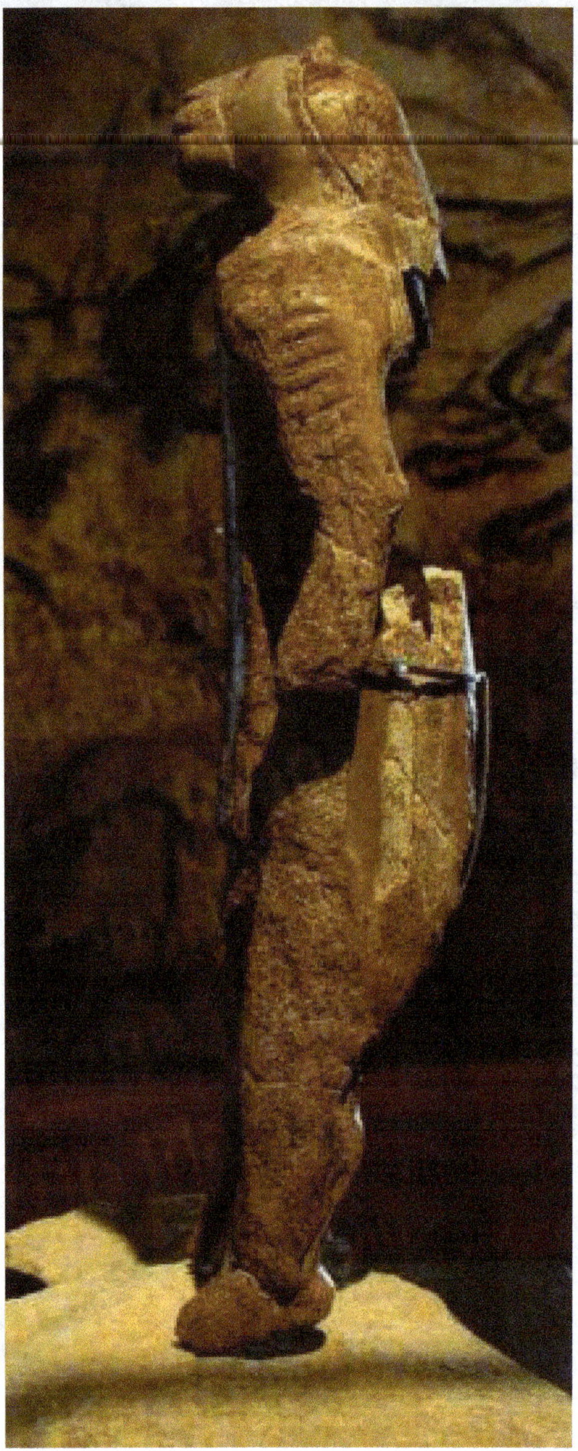

Figure 16.2: *Lion-Human* from Hohlenstein-Stadel, Germany, c. 30,000–26,000 BCE. Mammoth Ivory, 11 5/8 in, Ulmer Museum, Ulm, Germany.

Looking back at the Egyptian civilization, note that their sculptures appear very stiff and rigid. A case in point would be the sculpture of *Menkaure and His Wife* (not pictured). The figures are solid and immobile, each positioned with one foot forward to give the illusion of movement. But their bodies are in perfect balance. There is no weight shifting, no twisting; they appear to be robotic. In *Hermes and Dionysus*, the sculpture is presented in a contrapposto stance, with Hermes's body asymmetrical rather than symmetrical. The sculpture appears in a natural state, as if a person has been turned into stone.

After the fall of the Roman Empire, the contrapposto stance disappears, and artists revert back to the rigid, symmetrically balanced, frontally viewed sculpture. It would not be resurrected until the fifteenth century when the Italian artist Donatello used it in his bronze *David* (see fig 22.5), which has become one of the most famous of the Renaissance sculptures.

MODELING

The additive process of sculpture is broken down into three subcategories: modeling, casting, and assemblage. As you may have guessed, the additive process is the exact opposite of the subtractive process—just as in math. With the additive process, artists build up, or "add," material until the desired form is achieved.

With modeling, artists work with a pliable material, such as clay. Once formed, objects can be placed into a kiln and fired at high temperatures for a specific amount of time. When the clay emerges from the kiln, it is considered a ceramic. A more detailed description of this process appears in chapter 20.

CASTING

Casting was an invention of the Bronze Age, dating back to 2500 BCE. With casting, liquid metal, such as bronze, is poured into molds. Using metal

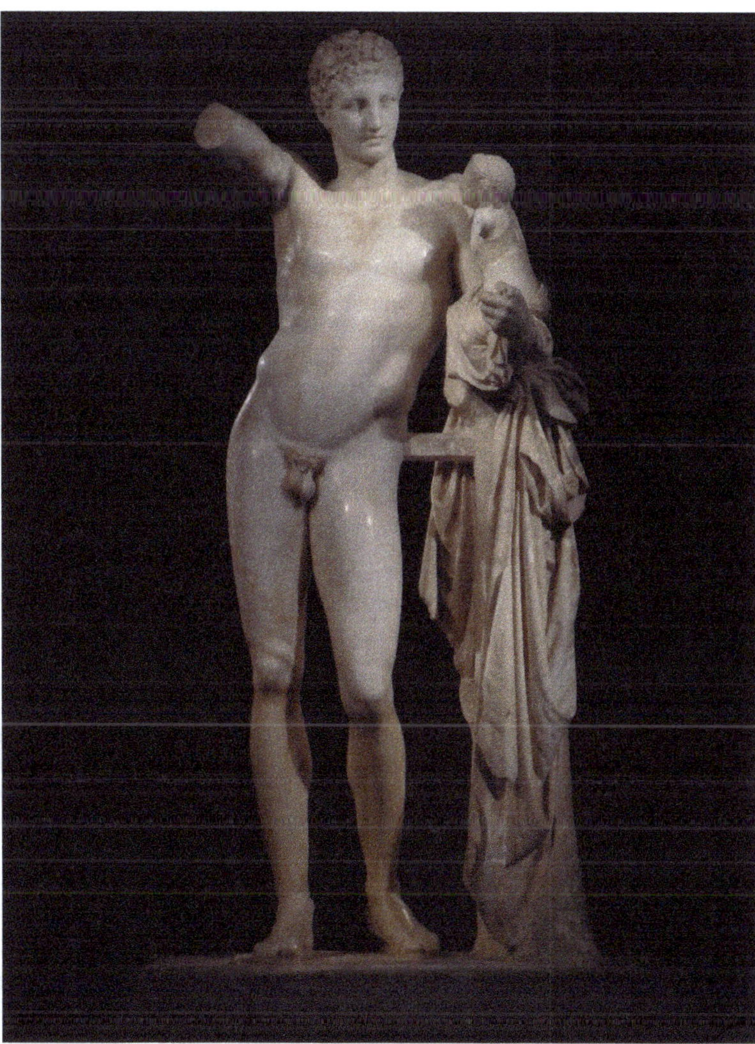

Figure 16.3: Praxitiles, *Hermes and Dionysus*, c. 330 BCE. Height 7'1", National Archeological Museum, Athens.

to create sculpture is extremely expensive, much more so than using materials such as clay or marble. One technique to help reduce this expense is the **lost-wax casting method**. An artist can use the lost-wax casting method to create a hollow sculpture. With a hollow sculpture, less material is used, thus reducing the cost of materials, as well as the weight of the sculpture.

Among the most talented artists to work in bronze was Auguste Rodin. His sculpture *The Burghers of Calais* (**fig 16.1**) was created using the lost-wax casting method. The story it relates comes from the Hundred Years War between England and France. The English had seized the French port city of Calais. In order to free their city from the siege, the six leaders of Calais agreed to sacrifice themselves. We see them in this sculpture walking "barefoot, and clad in sackcloth, with ropes around their necks."[3]

The expressions of the six individuals vary from anger and resentment to fear and sadness. The sculpture rests on a low base that allows the viewer the unique advantage of interacting with these figures on a more personal level, to look into their faces and see the emotions as well as the sensation of walking with them to what they thought was their demise.[4] Another interesting aspect of this sculpture is that it does rest on the ground, or a small base, rather than being elevated above one's head. It seems more common to view sculptures that are placed on high pedestals, such as Michelangelo's *David* (see fig 22.7) or Donatello's *Equestrian Sculpture of Gattamelata* (not pictured). Perhaps a reason for the sculpture's placement on the ground is that it commemorates a military loss rather than a victory.

ASSEMBLAGE

Assemblage is the newest way of creating sculpture. Artists construct these works placing non-art-related objects (many would call these objects trash) together by means of construction techniques such as welding or gluing. While early examples can be seen from the Surrealist artists, assemblage sculpture rose to prominence in the post–World War II art scene.[5] There is a juvenile quality seen in the construction of many of these sculptures, as they look like the creations of an overly creative child. It would even be fair to call some of these works into question, asking, "Is this art?" This element makes assemblage sculpture both fun and intriguing.

Edward Kienholz was an assemblage artist from Southern California. He would frequent junkyards and bring home a wide variety of props to use in his works. One of the more haunting works he created was *The Illegal Operation*

(**fig 16.4**), which is on display at the Los Angeles County Museum of Art. It is one of those works that needs to be seen in person, as a photograph can't do it justice, nor purvey the same feeling as being in its presence. The work places you at the scene of a backroom abortion. The art historian David Joselit suggests that this work serves as an association "between discarded objects and discarded lives."[6] A shopping cart is transformed into a chair, and a cement bag represents the form of a female body. The bedpan and bucket beneath are filled with old, dirty, rusted tools. The entire scene is cast in a sickly glow from a single light bulb.

RELIEF

Sculpture can be experienced in three ways: in relief, in-the-round, and as an environment. We will look at relief sculpture first. Sculpture that

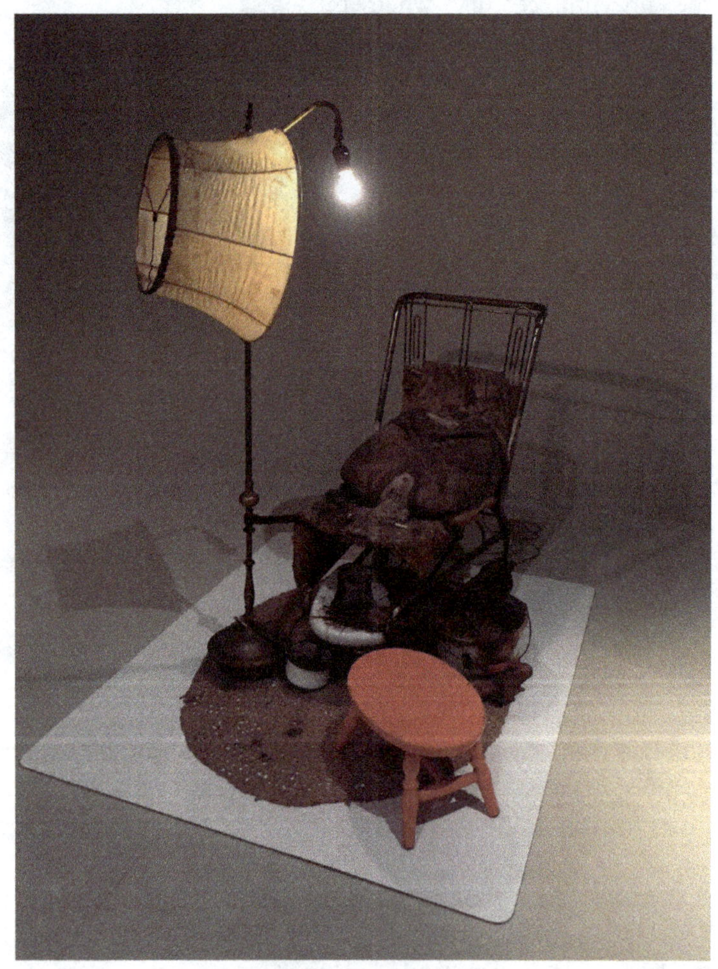

Figure 16.4: Edward Kienholz, *The Illegal Operation*, 1962. Mixed Media, 59 in × 48 in × 54 in, Los Angeles County Museum of Art.

is in relief is seen from one side, as it is literally carved from its background. Objects can be in high relief, or more commonly, in low relief, which is sometimes referred to as *bas relief.*

The *Palette of King Narmer* (**fig 16.5**) is considered to be in low relief. The key to identifying a sculpture in low relief is that the figures are firmly attached to their background, as seen with coins or medals, compared to the three-dimensionality seen in high-relief sculpture. The palette in this case is not an artistic palette for mixing paint, but for mixing eye makeup. A circular concave area on the top of the palette (at right) is formed by the intertwining necks of the animals. These figures denote the merging of Upper and Lower Egypt, which took place under Narmer's rule. Above this scene we see Narmer, in hieratic scale, in a processional led with banners, the dead bodies of his enemies lined up at the right. In the bottom register, a bull is menacing a fallen foe. On the bottom side of the palette, we see Narmer, with a club in his hand, taking up almost the entire length of the palette, as he is about to finish off one of the enemies. Narmer's assistant stands off to the left holding his sandals while the god Horus oversees the event. In the bottom register, two individuals are seen running away.

High-relief sculpture is easily identified in the three-dimensionality of the figures or objects the artist creates. They literally look as if they have been carved separately and placed against a backdrop. They are created in the same fashion as low-relief sculpture in that they are still carved from the background. But, as you can imagine, the creation of high-relief sculpture would take a much longer time, not

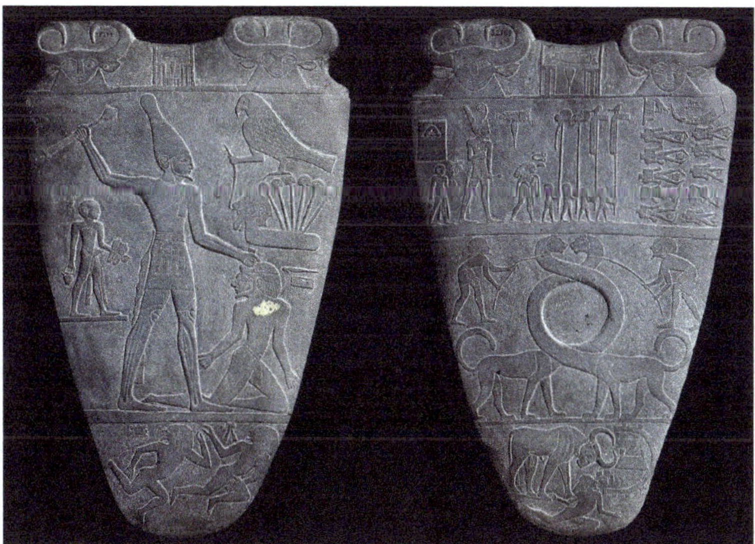

Figure 16.5: *The Palette of King Narmer*, c. 3000 BCE. Slate, Height 63.5 cm, Egyptian Museum of Cairo.

to mention a very talented artist, to produce. The *Triumph of Dionysus and the Seasons* (**fig 16.6**) is carved along the sides of the marble sarcophagus. It is sculpted with such precision and accuracy that the figures look as if they can step down from their scene onto the floor below.

A third form of relief sculpture is *repoussé*. It is extremely rare and is created differently than the other forms discussed above. With both low relief and high relief, the artist is using the subtractive process by carving from a block of material. In *repoussé* the artist is hammering

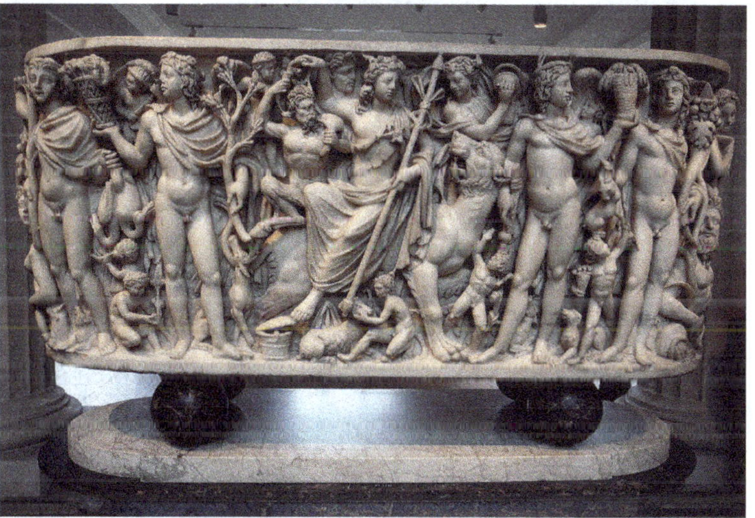

Figure 16.6: Roman Sarcophagus, *Triumph of Dionysus and the Seasons*, 260–270 CE. Phryglian Marble, 34 in × 85 in × 36.25 in, Metropolitan Museum of Art.

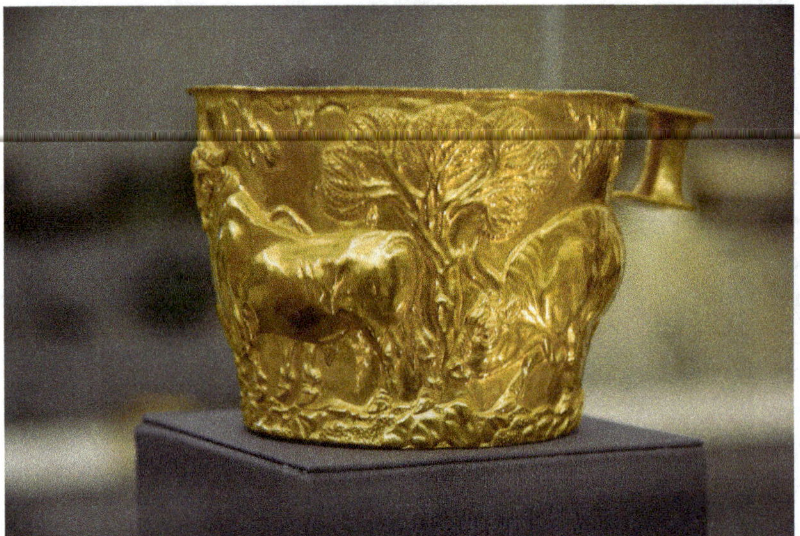

Figure 16.7: *Vapheio Cup*, C. 1400–1200 BCE. Gold, Height 3.5 in, National Museum of Archaeology, Athens.

metal from behind in order to create a viewable scene. No material is removed; rather, the shape of the metal is transformed. With this technique, the artist uses material that is soft and malleable, such as gold, which is what the *Vapheio Cup* (**fig 16.7**) is created from. The artist of this work was probably a Minoan craftsman working in Mycenaean mainland (where the cup was found), as they were the most accomplished metalworkers during this time.[7] The scene depicts young men trying to capture bulls, which were sacred animals in the Minoan culture.

IN-THE-ROUND

Sculpture in-the-round is exactly as it sounds. It is a sculpture that is viewable from all sides. It invites you, the viewer, to walk around and experience it from all angles. This is the type of sculpture one would expect to encounter at a museum or gallery, standing on a pedestal in the center of the room. Some of the most famous sculptures were created in-the-round. These include the statues of *David* by Michelangelo and Bernini (see figs 22.4 and 7.4) and *The Burghers of Calais* mentioned earlier in this chapter.

INSTALLATIONS

Sculptures can also be viewed as an environment. The most common environments are installations and earthworks. Both installations and earthworks can be considered **site specific**, because they are created for a specific area or location. They are not placed based on convenience or last-minute thought. Usually, these spaces are examined by the artist months or even years in advance of the artwork's creation.

Installations are created using multiple objects, but they should be viewed as one artwork, similar to an ensemble. They can be created inside a building, usually a gallery set aside specifically for that work, but they can also be created outside, as in the case of Chris Burden's *Urban Light* (**fig 16.8**). One of the most photographed spots in Los Angeles, this installation sits in front of the

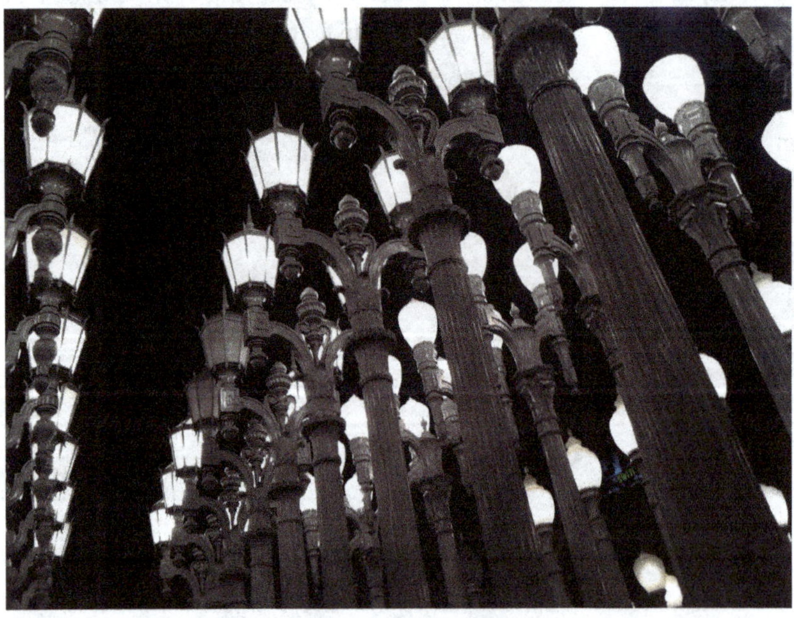

Figure 16.8: Chris Burden, *Urban Light*, 1962. 202 Cast-Iron Street Lamps, 320.5 in × 686.5 in × 705.5 in, Los Angeles County Museum of Art.

Los Angeles County Museum of Art on Wilshire Boulevard, near Fairfax. This artwork consists of street lamps, which the artist purchased from the city as they were being replaced.[8] The streetlights vary in form and ornateness. The plain lights at the edges of the work were recovered from the less prominent parts of Los Angeles, whereas the tall, multi-lamp posts at the center came from the more affluent neighborhoods.[9] Chris Burden will be discussed more in the next chapter on performance art, as he was a key figure in this medium in the 1970s.

EARTHWORKS

Earthworks, *earth art*, and *environmental art* are all synonymous terms and reflect the correlation of art with the rising environmental movement of the 1970s. The artists were inspired by ancient land art, such as the *Great Serpent Mound* in Ohio, which dates back to 600 BCE. Earthworks can either change the way we view or interpret the environment, such as seen in *Sun Tunnels* by Nancy Holt or *Lightning Field* by Walter de Maria (neither pictured), or they can transform the landscape itself, as seen in Robert Smithson's *Spiral Jetty* (**fig 16.9**). The *Spiral Jetty* extends into Utah's Great Salt Lake. If unfurled it would reach about 1,500 feet in length. Smithson felt that the spiral is the most fundamental form in nature, that shells, galaxies, and DNA molecules are based on the spiral shape.[10]

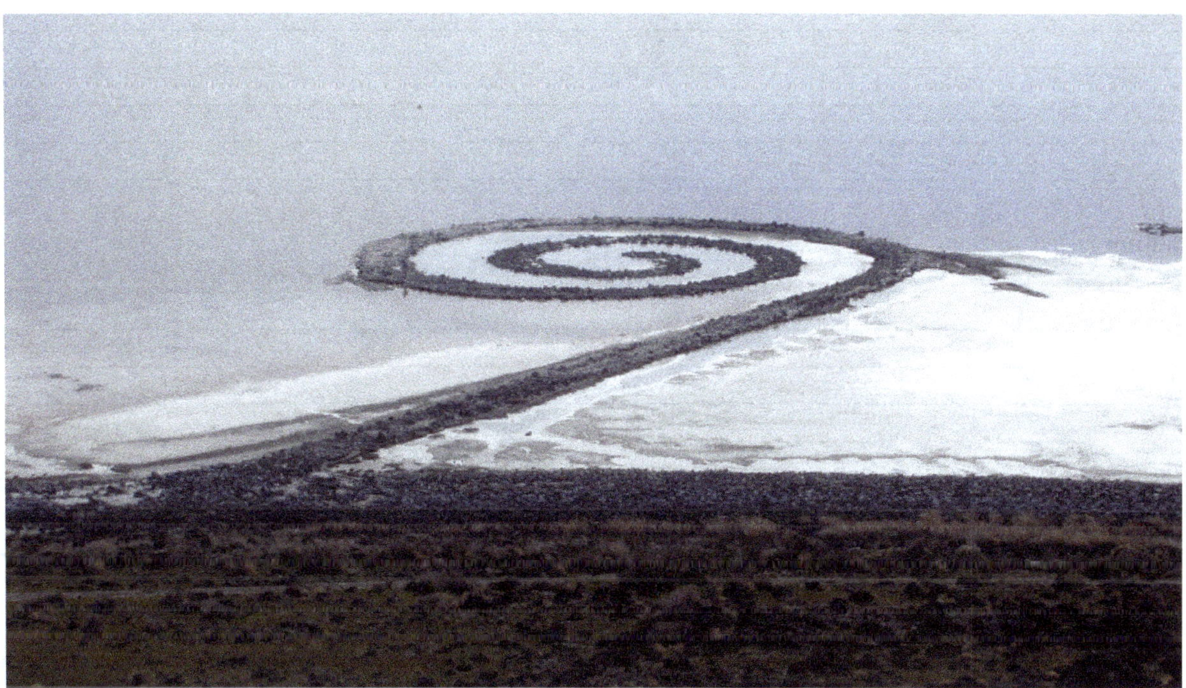

Figure 16.9: Robert Smithson, *Spiral Jetty*, 1970. Rocks, earth, algae, salt, 1550 ft × 15 ft, Great Salt Lake, Utah.

PROCESSES OF CREATING SCULPTURE

Subtractive process:

Carving:

Additive process:

Modeling:

Casting:

Assemblage:

In relief:

Low relief (*bas relief*):

High relief:

Repoussé:

In-the-round:

As an environment:

Installation art:

Earthworks:

ASSORTED TERMS

Contrapposto:

Lost-wax casting method:

Site specific:

ENDNOTES

1. Among the most famous sculptural works from the Paleolithic era are the *Woman of Willendorf*, measuring 4 3/8"; *Woman of Brassempouy*, measuring 1 1/4", and *Woman of Ostrava Petrkovice*, measuring 1 3/4".
2. The Roman equivalent of these gods would be Mercury and Bacchus.
3. H. H. Arnason and Elizabeth Mansfield, *History of Modern Art*, 7th ed. (Upper Saddle River, NJ: Pearson Education, 2013), 56.
4. The King of England's wife asks him to spare their lives, which he does.
5. Joan Miró and Salvador Dalí called these early assemblage sculptures, *Objects*.
6. David Joselit, *Art Since 1945* (New York: Thames and Hudson, 2003), 100.
7. Marilyn Stokstad, *Art History*, revised ed. (New York: Harry N. Abrams, 1999), 138.
8. Lecture by the Chris Burden, Pomona College, March 24, 2012.
9. Lecture by the Chris Burden, Pomona College, March 24, 2012.
10. Henry Sayre, *A World of Art*, 7th ed. (Boston: Prentice Hall, 2013). 9.

IMAGE CREDITS

- Fig. 16.1: Copyright © Auguste Rodin; Photo by AgnosticPreachersKid (CC BY-SA 3.0) at https://commons.wikimedia.org/wiki/File:The_Burghers_of_Calais_-_Hirshhorn_Sculpture_Garden.JPG.
- Fig. 16.2: Jduckeck, "Lion-Human," https://commons.wikimedia.org/wiki/File:Lion_man_photo.jpg. Copyright in the Public Domain.
- Fig. 16.3: Copyright © Praxiteles; Photo by Laitue (CC BY-SA 3.0) at https://commons.wikimedia.org/wiki/File:Hermes_portant_Dionysos_par_Praxitèle.JPG.
- Fig. 16.4: Edward Kienholz; Photo by David Plouffe, "The Illegal Operation."
- Fig. 16.5: Nicolas Perrault III, "Palette of King Narmer," https://commons.wikimedia.org/wiki/File:Narmer_Palette.jpg. Copyright in the Public Domain.
- Fig. 16.6: Copyright © Wikipedia Loves Art (CC by 2.5) at https://commons.wikimedia.org/wiki/File:WLA_metmuseum_Marble_sarcophagus_with_Triumph_of_Dionysos.jpg.
- Fig. 16.7: Copyright © Zdenek Kratochvil (CC BY-SA 3.0) at https://commons.wikimedia.org/wiki/File:Golden_cup_from_Vafio_1500_to_1450_BC,_NAMA_1759_080868.jpg.
- Fig. 16.8: Chris Burden; Photo by David Plouffe, "Urban Light."
- Fig. 16.9: Copyright © Robert Smithson (CC BY-SA 2.0) at https://commons.wikimedia.org/wiki/File:Spiral-jetty-from-rozel-point.png.

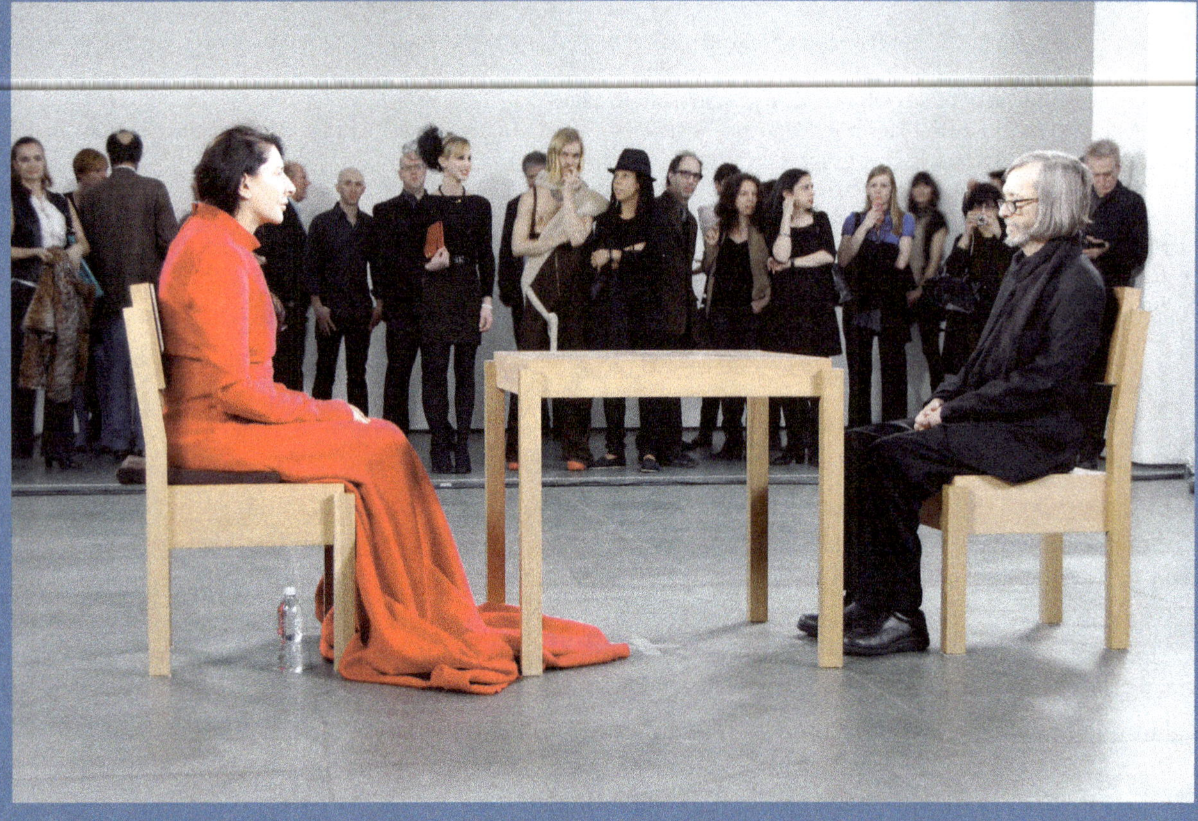

Figure 17.1: Marina Abramović, *The Artist is Present*, 2010. Performance at the Museum of Modern Art, New York.

PERFORMANCE ART

PERFORMANCE ART

Back in chapter 7 there was a quote from Harold Rosenberg that read: "At a certain moment, the canvas began to appear to one American painter after another *as an arena in which to act*."[1] The quote was used to describe how the Abstract Expressionists, or "action painters" as they were called, had been able to transform the passive duty of painting into a more active, dynamic, and gestural act. Artists such as Jackson Pollock would create their paintings through performative gesture (see fig 7.7). Pollock would apply paint using sweeping arm motions as he walked around the canvas, sometimes stepping onto the canvas itself as it lay on the ground. Artists were no longer static—they had become mobile.

Allan Kaprow, the father of performance art, viewed Pollock's paintings as being important to the evolution of art because the edges of the canvas no longer seemed to matter. They were being eliminated, not unlike what was happening in the drawings and paintings of Edgar Degas (see fig 7.5) during the late nineteenth century. Prior to the modern era, events happened within the frame of the painting. With Pollock and Degas, art begins to lose its borders and extend into our world.

Performance art becomes the next logical step for artists after Abstract Expressionism. Performance allows the artist to communicate more directly to the viewer than any other medium, such as painting or sculpture, could allow.[2] A performance might encompass elements of music, dance, theatre, poetry, and video, but it was not exclusively any of these. We cannot make the mistake of calling a performance artwork "theatre." In theatre there is a script, character development, narrative, rehearsals, repeat performances, and specific time allotments for the event to happen within. Not true with performance art.

Allan Kaprow was responsible for **Happenings**, which were the very first form of performance art. In Kaprow's words:

> A happening, unlike a stage play, may occur at a supermarket, driving along a highway, under a pile of rags, and in a friend's kitchen, either at once or sequentially. If sequentially, time may extend for more than a year. The Happening is performed according to a plan but without rehearsal, audience, or repetition. It is art but seems closer to life.[3]

These events included a live audience, which often participated in the Happening itself.

The very first Happening took place in 1959 at the Reuben Gallery in New York.[4] It was titled *18 Happenings in 6 Parts*. The gallery was divided into three rooms using transparent plastic sheeting so you could get a sense of what was happening in the other rooms. Kaprow, who was an Abstract Expressionist painter, painted some of the plastic sheeting.[5] Three Happenings took place simultaneously, one in each room. Six times a bell would ring, signaling the ending of one part and the beginning of another.

One of Kaprow's most famous Happenings was called *Household*, which took place in 1964. In this work a group of individuals showed up at a dump in Ithaca, New York. They separated out by gender. The women gathered at one area in the dump and began building a "nest" from the refuse. In another area the men began building a tower. A car was pushed out and the hood covered with strawberry jam. The women then ate the jam off the hood of the car while the men destroyed the nest. When it came the men's turn to eat the jam, the women destroyed the tower. The car was then destroyed with sledgehammers and set on fire. Everyone sat around and watched the car burn. Afterwards they left the dump.

The above performance might have sounded like it came from someone's dream or imagination, but there is photographic evidence of this event. This brings up one of the issues with performance art. Most of the time the artist fails at transferring the meaning of the work to the audience. The meaning of these works is extremely important, because performance art is considered a conceptual activity; that is, the meaning behind the artwork is more important than the physical work. If you saw *Household* for the first time, you would be left wondering what you had just seen, or why these people had acted the way they did, or what was with the jam. Henry Sayre, author of *A World of Art*, suggests that this work calls attention to the violence of relationships between the sexes: "It is a force that can drive us apart and bring us together."[6]

Note that in *Household* everyone took part in the work. There was an absence of a true audience. Instead, there were only participants. While this is common with performance art, it is not a strict rule. Many times an audience might be called in to witness an event. This is true for many of Chris Burden's works, including his landmark performance, *Shoot*. During the 1970s Chris Burden was among the most important and noteworthy performance artists. Today, he is known for his amazing sculptures, such as *Urban Light* (see fig 16.8) from the previous chapter; *Beam Drop*; and *Metropolis II*, which is a kinetic sculpture, also on display at the LA County Museum of Art. *Metropolis II* is a miniaturized version of a bustling city, with hundreds of vehicles running on 18 different tracks whipping around a city full of skyscrapers and other buildings.[7]

Shoot took place in "F Space," an industrial space in Santa Ana, California, on November 19, 1971. In this performance Burden was shot in the arm by one of his friends, Bruce Dunlap.[8] Burden invited a handful of friends to witness the event, telling them that he was going to be shot. The entire performance lasts only a few seconds: Chris Burden stands against one wall with his left arm hanging loosely, but extended out from his body. He visibly stiffens as Bruce Dunlap raises the .22 rifle, aims, and fires. Burden flinches as he is hit, the bullet passing through his arm. He is seen on camera walking back toward the shooter, checking his arm out as he walks off camera. According to a *New York Times* video article by Eric Kutner, Burden was taken to the hospital afterwards to be checked out.

Shoot made Chris Burden internationally famous. The media seemed to grasp exclusively on the violence of the event. Perhaps equaling the event to the violence seen on TV during coverage of the Vietnam War. However, in a 1979 interview with Jim Moison, Burden stated that it wasn't about the violence. It was about "how you dealt with the anticipation … like knowing at 7:30 you're going to stand in a room and a guy's going to shoot you."[9] However, one would have to argue that violence, or at least physical pain, permeated much of Burden's work during the early 1970s. For example, in *Transfixed* he was literally crucified on a Volkswagen. He stood on the car's rear bumper, leaned back onto the roof with his arms placed in the fashion of a goal post, and had friends drive nails into the palms of his hands. This work (along with many others that he has done) backfired, because when the nails hit the metal of the car the tips bent and could not be removed. They ended up being cut off. In another work, *Doorway to Heaven*, Burden pushed live electrical wires into his chest, electrocuting himself. And finally, in *Through the Night Softly*, late night television viewers witnessed Chris Burden crawling on the ground, nearly naked, through broken glass.[10]

While the work of Chris Burden might seem extreme, even by today's standards, it would be worthwhile to note here that most performance art is usually done one time. Burden wasn't shot at 7:30 with repeat performances at 8:30 and 9:30. The performance becomes more powerful because it is ephemeral, a fleeting moment in time never to be recaptured or recreated. There is no commodification like we see in other mediums, such as painting or sculpture, as there is nothing to sell. All that is left at the end of the performance is the experience of the viewer, as well as photographs and video.

While many famous artists populated the performance art scene in the 1960s and 1970s, it is a viable, if not expanding, medium today, with artists such as Marina Abramović. She calls herself not just the mother, but the grandmother, of performance art, having begun her work in the 1970s and continuing to create significant works today.[11]

Among her most recent works is *The Artist Is Present* from 2010 (**fig 17.1**). It took place at the Museum of Modern Art in New York. The performance lasted three months, from March until May, lasting a total of 716.5 hours. During the museum's visiting hours, Abramović sat motionless at a small wooden table, silently staring ahead, while spectators waited in line to sit opposite her. When the spectator, now participant, had his or her turn to sit, no words would be spoken between the two individuals, instead they would engage one another by staring into each other's eyes.

The appeal of this performance was incredible. People camped out overnight in front of the museum to guarantee their chance of sitting in front of Abramović. Those attending the exhibit included artist Chuck Close, actor James Franco, and Ulay, who had once been Abramović's artistic collaborator and romantic partner.[12] The final sitter was Klaus Biesenbach, who curated the exhibition.

Performance art:

Happening:

ENDNOTES

1. Harold Rosenberg, "The American Action Painters," *Art News*, December 1952, 22.
2. Robert Atkins, *Art Speak: A Guide to Contemporary Ideas, Movements, and Buzzwords, 1945 to the Present*, 2nd ed. (New York: Abbeville Press, 1997), 142–144.
3. Fred S. Kleiner, *Gardner's Art Through the Ages* 14th ed. (Boston: Wadsworth, Cengage Learning, 2014), 822.
4. Kristine Stiles and Peter Selz, ed., *Theories and Documents of Contemporary Art: A Sourcebook of Artists' Writings* (Berkeley: University of California Press, 1996), 682.
5. David Joselit, *Art Since 1945* (New York: Thames and Hudson, 2003), 51.
6. Henry Sayre, *A World of Art*, 7th ed. (Boston: Prentice Hall, 2013), 328.
7. "Metropolis II," accessed July 20, 2016, http://www.lacma.org/art/exhibition/metropolis-ii.
8. "Shot in the Name of Art," *New York Times*, video article, accessed July 21, 2016, http://www.nytimes.com/2015/05/20/opinion/shot-in-the-name-of-art.html?_r=1.
9. Kristine Stiles and Peter Selz, ed., *Theories and Documents of Contemporary Art: A Sourcebook of Artists' Writings* (Berkeley: University of California Press, 1996), 772.
10. https://youtu.be/cxmy4aQ1dZY.
11. *The Artist Is Present*, directed by Matthew Akers (2012, Music Box Films), DVD.
12. *The Artist is Present*, directed by Matthew Akers (2012, Music Box Films), DVD.

IMAGE CREDIT

- Fig. 17.1: Copyright © Marina Abramović; Photo by Andrew Russeth (CC BY-SA 2.0) at https://commons.wikimedia.org/wiki/File:Marina_Abramović,_The_Artist_is_Present,_2010_(2).jpg.

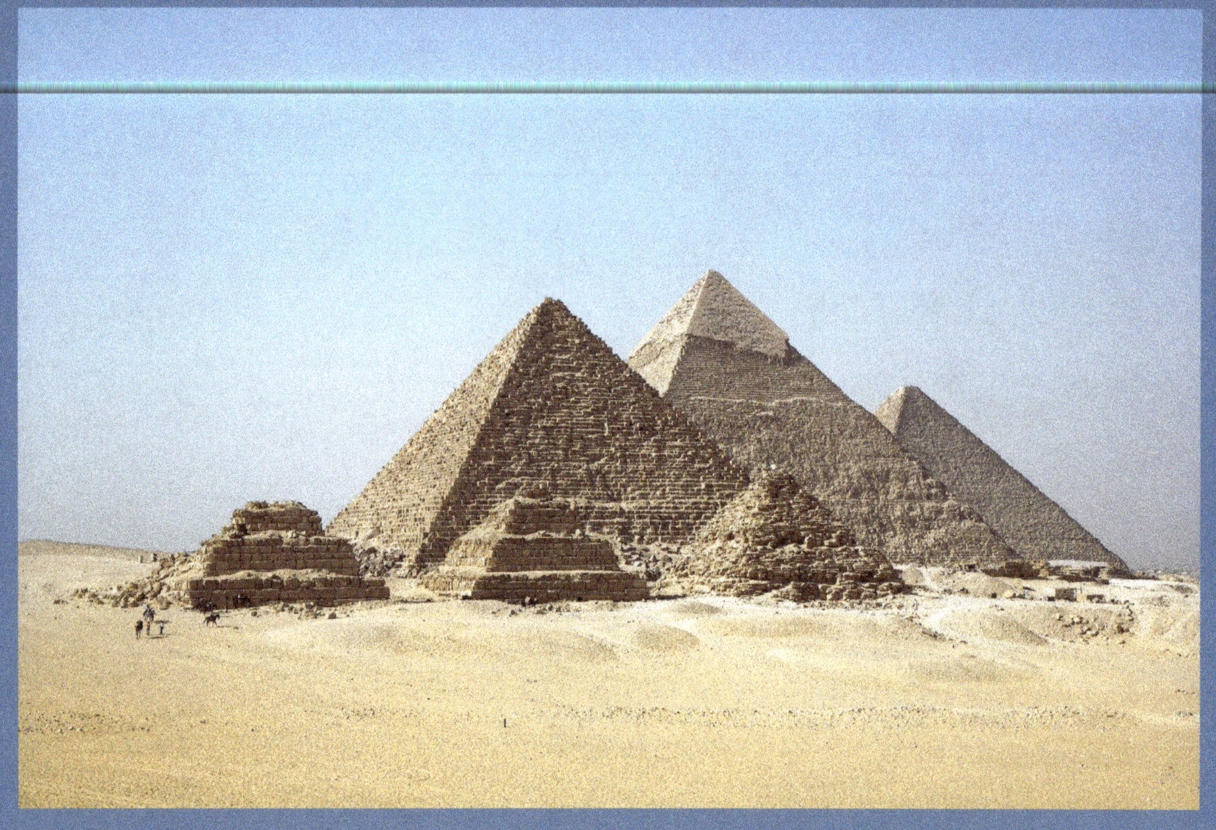

Figure 18.1: Pyramids at Giza: Menkaure (c. 2470 BCE), Khafre (c. 2500 BCE), and Khufu (c. 2530 BCE). Egypt, Old Kingdom.

ANCIENT VERSUS MODERN ARCHITECTURE

As noted by the chapter title, this chapter specifically covers ancient architecture. Our next chapter will examine modern architecture. But where does one place the dividing line between the two, and why? The answer to both questions is the difference in construction techniques. Just as we saw an advancement in painting mediums, moving from tempera to oil paint, so, too, do we have advancement in construction techniques. In fact, construction techniques have advanced so rapidly that it would be probable in the near future to consider a third chapter on this subject entitled "Contemporary Architecture."

In the study of ancient architecture, we are concerned with the **shell system** method of construction. With this method one basic building material is used throughout the entire structure. The chosen material serves as both the structural support and as the outer covering for the building. For instance, the Pyramids at Giza (**fig 18.1**) were made from limestone, the Greek Parthenon (**fig 18.6**) was made from marble, and the Roman Pantheon (**fig 18.14**) was made from concrete.

In comparison, modern architecture (discussed more thoroughly in the next chapter) utilizes the skeleton-and-skin method of construction. Here, a strong framing material, such as steel or cast-iron, is used for the interior (*skeleton*) of the building, while a lighter protective covering is used for the exterior (*skin*).

PREHISTORIC ARCHITECTURE

Ever since man has walked this planet he has had the innate sense to build. Throughout every populated continent, monuments stand to support this testament. We watch toddlers as they play with building blocks and learn how to construct, through trial and error, towers and houses. Later, as children, they will build sand castles in the summer and snow forts during the winter.

It is no surprise that architecture would originate in prehistoric times. What we first note as man-made structures emerged during the Stone Age. The Stone Age can be broken down into two eras: the Paleolithic and the Neolithic. During the Paleolithic era (40,000–8,000 BCE), man was a hunter-gatherer and constructed temporary shelters, such as the Mammoth-Bone House (**fig 18.2**). Remnants of these sites have been found in areas of Russia and Ukraine.[1] These crude homes

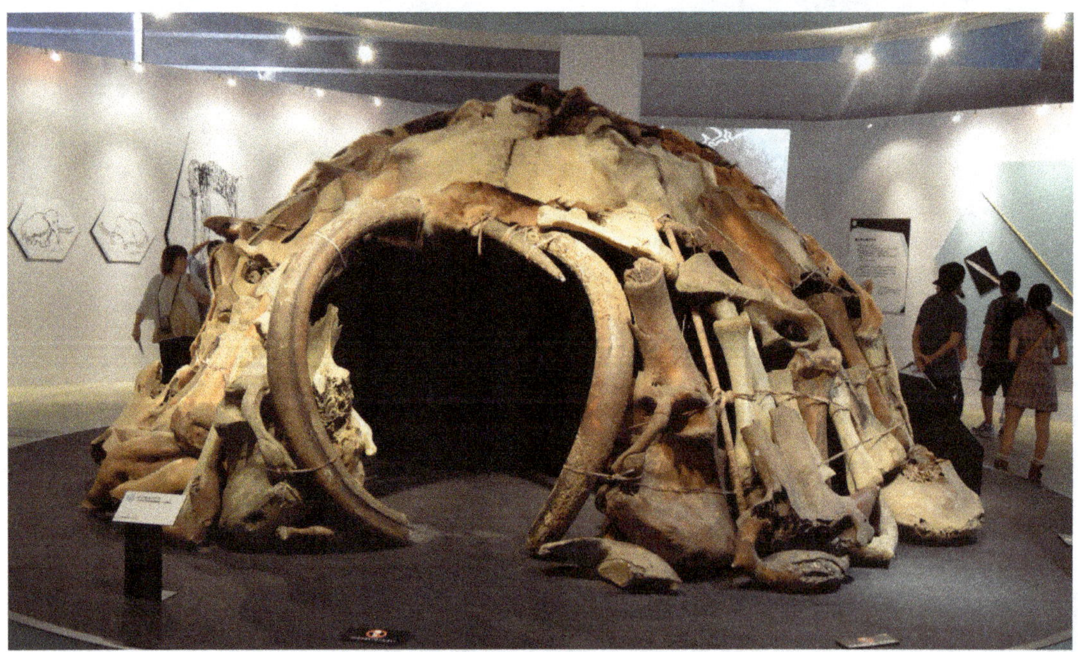

Figure 18.2: *Reconstruction of a Mammoth-Bone House,* c. 16,000–10,000 BCE.

were made from the bones of woolly mammoths, with animal skins on the outermost layer serving as insulation. These shelters were not very large, measuring only about 15 feet in diameter.

With the transition to the Neolithic era (8,000–2,000 BCE), man became more agrarian and began living in small communities. Among the best preserved of these Neolithic sites is off the coast of Scotland. In the Orkney Islands sits the settlement of Skara Brae. This settlement includes seven homes or rooms, with passageways leading between them. In the largest room (**fig 18.3**) we see a couple of very important early structural systems: corbeling and post and lintel.

The walls of the rooms are constructed using many courses of flat stones. Each layer, or *course*, of stones projects slightly inward from the previous layer. The walls could eventually meet at the center of the room. According to Marilyn Stokstad, author of *Art History*, the walls of the rooms of Skara Brae stopped short of meeting in the center, with the remaining space being covered by animal hides.[2] This structural system is called **corbeling**, and it allows for construction of enclosures approximately 15 to 20 feet in diameter. Rather than buckling in the center, the weight of the material is transmitted down the sides to the ground, similar to an arch.

The room at the settlement of Skara Brae contains another important structural system. Looking across the room to the far wall is a cabinet-like object. This structure was built using the **post-and-lintel** system. The posts consist of two blocks of material placed in an upright or vertical position, while another block of material, the lintel, is placed horizontally above the posts. The posts support the lintel, while the weight of the lintel keeps the upright posts in place. The tensile strength of the material being used determines the space between the posts.

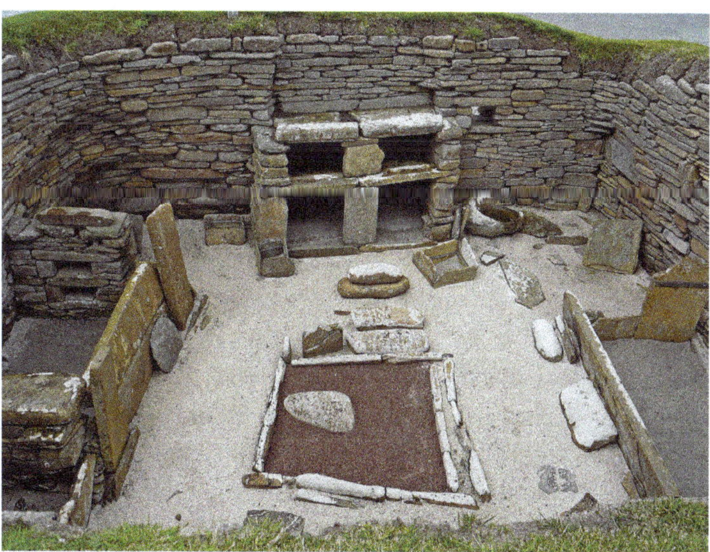

Figure 18.3: *Settlement of Skara Brae*, House Interior (Detail), c. 3,100–2,600 BCE. Orkney Islands, Scotland.

The greater the tensile strength of the material, the farther apart the posts can be placed.

We see many famous examples of post-and-lintel architecture throughout early civilizations. The Mycenaeans used it for the construction of the Lion's Gate (not pictured), which guarded the entranceway into the citadel at Mycenae. The Greeks used it in the construction of the Parthenon (**fig 18.6**).

One could argue that one of the most noted uses of post-and-lintel architecture in the ancient world is at Stonehenge (**fig 18.4**). This famous

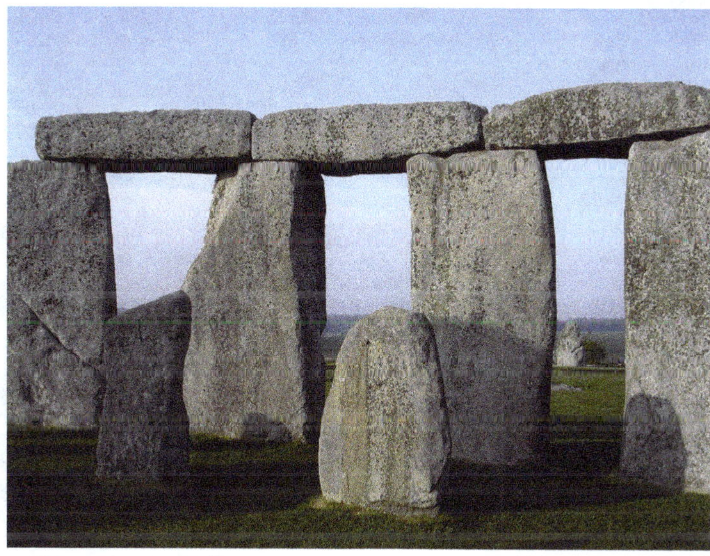

Figure 18.4: *Stonehenge*, c. 2750–1500 BCE. Salisbury Plain, Wiltshire, England.

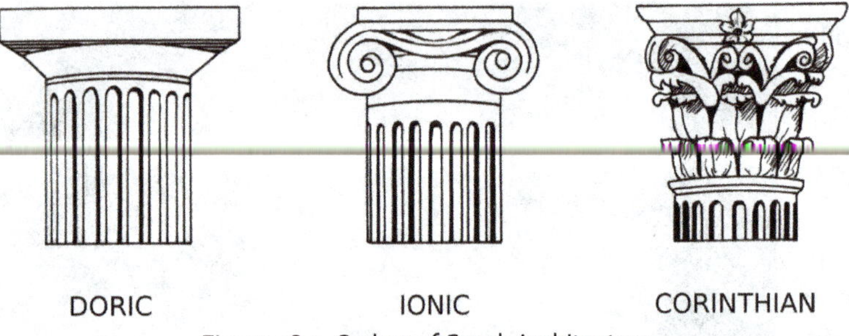

Figure 18.5: Orders of Greek Architecture.

site has always been shrouded in mystery, but one thing is clear—it took an advanced culture to quarry, transport, and raise these stones. Cooperation and organization were essential elements in the construction of this site, as the average stone weighed 26 tons and was moved 23 miles to this site through marshland and forest.

GREEK ARCHITECTURE

The Greeks developed the **classical orders of architecture**. These orders help to identify the aesthetic style of a temple or building. The three orders are: Doric, Ionic, and Corinthian (**fig 18.5**). Each of these styles is unique and easy to identify simply by looking at the top of the column, the area of which is called the *capital*.

The Doric order is the oldest of the orders of architecture and dates back to the seventh century BCE. The Doric order is unique in that the columns sit directly on the floor, or *stylobate*, rather than up on a base, as with the other two styles. The column itself appears rather wide and heavy at the base, with a gradual tapering to the top. The capital has a semicurved portion, called the *echinus*, which leads to a square slab, the *abacus* (**fig 18.6**).[3] Among the notable temples featuring this order is the Parthenon. The temple, dedicated to Athena Parthenos, sits atop the highest point of the Acropolis overlooking Athens.

The Ionic order is an imported style from Ionia, an area of Anatolia, in present-day Turkey. The order is more slender and elegant than the Doric order with its notable spiral scrolls, or *volutes*, adorning the capital. The order became popular during the fifth century BCE and serves as the style for many of the temples to the female goddesses, such as the Temple of Athena Nike (**fig 18.7**).

The final order is the Corinthian style. It is by far the most famous order and is incredibly popular even today. The distinguishing feature is how extremely ornate the capitals are, usually in the form of Acanthus leaves or rosettes. The Greeks prized this order and reserved its use for the interiors of temples, their most sacred spots. The Romans placed Corinthian columns everywhere, including colonnades, where they could be seen and admired.[4] This difference in use helps us to determine whether a building was built by the Romans or the Greeks. When we look at a structure, such as the Maison Carrée (**fig 18.8**), and see the Corinthian columns along the colonnade, we can immediately identify it as Roman. Further research proves that it

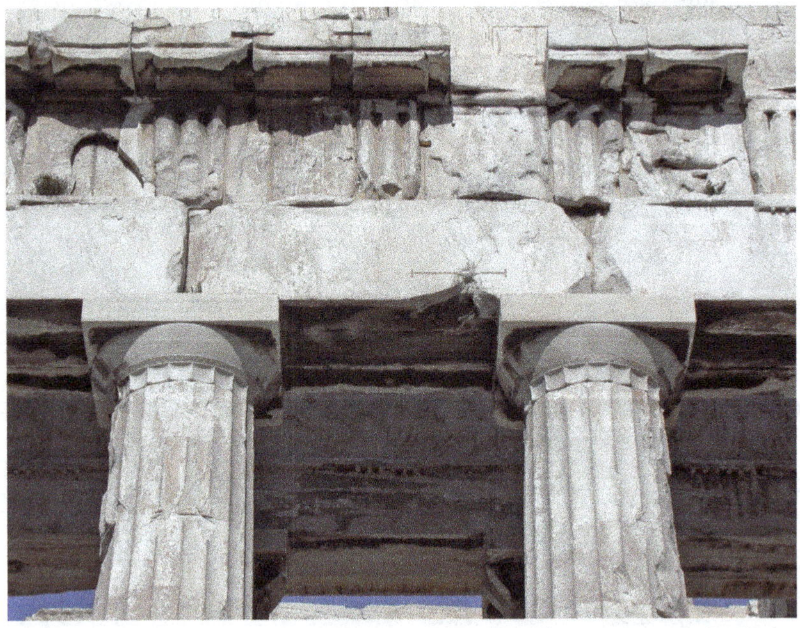

Figure 18.6: Kallikrates and Iktinos, Parthenon (Detail), 447–432 BCE. Greek, Akropolis, Athens.

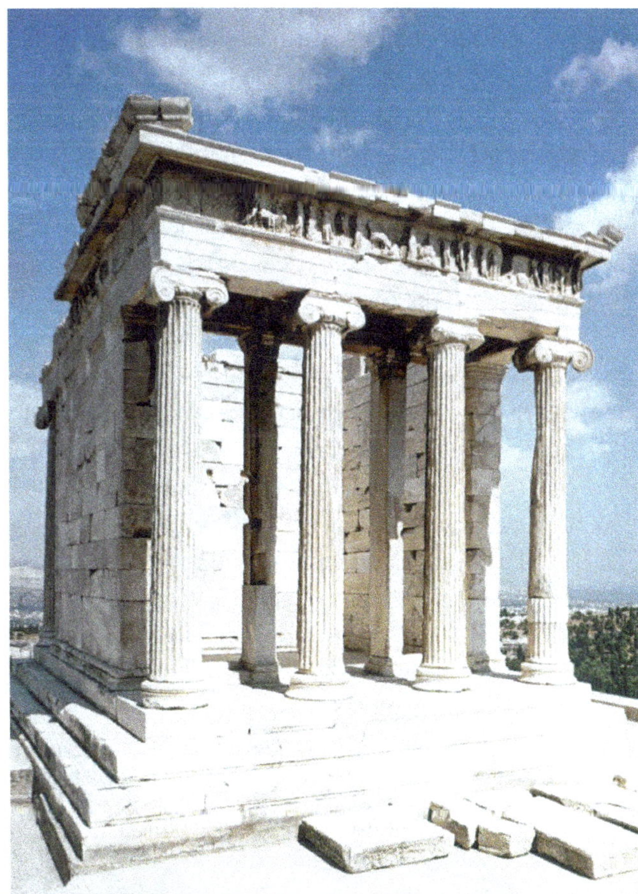

Figure 18.7: Kallikrates, Temple of Athena Nike, c. 425 BCE. Greek, Akropolis, Athens.

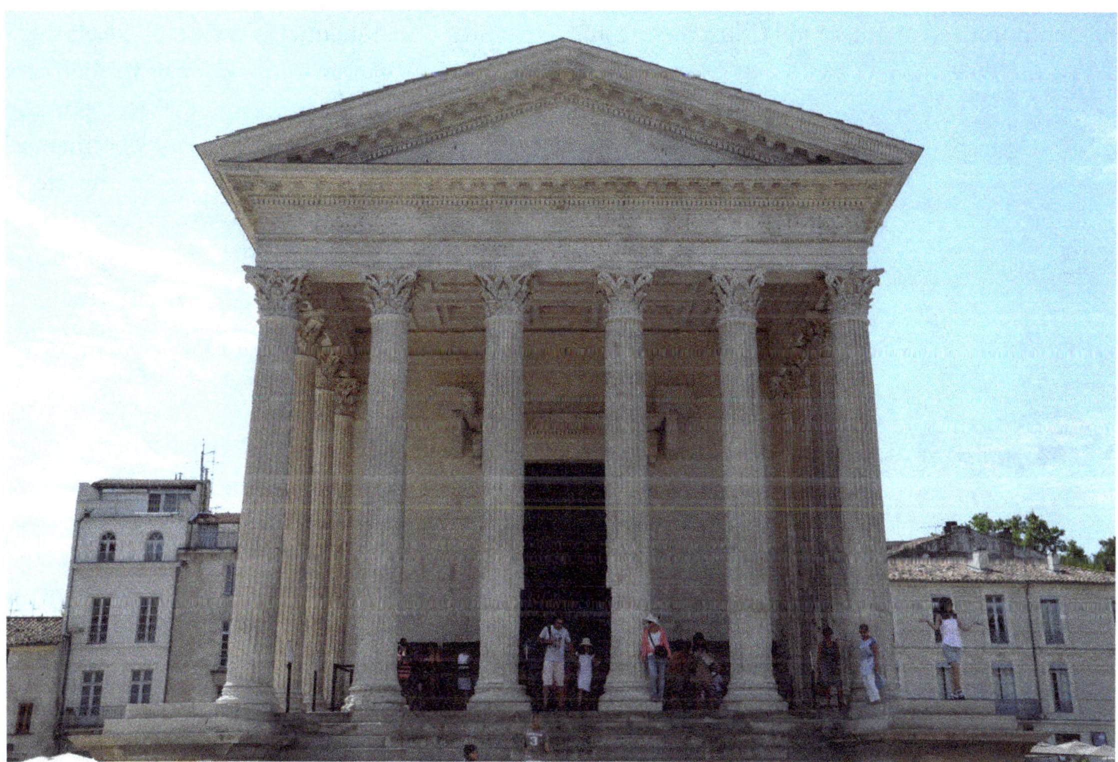

Figure 18.8: Maison Carrée, 1st Century BCE. Roman, Nîmes, France.

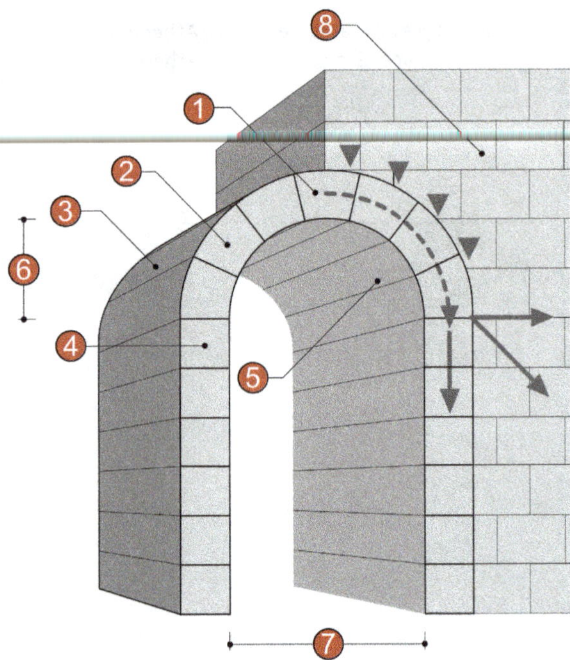

Figure 18.9: Segments of an Arch.

is indeed Roman, having been commissioned by Marcus Agrippa in the first century BCE.

ROMAN ARCHITECTURE

The Greeks gave us the orders of architecture, but it was the Romans that gave us the **arch**. The arch revolutionized architecture! Constructing an arch is pretty simple. Wedge-shaped stones called *voussoirs* (labeled 2 in **fig 18.9**) are fitted into place above posts, very similar to post-and-lintel construction. The last stone to go into place is the *keystone*, which sits at the center (labeled 1 in fig 18.9). The arch, as seen with corbeling earlier in this chapter, transmits the weight of the structure down its sides to the ground. The advantage of using an arch over corbeling is that it allows for much larger uninterrupted areas of space. You might be able to construct a room 15 to 20 feet in diameter with corbeling, but with arches spaces of 60 feet and larger in diameter could be formed without any visible means of support.

The first major building project to utilize arches was the Pont du Gard (**fig 18.10**) located in Nîmes, France. This is one of the most significant works of ancient architecture, as it marks man's mastery over nature. Up until this time in history, man had to live close to a water source. When we look at the Middle East, we see how cities grew along the Tigris and Euphrates rivers. In Egypt, cities grew along the Nile. The Romans were able to build the Pont du Gard and transport water over 20 miles from its source to where it was needed. The aqueduct is massive, measuring 150 feet in height and 800 feet across. The blocks themselves weigh up to two tons each and are fitted together without mortar (except for the top level, the actual aqueduct).

Arches are an extremely versatile tool for architects and can be used in several ways. By rotating an arch 360 degrees you can create a **dome** or hemisphere. The largest dome created in the ancient

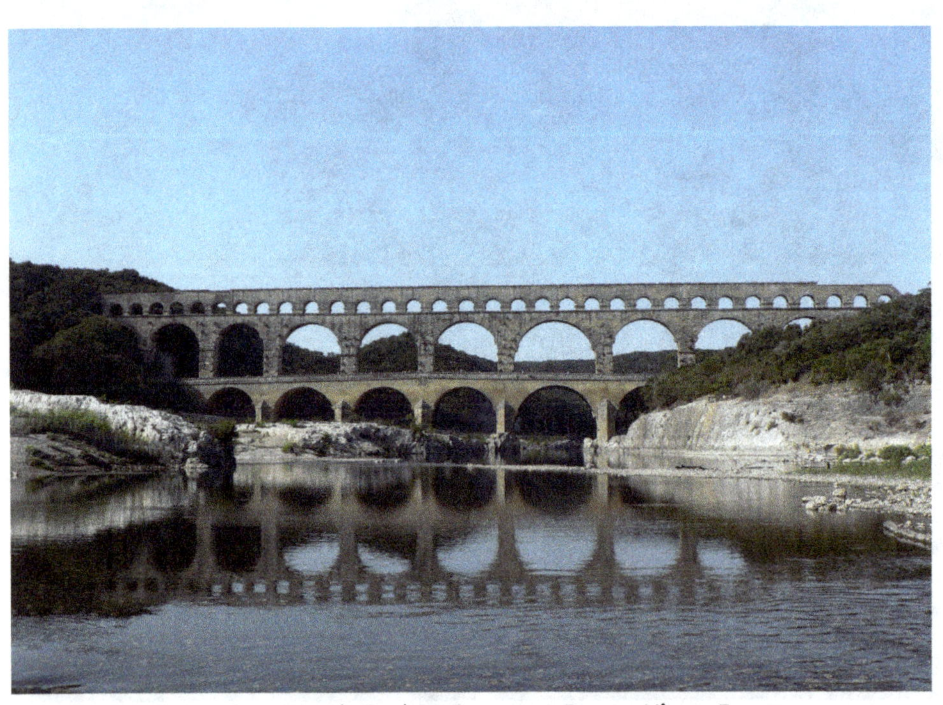

Figure 18.10: Pont du Gard, 1st Century CE. Roman, Nîmes, France.

world was the one that sits atop the Pantheon in Rome (**fig 18.11**). It measures 140 feet in diameter and is made from concrete. The weight of the dome is so great that the walls supporting it are 20 feet thick. No one was able to create another dome this large for the next 1,300 years, until the dome of the Florence Cathedral was completed in 1436 (see chapter 22).

Emperor Hadrian was responsible for the

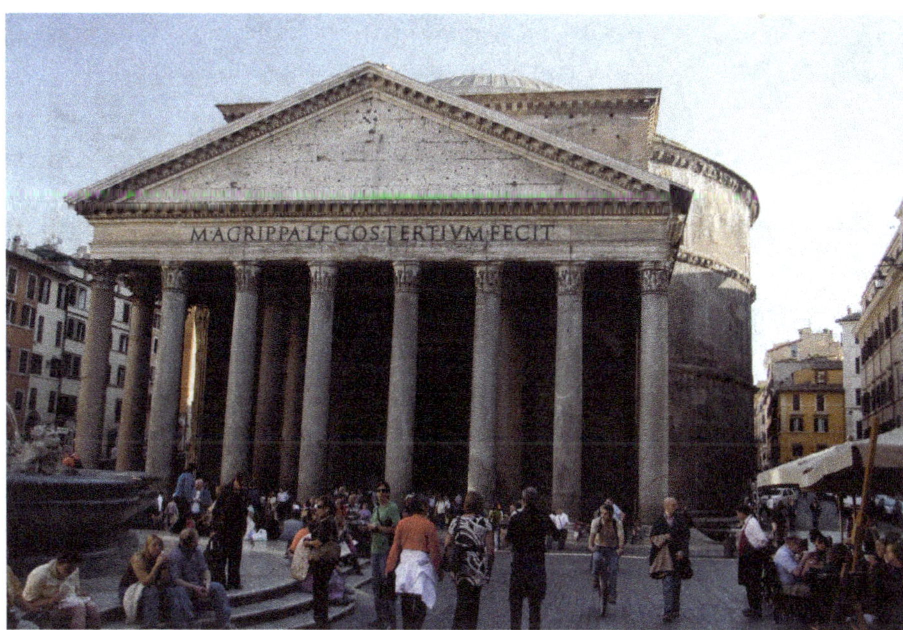

Figure 18.11: Pantheon, 118–128 CE. Roman, Rome, Italy.

construction of the Pantheon.[5] It was his favorite location at which to meet visiting diplomats.[6] During the Roman Empire you would enter the Pantheon through a narrow courtyard, which masked the curvature of the building. Visitors would feel as if they were entering through the front of a standard Greek temple, but once on the inside the space would open up into a gigantic circular room. In the center of the dome is the *oculus*, or "eye," of the building. This 27-foot opening serves as the light source for the building.[7]

Another large dome created during the Roman Empire was the one placed on the Hagia Sophia (**fig 18.12**). Construction of this church began in 532, which was commissioned by Emperor Justinian. What is different about this dome compared to the one on the Pantheon is that this dome sits atop a square building. The Pantheon is a circular building, and there is support for the dome along its circumference. With the dome of the Hagia Sophia being on a square building, the dome would only touch the edges of the structure in four specific places, and that would not be enough to support its weight. The solution was the

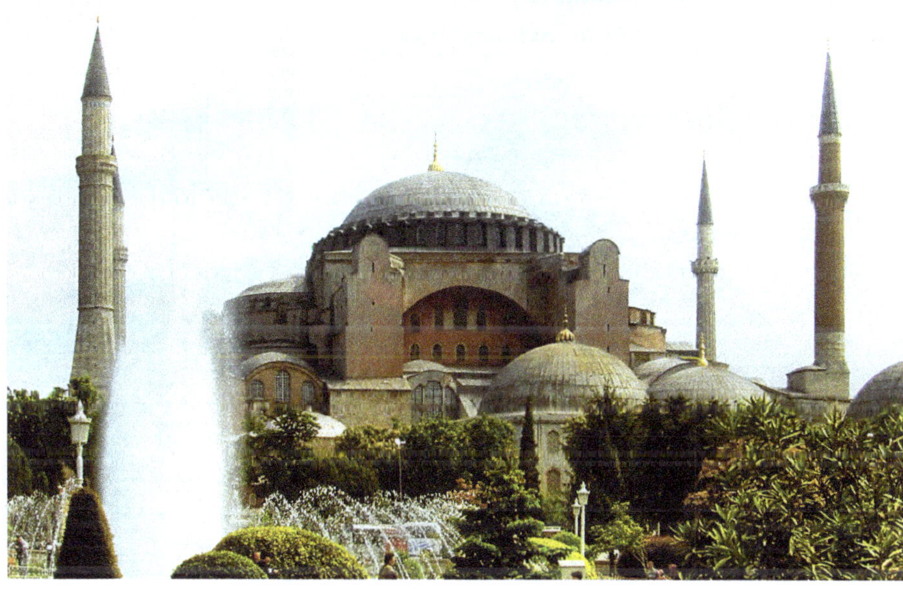

Figure 18.12: Anthemius of Tralles and Isidorus of Miletus, Hagia Sophia, 532–537. Byzantine, Istanbul (Constantinople), Turkey.

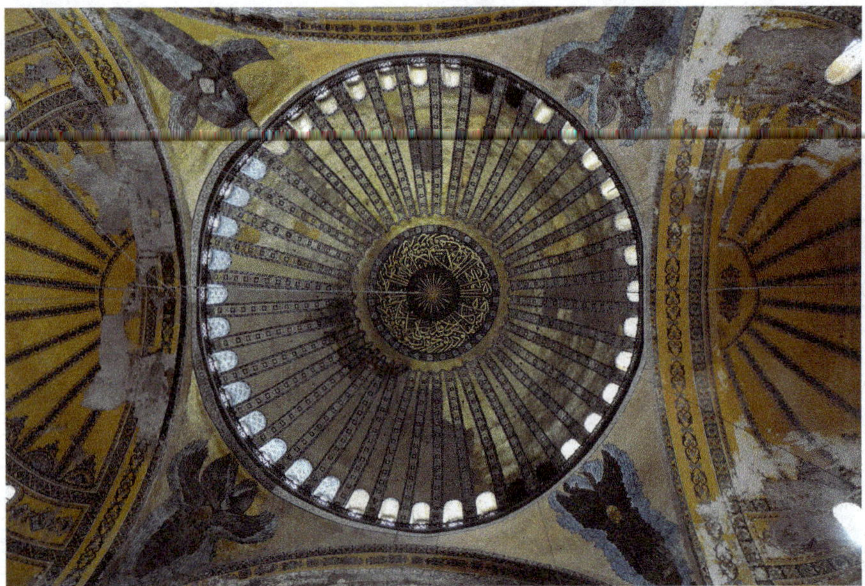

Figure 18.13: *Hagia Sophia* (pendentive).

development of a new form called a **pendentive** (**fig 18.13**). Pendentives are triangular inward-curving wall sections placed between arches in order to support a dome. This was the first time pendentives were used in a major building project.[8] It is still the way that domes are supported on square structures today.

MEDIEVAL ARCHITECTURE

If arches are lined up one after the other in a row they create a **barrel vault** (**fig 18.14**). These vaults were used as early as Roman times, but were used extensively in early Christian churches of the Romanesque and Gothic periods of the Middle Ages. The **nave** (**fig 18.15**), where the congregation sits, and the **transept**, the crossing or arms of the church, are created using barrel vaults.

Remember that arches provide large areas of uninterrupted space and that the weight of the structure is transmitted down the sides of the arch to the ground. You can see in both the barrel vault illustration (**fig 18.4**) and the Church of St. Mary Redcliffe (**fig 18.15**) that the arch is not rounded, but pointed. **Pointed arches**

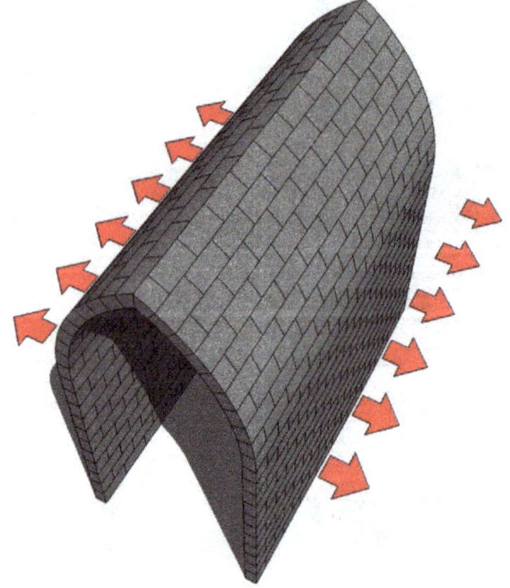

Figure 18.14: Barrel Vault.

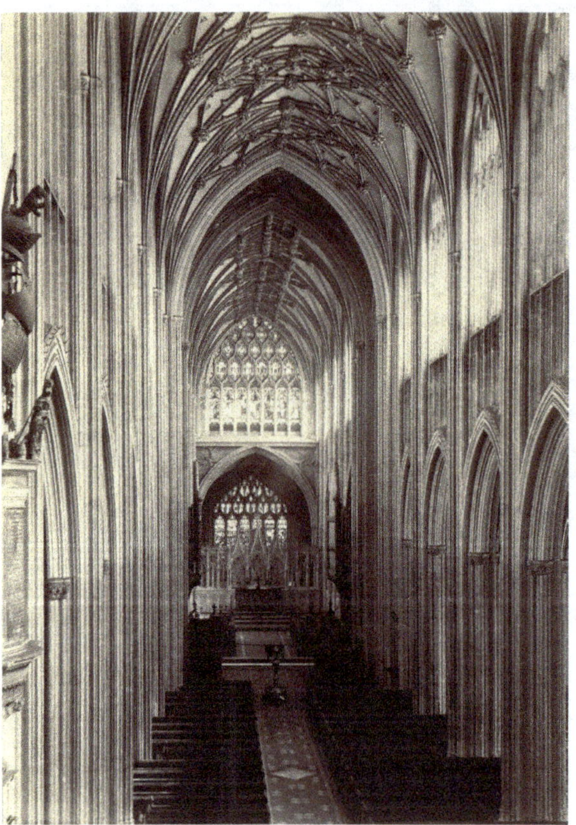

Figure 18.15: *Church of Saint Mary Redcliffe* (Nave), c. 1185–c. 1380. English Gothic, Bristol, England.

were invented in the Middle Ages. They allow for the building of even taller structures than the previously used rounded arches could permit. However, with pointed arches the weight descends to the ground more directly. In some cases it was too much pressure for the walls to handle, and several churches ended up collapsing under the strain.[9] In order to prevent the walls from collapsing, **flying buttresses (fig 18.16)** were invented. These features are defined as extensions of interior arches. They have very ornamental qualities, some similar in look to a spider's web, which added to the look of the Gothic age. Flying buttresses counteracted the stress points of the pointed arch by providing additional support and helped transmit the weight of the structure to the ground.

The final architectural element we will look at in this chapter is called a **tympanum**. These are semicircular relief sculptures that were placed above doorways to churches. The majority of people during the medieval period would have been illiterate, so these works told stories through icons. Tympanums would relate stories from the Bible, such as the *Last Judgment* (**fig 18.17**) by the artist Gislebertus. Christ is placed in the center of the work in hieratic scale. Beneath his feet is a row of figures who have been awakened and placed in line to be judged. To Christ's left is Saint Michael conducting the weighing of souls, while to his right are the saved.

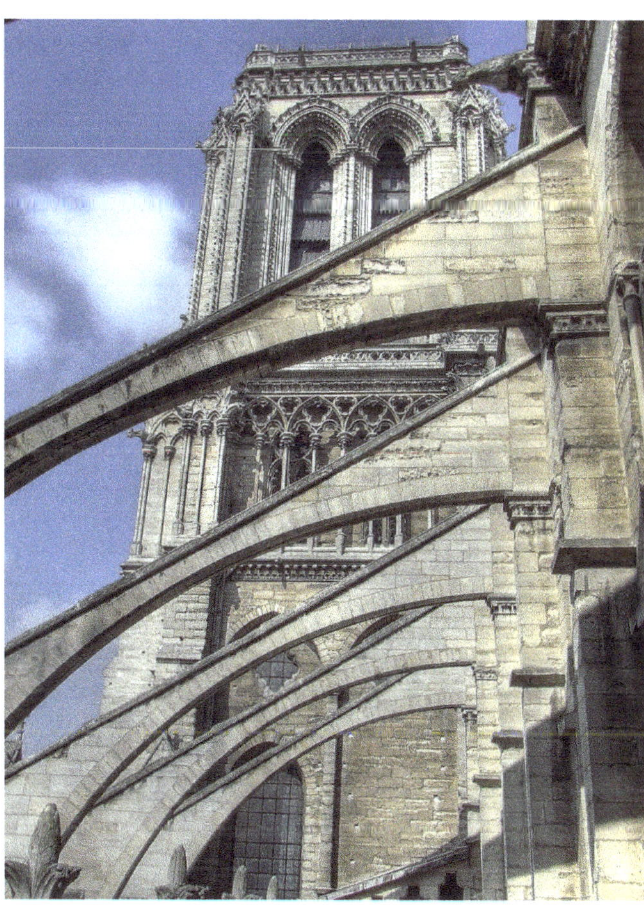

Figure 18.16: Notre Dame Cathedral (Flying Buttress), Begun c. 1215. French, Early Gothic, Paris, France.

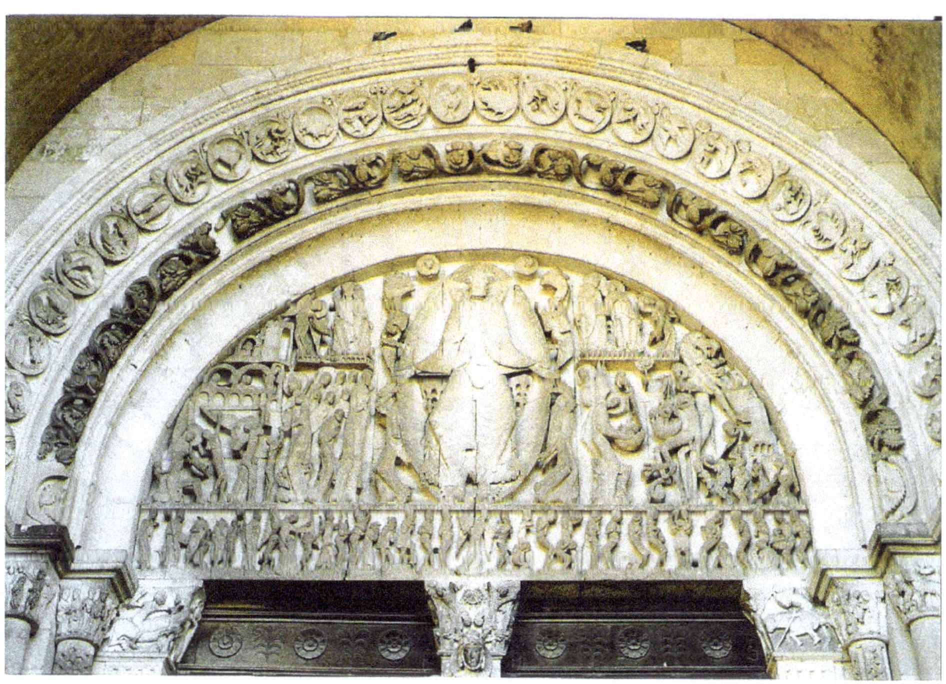

Figure 18.17: Gislebertus, *Last Judgment*, Tympanum from Cathedral of Saint-Lazare, c. 1120–35. 1970. Romanesque, Autun, France.

Shell system:

Corbeling:

Post and lintel:

Orders of Greek architecture:

Arches, barrel vaults, and domes:

Pendentives:

Naves and transepts:

Pointed arches and flying buttresses:

Tympanum:

ENDNOTES

1. Marilyn Stokstad, *Art History*, 5th ed. (New York: Harry N. Abrams, 2014), 4.
2. Marilyn Stokstad, *Art History*, revised ed. (New York: Harry N. Abrams, 1999), 50.
3. Marilyn Stokstad, *Art History*, revised ed. (New York: Harry N. Abrams, 1999), 165.
4. The colonnade is the outermost row of columns that run along the edge of a temple.
5. Khan Academy, "The Pantheon, Rome," https://youtu.be/KaY8zqYfQI0.
6. Khan Academy, "The Pantheon, Rome," https://youtu.be/KaY8zqYfQI0.
7. Fred Parker, "The Pantheon–Rome–126 AD," accessed August 14, 2016, http://www.monolithic.org/domes-more/the-pantheon-rome-126-ad.
8. Marilyn Stokstad, *Art History*, 5th ed. (New York: Harry N. Abrams, 2014), 236.
9. NOVA, "Building the Great Cathedrals," https://youtu.be/Lq1UXNjA3gQ.

IMAGE CREDITS

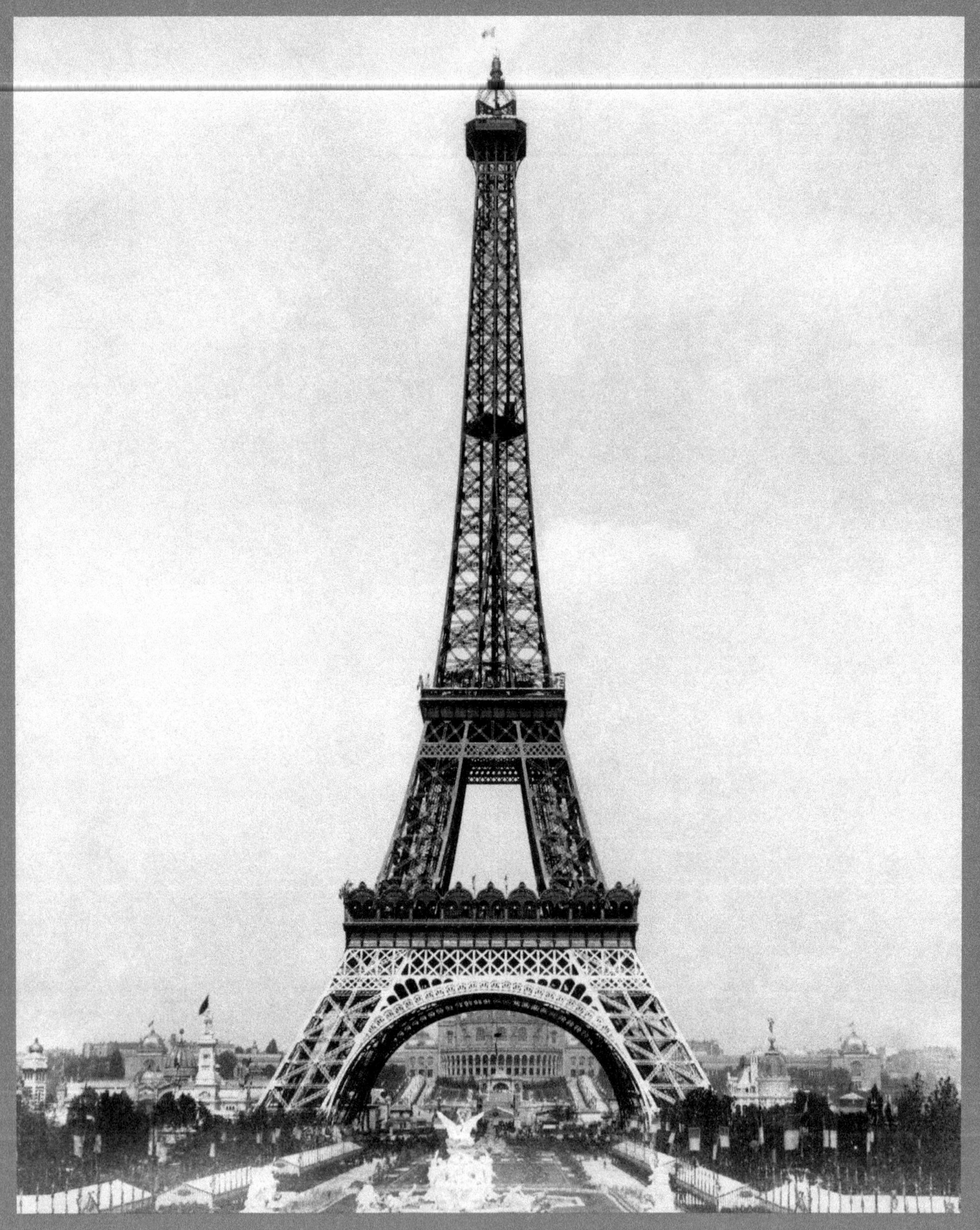

Figure 19.1: Gustave Eiffel, *Eiffel Tower*, 1887–89. Paris, France.

MODERN ARCHITECTURE

CHAPTER
19

In the previous chapter on ancient architecture, we learned that early architects built structures using the shell system. This meant that only one basic building material, such as limestone, would be used for both the building's structural support and the outer covering. With modern architecture, architects use a different construction system, called the **skeleton-and-skin system**. Here, a strong framing material, such as steel or cast-iron, is used for the structure's interior (*skeleton*) while another material, such as plaster or glass, is used for the building's exterior coating (*skin*).

The Crystal Palace (**fig 19.2**), located in London, was the first building constructed using this new method. It looked unlike any other building built up to that point. The recently invented cast-iron alloy was able to support the building, opening up the walls to allow for the tremendous amount of glass, its signature feature. The building featured more than 900,000 square feet of glass, which made it look somewhat like a greenhouse. That was no mistake, as the architect, Joseph Paxton, was a horticulturalist by trade.[1]

The purpose behind building the Crystal Palace was for it to serve as the venue for the very first World's Fair, which took place in 1851. The building was constructed for the event in a period of just over six months, and it served as a symbol of England's industrial might.[2]

As amazing as this new architecture was, not everyone was on board with the look of these

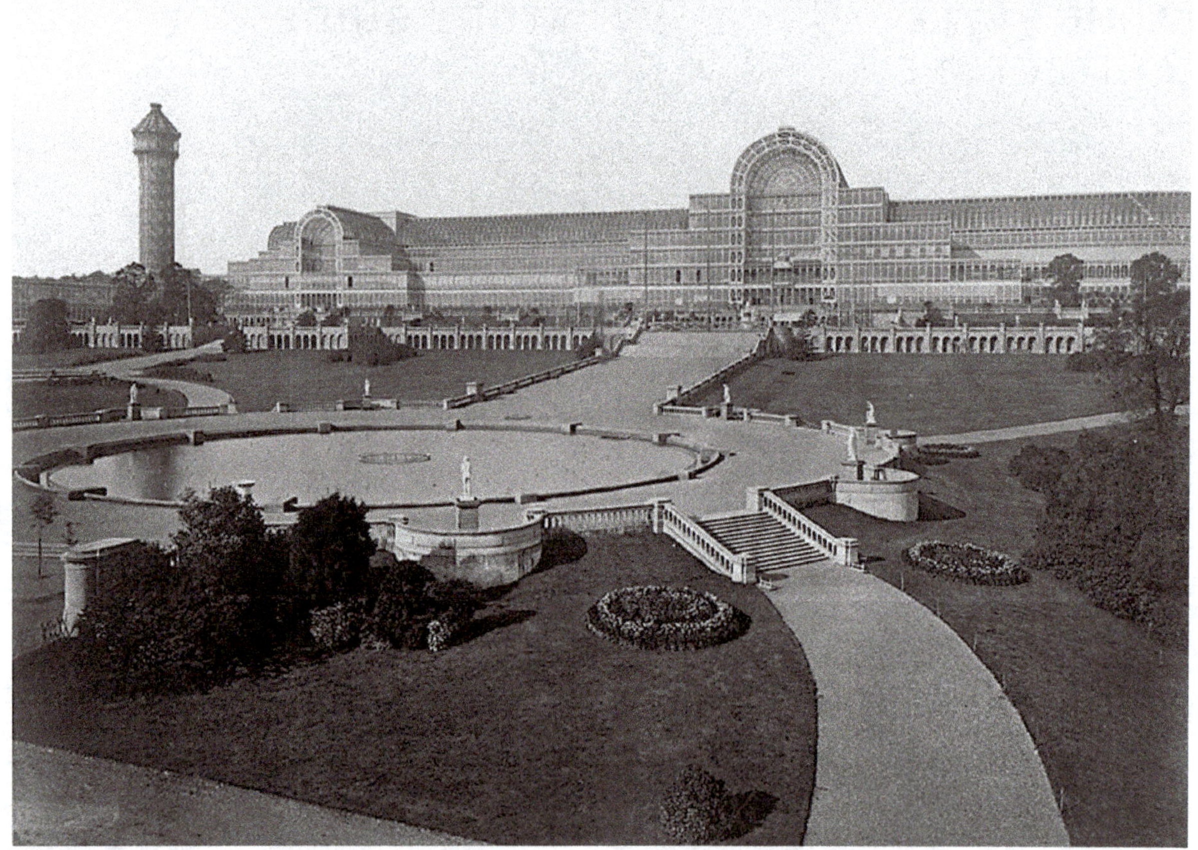

Figure 19.2: Joseph Paxton, Crystal Palace, 1850–51. London, England.

new modern buildings. Among these people was William Morris, who, along with Philip Webb, built the Red House (**fig 19.3**). This home was constructed eight years after Paxton had completed the Crystal Palace. The Red House serves as an example of Gothic Revival architecture, a return to simplicity and craftsmanship. We will learn more about Morris and his followers in the chapter entitled "Design Styles, 1850–1950," which covers the Arts and Crafts movement.

Probably the most famous structure of modern architecture is the Eiffel Tower. It was constructed to serve as the entrance gateway to the Exposition Universelle of 1889. It was originally intended to be a temporary structure, lasting for only 20 years, but it has become a permanent fixture of the Paris skyline.[3] The tower allows us to see the skeletal framework of the skeleton-and-skin system.

While it is hard to imagine Paris without the tower today, when it was first constructed people despised it. A group of artists circulated a petition stating, "We [the] writers, painters, sculptors, architects, lovers of the beauty of Paris … do protest with all our strength and indignation … against the [building], in the very heart of our capital, of the useless and monstrous, Eiffel Tower … this odious column of bolted metal."[4] French politician Pierre Tirard went further, stating that it was "a project more in character with America, where taste is not yet very developed."[5]

At its completion it became the world's tallest building, nearly doubling the record of its predecessor, the Washington Monument. America would recapture the title of constructing the world's tallest building in the early twentieth century with the completion of the Chrysler Building (not pictured) in New York.

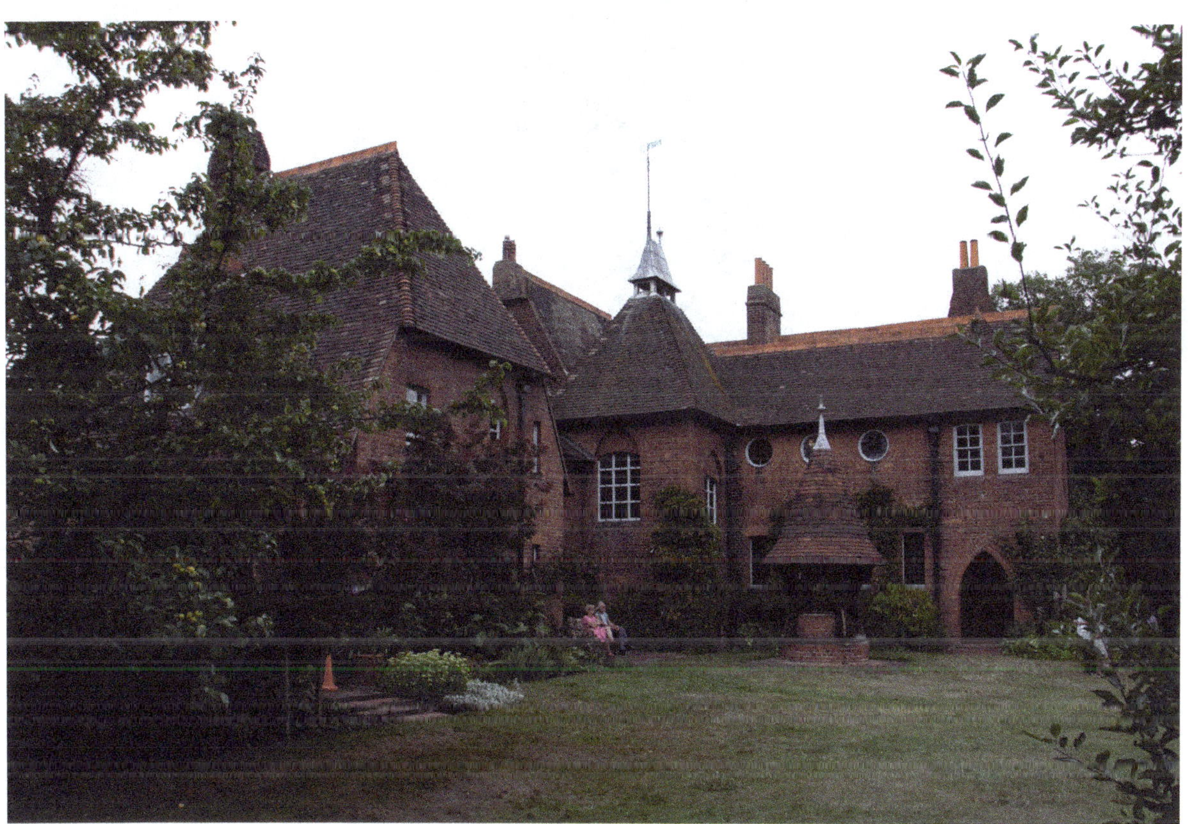

Figure 19.3: Philip Webb and William Morris, The Red House, 1859–60. Kent, England.

MODERN ARCHITECTURE IN AMERICA

Although the first modern structures were built in Europe, modern architecture established a foothold in America.[6] The city of Chicago is considered the birthplace of modern architecture in the United States. There are several reasons for this. First, the Great Chicago Fire of 1871 destroyed the entire downtown area, leaving architects with a clean slate to build upon. Second, city planners employed a gridlike road system. And finally, there were no significant historical monuments that would have gotten in the way of construction, as was an issue in many parts of Europe.

Among the first skyscrapers to be built in Chicago was the Marshall Field's Wholesale Store (**fig 19.4**). It looked nothing like the skyscrapers we have today, as it was heavy and bulky, rather than sleek and slender. It did not transcend its environment. What then made this building so modern? The skeleton of this structure was similar to that of the Crystal Palace in that it used cast-iron columns to support the weight of the floors and wrought-iron beams to provide large uninterrupted interior spaces.[7] However, the exterior walls were weight-bearing and created using large sandstone blocks. This made the structure look more like a traditional building, weighing it down to the city block that it occupied.

During the decade following the completion of the Marshall Field's Wholesale Store, skyscrapers began taking on their more familiar

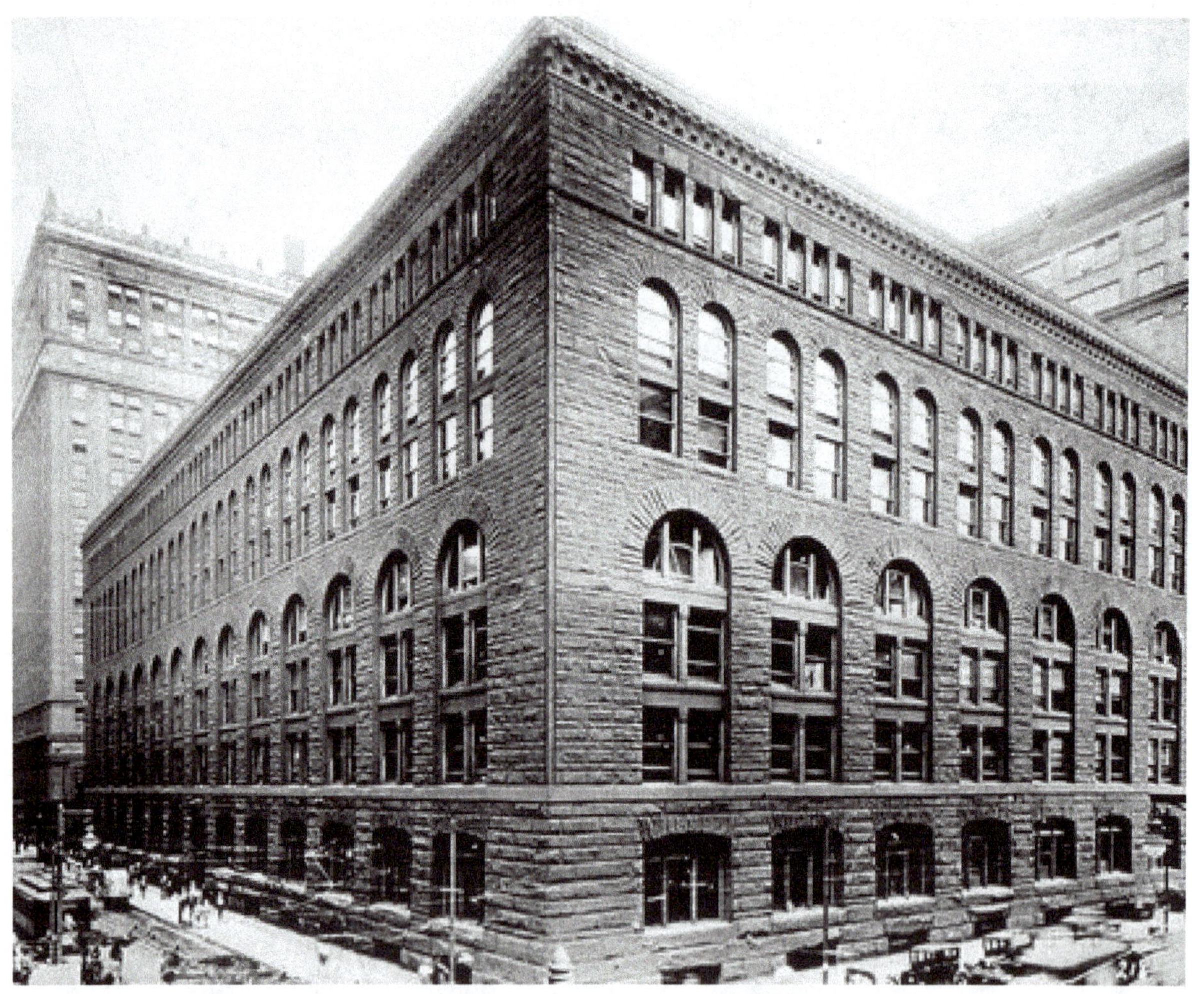

Figure 19.4: Henry Hobson Richardson Marshall Field Wholesale Store 1885–87 (demolished c. 1935). Chicago, Illinois.

shape. One of America's leading architects, Louis Sullivan, worked with a standard design seen in the Guaranty Trust Building (**fig 19.5**): retail shops would occupy the ground floor, above that a mezzanine level, then several floors of office space, and then the building would be capped off by an attic. What is unique to Sullivan's buildings is the tremendous amount of ornamental detail. Instead of hiding the structural elements of the building, he enhanced them. This beauty that Sullivan invoked on the exterior of his buildings confirmed his belief that "the primary function of a building was to elevate the spirit of those who worked in it."[8]

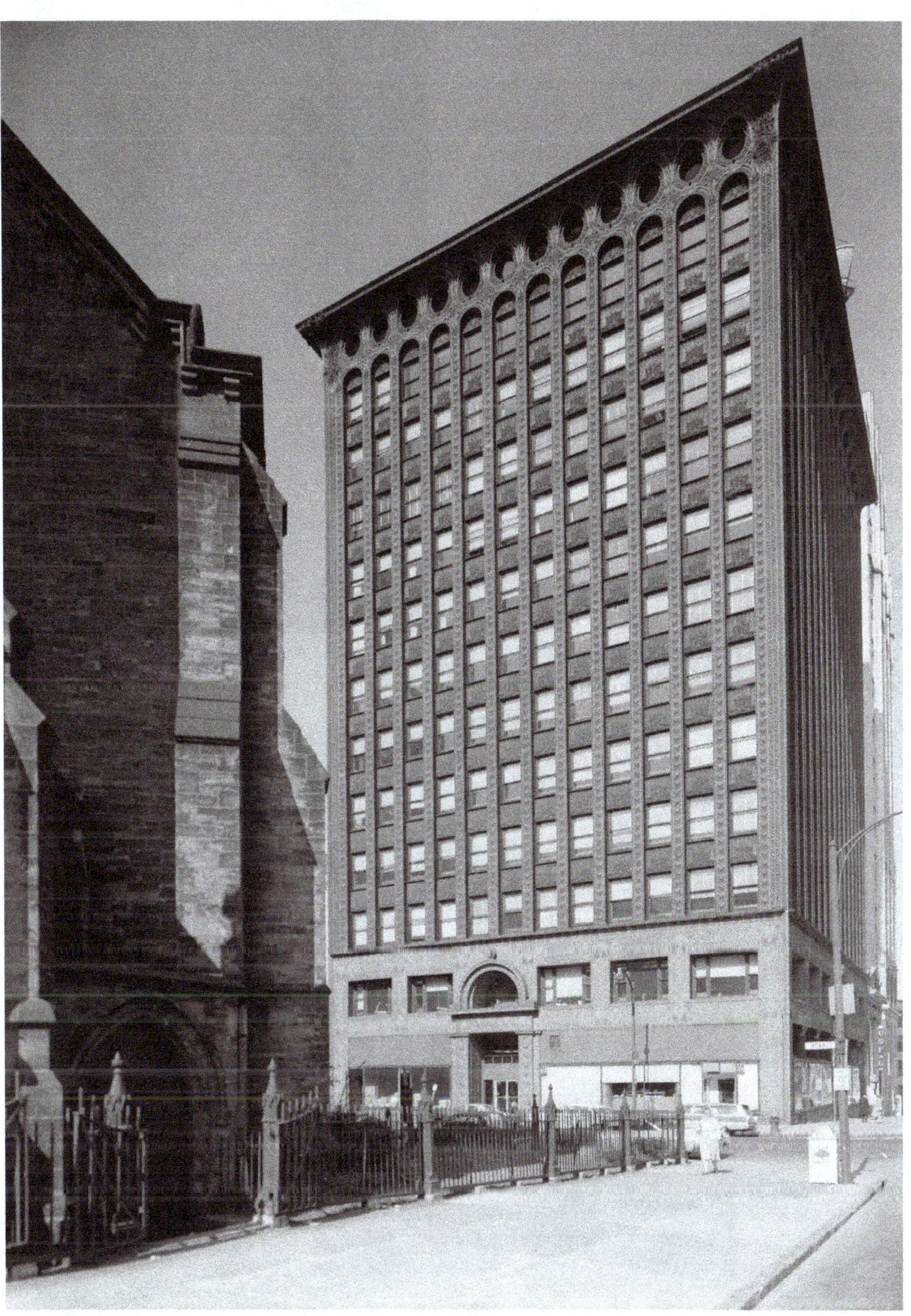

Figure 19.5: Louis Sullivan, *Guaranty Trust Building* (Prudential Building) 1894–95. Buffalo, New York.

As important as Sullivan's buildings are to the history of architecture, he has an infamous claim to fame that falls in the category of human resources. He fired an employee, a draftsman, by the name of Frank Lloyd Wright (**fig 19.6**).[9] Wright would of course go on to become the most famous American architect of the twentieth century, having a long and distinguished career. Wright was born shortly after the Civil War and designed his first residential house in 1902–1903, the Ward Willits House. This home features some of the common characteristics seen in Wright's later designs. These characteristics include a strong horizontal element, as well as a hip roof, where each of the four sides of the roof slope down, compared to the common gable roof, which slopes on two sides, similar to a camping tent.

In 1910 Frank Lloyd Wright would complete the Robie House (**fig 19.7**). This home for Frederick C. Robie is considered the epitome of **Prairie style architecture**. The homes created in this style echo the look of their neighboring Midwestern prairies. The cantilevered roof is one of the most poignant elements of this home, as it seemingly juts out into space without any visible means of support. There is also a preponderance of windows that let in natural light, keeping artificial light to a minimum. Today, the Robie House is a National Historic Landmark.

Many of the modern architects, such as Frank Lloyd Wright,

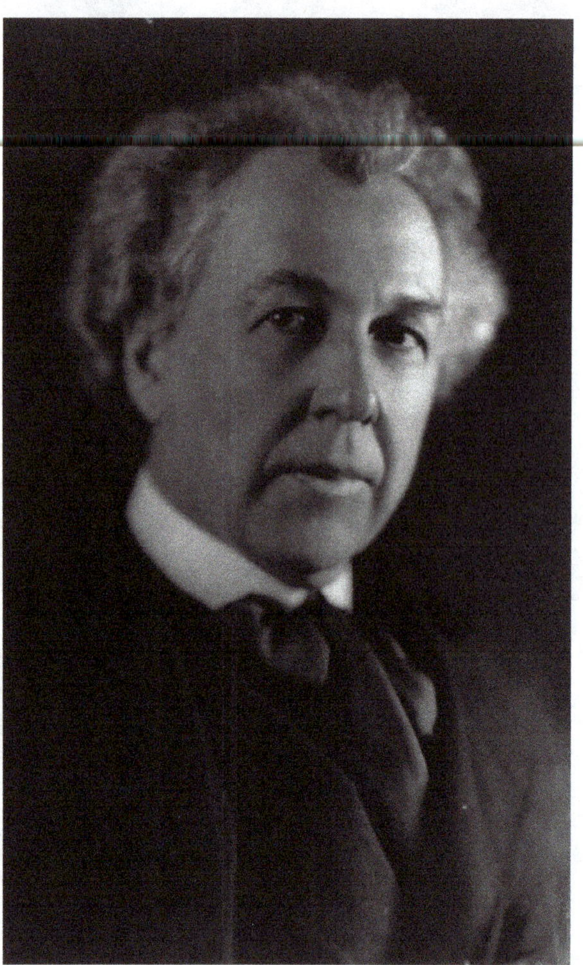

Figure 19.6: Frank Lloyd Wright.

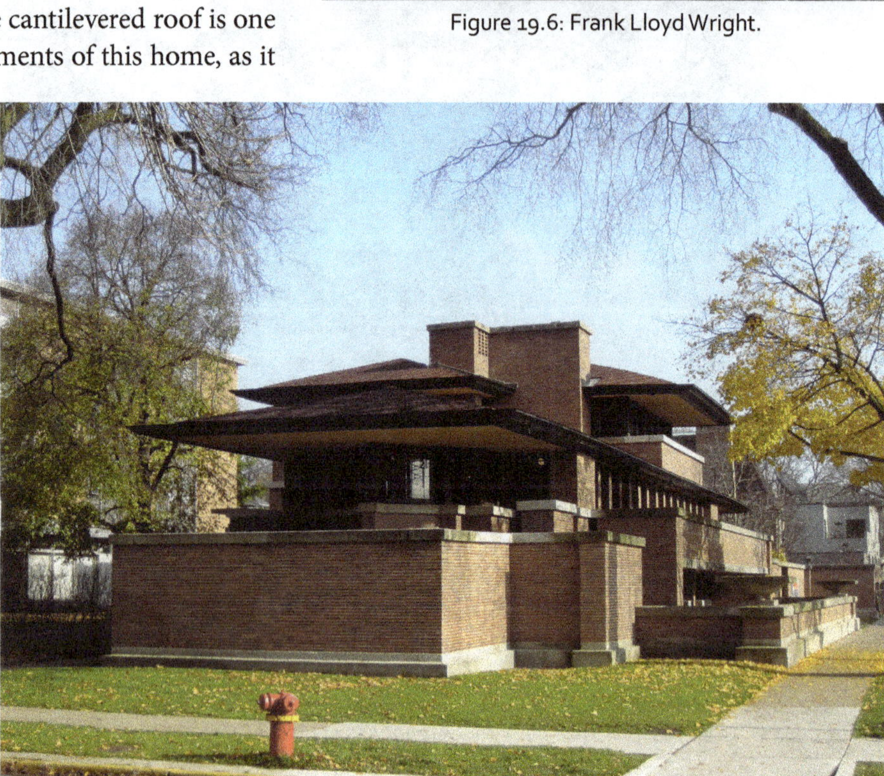

Figure 19.7: Frank Lloyd Wright, Robie House, 1908–10. Chicago, Illinois.

Antonio Gaudi, and Rudolph Schindler, would also be forced to design the furniture for their homes, because the furniture that was available in stores did not match the style of these new, modern buildings.

The Robie House and other buildings that Frank Lloyd Wright designed tend to have an Eastern sensibility to them. Wright worked on several commissions in Japan in the early part of the twentieth century when he had a difficult time getting work in America. With Eastern art the center of the work is where the artist normally begins, and then works outward. Wright begins his designs with the fireplace, or hearth, at the center of the home and works outward. He considers the area around the fireplace as the "spiritual and psychological center of the house," a place where family interaction occurs.[10]

The troubling aspect of architecture, especially modern architecture, is that people seem so eager to destroy it. People go to great lengths to preserve and protect other forms of art, such as painting or sculpture. Think of the restoration effort given to Leonardo da Vinci's *The Last Supper* (see fig 22.8). It went through an extensive 20-year restoration beginning in 1979 and ending in 1999.

Built in 1904, Wright's Larkin Building (**fig 19.8**), was a fortress-like complex from the outside. The inside contained a center atrium that rose unobstructed through its five stories to the ceiling's skylights, with office space situated around the building's perimeter. This was the first building to be specifically designed for air conditioning.[11] It was demolished in 1950. Also destroyed was Wright's Imperial Hotel in Tokyo

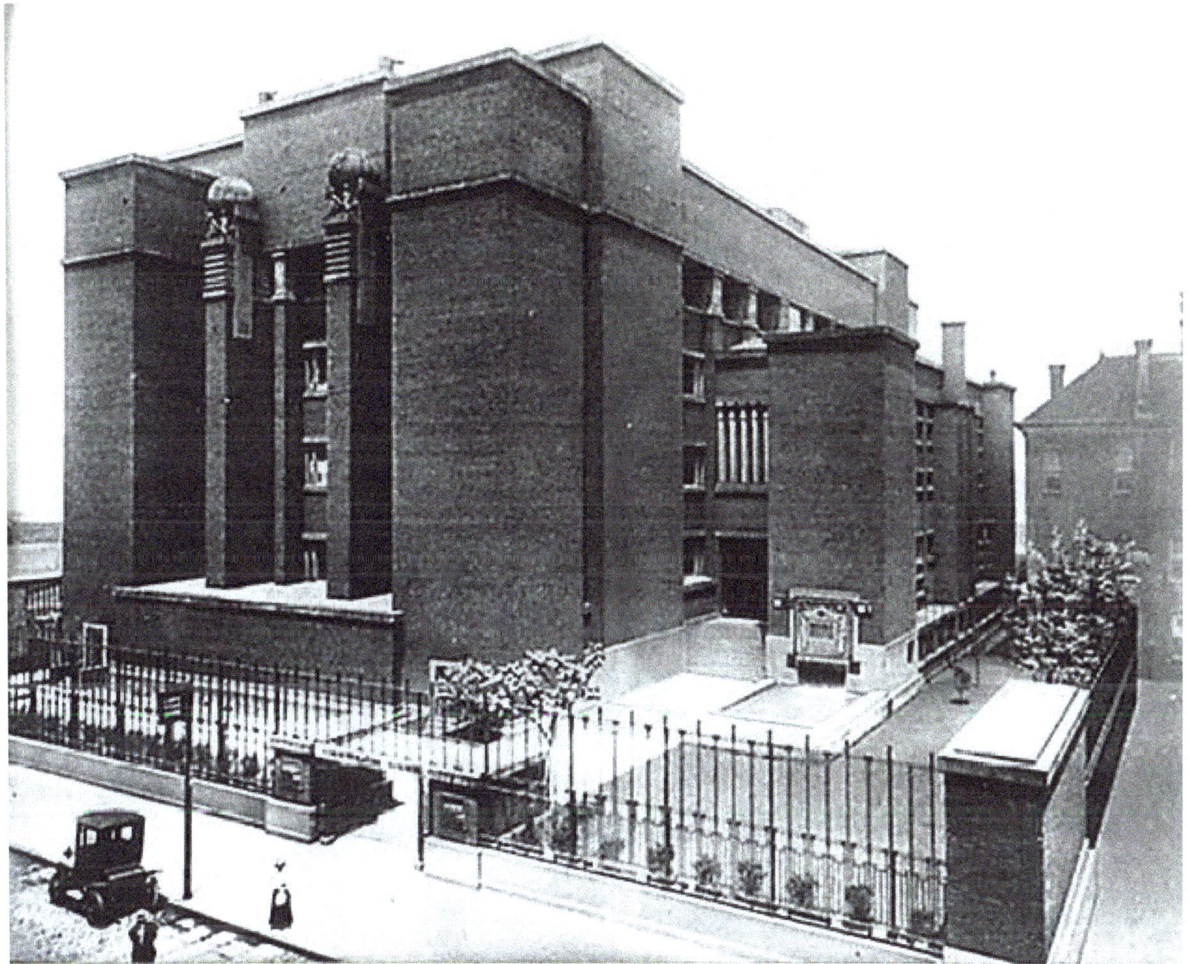

Figure 19.8: Frank Lloyd Wright The Larkin Building, 1904 (demolished 1950). Buffalo, New York.

(see fig 9.3). Part of this structure has been relocated and preserved.

The pinnacle of Frank Lloyd Wright's architectural accomplishments can be found with Fallingwater (**fig 19.9**). Built in Bear Run, Pennsylvania, it served as a summer retreat for Edgar J. Kaufman, whose family owned the land. Kaufman had fond memories of this place from vacationing there when he was a child and commissioned Wright, then in his 60s, to design this summer home. Several plans were passed over that situated the home on one side of the river and then the other. They finally decided that the home's resting place would be on top of the river and falls. The home is supported by six large "I" beams that span the river. Natural elements, such as boulders, were incorporated into the structure in such a way as to help anchor the home to the land.

Besides the proximity to the water, the other unique factor of Fallingwater is the cantilevered terraces. The home itself seems to look like several interconnected trays. Some of the terraces reach out 18 feet. The construction workers, and even Kaufmann himself, questioned the sustainability of these elements, which infuriated Wright.[12]

According to the Fallingwater website, over 4.5 million people have visited the home,[13] including celebrities such as Tom Hanks, Ron Howard, Angelina Jolie, Brad Pitt, and Christopher Nolan. Like the Robie House, Fallingwater is also a National Historic Landmark.

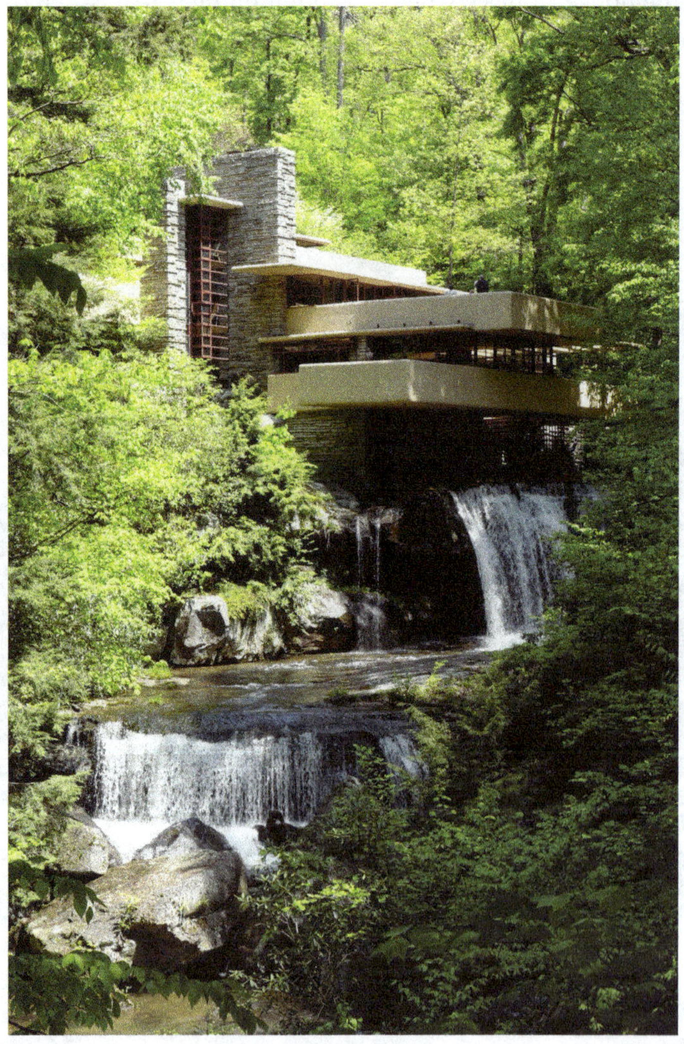

Figure 19.9: Frank Lloyd Wright, Fallingwater, 1934–37. Bear Run, Pennsylvania.

INTERNATIONAL STYLE ARCHITECTURE

While all these wonderful buildings were being produced in America, let us take a moment to look back at Europe to see how modern architecture was evolving in the early part of the twentieth century. The **International Style** became the dominant force of European architecture during the 1920s and 1930s. The International Style is characterized by seven components, all of which are seen in the Villa Savoye (**fig 19.10**), which is located in France. The first notable feature of this home are the *pilotis*. These are the slender columns placed around the perimeter of the home, very similar to how Greek columns would be placed along the colonnade. Because the columns look as if they support the home, we consider the façade to be non-weight-bearing or free-floating. The windows along the second story are called *ribbon windows*. The home has an open floor plan, which means that there are few walls, so that family interaction is encouraged. We know immediately that Louis Sullivan would not have built nor cared much for this home, as there is no ornamentation upon its exterior. Buildings done in the International Style have a rather bland look to them in terms of color, usually being painted white or beige. The rooftop garden is the final element that signifies the International Style. The curved wall feature on the roof—the Villa Savoye's most notable feature—mimics the sail of a vessel.

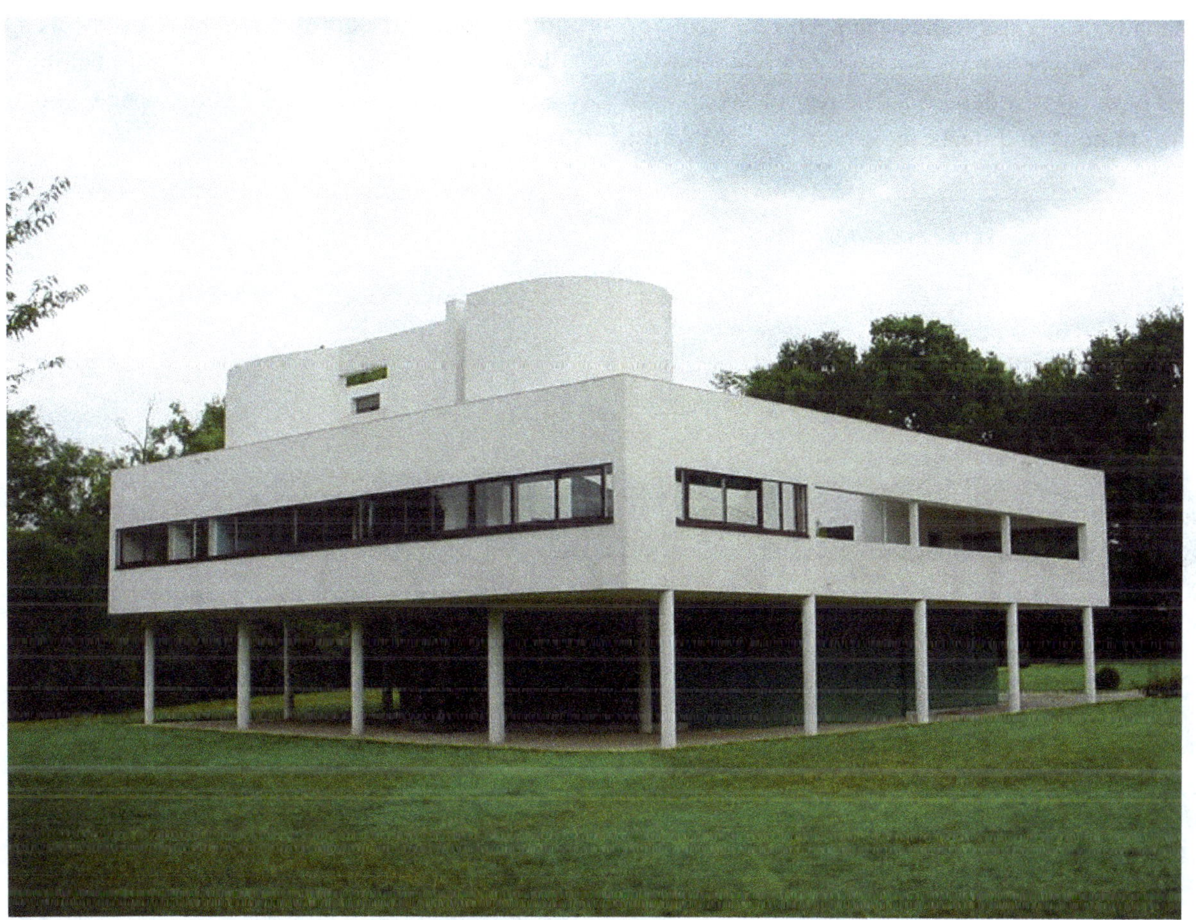

Figure 19.10: Le Corbusier, Villa Savoye, 1928–30. Poissy-sur-Seine, France.

CASE STUDY HOUSE PROJECT

The **Case Study House Project** ran from 1945 to 1966. These were experiments in residential architecture. World War II had ended and there was a housing shortage, so builders were looking for home designs that could be built quickly with readily available and economical materials. A total of 36 designs were created, but the program shouldn't be considered a success, as none of the designs were carried out in terms of mass housing. What we are left with throughout Southern California are incredible examples of unique modern houses. Of the 36 designs, roughly 24 homes were constructed. Some of these homes have seen extensive remodeling that has transformed their original design. An example of this is Case Study House #15 in La Cañada. The glass walls have been removed, and the home's square footage has been nearly doubled as rooms have been added on to the rear of the house.[14] Several famous architects took part in this project, including Charles and Ray Eames, Pierre Koenig, and Richard Neutra.

The most famous of the Case Study Houses is #22 (**fig 19.11**), which sits atop a hill overlooking the Los Angeles basin.[15] The 280-degree view on a clear day is amazing! The photograph provided in this book only shows the kitchen and living room, the most famous parts of the house. The home is "L" shaped, and the two bedroom areas are located just to the left of the pool. One side of the rooms is glass; the other side faces the street and is a solid wall. The front of the house, facing the street, is nothing more than windowless aluminum siding. The house does not have a garage, but the carport holds two cars comfortably. Due to building codes, a home like this could no longer be constructed in Los Angeles. This makes this home a gem in the community. Many movies, television shows, and photo shoots have used this site as a location and backdrop. Like Wright's Fallingwater, CSH #22 has a website, Facebook page, and offers tours to the public.

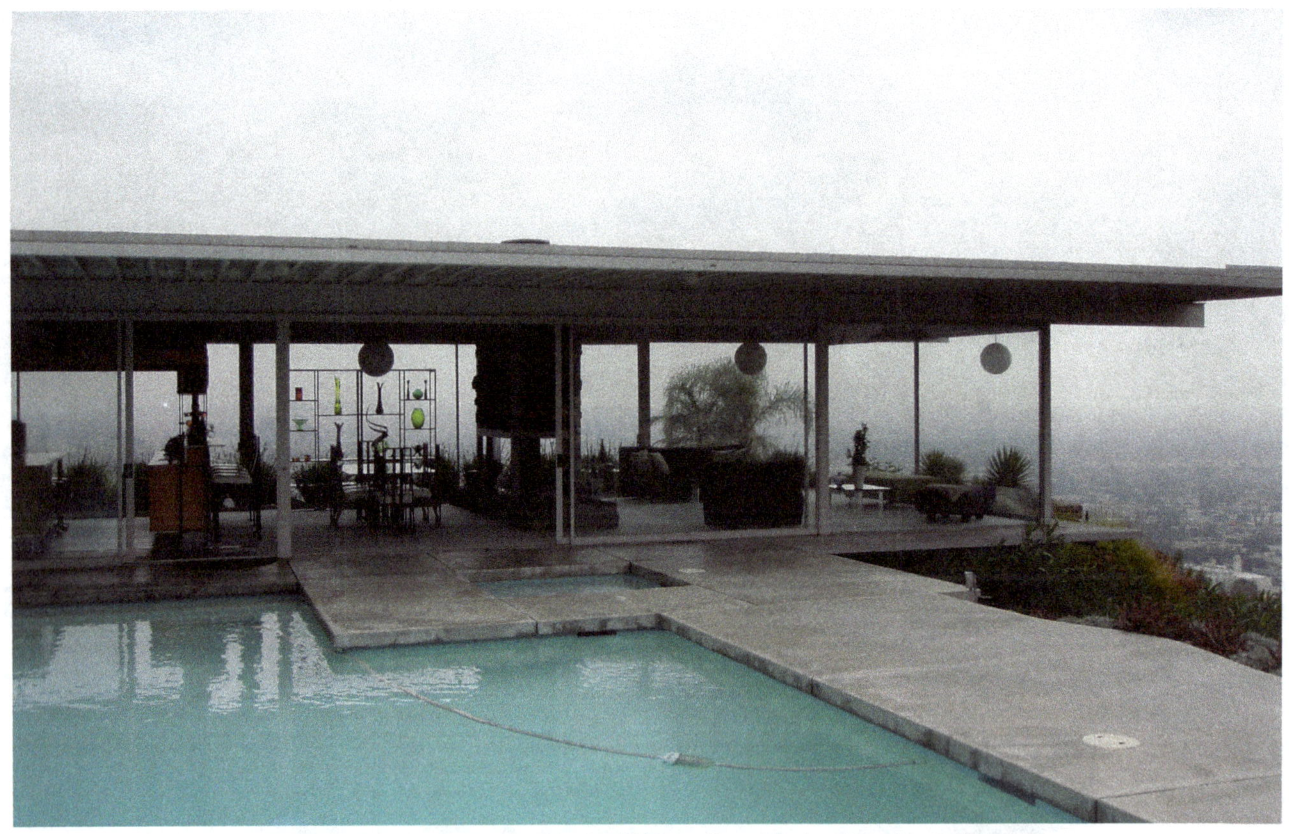

Figure 19.11: Pierre Koenig, *Case Study House #22* 1959, Los Angeles, California.

Skeleton-and-skin system:

Prairie style architecture:

International style architecture:

Case Study House Project:

ENDNOTES

1. William J. R. Curtis, *Modern Architecture Since 1900*, 3rd ed. (New York: Phaiden, 1996), 36.
2. Marilyn Stokstad, *Art History*, revised ed. (New York: Harry N. Abrams, 1999), 980.
3. Jill Jones, *Eiffel's Tower* (New York: Viking, 2009), 22.
4. Elaine Sciolino, *La Seduction: How the French Play the Game of Life* (New York: Times Books, 2011), 66.
5. Jill Jones, *Eiffel's Tower* (New York: Viking, 2009), 23.
6. It is an interesting juxtaposition that Americans embraced modern architecture while simultaneously rejecting modern art, as seen in the reception of the Armory Show of 1913.
7. William J. R. Curtis, *Modern Architecture Since 1900*, 3rd ed. (New York: Phaiden, 1996), 42.
8. Henry Sayre, *A World of Art*, 7th ed. (Boston: Prentice Hall, 2013), 377.
9. Marilyn Stokstad, *Art History*, revised ed. (New York: Harry N. Abrams, Inc., 1999), 1067.
10. H. H. Arnason and Elizabeth Mansfield, *History of Modern Art*, 7th ed. (Upper Saddle River, NJ: Pearson Education, 2013), 173.
11. Great Achievements, "Air Conditioning and Refrigeration Timeline," accessed August 31, 2016, http://www.greatachievements.org/?id=3854.
12. Henry Sayre, *A World of Art*, 7th ed. (Boston: Prentice Hall, 2013), 378–379.
13. Fallingwater, "Fallingwater Facts, House," accessed August, 31, 2016, http://www.fallingwater.org/38/fallingwater-facts.
14. Personal interview with the owners.
15. The home is also known as the Stahl home. This is the name of the original owners, and it is still held by the family although they do not live there.

IMAGE CREDITS

- Fig. 19.1: Gustave Eiffel, "Eiffel Tower," https://commons.wikimedia.org/wiki/File:Tour_Eiffel_3c02660.jpg. Copyright in the Public Domain.
- Fig. 19.2: Joseph Paxton; Photo by Philip Henry Delamotte, "Crystal Palace," https://commons.wikimedia.org/wiki/File:Crystal_Palace_General_view_from_Water_Temple.jpg. Copyright in the Public Domain.
- Fig. 19.3: Copyright © Philip Webb and William Morris; Photo by Tony Hisgett (CC by 2.0) at https://commons.wikimedia.org/wiki/File:Red_House_home_of_William_Morris_(1).jpg.
- Fig. 19.4: Henry Hobson Richardson, "Marshall Fields Wholesale Store," https://commons.wikimedia.org/wiki/File:Marshall_Field_Warehouse_Store.jpg. Copyright in the Public Domain.
- Fig. 19.5: Louis Sullivan; Photo by Jack E. Boucher, "Guaranty Trust Building (AKA Prudential Building)," https://commons.wikimedia.org/wiki/File:Prudential_buffalo_louis_sullivan.jpg. Copyright in the Public Domain.
- Fig. 19.6: "Frank Lloyd Wright," https://commons.wikimedia.org/wiki/File:Frank_Lloyd_Wright_LC-USZ62-36384.jpg. Copyright in the Public Domain.
- Fig. 19.7: Copyright © Frank Lloyd Wright; Photoby Teemu08 (CC BY-SA 3.0) at https://commons.wikimedia.org/wiki/File:Frederick_C._Robie_House.JPG.
- Fig. 19.8: Frank Lloyd Wright, "The Larkin Building," https://commons.wikimedia.org/wiki/File:LarkinAdministrationBuilding1906.jpg. Copyright in the Public Domain.
- Fig. 19.9: Frank Lloyd Wright; Photo by Daderot, "Fallingwater," https://commons.wikimedia.org/wiki/File:Fallingwater_-_DSC05639.JPG. Copyright in the Public Domain.
- Fig. 19.10: Copyright © Le Corbusier; Photo by Valueyou (CC BY-SA 3.0) at https://en.wikipedia.org/wiki/File:VillaSavoye.jpg.
- Fig. 19.11: Pierre Koenig; Photo by Ovs, "Case Study House #22," https://commons.wikimedia.org/wiki/File:Case_Study_House_No._22.JPG. Copyright in the Public Domain.

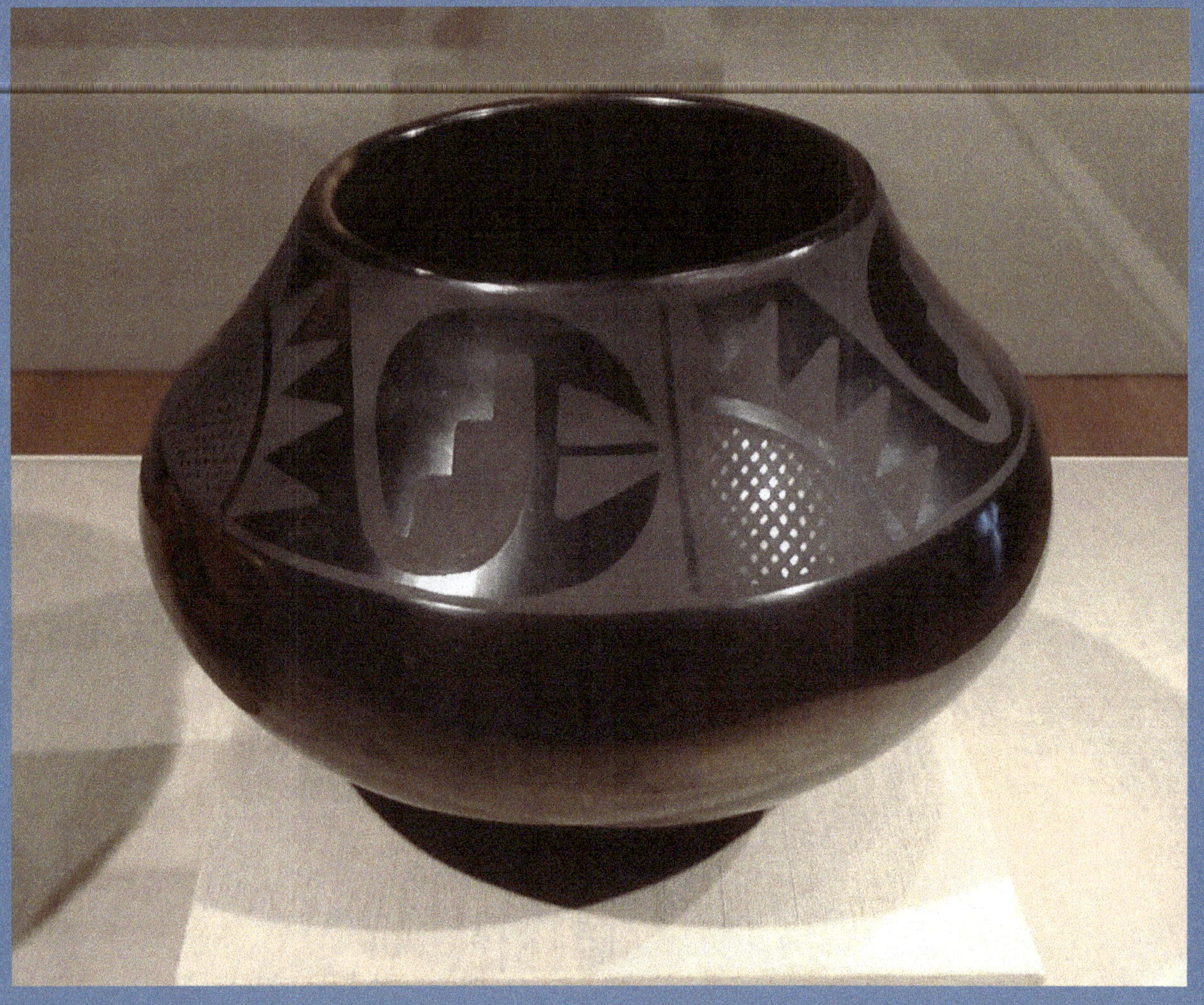

Figure 20.1: María Martinez Montoya, *Jar*, c. 1945. Ceramic, de Young Museum, San Francisco.

CRAFT VERSUS FINE ART

CHAPTER 20

CRAFT VERSUS FINE ART

Since chapter 12 we have been discussing mediums such as drawing, painting, and sculpture. There has been little doubt whether to call these works *art*, but now we will venture into some questionable areas. Historically, the mediums discussed within this chapter fall under the category of *craft*.

What sets craft apart from fine art? The primary difference between the two is the functionality of the object. If there is a utilitarian use of the object in one way or another, the work is deemed as craft. This might include chairs to sit on, dishes to eat off of, or clothes to wear.

The Industrial Revolution of the eighteenth and nineteenth centuries played a significant role in the struggle between the arts and crafts. With the Industrial Revolution came the advent of mass production. Before the Industrial Revolution utilitarian objects, such as plates and bowls, would have been handmade by individuals or craftsmen. Now, these objects were made by machine, thereby removing any artistic significance they might have carried.

Among the first to attempt to raise craft to the level of fine art was the eighteenth-century pottery maker Josiah Wedgewood. Wedgewood's factory manufactured two distinctive lines of pottery. The first was called "useful ware," and was made by machine.[1] These plates, cups, and saucers were all made from pouring liquid clay into molds and were rather plain in appearance. The other line of pottery was called "ornamental ware."[2] Skilled craftsmen created these works with incredible attention to detail. The name alone reminds us that these objects are supposed to be looked at and admired as works of art rather than used.

CERAMICS

Ceramics are made through one of the additive processes of sculpture: modeling (chapter 16). Artists take a pliable material, such as clay, and form it into the desired shape. The newly formed object is then fired in a kiln, which is an oven or furnace where the clay is baked at high temperatures.

Once the clay is hardened and removed from the kiln, it is reclassified as a ceramic. The three ways that ceramics are commonly created are slab construction, coiling, and throwing.

Most of us are already familiar with **slab construction**, especially if we played with Play-Doh as a kid. The clay is pounded out into a flat circular shape and then the edges are drawn up, similar to forming a piecrust. The *Tea Bowl* (**fig 20.2**) is an example of slab construction. The bowls themselves are not very large, as they are meant to fit in the palm of the hand. Another example of slab construction, which may not seem culturally correct today, comes from the 1970s. Many of us who attended grade school during that period had "arts and crafts time" where we would work on different projects. Usually, the outcome would be a gift for our parents or grandparents. One such project was creating an ashtray, as much of the population smoked during that time. We would pound out the clay with our little fists and bring the edges up, crimping them occasionally so that they were able to effectively hold a cigarette or pipe.

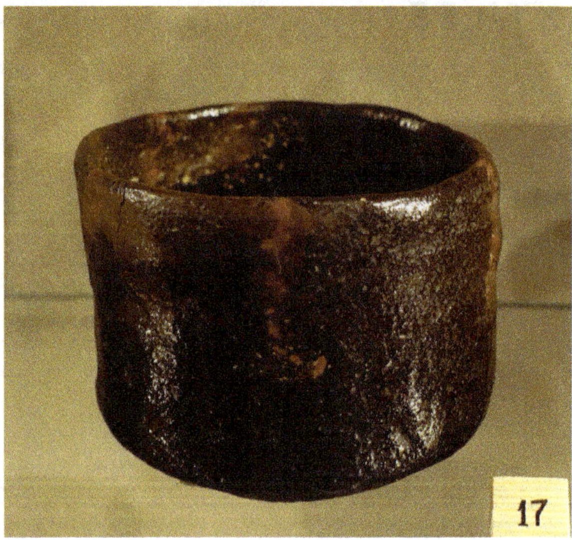

Figure 20.2: *Tea Bowl*. Ceramic, Museum of Far Eastern Antiquities, Stockholm.

The second construction technique for making ceramics is through **coiling**. Here the ceramicist rolls out long ropelike strands of clay. The ends are attached and then the coils are stacked one on top of the other. The sides, both inside and out, are smoothed as the layers increase and the shape of the pottery begins to take form.

This process was common to Native American Indians of the Southwestern United States. One of the most famous artists to emerge from that culture was María Montoya Martinez. She, along with her husband Julián, produced an extensive amount of work during the first half of the twentieth century. Her work *Jar* (**fig 20.1**) was created using the coiling technique.

The final process of creating ceramics, **throwing**, is also the most common. Throwing is done using a potter's wheel (**fig 20.3**). The use of a potter's wheel can be dated to as early as 4000 BCE.[3] The potter's wheel is made up of a circular disk connected to a flywheel below. The objects created using this method are symmetrically balanced. Most of us are familiar with seeing pottery created in this way. The process was popularized in the 1990 movie *Ghost* starring Patrick Swayze and Demi Moore.

Ceramics come in three quality levels: earthenware, stoneware, and porcelain. Earthenware is considered the lowest grade of ceramics. It has the least strength and toughness compared to other types of ceramics because it is fired at low temperatures. It is porous and cannot hold liquid unless it has first been glazed. That is why one of the more common uses for earthenware pottery is as planters for potted plants. The porousness of the container prevents the plants from rotting due to overwatering, which is common with plastic plant containers.

The middle grade of ceramics is stoneware. It is also the most familiar to people because this is the grade used for dinnerware and coffee mugs.

The highest grade of ceramics is porcelain. It is fired at the highest temperatures compared to the other grades of ceramics. Porcelain was first invented by the Chinese around 900 BCE. Artists would hand paint plates and vases made of porcelain, which would then be exported.

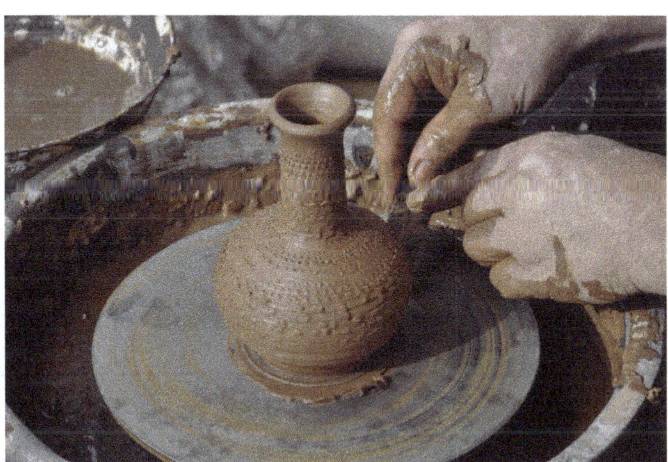

Figure 20.3: Potter's Wheel.

GLASS

One ancient form of art that has seen a resurgence in the modern era is glass. Glass can be formed in a couple of different ways. The *Mosaic Bowl* made by Salviati & Co. (**fig 20.4**) is an example of fusing. This process dates back to early Roman times. Chips of colored glass would be placed on a ceramic core and then placed in a kiln. The glass would melt and the pieces would fuse together.

Much of the early glasswork is both aesthetically pleasing and functional. When we

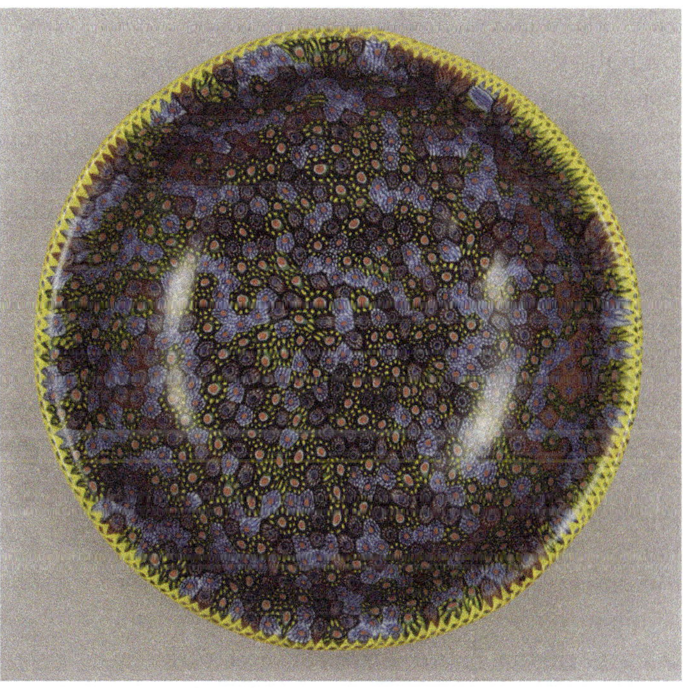

Figure 20.4: Salviati & Co. (Italian), *Mosaic Bowl*, late 19th-early 20th century. Glass, 6.8 in diameter, Walters Art Museum, Baltimore.

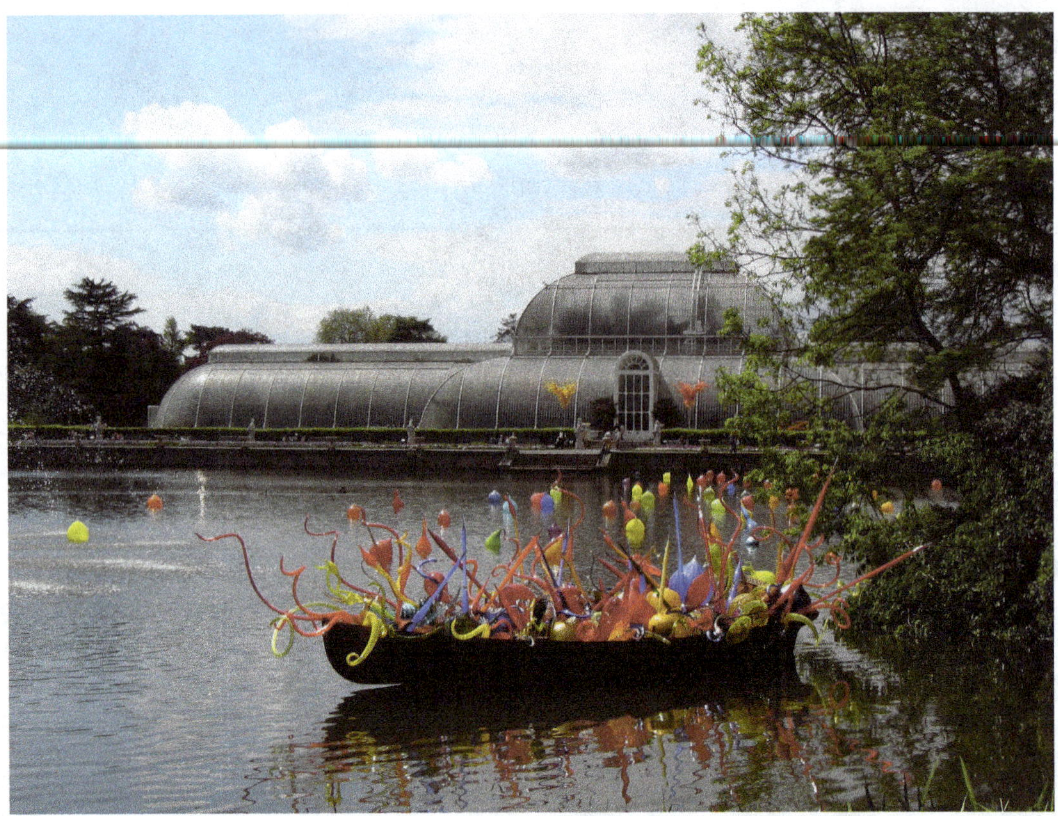
Figure 20.5: Dale Chihuly exhibit at the Royal Botanic Gardens, Kew, United Kingdom, 2005.

consider the glasswork that is being produced in the contemporary era, we see a trend toward aesthetic fulfillment. Among the foremost glassmakers in the world today is Dale Chihuly. Chihuly creates his works through the technique of glassblowing.[4] Here, molten glass is placed at the end of a long pipe that is constantly twirled as the artist blows into the other end, expanding the glass like a bubble. The glasswork is formed and cut quickly, before it cools. Chihuly's works (**fig 20.5**) are purely aesthetic and are extremely popular, as they are celebrated in books, calendars, and documentaries, such as *Chihuly over Venice*.

TEXTILES

An area that is receiving more and more attention in both galleries and museums is textiles. Museums, such as the Los Angeles County Museum of Art, have entire departments dedicated to this medium.[5] Artists such as William Morris and Anni Albers are known almost solely for their production of textiles.

The basis for textiles is weaving, which most of us did as kids, interlacing horizontal threads through vertical ones. This direction of the threads, the **warp** and the **weft** (**fig 20.6**), is one of the important elements to know about textiles. *Warp* threads are the vertical threads, running in a north and south direction on the loom. The horizontal threads shuttled between the warp are called the *weft*.

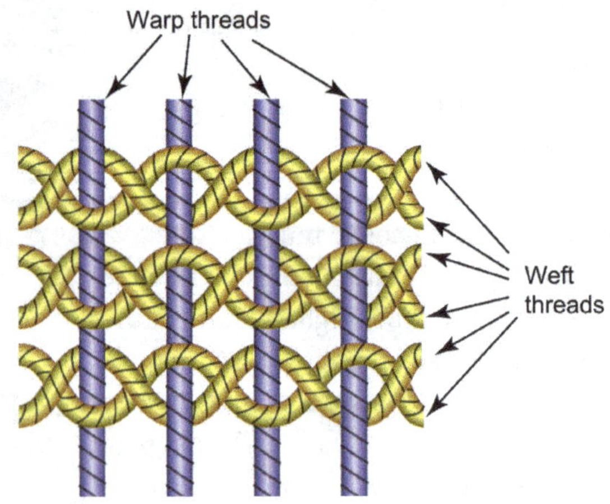

Figure 20.6: Warp and Weft Threads.

Why is it important for anyone to know the direction of the threads? There are a couple of answers to this question. First, if you are going to hang a textile for display it must be done using the warp threads, as they are taut. If the weft is used, the textile will be disfigured because of the amount of slack in those threads. Another reason it is important to know the direction of the warp and weft is when fabric is being pieced together to make clothing. The warp must be going in the same direction, otherwise the clothing will stretch oddly.

A contemporary artist who uses textiles in his work is Christo and his wife Jeanne-Claude. *The Gates, Central Park, New York City* (**fig 20.7**), which came to fruition in 2005, is one of their more recent works. The artists and their assistants created 7,503 "gates" and spaced them 12 feet apart. If you work the math, that means that this artwork covered roughly 17 miles of pathway in Central Park. The bright orange fabric was eye-catching, even more so in the snow. While this was a temporary artwork, lasting only two weeks, it made visitors to the artwork reexamine the familiar surroundings of Central Park.

MOSAIC

Mosaics are very reminiscent of paintings, particularly fresco paintings, except that instead of paint pieces of stone, glass, or tile are used to create the image or pattern. Many times you will see the interior of buildings covered from floor to ceiling with them. This is the case with the Church of San Vitale, located in Ravenna, Italy. While the church contains a multitude of mosaics, the two most important flank the altar: *Justinian and His Attendants* (**fig 20.8**) and *Theodora and Her Attendants* (**fig 20.9**).

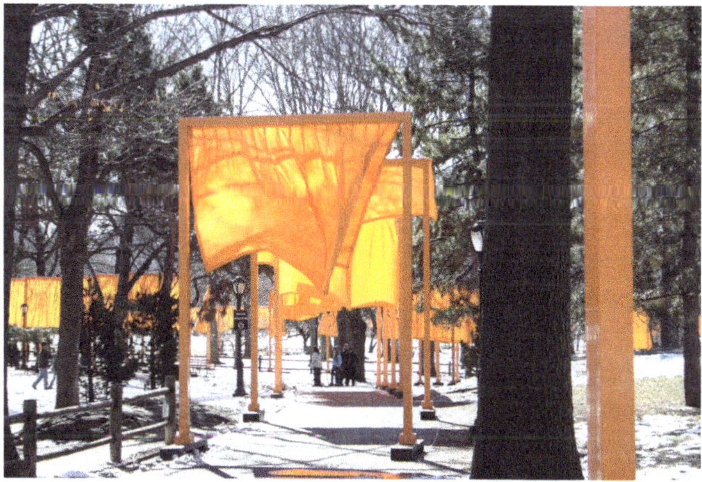

Figure 20.7: Christo and Jeanne-Claude, *The Gates, Central Park, New York City*, 1979–2005.

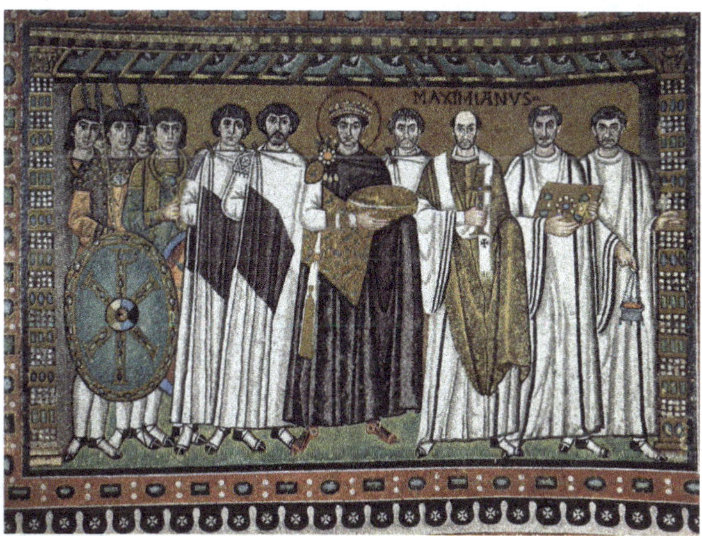

Figure 20.8: *Emperor Justinian and His Attendants*, c. 547. Mosaic on north wall of the apse, 8 ft 8 in × 12 ft, Church of San Vitale, Ravenna, Italy.

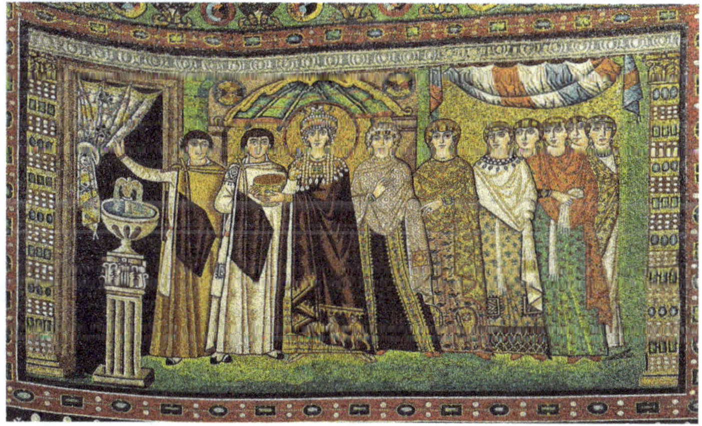

Figure 20.9: *Empress Theodora and Her Attendants*, c. 547. Mosaic on south wall of the apse, 8 ft 8 in × 12 ft, Church of San Vitale, Ravenna, Italy.

Mosaics were one of the most common artistic mediums of the Roman Empire. Emperor Justinian was the leader of the Eastern Roman Empire between 527 CE and 565 CE. He ruled from Constantinople, and neither he nor his wife, Theodora, ever set foot in the city of Ravenna.[6] These mosaics were created to serve as a form of propaganda, reminding people that he ruled this area and that he was the leader of the church. In the mosaic, Justinian is portrayed as Christ with a halo around his head. He is surrounded by his attendants, which include both religious and military figures. He holds a bowl that would be used for holding the bread used in the Eucharist.

Across from Justinian's mosaic is one of his wife, the Empress Theodora. She personifies Mary, and her dress has the three magi embroidered on it. Attendants surround her as she carries a goblet for wine, another element of the Eucharist.

COLLAGE

Collages are works of two-dimensional art. They are created by attaching pieces of material, such as paper, photographs, or textiles, onto a canvas, board, or panel. Collage is a rather new medium for artists to work in, emerging in the early twentieth century. Artists such as Pablo Picasso and Romare Bearden are known for their works in this medium. *Keep Your Mind on the Road* (**fig 20.10**) is a collage created by pasting images from sports magazines onto paper. In the image a driver seems to gaze blankly at the road before him, while his mind fills the windshield with sporting events.

MIXED MEDIA

As the name suggests, this term denotes an artwork that is created using various sorts of media. Normally when we see artwork at a museum the materials used to create them tend to be very limited, such as oil on canvas, tempera on panel, or just simply marble. However, in the twentieth century sculptors began to use several objects in order to create assemblages. One we looked at in an earlier chapter was Edward Kienholz's *The Illegal Operation* (see fig 16.4). This work includes such articles as a shopping cart, bedpan, bag of cement, milking stool, rug, lamp, etc. Instead of listing all the material used in this artwork on the didactic label, we can use the term *mixed media*.[7]

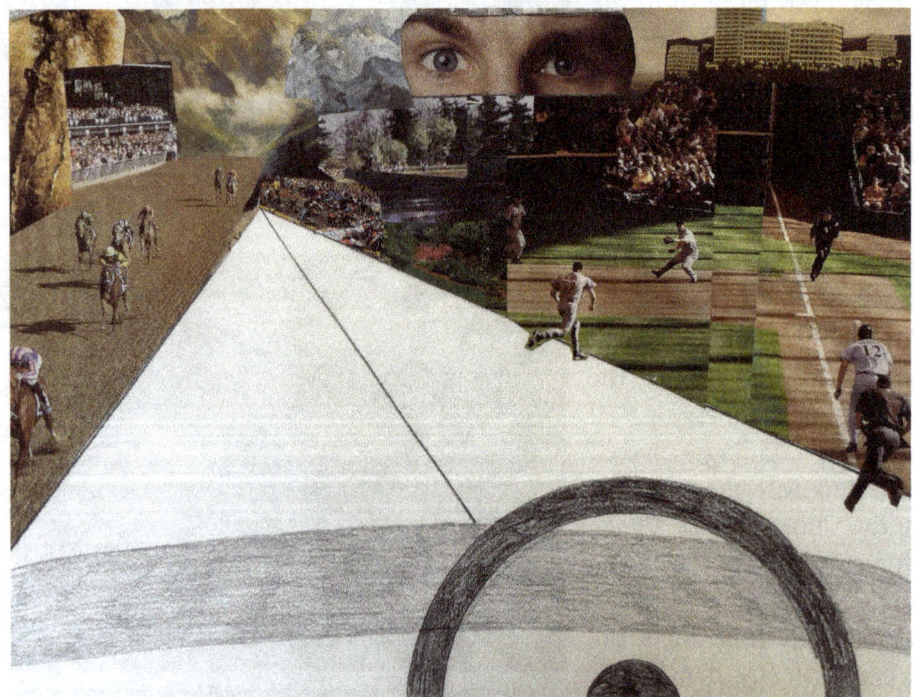

Figure 20.10: David Plouffe, *Keep Your Mind on the Road*, 2004. Magazine Cutouts on Paper, 16 in × 20 in.

Ceramics:

Glass:

Textiles:

Mosaic:

Collage:

Mixed media:

ENDNOTES

1. Henry Sayre, *A World of Art*, 7th ed. (Boston: Prentice Hall, 2013), 335.
2. Henry Sayre, *A World of Art*, 7th ed. (Boston: Prentice Hall, 2013), 335.
3. Henry Sayre, *A World of Art*, 7th ed. (Boston: Prentice Hall, 2013), 338.
4. Chihuly now serves as a director to those creating his works rather than an active participant in glassblowing since a car accident in 1976 caused him to lose sight in his left eye. "Chihuly: FAQs," accessed September 13, 2016, www.chihuly.com/learn#n2380.
5. The Los Angeles County Museum of Art has over 30,000 objects located within the Department of Costume and Textiles. The author was employed in this department from 2005–2007.
6. Khan Academy, "San Vitale, Ravenna," accessed September 13, 2016, https://www.khanacademy.org/humanities/medieval-world/byzantine1/venice-ravenna/v/justinian-and-his-attendants-6th-century-ravenna.
7. The *didactic label* is the placard situated next to the artwork in a museum or gallery that contains information about the artwork and the artist who created it.

IMAGE CREDITS

- Fig. 20.1: Copyright © María Montoya Martinez; Photo by Jim Heaphy (CC BY-SA 3.0) at https://commons.wikimedia.org/wiki/File:Maria_Martinez_pot.jpg.
- Fig. 20.2: Daderot, "Tea Bowl," https://commons.wikimedia.org/wiki/File:Tea_bowl_17_-_Östasiatiska_museet,_Stockholm_-_DSC09164.JPG. Copyright in the Public Domain.
- Fig. 20.3: Copyright © Caaman (CC BY-SA 4.0) at https://commons.wikimedia.org/wiki/File:Working_on_pottery_wheel.JPG.
- Fig. 20.4: Copyright © Salviati & Co.; Photo by Walters Art Museum (CC BY-SA 3.0) at https://commons.wikimedia.org/wiki/File:Salviati_%26_Co_-_Mosaic_Bowl_-_Walters_47298_-_Interior.jpg.
- Fig. 20.5: Dale Chihuly; Photo by Patche99z, "Dale Chihuly exhibition, Royal Botanical Gardens, Kew, United Kingdom," https://commons.wikimedia.org/wiki/File:Chihuly_at_Kew_Gardens_031.jpg. Copyright in the Public Domain.
- Fig. 20.6: Copyright © KDS444 (CC BY-SA 3.0) at https://commons.wikimedia.org/wiki/File:Gauzeweave.svg.
- Fig. 20.7: Copyright © Christo and Jeanne-Claude; Photo by Morris Pearl (CC BY-SA 3.0) at https://commons.wikimedia.org/wiki/File:Gates_f.jpg.
- Fig. 20.8: "Emperor Justinian and His Attendants," https://commons.wikimedia.org/wiki/File:Meister_von_San_Vitale_in_Ravenna_003.jpg. Copyright in the Public Domain.
- Fig. 20.9: Petar Milošević, "Empress Theodora and Her Attendants," https://commons.wikimedia.org/wiki/File:Mosaic_of_Theodora_-_Basilica_San_Vitale_(Ravenna).jpg. Copyright in the Public Domain.

CASE STUDIES

IN ART HISTORY

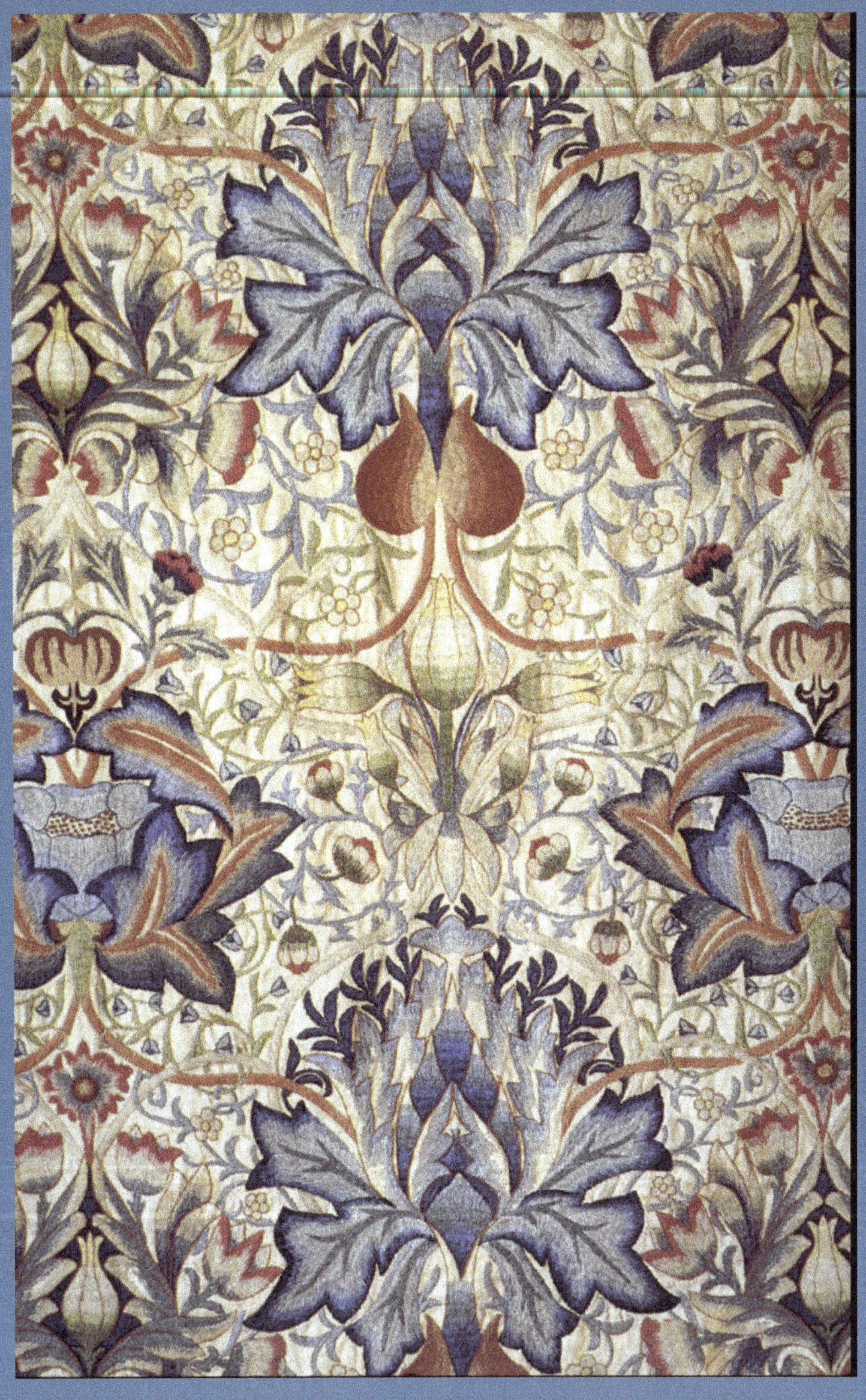

Figure 21.1: William Morris, *Artichoke*, 1890. Embroidery in wool, Victoria and Albert Museum, London.

DESIGN STYLES, 1850–1950

DESIGN STYLES

Several prominent design or stylistic changes can be seen in the artwork produced between 1850 and 1950. These design styles tend to be binary, seemingly paddling back and forth between two extremes, as if someone were playing a game of tennis or ping-pong. One of these extremes revolves around the use of curvilinear line, which is the basis for the implementation of organic and natural forms. The other extreme is rectilinear line, a line that is strict, mechanical, and man-made.

Is there a difference between a design style and an art movement? There is! An *art movement* such as Impressionism or Futurism has at its base a shared ideology of the members involved. This will be discussed in more detail in chapter 23, which takes a look at modern art movements. The term *style* is more directly tied to the outward appearance of an object. The terms are not exclusive, as we will see with the Arts and Crafts movement and de Stijl.

ARTS AND CRAFTS MOVEMENT

The Arts and Crafts movement began as a rebellion against industrialization. As mentioned in chapter 20, the Industrial Revolution threatened artistic accomplishment. Previously handmade objects were now being mass produced by machine. The artist or craftsman was literally removed from the creative process. The Arts and Crafts movement sought to resurrect the importance of craftsmanship and reinstate the tie between artist and object.

William Morris (**fig 21.2**) is considered by many to be the leader of the Arts and Crafts movement, or at least its most prominent member. Morris was an artist, craftsman, designer, social reformer, and writer. He was mentioned briefly in chapter 19, along with his friend Philip Webb, who helped design and build the Red House, which was Morris's home. When Morris could not find the high-quality handmade goods he desired to fill his home with, he opened his own company, Morris and Company, in 1861.[1]

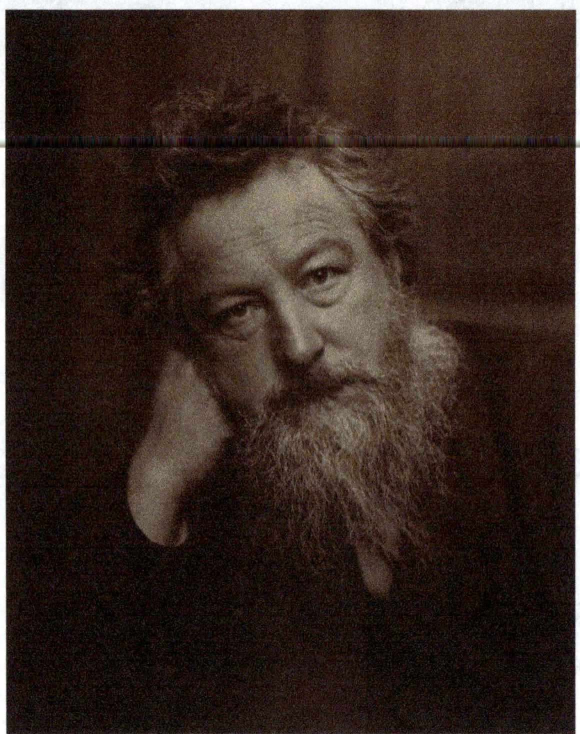

Figure 21.2: Frederick Hollyer, *Portrait of William Morris,* c. 1887.

Morris and Company would serve as the catalyst for the Arts and Crafts movement. Like Morris's Red House, his company rejected the modern age and focused instead on the renewal of beauty and craftsmanship of handmade goods. The belief was that true art should be both beautiful and useful and base its forms on those found in nature.

Morris and Company created a tremendous array of household furnishings, including furniture, tile, glasswork, and metalwork. But its most celebrated commodity was textiles, such as *Artichoke* (**fig 21.1**). Today, these celebrated artworks grace museum and gallery display cases worldwide and are highly sought after by collectors. *Artichoke* incorporates curvilinear line and natural forms through its systematic placement of flowers, leaves, and stems. The color, created from hand-dyed threads, provides points of emphasis and establishes a sense of space.

Morris founded the Kelmscott Press in 1888. It was originally intended to publish the writings, particularly poetry, of Morris and his friends. However, the most famous book to emerge from the press was *The Works of Geoffrey Chaucer*. In 1894, just two years before his death, Morris would publish *The Wood Beyond the World*, an early fantasy book (**fig 21.3**).[2] One can see that both the illustrations and the design work around the illustrations and text are similar to the textiles Morris and Company produced.[3] Even the font designed by Morris, called Chaucer, can be described as natural, organic, and flowing.[4]

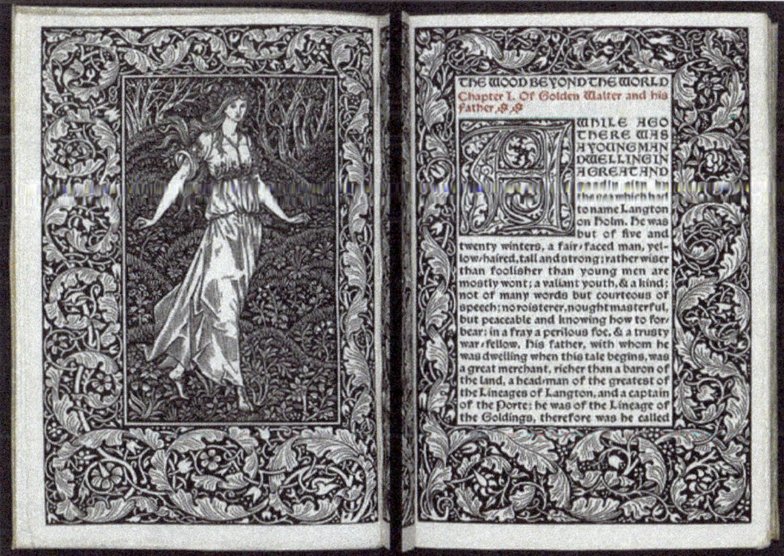

Figure 21.3: Page from *The Wood Beyond the World* by William Morris, illustrations by Edward Burne-Jones, Kelmscott Press, 1894.

ART NOUVEAU

While the Arts and Crafts movement was centered in England, a similar art style, called *Art Nouveau*, began to emerge in France. The name is derived from the Galeries de l'Art Nouveau, which was opened in Paris in 1895 by Siegfried Bing. Art Nouveau can definitely be considered an extension of the Arts and Crafts movement, as the artworks from both look similar in form, with attention to curvilinear aspects and the incorporation of organic motifs.

The major difference between the two styles is that the Arts and Crafts movement embraced the past, whereas Art Nouveau embraced the future. The artists and designers involved in this style sought out new and innovative materials and embraced the new technologies of the late nineteenth and early twentieth centuries. For instance, *Wisteria Lamp* (**fig 21.4**) utilized electricity, the new "modern" way of lighting the interior of a home. The colors that these stained glass lamps gave off would have been incredibly unique and different than anything previously seen.[5]

The design styles covered in this chapter are not restricted to one or two artistic mediums, but instead they spread to all mediums of art. The Art Nouveau style can be seen in the paintings of Gustave Klimt, such as the *Portrait of Adele Bloch-Bauer* (not pictured), the sculptures of Alphonse Marie Mucha, and Jan Troop's commercial graphic designs. The style of Art Nouveau was even powerful enough to infiltrate and transform the aesthetics of architecture. One of the first and best examples of Art Nouveau architecture is the

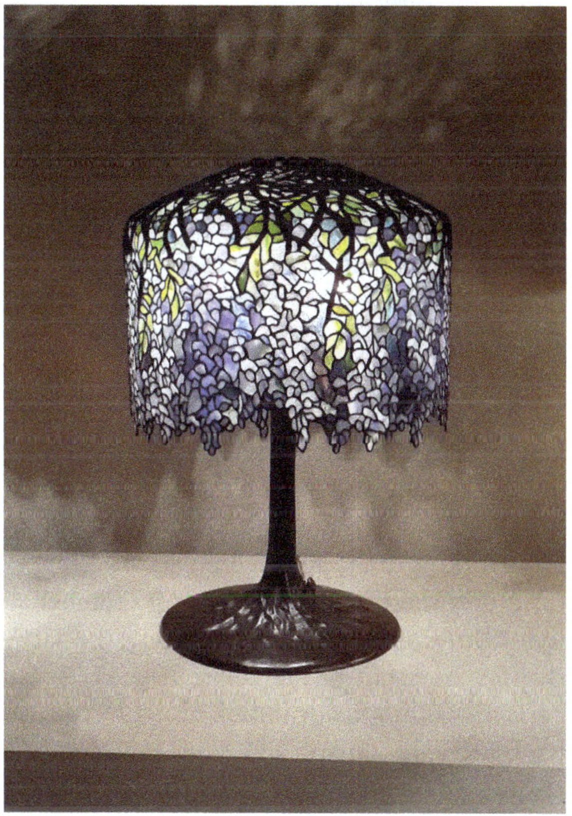

Figure 21.4: Clara Driscoll, Tiffany Studios, *Wisteria Table Lamp*, c. 1902. Virginia Museum of Fine Arts.

Hôtel Tassel in Brussels (**fig 21.5**). The flow of lines throughout the building's interior seems never-ending. It is like a vining plant whose tendrils have taken over the floors, walls, banisters, and ceilings. Normally when one considers architecture, space is the biggest concern and interest, but here line trumps space. The Hôtel Tassel is considered "outstanding for its synthesis of architecture and the decorative arts and its declaration of new formal principles."[6]

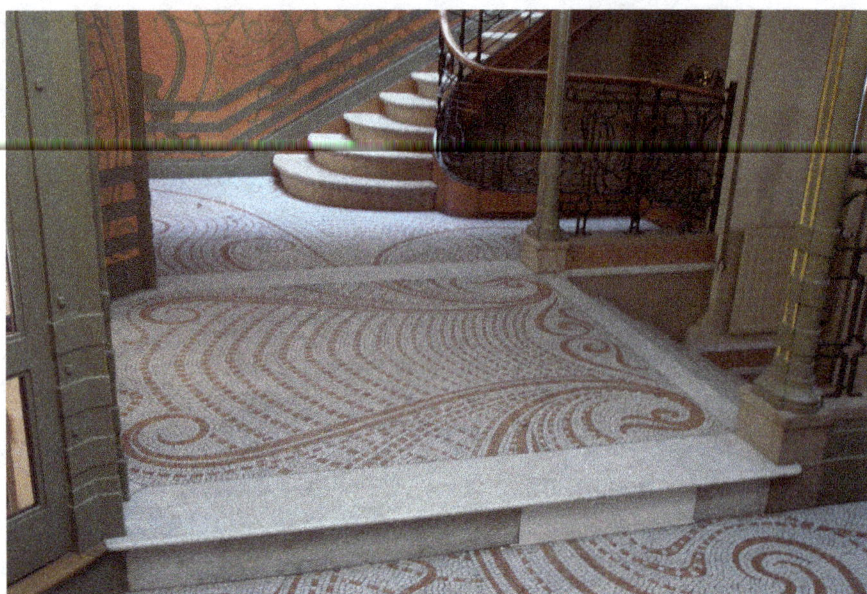

Figure 21.5: Victor Tassel, Hôtel Tassel, Brussels, 1892–93.

ART DECO

Art Nouveau would remain the dominant style during the early 1900s, but the curvilinear lines and organic qualities people had become accustomed to over the past decades would soon disappear, giving way to the geometric abstraction of a new style called *Art Deco*. The name originated from the International Exposition of Modern Decorative and Industrial Arts, a World's Fair that was held in Paris in 1925 (**fig 21.6**).

The defining characteristics of Art Deco are sharp 90-degree angles, rectilinear lines, geometric shapes, and the incorporation of modern materials, such as Bakelite, the world's first synthetic plastic.[7] The style was prevalent in both Europe and in America. The American designer Paul T. Frankl, whose studio was in New York, is noted for his line of "skyscraper" furniture. These new modern designs mimicked the architecture that was redefining the city's skyline. *Skyscraper End Table* (**fig 21.7**) fits perfectly within the definition of Art Deco with its noticeable square and rectangular forms creating 90-degree angles. The curving fluidity of Art Nouveau vanished in the wake of the meticulous exactness of Art Deco.

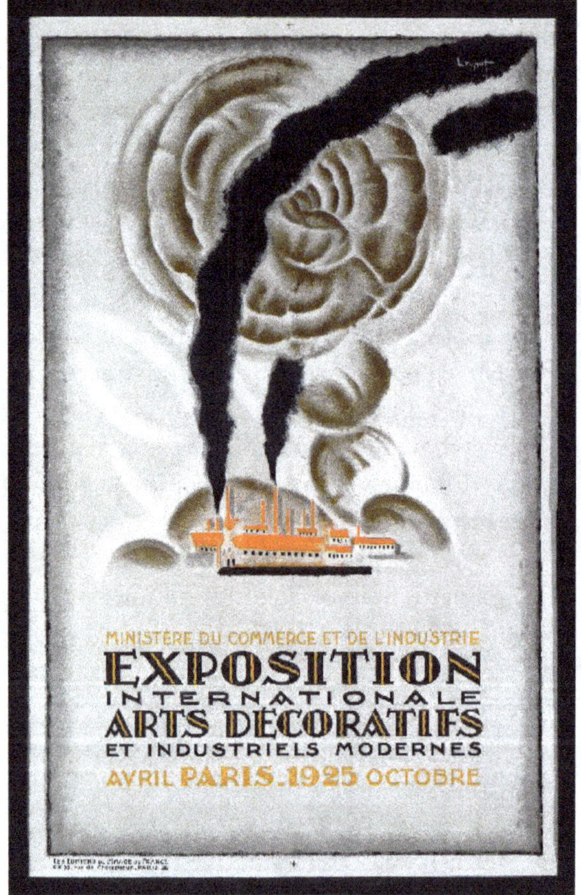

Figure 21.6: Poster, The International Exposition of Modern Decorative Industrial Arts, 1925. The Wolfsonian-Florida International University, Miami Beach, Florida, The Mitchell Wolfson, Jr. Collection.

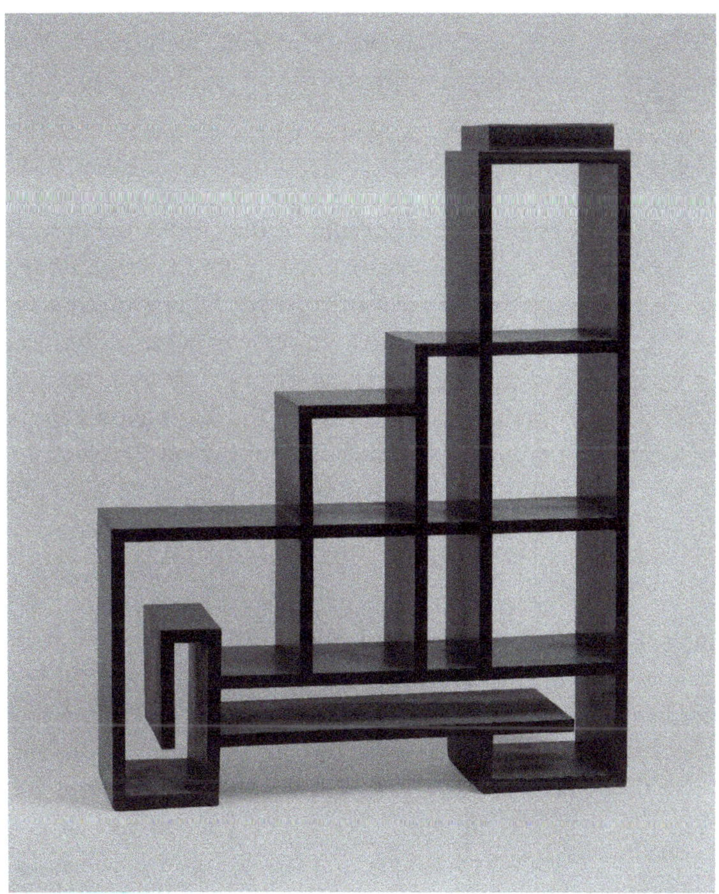

Figure 21.7: Paul T. Frankl, *Skyscraper Step Table*, 1920s. Painted Wood, 38.75 in × 30.5 in × 9 in, Brooklyn Museum.

DE STIJL

Running concurrently with Art Deco was the Dutch movement called *de Stijl*, which translates into "The Style." It emerged from Holland at the end of World War I and looks remarkably similar in style to Art Deco. However, Art Deco is looked at as a design style and is usually associated with the world of opulence and elegance, as described in F. Scott Fitzgerald's *The Great Gatsby*. In contrast, de Stijl was a response to the horrors of World War I. The Great War was the first to use airplanes, tanks, poison gas, and trench warfare. It also saw the genesis of plastic surgery to help those who had been wounded and disfigured. To say it did not have a significant impact on artists would be a misnomer.

Artists responded to the war with the use of basic geometric shapes and the incorporation of primary colors, along with black and white, to create artworks that were "dedicated to purity, logic, balance, proportion, and rhythm."[8] These artworks became a source of certainty in a very uncertain world. Among the most important artists from this movement was Piet Mondrian, and his work *Composition with Red, Blue, and Yellow* (see fig 4.1) is among the most popular de Stijl paintings.

Another artist who emerged from de Stijl was Gerrit Rietveld. The *Red-Blue Chair* (**fig 21.8**) could be considered a three-dimensional version of a Mondrian painting, as it incorporates geometric shapes along with the primary colors. While most of the output of the de Stijl artists dealt with painting, de Stijl also influenced architecture, with works such as the Schröder House (not pictured), also by Rietveld.

RUSSIAN CONSTRUCTIVISM

In 1917 the Czarist monarchy fell in Russia and Vladimir Lenin rose to power. The artwork produced after this event is categorized as Russian Constructivism, which, in turn, is reclassified as Russian Suprematism after 1921.[9] Among the

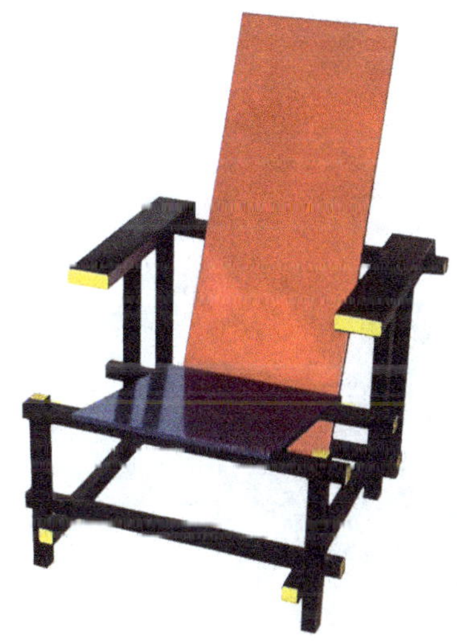

Figure 21.8: Gerrit Rietveld *Red-Blue Chair*, 1918 (prototype). Painted Wood, 23 5/8 in × 33 1/16 in × 33 1/16 in, Los Angeles County Museum of Art.

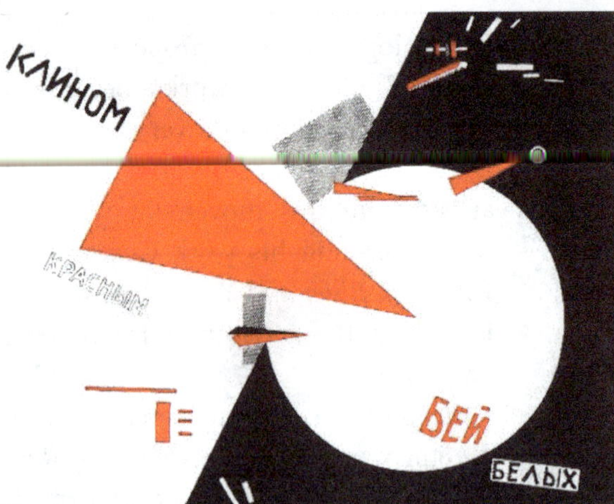

Figure 21.9: El Lissitzky, *Beat the Whites with the Red Wedge*, 1919. Lithograph 70 cm × 50 cm, Stedelijk van Abbemuseum, Eindhoven, The Netherlands.

most influential artists of this movement is El Lissitzky, whose most noted works encompass geometric forms floating in space. His poster *Beat the Whites with the Red Wedge* (**fig 21.9**) is read as propaganda, where the aggressive "red" triangle represents the Bolsheviks piercing the passive circle.

The reason this movement is brought into this chapter is to provide a point for comparison with de Stijl and Art Deco. While the underlying beginnings/meanings of the three movements/styles are completely different, we can see how their design aspects duplicate one another.

STREAMLINING

The beginning of the 1930s ushered in a familiar design style of curvilinear line. This time though there was a lack of organic motif. *Streamlining* is defined as a teardrop-shaped line of contour that offers the least amount of wind resistance. Streamlining became firmly entrenched in Americana in 1934 when the *Burlington Zephyr* (**fig 21.10**) departed Denver bound for Chicago. This 1,015-mile trip normally takes 26 hours to complete, but because of the *Burlington Zephyr*'s design, material, and low center of gravity, it was able to make the trip in 13 hours and 5 minutes![10]

Once news of the train's accomplishment spread the word of the day became *streamlining*. It was the style of the future, and the future was what people were looking forward to, having been mired in the Great Depression of the late 1920s and early 1930s. Everywhere you looked products were streamlined, from cars, such as the Chrysler Airflow, to cigarette packaging. Even architecture, such as the Pan-Pacific Auditorium in Hollywood, California, was created with this new design style.

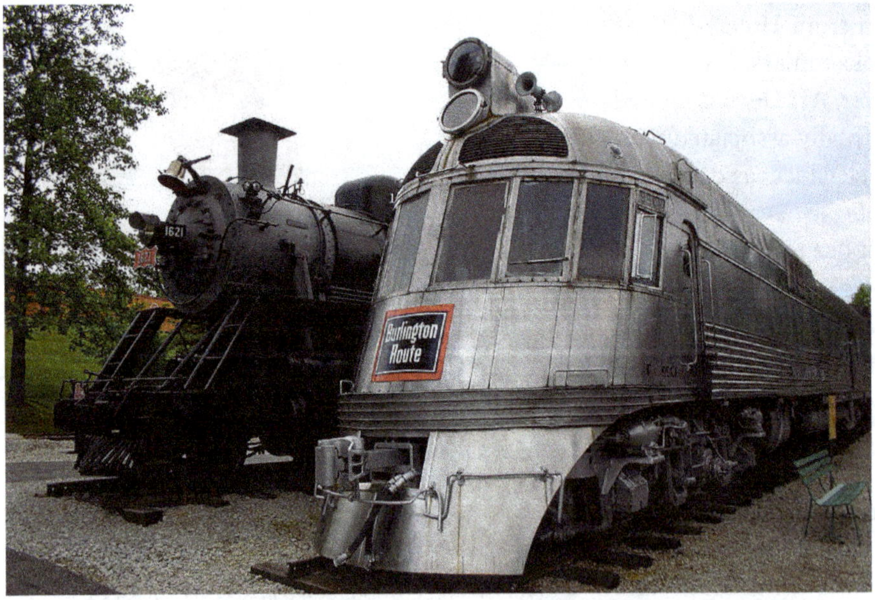

THE BAUHAUS

The Bauhaus was a school of art and design that opened in the Weimer Republic of Germany in 1919. It embodied a new approach to art education. Up to this time, modernist artists, such as Édouard Manet, Auguste Renoir, and Henri Matisse, would have had very traditional schooling in the arts. Their avant-garde nature would not take form until later in their careers. When

Figure 21.10: Burlington Northern Company, *Burlington Zephyr*.

the Bauhaus opened it became the first school to teach an avant-garde, rather than traditional, approach to the arts from the outset.

What was also important about this school was that all forms of art were considered to have equal importance. There was no distinction between the fine arts, such as painting and sculpture; crafts, such as ceramics and glass making; and the mechanical arts, such as graphic design and photography.

The location of the Bauhaus would be moved several times until its most famous location in Dessau (**fig 21.11**) was built in 1926. The Bauhaus was closed in 1933 when the Nazi party rose to power and claimed Hitler as its chancellor.[11] Hitler was a classicist and disliked modernism. He would eventually label both modern artists and modern artworks as degenerate. With the Bauhaus as an institution based on the teaching of modernist art, there was no chance of it reopening. Teachers and students immigrated to other countries in Europe, and many made their way to America, such as Ludwig Mies van der Rohe, the last director of the Bauhaus.

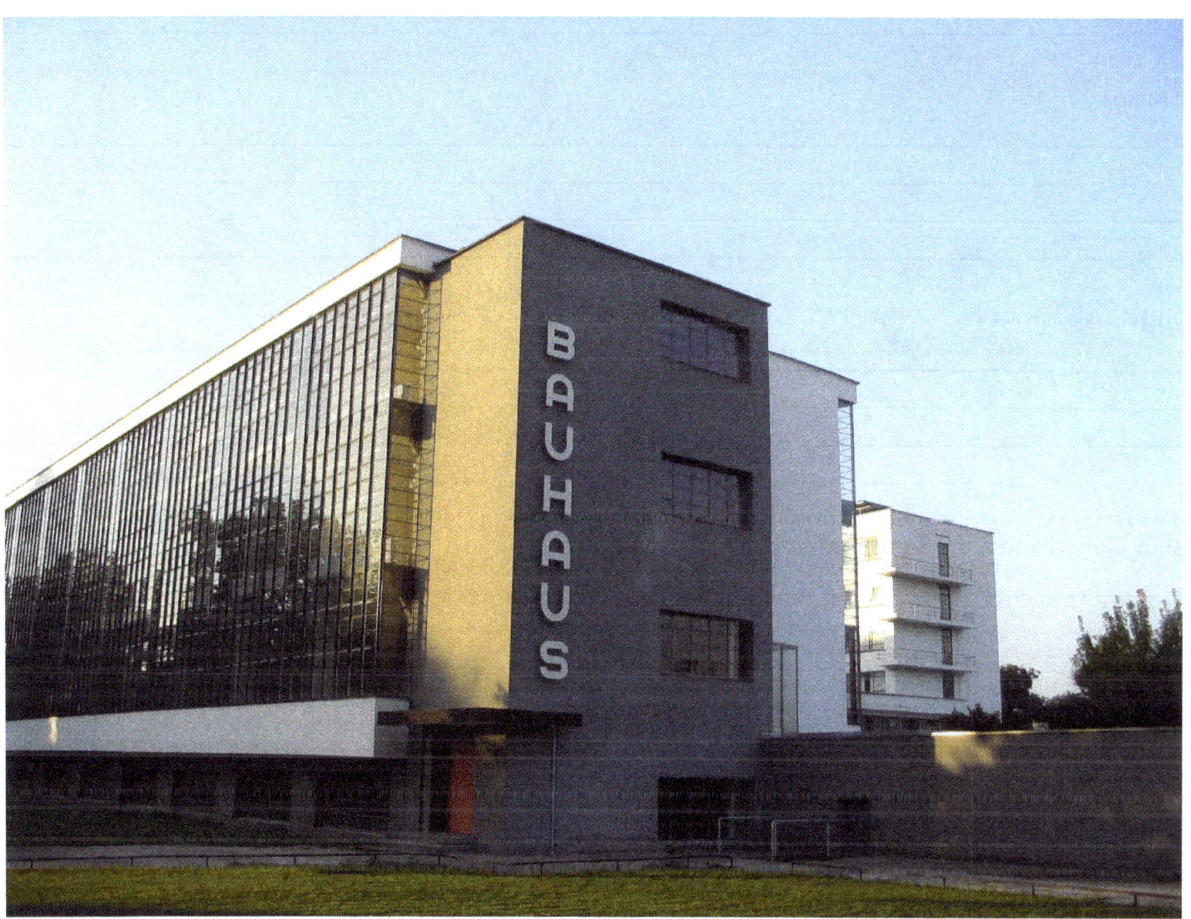

Figure 21.11: Walter Gropius, *Bauhaus, Dessau*, 1926.

Arts and Crafts movement:

Art Nouveau:

Art Deco:

De Stijl:

Russian Constructivism/Suprematism:

Streamlining:

The Bauhaus:

ENDNOTES

1. Morris and Company was originally called Morris, Marshall, and Faulkner. Marilyn Stokstad, *Art History*, revised ed. (New York: Harry N. Abrams, 1999), 1006.
2. Morris is considered one of the early authors in the realm of science fiction, fantasy, and utopian literature.
3. The illustration mentioned here, as well as those in *The Works of Geoffrey Chaucer*, are credited to Edward Burne-Jones. National Library of New Zealand, accessed September 27, 2016, http://natlib.govt.nz/records/20427541.
4. Henry Sayre, *A World of Art*, 5th ed. (Boston: Prentice Hall, 2013), 399.
5. Siegfried Bing visited Tiffany Studios in 1894 when he visited the United States. Henry Sayre, *A World of Art*, 5th ed. (Boston: Prentice Hall, 2013), 401.
6. William J. R. Curtis, *Modern Architecture Since 1900*, 3rd ed. (New York: Phaiden, 1996), 55.
7. ACS, "Leo Hendrick Baekeland and the Invention of Bakelite," accessed October 2, 2016, https://www.acs.org/content/acs/en/education/whatischemistry/landmarks/bakelite.html.
8. H. H. Arnason and Elizabeth Mansfield, *History of Modern Art*, 7th ed. (Upper Saddle River, NJ: Pearson Education, 2013), 263.
9. Ingo F. Walther, ed., *Masterpieces of Western Art* (Köln, Germany: Taschen, 2002), 553.
10. "Zephyr Makes World Record Run, 1017 Miles at an Average of 78 Hour," accessed October 2, 2016, https://web.archive.org/web/20050208015948/http://www.msichicago.org/exhibit/zephyr/history/nytimes/nytimes.html.
11. William J. R. Curtis, *Modern Architecture Since 1900*, 3rd ed. (New York: Phaiden, 1996), 311.

IMAGE CREDITS

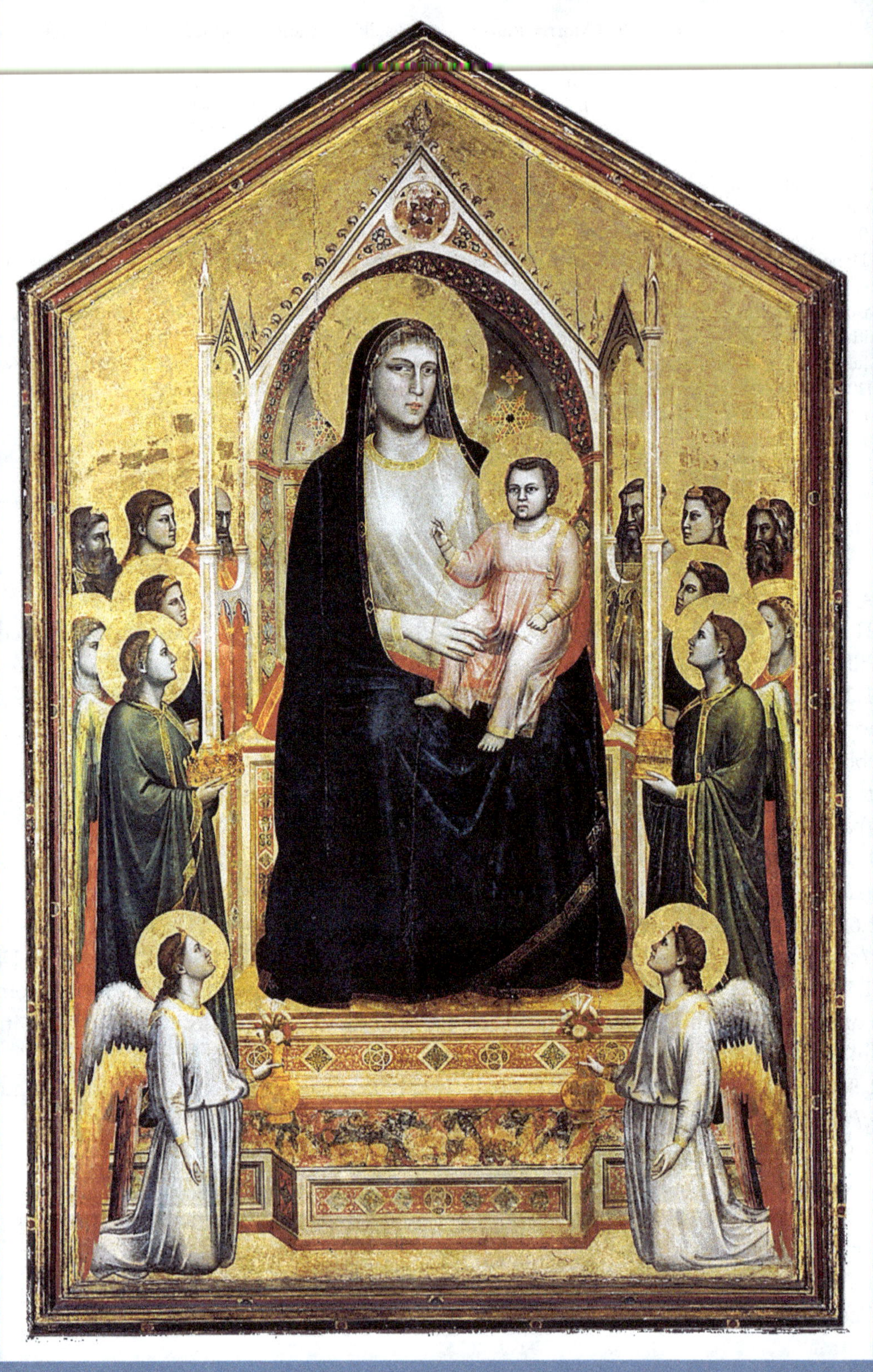

Figure 22.1: Giotto, *Enthroned Madonna with Saints*, c. 1305–10. Tempera on panel, 10 ft, 8 in × 6 ft, 8 in, Uffizi Gallery, Florence.

RENAISSANCE ART

THE RENAISSANCE

We have completed our study of both the formal elements and the mediums used to create art. This chapter, along with the next, concentrate on specific time frames in art. In this chapter we are going to focus on the Renaissance, which was one of the most prolific periods of artistic production. No single chapter can do this time period justice, as entire books have been dedicated to the subject. Therefore, this chapter will give a general overview of the topic at hand and then examine several works of art that demonstrate artistic development during this era.

The word *renaissance* translates to "rebirth," and that is exactly what was happening during this time period. It was the rebirth of knowledge and learning, particularly in the arts and sciences, as Europe emerged from the Dark Ages. The Dark Ages, also known as the Middle Ages or Medieval Ages, is the time period between the fall of the Roman Empire and the beginning of the Renaissance.

The Renaissance itself can be broken down into three distinct periods. The Early Renaissance, or Proto-Renaissance, takes place during the 1300s. This is not to say that the Early Renaissance begins exactly on January 1, 1300, and ends on December 31, 1399. The dates presented here are meant as general guideposts that mark the significant technical and stylistic changes we see during this time period. The Middle Renaissance takes place during the 1400s, and the final period, the Late, or High, Renaissance, takes place during the 1500s.

The Renaissance occurred throughout Europe, but this chapter focuses specifically on the artistic development seen in Italy. We will first look at the emergence of this new style of art in the city of Padua, and then transition to Florence during the 1400s, and eventually to Rome during the early 1500s. After the Sack of Rome in 1527, the last vestiges of the Renaissance are seen in the city of Venice.

The individuals of note during the era are as significant as the artworks being produced. Imagine a time when many of the greatest artists, scientists, adventurers, and thinkers are alive and walking the Earth. These are people like Michelangelo, Leonardo da Vinci, Raphael, Donatello, Martin Luther, Machiavelli, Christopher Columbus, and Galileo.

As wonderful as this time period sounds, we must also consider the harshness of life. Europe did not exist as it does today. There was no unified political system. Most of Europe, and all of Italy, was nothing more than a group of loosely aligned city-states, which were usually at war with one another. It was a male-dominated society. In fact, we will not begin to attribute any works to female artists until the early 1600s. It was also a time of religious persecution, famine, floods, and disease. Among the worst diseases was the Plague, or the Black Death. It would strike several times throughout the Renaissance, with the worst year being 1348. During that year, as much as half the population of Europe would fall victim to the disease.

EARLY RENAISSANCE

What creates the dividing line between the Renaissance and the Dark Ages? First, we see attention being given once again to individual artists. Artists' names lost their importance after the fall of the Roman Empire. In the Early Renaissance, we begin to see individuals being associated with the work they produced. We've moved away from the technical skill that was looked upon so highly to a more individual, God-given, talent. Second, the artworks were being created with attention to mimesis. The term *mimesis* means to mimic or to reproduce. During the Renaissance artists focus on how well they can reproduce nature. The better an artist is able to reproduce the natural appearance of an object, the better the artist he is considered.

To help illustrate the transformation that we see in artwork at the beginning of the Renaissance, take a look at the two altarpieces created by Cimabue and Giotto (**figs 22.1** and **22.2**). Both contain similar subject matter, an enthroned Madonna holding the Christ Child, saints, and angels. Cimabue is considered among the last of

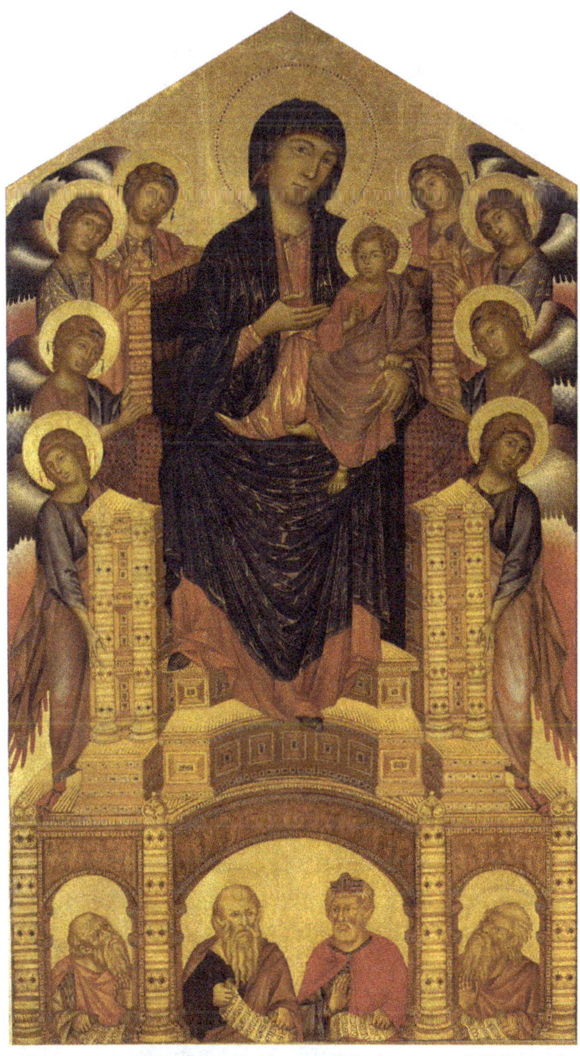

Figure 22.2: Cimabue, *Enthroned Madonna and Child with Angels and Prophets*, c.1280. Tempera on Panel, 11 ft 7 in × 7 ft 4 in, Uffizi Gallery, Florence.

the Byzantine artists.[1] His altarpiece, *Enthroned Madonna and Child with Angels and Prophets*, shows a very flattened scene. The Madonna in the center looks as if she might slide right out of her throne onto the saints below her. The saints also block our ability to access the Madonna. The angels on either side of her, holding the throne, appear in a jack-in-the-box fashion, with seemingly no space between them, as each angel appears higher than the previous one. The angels and saints appear to be caught up in their own worlds, not paying attention to or acknowledging the person next to them.

Giotto's altarpiece, *Enthroned Madonna with Saints*, presents a more natural composition. The Madonna sits firmly on her throne holding the Christ Child, who gives the benediction. She is created in a more sculptural, three-dimensional form. The fall of her clothes is even more realistic than those in the previous altarpiece. There are steps to make her accessible, and although there are more figures around the Madonna, there is also more room for them. Note how all the surrounding figures are concentrating their gaze on the Madonna and Child. This helps to establish her as the focal point of this work and lets us know that this is where we should be looking as well. Giotto has mimicked nature much more accurately than Cimabue. Giotto is considered by many to be the first artist of the Renaissance.

In 1305 a wealthy merchant, Enrico Scrovegni, commissioned Giotto to paint the inside of his newly built Arena Chapel.[2] Giotto would fill the interior with 38 fresco scenes depicting the lives of the Virgin and Christ, along with the seven virtues and seven vices. While many of the fresco paintings from this chapel are famous, we will concentrate on two specific works.

First, the *Meeting at the Golden Gate* (**fig 22.3**) shows an emotional reunion of husband and wife. This emotional, and very human, element helps to differentiate this new style of art. While we can consider the work of Giotto as a huge step in

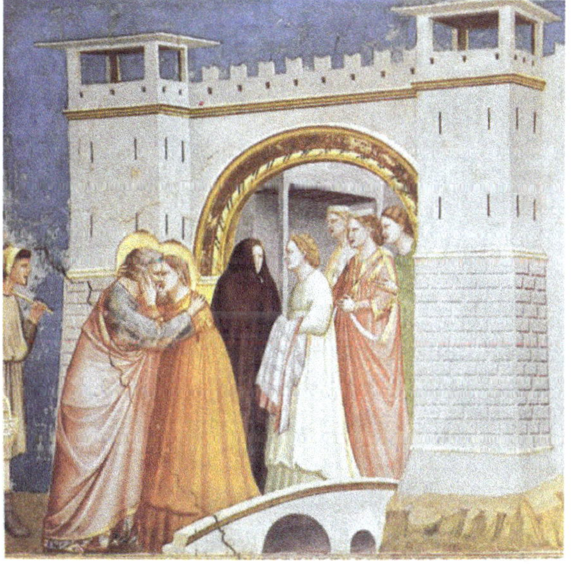

Figure 22.3: Giotto, *Meeting at the Golden Gate*, c. 1305. Fresco, 78.75 in × 72.87 in, Arena Chapel, Padua.

artistic development, there are some issues with his work that need to be considered. The primary issue is the use of light. Everything in this painting is bathed equally in light; the light does not have a single point of origin. Note that none of the figures cast any shadows. The secondary issue with Giotto's work is the representation of space. The scale of the characters and the architecture are at odds with one another. The building is too small or the characters are too big. We have to keep in mind when looking at works from the Early Renaissance that linear perspective (chapter 5) has yet to be invented.

As people leave the Arena Chapel, they are confronted with the *Last Judgment* (**fig 21.4**) painted just above the doorway. This work is symmetrically balanced and quite organized, with an emphasis on linear rows. Christ is positioned in the center with a mandorla around his body. The saved are shown to Christ's right (our left), while the damned are on his left. Near the base of the cross, we see the patron, Enrico Scrovegni, offering the Arena Chapel to Mary as a gift, or more accurately as repentance for the crimes of usury that he and his father committed.[3] Notice how Scrovegni has been painted on the side of the saved. Through his offering he is being allowed entrance to heaven. It was not uncommon for patrons to be painted into an artwork, usually at a religious event, such as the Last Judgment, Adoration, or Annunciation.

Purchasing artwork during the Renaissance (as well as the later Baroque era) was much different than how artwork is purchased today. If someone wants to purchase artwork today, all they have to do is go to a retail store or order a work online. Art, for the most part, is already produced; it is just an issue of getting that work from the artist to the buyer. But during the Renaissance artwork was made to order and relied on the patronage process. Contracts were drawn up between the patron and the artist explaining in detail what would be created. It would take several months or longer for the artwork to be made and delivered. As seen in the Arena Chapel, wealthy families were common patrons of the arts. But there were also other patrons, such as the Pope, guilds, and city government.[4]

MIDDLE RENAISSANCE

The Middle Renaissance centers on the city of Florence. Author Dale Kent states that, "Every age has a place. In the late nineteenth century it was Paris. In the late twentieth century maybe it was New York."[5] During the fifteenth century that place was definitely Florence. One of the most influential families who lived in this city was the Medici family. They are looked upon as the "godfathers" of the Renaissance and were tremendous patrons of the arts.

Among the talented artists who worked for the Medici family was Donatello. He was a successful and highly sought after sculptor. He also had a bit of a temper and was known to smash his creations.[6] He was obsessed with perfection; he had actually

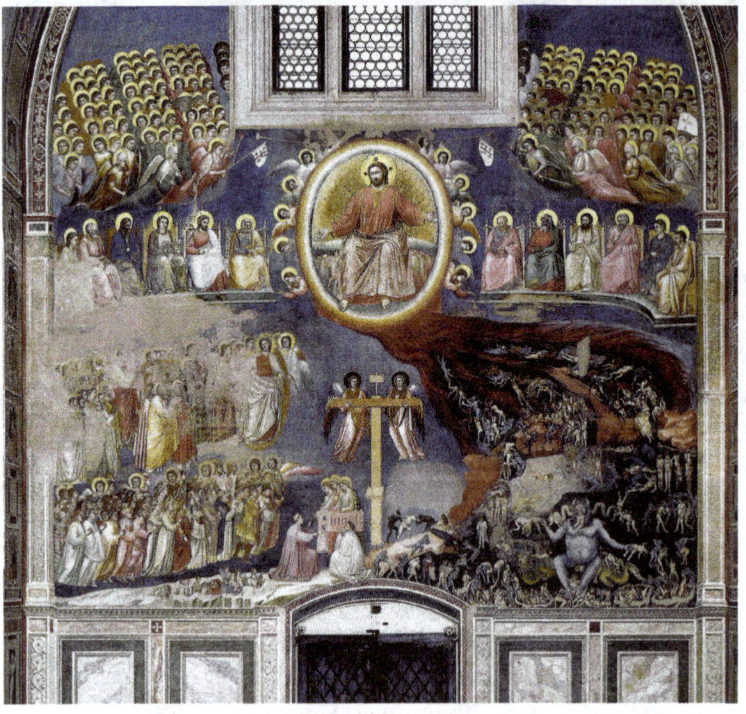

Figure 22.4: Giotto, *Last Judgment*, c. 1305. Fresco, 6 ft 6.75 in × 6 ft 1 in, Arena Chapel, Padua.

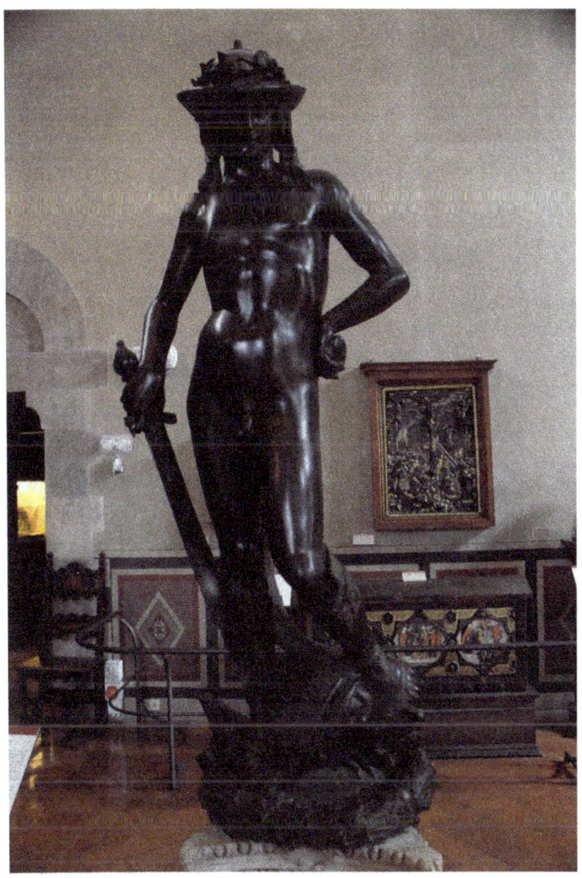

Figure 22.5: Donatello, *David*, c. 1446–60. Bronze, height 62.25 in, Museo Nazionale del Bargello, Florence.

been seen yelling at his sculpture *Zuccone* (not pictured), saying, "Speak damn you, speak!"[7] He created a sculpture of *David* (**fig 22.5**), the patron saint of Florence, for the Medici family's courtyard. It turned out to be one of the most important sculptures created during the Renaissance. It was the first time someone had created a bronze "nude, freestanding sculpture in-the-round since antiquity."[8]

Most of us are already familiar with Michelangelo's version of *David* (see fig 22.7), which will be discussed later, but Donatello's is radically different. Donatello's version shows a young adolescent boy of 12 or 13 years of age. The sculpture has an effeminate quality, as the boy seems to sway in a sinewy pose with the back of his hand resting upon his hip. He wears a bonnet crowned with laurel, under which emerges long locks of curly hair. We're not quite sure whether this boy could win against Goliath, but the part of the story being depicted is that the battle has already been fought and the severed head of Goliath rests under David's foot. The sculpture also differs from Michelangelo's version because it is made from a different medium, bronze. When you see bronze, think money. It is much more expensive to make a sculpture out of bronze than it is marble.

During the Middle Renaissance we see tremendous technical advancement in the art being produced. The codification of linear perspective (chapter 5) was the most significant achievement of the time. It revolutionized the way two-dimensional artworks were rendered. The first work to be painted in linear perspective was *The Trinity with Mary, John the Evangelist, and Two Donors* (see fig 5.9) by Masaccio.

In the Church of the Santa Maria del Carmine is the Brancacci Chapel. Along the left wall of the chapel, in the upper register, resides another of Masaccio's important works, *The Tribute Money* (**fig. 22.6**). When Christ and the apostles arrive

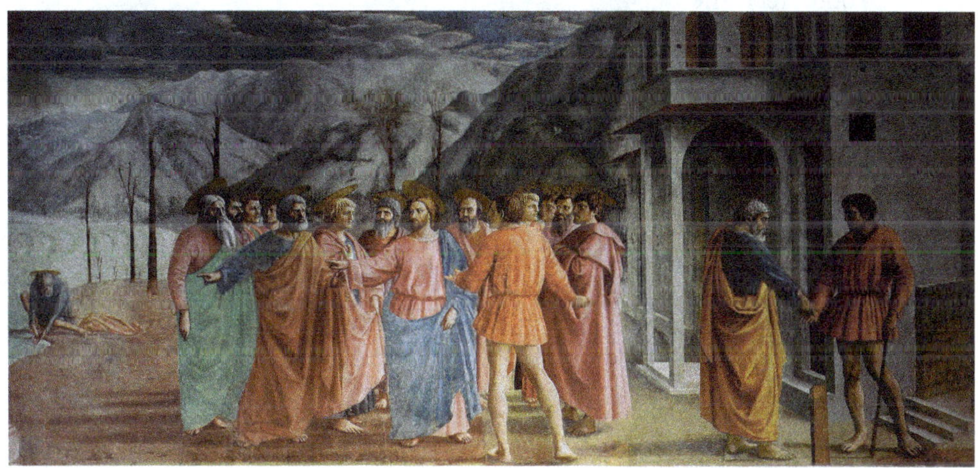

Figure 22.6: Masaccio, *Tribute Money*, c. 1420s. Fresco 8 ft 1 in × 19 ft 7 in, Brancacci Chapel, Santa Maria del Carmine, Florence.

at the city of Capernaum, a Roman tax gatherer confronts Peter and demands a half-drachma tribute. Peter, returning to Christ for instructions, is told that he would find the money in the mouth of the fish near the shore of Lake Galilee. Peter catches the fish, collects the coin, and pays the tax gatherer.

The subject matter of this painting is taxation, which was becoming an issue in Florence during the 1420s when this painting was completed. *The Tribute Money* points specifically to a biblical precedent about taxation.

What is the most important aspect of this painting is how different it is compared to the work of Giotto only a century before. The building to the right is created in linear perspective. Distance is also created by the use of atmospheric perspective (chapter 5). The figures are more sculptural because the artist used the technique of chiaroscuro (chapter 6). They also cast shadows, as Masaccio has placed a light source off to the right side of the image. All of these advancements show a clear distinction between the artwork produced during the fourteenth century versus the fifteenth century.

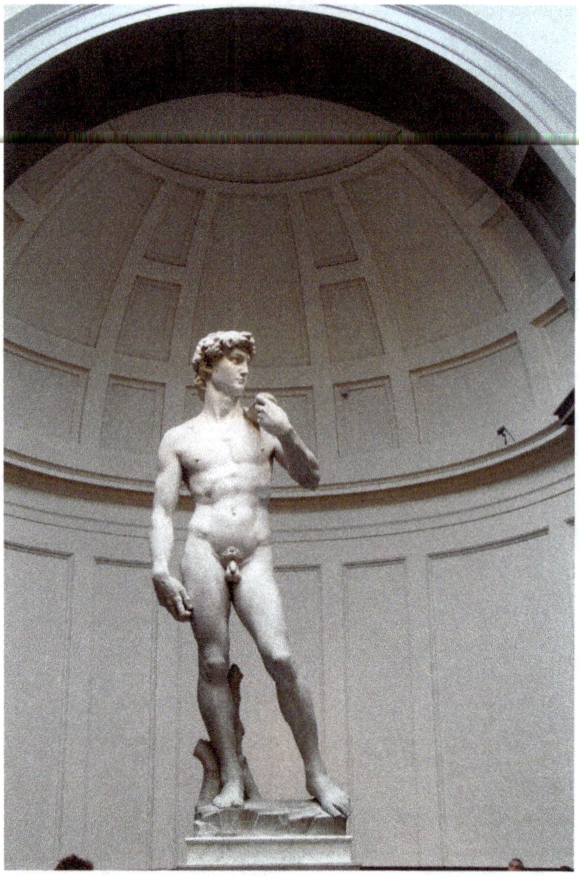

LATE (HIGH) RENAISSANCE

The Late, or High, Renaissance is one where people feel the most comfortable. We are familiar with both the artists and the artworks that were produced during this time period. Perhaps the most famous of the Renaissance artists is Michelangelo. During the Renaissance he produces one of the icons of Western art, the monolithic sculpture of *David* (**fig 22.7**).

Figure 22.7: Michelangelo Buonarroti, *David*, 1501–04. Marble, height 17 ft × pedestal 6 ft, Accademía, Florence.

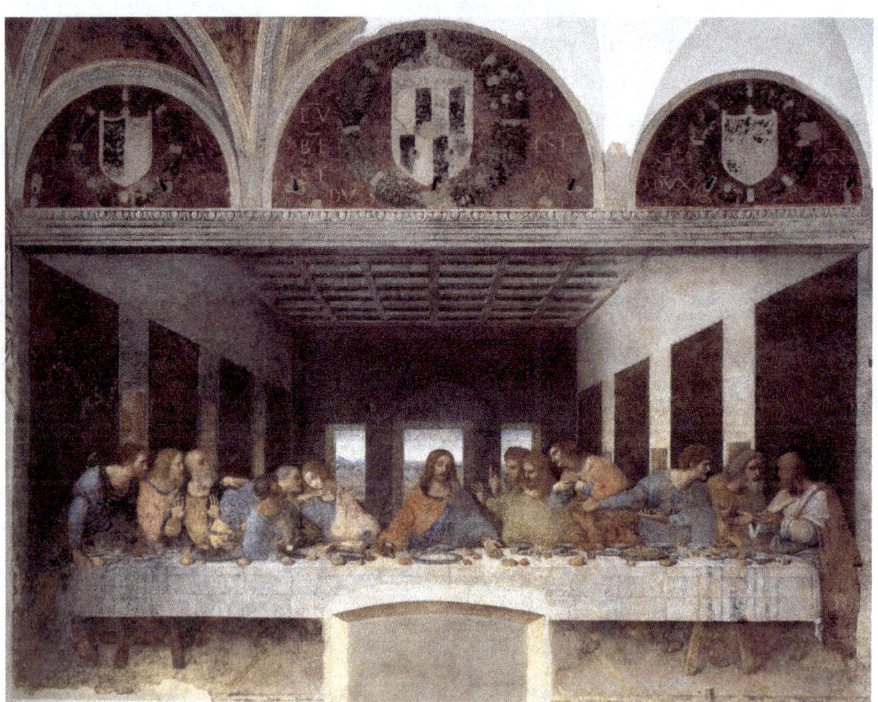

Figure 22.8: Leonardo da Vinci, *The Last Supper*, 1495–98. Fresco Secco, 13 ft 9 in × 29 ft 10 in, Refectory of Santa Maria della Grazie, Milan.

The sculpture is 17 feet tall, roughly three times the height of an average person. The reason it is so tall is because it was originally going to be placed atop the Florence Cathedral, and it needed to be visible from the ground.[9] However, when it was unveiled it "was so admired that the Florentine city council placed it in the square next to the seat of Florence's government."[10]

But Michelangelo's *David* was not the first work of the Late Renaissance. That distinction belongs to Leonardo da Vinci who, in 1498, completed *The Last Supper* (**fig 22.8**) inside the refectory of the Santa Maria della Grazie in the city of Milan. Sadly, even with heroic reconstruction attempts this work remains in disrepair because of the technique that was used when it was painted. The work is painted in *fresco secco*, which is the painting on already dried plaster (chapter 15). If it had been completed in the traditional fresco technique, it would look as pristine as the paintings inside the Arena or Sistine Chapels. We are lucky to have this work at all as the building it is in was nearly destroyed during World War II when a bomb fell on the room it was painted in. The painting was spared because a wall of sandbags had been placed in front of it.

Pope Julius II began to call influential artists to Rome to produce work for the church. Michelangelo was called to paint the ceiling of the Sistine Chapel (**fig 22.9**) with nine images from the book of Genesis. The scenes begin over the altar with the *Separation of Light from Darkness* and end with the *Drunkenness of Noah* positioned over the entrance to the chapel.[11]

At the same time that Michelangelo was painting the ceiling of the Sistine Chapel, a young artist by the name of Raphael was completing another important fresco cycle right next door in the papal apartments. He was awarded a commission in 1508 to paint the four walls of the *Stanza della Segnatura*.[12] The subject matter for this room was the four domains of knowledge: theology, law, poetry, and philosophy. The last domain's image is more

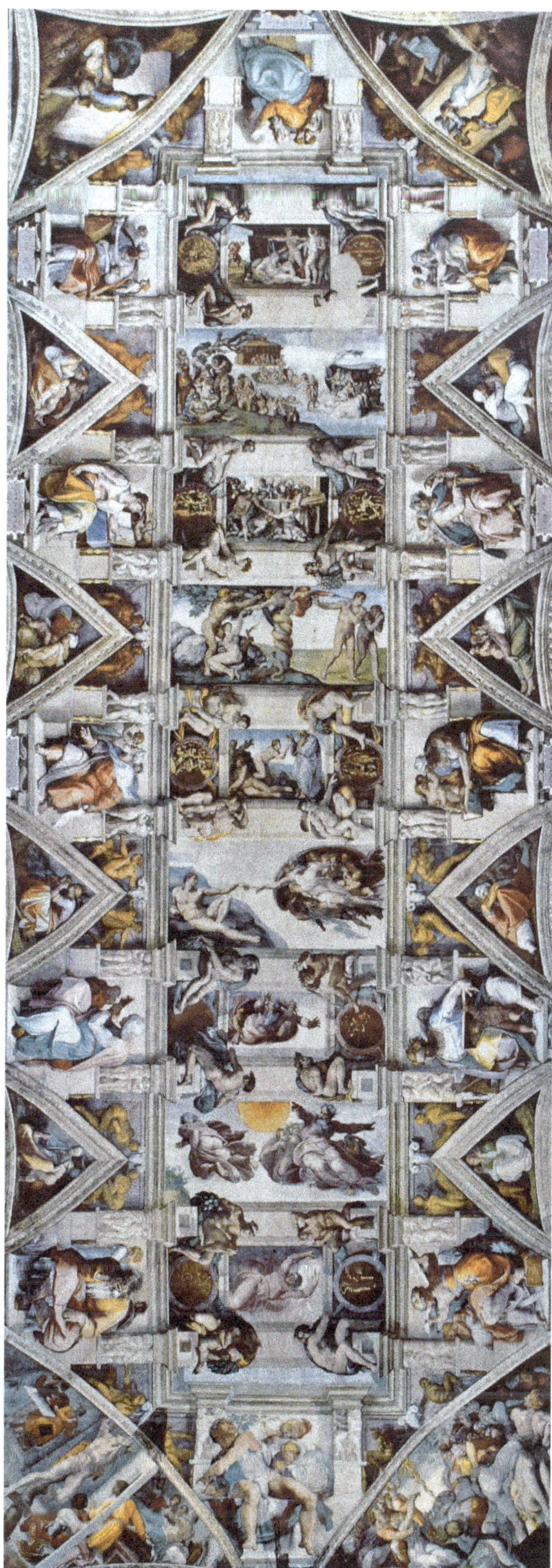

Figure 22.9: Michelangelo Buonarroti, *Sistine Ceiling*, 1508–12. Fresco, 45 ft × 128 ft, Sistine Chapel, Vatican, Rome.

commonly referred to as the *School of Athens* (**fig 22.10**).

The painting depicts a gathering of the greatest philosophers, mathematicians, astronomers, and naturalists of the ancient world. Among the individuals depicted are Plato, Aristotle, Ptolemy, Socrates, Euclid, and Pythagoras. Raphael painted them in the likenesses of his friends. For example, the image of Plato, walking toward us at the left-center of the work, is a portrait of Leonardo da Vinci.[13] Raphael has included himself at the lower-right-hand side of the scene. He is the second figure who is peering out at the viewer.

An interesting part of this painting is the depiction of Michelangelo in the lower portion of the work, near the center. He does not appear on any of the preliminary drawings for this painting, so he was a last-minute addition. He sits leaning against a block of marble in contemporary clothing. He looks out of place amongst the other individuals.

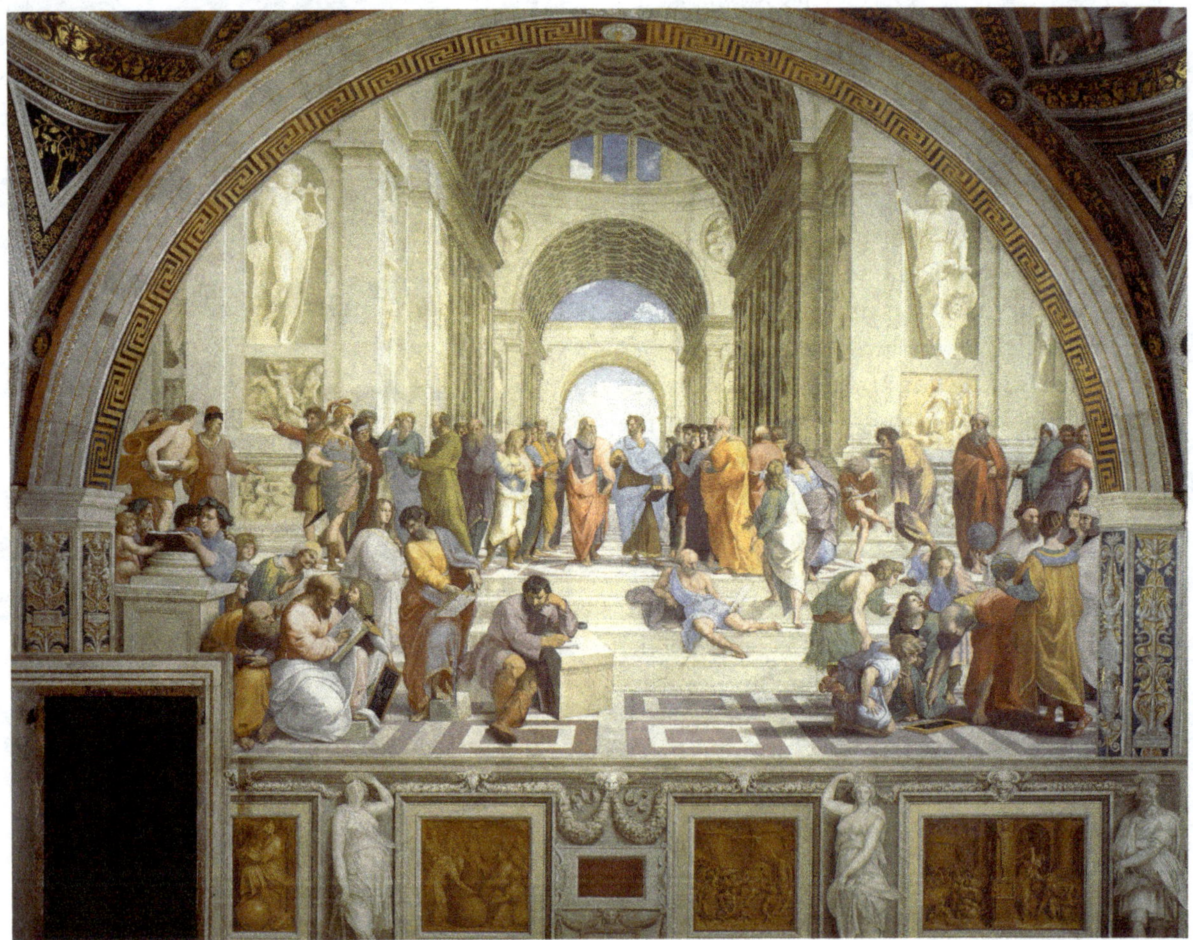

Figure 22.10: Raphael, *School of Athens* 1510–11. Fresco, 19 ft × 27 ft, Stanza della Segnatura, Vatican, Rome.

Renaissance:

Early Renaissance:

Middle Renaissance:

Late (High) Renaissance:

ENDNOTES

1. The Byzantine period is considered the final stage of the Dark Ages. The first stage is the Romanesque period, and the middle stage is the Gothic period.
2. Marilyn Stokstad, *Art History*, revised ed. (New York: Harry N. Abrams, 1999), 615.
3. Frederick Hartt and David G. Wilkins, *History of Italian Renaissance Art* (Upper Saddle River, NJ: Prentice Hall, 2003), 95, 107.
4. Guilds are independent associations of bankers, artisans, merchants, and manufacturers that are similar to today's labor unions. The profession you were in determined the guild you belonged to.
5. *The Medici: Godfathers of the Renaissance*, directed by Justin Hardy (Hollywood: Paramount Home Entertainment, 2005), DVD.
6. *The Medici: Godfathers of the Renaissance*, directed by Justin Hardy (Hollywood: Paramount Home Entertainment, 2005), DVD.
7. Ross King, accessed October 14, 2016, http://library.fora.tv/2007/01/14/Ross_King.
8. Frederick Hartt and David G. Wilkins, *History of Italian Renaissance Art* (Upper Saddle River, NJ: Prentice Hall, 2003), 284.
9. Marilyn Stokstad, *Art History*, revised ed. (New York: Harry N. Abrams, 1999), 698.
10. Marilyn Stokstad, *Art History*, revised ed. (New York: Harry N. Abrams, 1999), 698.
11. A virtual tour of the Sistine Chapel can be found at http://www.vatican.va/various/cappelle/sistina_vr/index.html.
12. The *Stanza della Segnatura* is the library within the papal apartments.
13. Marilyn Stokstad, *Art History*, revised ed. (New York: Harry N. Abrams, 1999), 694.

IMAGE CREDITS

- Fig. 22.1: Giotto, "Enthroned Madonna with Saints," https://en.wikipedia.org/wiki/File:Giotto_Ognissanti_Madonna_white_ground.jpg. Copyright in the Public Domain.
- Fig. 22.2: Cimabue, "Enthroned Madonna and Child with Angels and Prophets," https://commons.wikimedia.org/wiki/File:Cimabue_-_Maest%C3%A0_di_Santa_Trinita_-_Google_Art_Project.jpg. Copyright in the Public Domain.
- Fig. 22.3: Giotto, "Meeting at the Golden Gate," https://commons.wikimedia.org/wiki/File:Giotto_-_Scrovegni_-_-06-_-_Meeting_at_the_Golden_Gate.jpg. Copyright in the Public Domain.
- Fig. 22.4: Giotto, "Last Judgement," https://commons.wikimedia.org/wiki/File:Last-judgment-scrovegni-chapel-giotto-1306.jpg. Copyright in the Public Domain.
- Fig. 22.5: Copyright © Donatello; Photo by Miguel Hermoso Cuesta (CC BY-SA 4.0) at https://commons.wikimedia.org/wiki/File:David_Donatello_01.JPG.
- Fig. 22.6: Masaccio, "[image]: Tribute Money," https://commons.wikimedia.org/wiki/File:Masaccio7.jpg, ~1. Copyright in the Public Domain.
- Fig. 22.7: Copyright © Michelangelo Buonarroti; Photo by Rabe! (CC BY-SA 4.0) at https://commons.wikimedia.org/wiki/File:Florenz_-_David_von_Michelangelo_01.JPG.
- Fig. 22.8: Leonardo da Vinci, "The Last Supper," https://commons.wikimedia.org/wiki/File:Leonarda_da_vinci,_last_supper_01.jpg. Copyright in the Public Domain.
- Fig. 22.9: Copyright © Michelangelo Buonarroti (CC BY-SA 3.0) at https://commons.wikimedia.org/wiki/File:CAPPELLA_SISTINA_Ceiling.jpg.
- Fig. 22.10: Raphael, "School of Athens," https://commons.wikimedia.org/wiki/File:Sanzio_01.jpg. Copyright in the Public Domain.

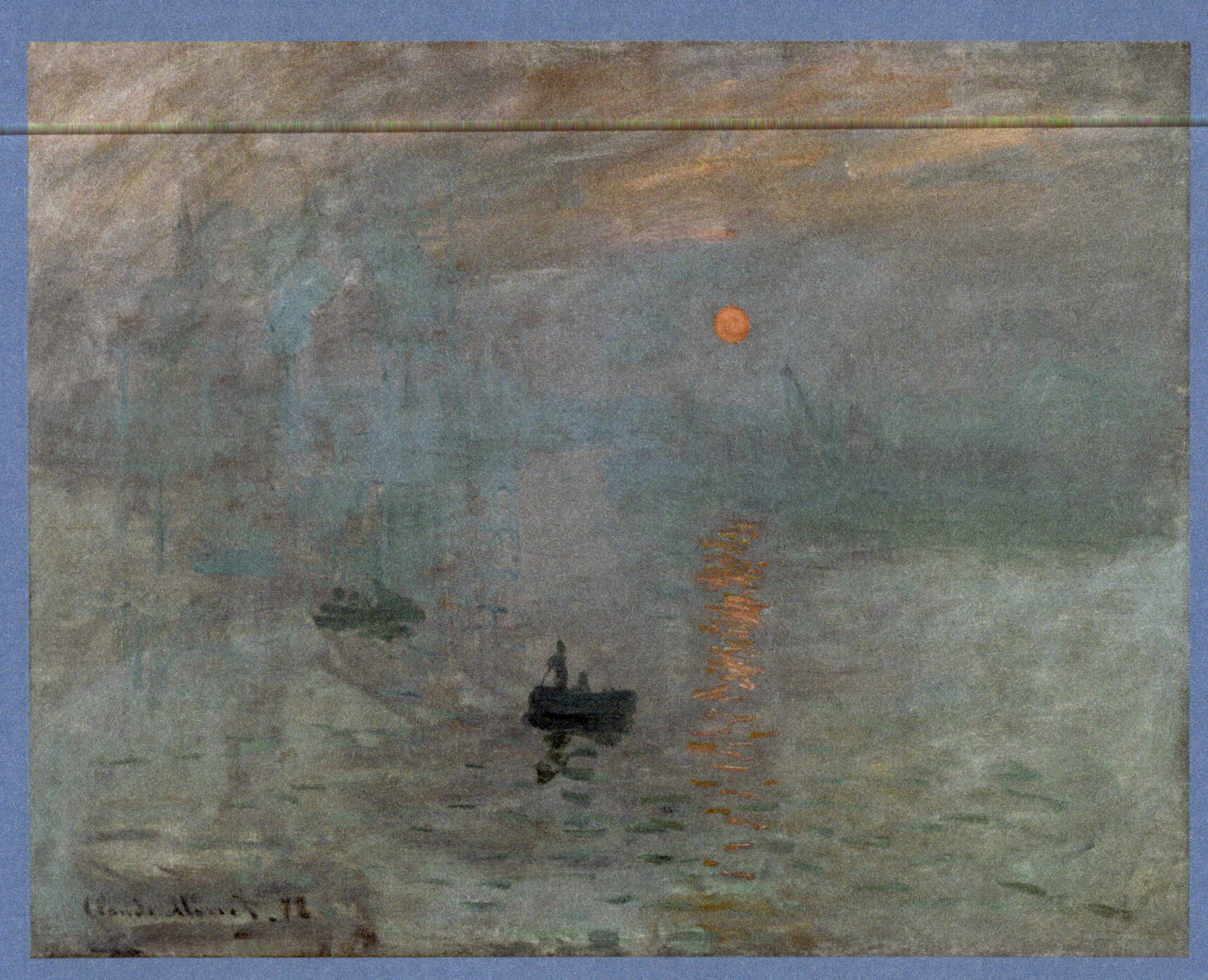

Figure 23.1: Claude Monet, *Impression, Sunrise*, 1872. Oil on canvas, 48 cm × 63 cm, Musée Marmottan Monet, Paris.

MODERN ART

MODERN ART

How does one define the term *modern art*? To some, the term relates to a specific time period. If that is true, then what marked the beginning of the modern age? Are we currently in modern times, or have those ended, and if so, when? Do we consider all art produced during the modern era to be modern art? Others consider modern art to be more of a style, works that can be described as cutting-edge, new-fangled, or abstract—a departure from the traditional.

Modern art can be defined both ways. First, we will take a look at the time period. This textbook considers the first work of modern art to be Édouard Manet's *Luncheon on the Grass* (see fig 2.1), which was created in 1863. The modern era continues to the end of World War II, when Abstract Expressionism emerged in New York.

Next, we will consider the stylistic aspects of modern art. A precursor to the modern era was the invention of the camera in 1839 (chapter 14). Due to its immense popularity, artists were needed less and less. Photography was able to capture the world much more quickly and accurately than artists could ever hope to. Traditional mediums, such as painting and sculpture, needed to evolve in order to stay viable. This opened the door for many artists to experiment within these mediums, which hadn't changed much, technically speaking, since the mid-1400s. In less than a century, **avant-garde** artists would establish different ways of representing color, as well as eliminate the use of linear perspective. These artists would create artwork that would be classified as abstract and nonobjective, terms that would need to be invented in order to explain what they were producing.

IMPRESSIONISM

After completing *Luncheon on the Grass* (see fig 2.1), Édouard Manet began to develop a following of younger artists that included Edgar Degas, Camille Pissarro, Berthe Morisot, and Claude Monet.[1] These individuals were known as Manet's circle and would go on to become the Impressionists. Impressionism was the first secessionist art movement. The term *secessionist* means that these artists held their *own* art exhibitions, in direct opposition to the established Salon. The first Impressionist Exhibition was held in 1874 and was considered a failure in most aspects. The exhibition did not pull the desired percentage of the populace, nor did it create the sales needed to break even.[2] Seven more exhibitions would follow; none of the exhibitions met with critical success. Impressionism would not become popular until a couple of decades after its genesis.

The name *Impressionism* is derived from the title of Claude Monet's painting *Impression, Sunrise* (**fig 23.1**). Impressionism, as seen in this painting, is characterized by short, quick, visible brushstrokes that capture the elements of light. The painting possesses a certain sketch like quality, which happens to be the name sometimes used to address these artists, "the sketchers." One of the great things about Impressionist paintings is that they are enjoyable scenes rather than heavy or religious subject matter. They depict people at rest or leisure, playing, dancing, sailing, or merely walking down the street. The scenes of many Impressionist paintings give us a glimpse into what life was like in Paris in the late nineteenth century.

Impressionists were very experimental. As discussed in chapter 6, they were the first artists to leave the studio as common practice and paint en plein air. They needed to do this in order to capture the optical effects that color had on particular objects, such as grainstacks (see fig 6.11) or cathedrals.

POST-IMPRESSIONISM

Post-Impressionist artists, such as Paul Cézanne, Paul Gauguin, and Vincent van Gogh, continued the modernist theme of experimentation. Although not quite the next generation of artists, they were later contemporaries of the Impressionists. The Post-Impressionists moved away from the pursuit of capturing optical color and instead focused more on its expressive uses. An example of this is Paul Gauguin's painting

Vision After the Sermon (**fig 23.2**); most of the painting is composed of a red background upon which Jacob and an angel are wrestling. The red is not only eye-catching, but also invokes a sense of passion and energy to the battle that is taking place on the painting's surface.

Another artist during this time, Georges Seurat, was busy trying to prove his color theory in a painting entitled *Sunday Afternoon on the Island of La Grande Jatte* (see fig 6.1). In this painting, he places dots or points of pure color next to one another instead of mixing the paint in the traditional sense. His technique of Pointillism (chapter 6) is a success, but it will never see mainstream usage. Meanwhile, an unknown artist, Vincent van Gogh (chapter 24) begins producing soon-to-be iconic paintings in the cities of Paris and Arles.

Paul Cézanne also had an interest in the expressive usage of color, as seen in *The Great Bathers* (not pictured), but his work in the manipulation of spatial planes is even more noteworthy. Manet was the first artist to reject the use of linear perspective. Cézanne would take this effort even further with *Still Life with Basket of Apples* (**fig 23.3**). At first glance this painting looks like a normal still life. However, upon closer examination the painting is quite unsettling. The wine bottle at the center of the work—the stabilizing point of the artwork—is tilted off to the left. The lines that create the front and back edges of the table, although parallel, seem to change direction somewhere near the center of the painting

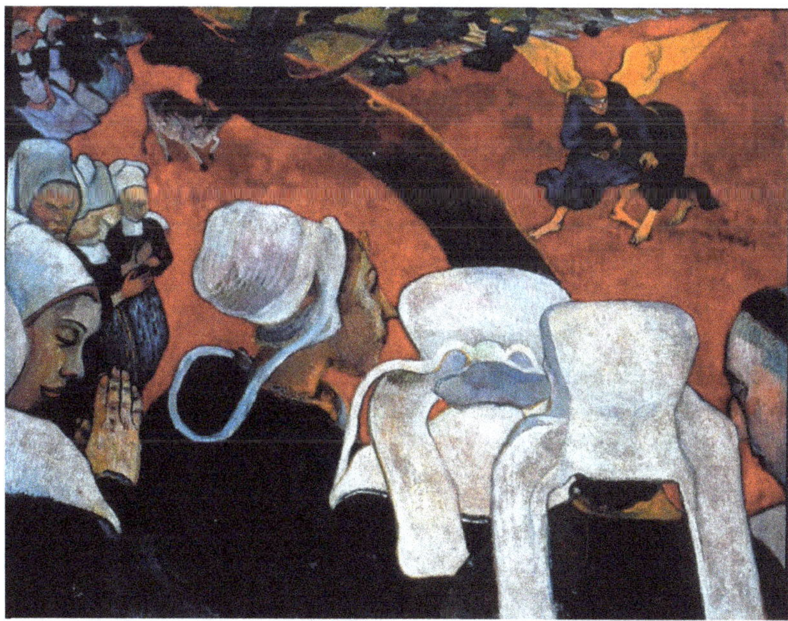

Figure 23.2: Paul Gauguin, *Vision After the Sermon*, 1888. Oil on Canvas, 72.2 cm × 91 cm, National Gallery of Scotland.

underneath the tablecloth and behind the basket of apples. The apples themselves look unstable on the table and appear as if they are about to roll off. The art historian Roger Fry considers Cézanne influential in establishing the "importance of form over content."[3] Due both to his work in color and his manipulation of spatial planes, Cézanne

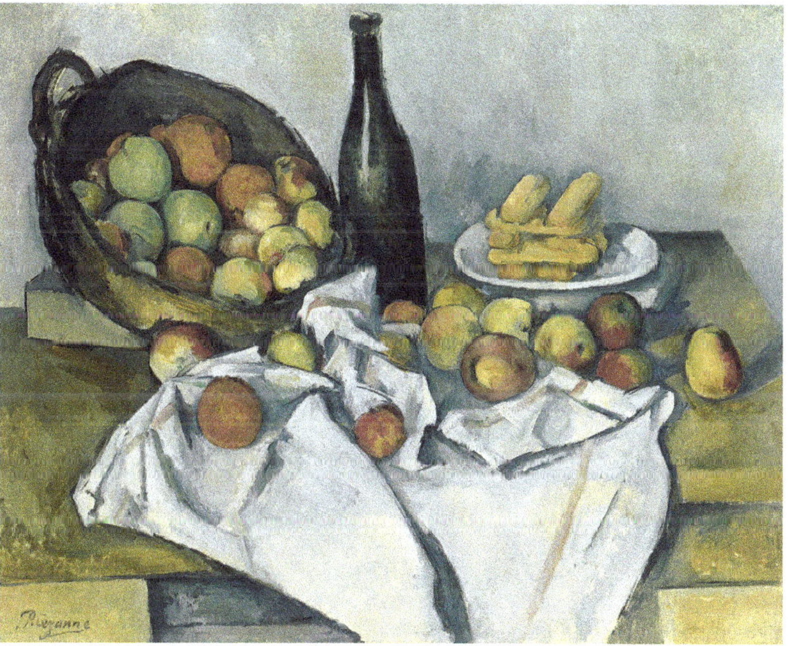

Figure 23.3: Paul Cézanne *Still Life with Basket of Apples*, c. 1890–94. Oil on Canvas, 65 cm × 81 cm, Art Institute of Chicago.

is considered to be the father of two of the early twentieth-century artistic movements: Fauvism and Cubism.

FAUVISM

The first Fauvist works were shown at the Salon d'Automne of 1905. This is also the event where Fauvism earned its name. Fauvist paintings by their very nature are loud and exciting works because of their use of arbitrary color (chapter 6). The brightly colored paintings were hung along the walls at the Salon d'Automne, but in the center of the room, definitely out of place, was a sculpture by the fifteenth-century sculptor, Donatello. The art critic Louis Vauxcelles wrote in his review, "*Donatello au milieu des fauves!*"[4] Translated: "Donatello among the wild beasts!"[5]

Henri Matisse was the leader of this short-lived art movement.[6] The painting of his wife, *Woman with a Hat*, also known as *Femme au Chapeau* (**fig 23.4**) exemplifies the Fauvist use of arbitrary

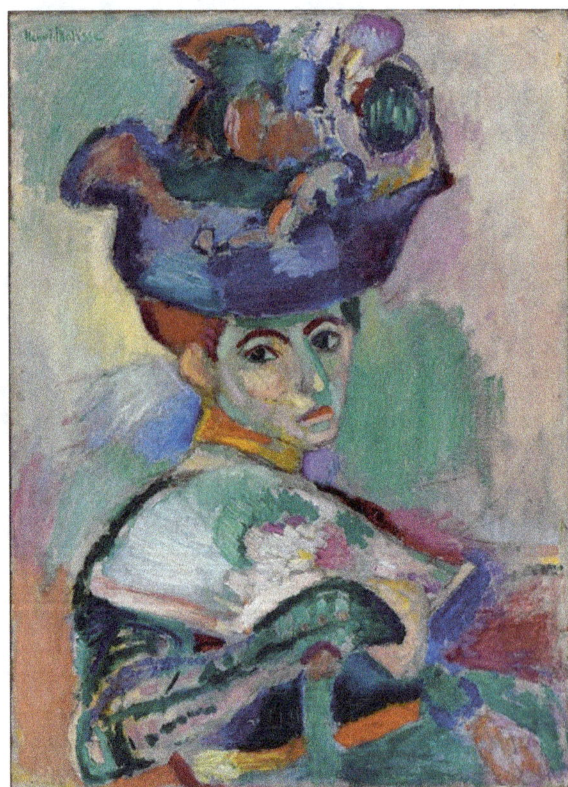

Figure 23.4: Henri Matisse, *Woman with a Hat*, 1905. Oil and Tempera on Canvas 31.75 in × 23.5 in, San Francisco Museum of Modern Art.

color. The portrait shows Matisse's wife looking over her right shoulder wearing an extremely large and colorful hat. Leo Stein, brother of Gertrude, purchased the work, calling it "a thing brilliant and powerful, but the nastiest smear of paint I had ever seen."[7]

CUBISM

In 1907 Picasso created one of the two most important paintings of modern art with *Les Demoiselles d'Avignon* (see fig 3.2).[8] Not only was this painting the first abstract work ever created, but it was also the first Cubist painting. While Pablo Picasso is the name most associated with Cubism, Georges Braque, originally a Fauvist painter, was also an important member and should be considered as cofounder.

Cubism continues the abandonment of linear perspective while emphasizing rectilinear line and geometric shapes. While the color of Cubist paintings would be categorized as arbitrary, it is not nearly as emphasized or spectacular as that of the Fauves. It is generally muted, and many of the paintings take on similar tonality. With respect to structure, Cubist works tend to divide the subject matter up into several planes and present them to the viewer at one time rather than in sequential order. In other words, the viewer is seeing the top, bottom, and sides of the object at the exact same moment. This breakdown of time and space is seen in Picasso's *Les Demoisselles d'Avignon* where a woman is sitting near the lower-left quadrant of the canvas. A frontal view of her face is presented although we see her back at the time.

FUTURISM

Futurism is a direct spin-off from Cubism. It differs from the other modern art movements because it originated in Italy rather than France. The leader of the Futurists, Filippo Marinetti, authored the *Futurist Manifesto*. The manifesto stated the intention and philosophy of the group. In this case the Futurists were interested in mechanization, violence, power, speed, and war. In fact they venerated war, calling it "the world's only hygiene."[9]

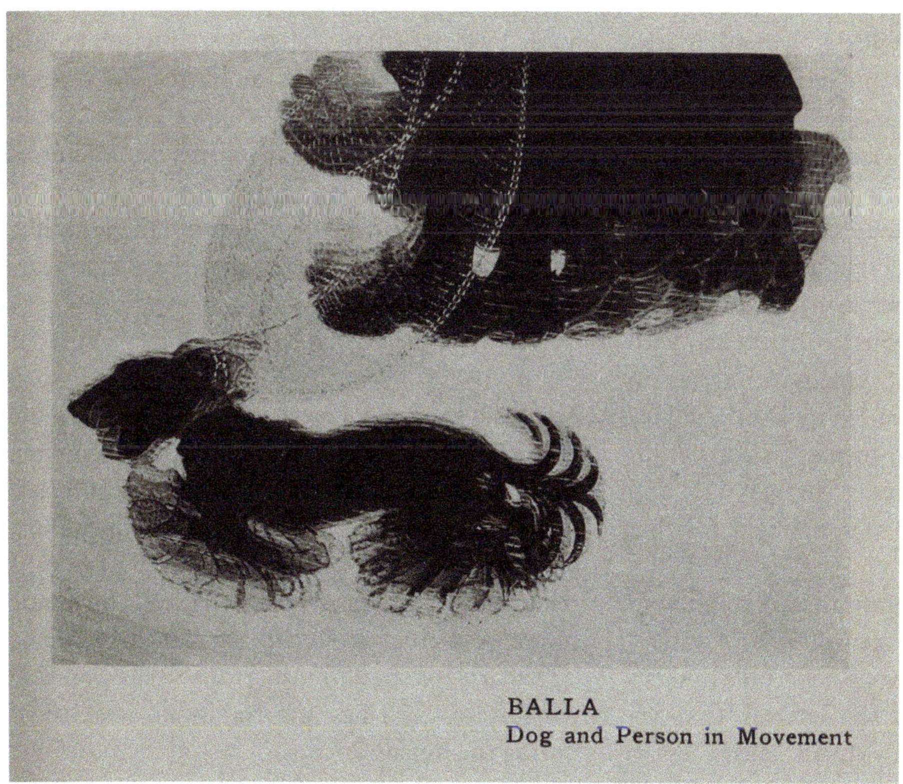

Figure 23.5: Giacomo Balla, *Dynamism of a Dog on a Leash*, 1912. Oil on Canvas, 35$^{3}/_{8}$ in × 43 1/4 in, Albright-Knox Art Gallery, Buffalo.

movement, but were in agreement as to its meaning.

Up until now the argument pertaining to modern art was simple and straightforward. It was an argument over how art was produced—either in a traditional format or in a manner that was innovative and experimental. However, Dada posed a much more serious question, asking us to consider "What is art?"

Originally a Cubist painter, Marcel Duchamp, becomes the most important voice in Parisian Dada. His work *Fountain* (**fig 23.6**) continues to bring forth extreme emotions from viewers. The work itself is a urinal turned on its side. Duchamp would

An exciting aspect of Futurism is that the artists did their best to depict movement through static art mediums, such as painting and sculpture. In *Dynamism of a Dog* (**fig 23.5**), Giacomo Balla superimposes the dog and the leash several times in order to give the illusion of movement. Balla's paintings were much tamer and less involved with violence than the other Futurists. He was a little bit older than most of the Futurists and lived in Milan rather than in Rome. Several Futurists, such as Umberto Boccioni, would go off to fight in World War 1 and were killed during the war, putting an early end to this art movement.

DADA

Emerging on the other side of World War I was the movement of Dada. It is a unique movement in that it emerged from different cities at the same time. It began in Zurich, where many artists immigrated at the beginning of the war, but it quickly found footing in other cities, including Paris, Berlin, and New York. Each city had its own unique take on the aesthetics and style of the

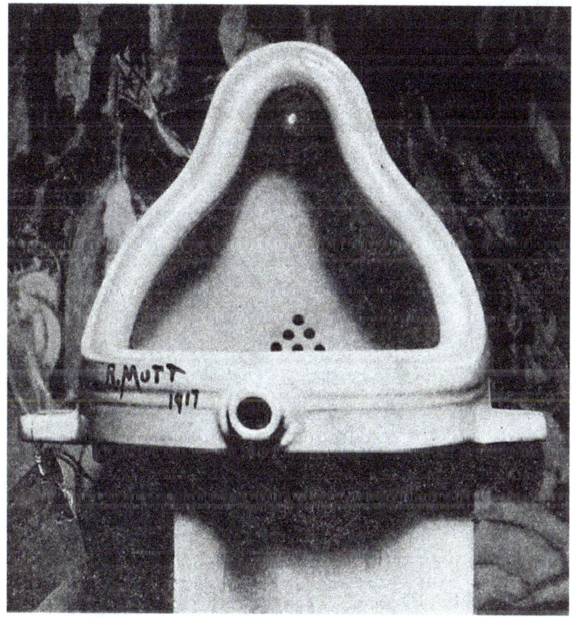

Figure 23.6: Marcel Duchamp, *Fountain*, 1917. Porcelain urinal turned on its back, Destroyed.

label this and similar objects as **readymade**, which were commonly manufactured items that had been transformed into works of art. *Fountain* was entered into "the 1917 exhibition of the New York Society of Independent Artists."[10] It was promptly removed from the exhibition. The jury of the art exhibit argued that this was not an artwork, but instead just an article of plumbing. Duchamp argued back, "whether [the artist] with his own hands made the fountain or not has no importance. He CHOSE it. He took an ordinary article of life, placed it so that its useful significance disappeared and under the new title and point of view—created a new thought for that object."[11]

The long-reaching effects of Dada are incredibly important to future generations of artists. Dada allows for art to become conceptual, meaning that the idea behind the artwork is much more important than the artwork itself. This is going to be of critical importance post World War II when we begin to enter the time period of contemporary art.

SURREALISM

Of all the modern art movements discussed in this chapter, Surrealism may have survived the longest, with artists actively producing work for approximately 30 years. Early Surrealist works appear in the 1920s, and artists continued creating Surrealist works into the 1950s. The Surrealists believed that their talent/inspiration came from the subconscious and reflected their impulses, desires, and fears. Most Surrealist works show a duality or juxtaposition between extremes: interior versus exterior, conscious versus unconscious, dream versus reality.

The most iconic work of Surrealism is Salvador Dalí's *The Persistence of Memory* from 1931 (not pictured). It is a barren landscape scene punctuated by melting clocks. Although Dalí is the artist most associated with the movement, he was actually kicked out of the Surrealist movement in 1936. Surrealism appeared as more of a club or organization at times rather than an art movement where members had to abide by strict rules. Artists were invited to join and, as just noted, could be kicked out if they didn't live up to the group's expectations. Pablo Picasso didn't even realize he was a member of the group. The founder of Surrealism, André Breton, wrote the *Surrealist Manifesto*, and, like Filippo Marinetti, never produced any noteworthy art himself.

AMERICAN MODERNISM

This chapter has taken a look at the incredible development of art seen in Europe during the late nineteenth and early twentieth centuries. Americans were not accepting of European art, as witnessed with the Armory Show of 1913 (chapter 2). Americans were critical and made fun of works such as Duchamp's *Nude Descending a Staircase* (see fig 2.6). American artists were still clinging to the rules and traditions established during the Renaissance.

Consider the painting *Nighthawks* (**fig 23.7**) by Edward Hopper. It depicts a scene from Greenwich Village in New York, where the artist lived. A diner sits on a virtually empty street, and it looks to be the middle of the night. Only a few customers are inside, and although they are huddled together a sense of isolation pervades the image. The two figures sitting together are not conversing or even acknowledging one another's presence. The figure with his back to us sits removed from the other patrons. The lone employee of the diner is set off from the customers because of the physical barrier of the bar. Finally, the viewer, too, is isolated, as we can peer into the diner but cannot enter because of the lack of a door.

This painting and others done by Hopper and other famous regionalist painters of the time, such as Grant Wood, are very traditional in form and function. The art itself is representational. All the elements appear as they should. The colors are local and the space is authentic with respect to linear perspective. The only thing we can address as being "modern" about this painting is that it shows a current scene and it relates current issues of isolation felt throughout New York and America during World War II.[12]

ABSTRACT EXPRESSIONISM

Europe was left decimated at the end of World War II, and New York became the center of the art world. During the war many artists immigrated to the United States, and many artworks were brought to its museums for safekeeping. Abstract Expressionism emerges as the first American art movement. Abstract Expressionism is also referred to as the *New York School* or the *action painters* (chapter 7).

Each of the artists associated with this movement had their own unique style of painting. It is not difficult to distinguish the difference between Jackson Pollock's "drip" paintings (see fig 7.7) and the "color field" paintings of Mark Rothko. Most Abstract Expressionist paintings fall into the category of nonobjective art because they lack subject matter or recognizable objects. So why weren't they called the "Nonobjective Expressionists"? The answer is quite simple. The term *nonobjective* had not been coined at the time they were active.

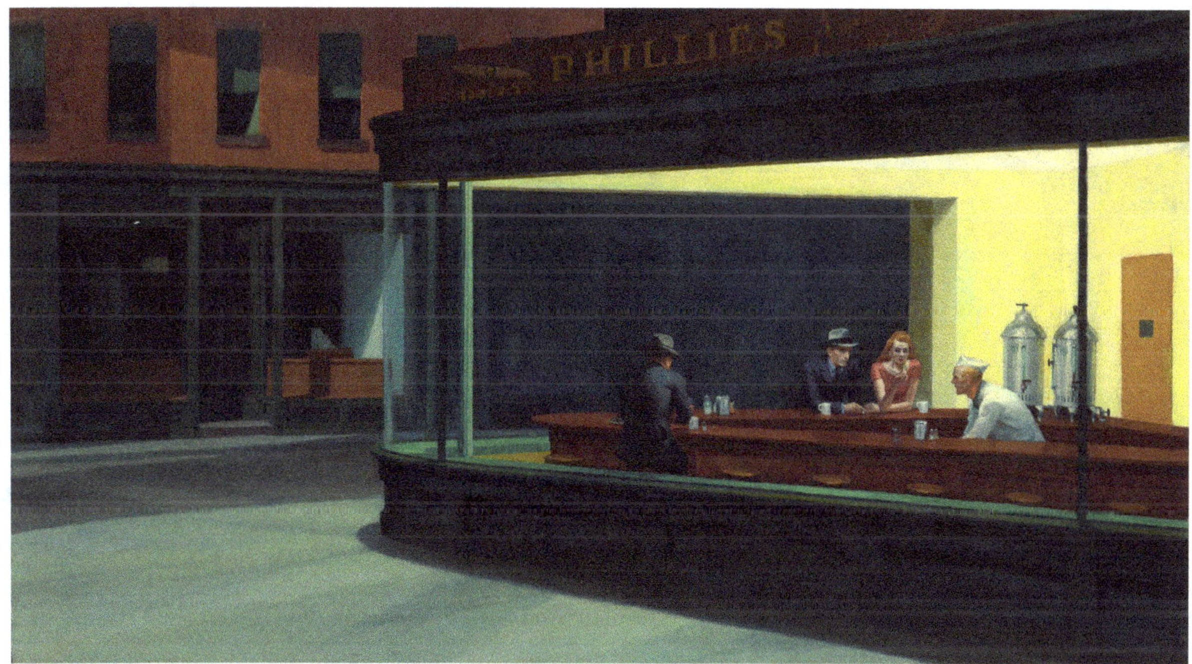

Figure 23.7: Edward Hopper, *Nighthawks*, 1942. Oil on Canvas, 33³/₁₆ in × 60¹/₈ in, Art Institute of Chicago.

Impressionism:

Post-Impressionism:

Fauvism:

Cubism:

Futurism:

Dada:

Surrealism:

American Modernism:

Abstract Expressionism:

Avant-Garde:

ENDNOTES

1. Ross King, accessed October 30, 2016, http://library.fora.tv/2007/01/14/Ross_King.
2. Peter Gay, *Modernism: The Lure of Heresy from Baudelaire to Beckett and Beyond* (New York: W. W. Norton, 2008), 76.
3. Laurie Schneider Adams, *The Methodologies of Art: An Introduction* (Boulder, CO: Westview Press, 1996), 34.
4. H. H. Arnason and Elizabeth Mansfield, *History of Modern Art*, 7th ed. (Upper Saddle River, NJ: Pearson Education, 2013), 90.
5. H. H. Arnason and Elizabeth Mansfield, *History of Modern Art*, 7th ed. (Upper Saddle River, NJ: Pearson Education, 2013), 90.
6. Fauvism lasts from 1903 to 1908.
7. Robert M. Crunden, *American Salons: Encounters with European Modernism, 1885–1917* (Oxford: Oxford University Press, 1993), 285.
8. The other important painting of modern art is Manet's *Luncheon on the Grass*.
9. Filippo Tommaso Marinetti, "The Foundation and Manifesto of Futurism" in *Art in Theory, 1900–2000: An Anthology of Changing Ideas*, eds. Charles Harrison and Paul Wood (Oxford: Blackwell Publishing, 2003), 147–149.
10. H. H. Arnason and Elizabeth Mansfield, *History of Modern Art*, 7th ed. (Upper Saddle River, NJ: Pearson Education, 2013), 221.
11. H. H. Arnason and Elizabeth Mansfield, *History of Modern Art*, 7th ed. (Upper Saddle River, NJ: Pearson Education, 2013), 221.
12. "Hopper, Nighthawks," accessed October 30, 2016, https://www.youtube.com/watch?v=j24uh8cZ3wA.

IMAGE CREDITS

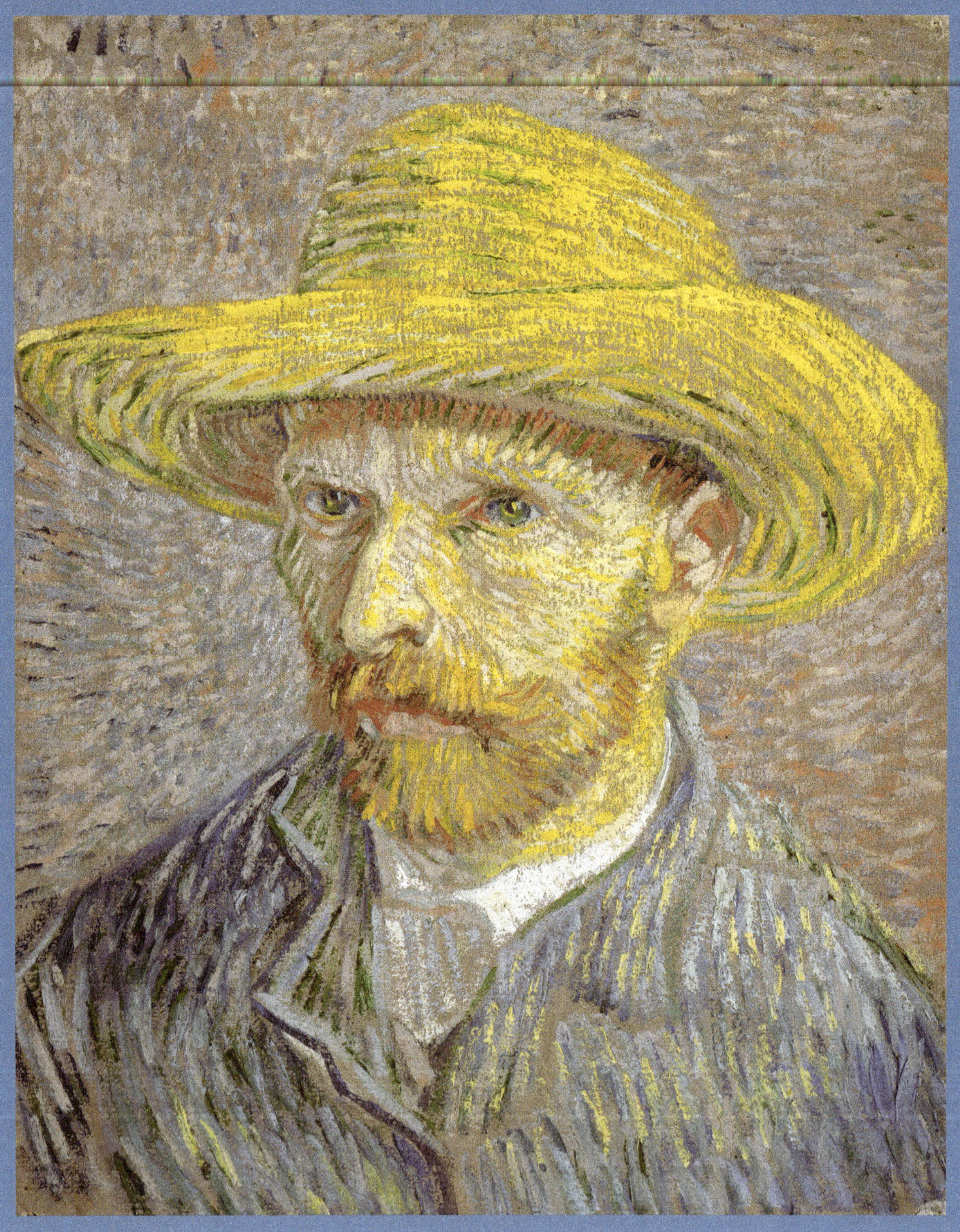

Figure 24.1: Vincent van Gogh, *Self-Portrait with Straw Hat*, 1887. Oil on canvas, 16 in × 12.5 in, Metropolitan Museum of Art, New York.

VINCENT VAN GOGH

As popular as Vincent van Gogh is, the average person actually knows little about him, save for the fact that he cut off his ear. This chapter's goal is to introduce you to an entirely different figure than the one you have created in your mind. Yes, it will cover the ear-cutting incident and his mental state, but it will also delve much deeper into van Gogh's life and artworks as well as trace the evolution of his unique style.

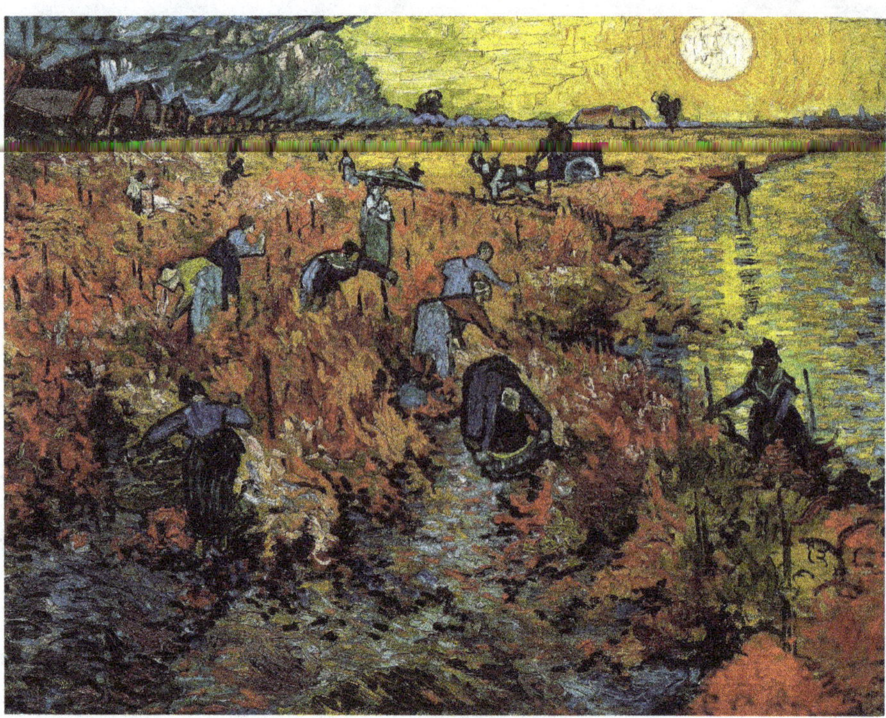

Figure 24.2: Vincent van Gogh, *The Red Vineyard*, 1888. Oil on Canvas, 29.5 in × 36.6 in, Pushkin Museum, Moscow.

Normally when artists are talked about we refer to them by their last name or full name. But in this chapter, in order to avoid confusion, at times we are going refer to Vincent van Gogh simply as "Vincent," because we will be dealing with other family members who would share the same last name.

During his lifetime Vincent van Gogh was basically ignored as an artist, only selling one work, *The Red Vineyard* (**fig 24.2**), for 400 francs.[1] Yet today his works sell for millions of dollars! One of his most noted works, *Sunflowers* (**fig 24.3**), sold at Christie's in 1987 for nearly 40 million dollars.[2] Later that same year *Irises* (**fig 24.4**) sold for nearly 54 million dollars.[3] And that isn't even van Gogh's highest-selling work at auction. That prize goes to *Portrait of Dr. Gachet* (**fig 24.5**). (Gachet was the doctor who cared for Vincent during the last couple of months of his life.) This painting went to auction in 1990 and brought a whopping sum of 82.5 million dollars![4]

Take a moment to note how Vincent van Gogh signs his name on the canvases of both *Sunflowers* and *Irises*. He signs the paintings with his first name only. Consider the paintings by another famous artists, Claude Monet; he signs his entire name, as seen in his *Grainstack* painting (see fig 6.11).

Other artists, such as Picasso, use their initials and last name or last name exclusively. Vincent

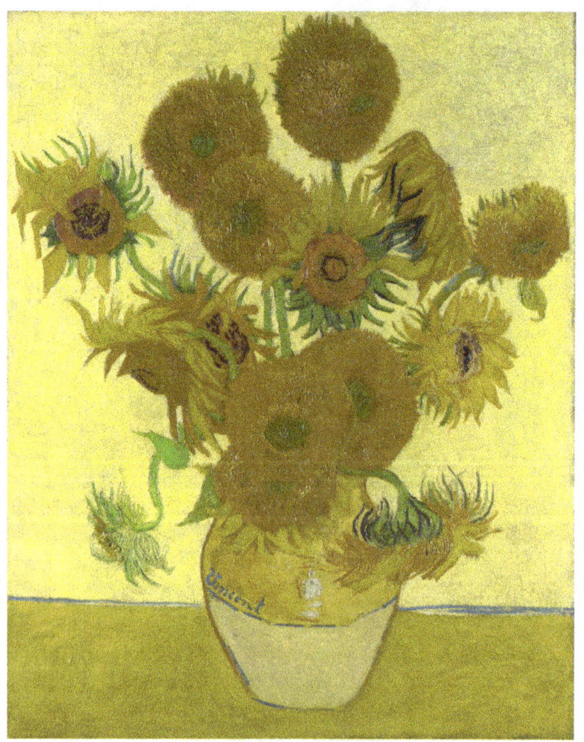

Figure 24.3: Vincent van Gogh, *Sunflowers*, 1888 Oil on Canvas, 36.3 in × 28.7 in, National Gallery, London.

gives one reason for not using his last name in a letter to his brother Theo, writing, "for the excellent reason that people here [Arles, France] wouldn't be able to pronounce that name."[5]

The lure of Vincent van Gogh's works is irresistible, and people will do anything to obtain one. If they can't afford one of his paintings, they might steal one. Such was the case in 2002 when thieves, using a ladder, climbed onto the roof of the Van Gogh Museum in Amsterdam, broke in through a window, and made off with two paintings: *Congregation Leaving the Reformed Church in Nuenen* and *View of the Sea at Schevengingen*.[6] A year later *The Fortification of Paris* was stolen (along with two other works not by van Gogh) from the Whitworth Gallery in Manchester, England. In this burglary, the thieves left a note explaining, "that they were only trying to highlight the poor security at the gallery."[7] The paintings were recovered the next day in a public restroom, but the upper-right-hand corner of the van Gogh painting had been torn. The paintings from the Van Gogh Museum were recovered only recently, in October 2016.[8]

Vincent van Gogh has a very interesting history. He was born in 1853, but doesn't begin painting until 1880 at the age of 27. His career is short—only 10 years—due to his suicide in 1890. But during this time he completes more than 1,700 works of art, with 463 of those being completed in the last 30 months of his life, from January 1888 to July 1890.[9] When you figure the math, that means he completed a painting every 46 hours! And we are not talking small, insignificant paintings. This was the time when he completed some of his most noted masterpieces, including

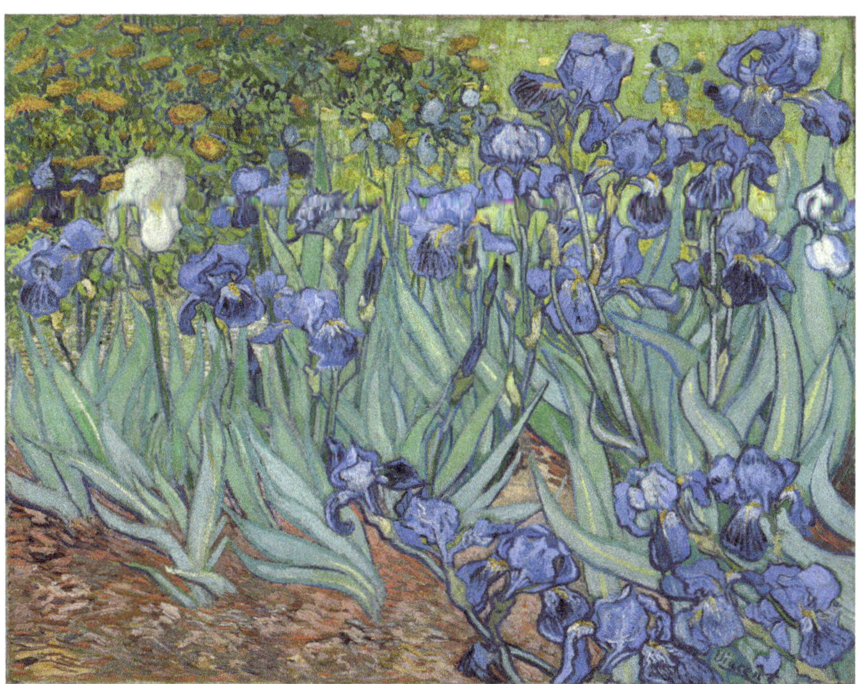

Figure 24.4: Vincent van Gogh, *Irises*, 1889. Oil on Canvas, 29.3 in × 37.1 in, Getty Museum, Los Angeles.

Sunflowers (**fig 24.3**), *Irises* (**fig 24.4**), *Portrait of Dr. Gachet* (**fig 24.5**), *Wheatfield with Crows* (see

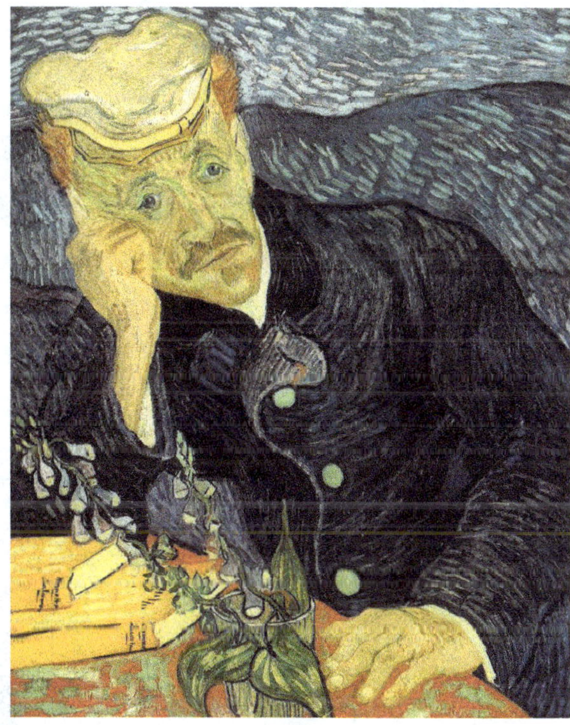

Figure 24.5: Vincent van Gogh, Portrait of Dr. Gachet, 1890. Oil on Canvas Mounted on Wood, 26.4 in × 22 in, Private Collection.

fig 4.10), *The Night Café* (see fig 6.7), and *Starry Night* (see fig 8.6).

Vincent van Gogh was a remarkable person. He studied both Greek and Latin. He was conversant in four languages: French, German, English, and his native Dutch.[10] He began his adult life as a Baptist minister, following in the footsteps of his father, and served the poor coal mining towns of Belgium, earning the nickname, "Christ of the Coal Mines."

Vincent was the eldest of six children of Theodorus and Anna-Cornelia van Gogh. Next in line was his sister Anna, followed by Theo. We will return to Theo in just a moment because of his importance in Vincent's life. Then came Elizabeth and Wilhelmina, and the last child to be born was Cornelius. It is interesting to look at the overall genetics of the family. The men—Vincent, Theo, and Cornelius—would all die in their 30s, while the women—Anna, Elizabeth, and Wilhelmina—would all live well into their 70s. None of them, with the exception of Theo, would have children. His progeny extends the family line to the current day.

Theo van Gogh was probably the most influential and important person in Vincent's life. Even though Theo was three years younger than Vincent, he was the one who financially supported him so he could pursue a career as an artist. A wealth of information about Vincent can be discovered in the letters written between the two brothers. These letters have been published in both single- and multivolume sets as well as being available to be viewed free of charge on the website vangoghletters.org. The brothers are buried next to one another at the cemetery at Auvers-sur-Oise in Northern France, about 20 miles outside of Paris.

In 1885 Vincent produced his first masterpiece, *The Potato Eaters* (**fig 24.6**). Consider how

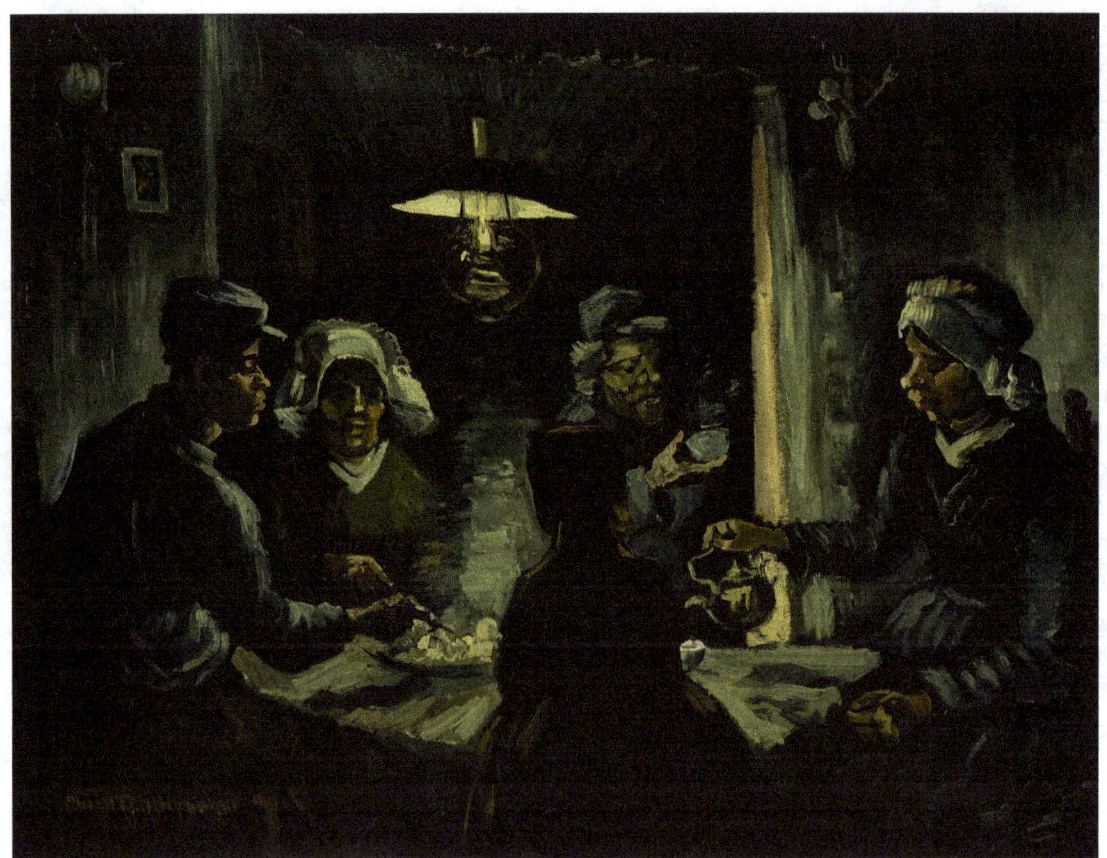

Figure 24.6: Vincent van Gogh, *The Potato Eaters*, 1885. Oil on Canvas Mounted on Wood, 28.3 in × 36.6 in, Kröller-Müller Museum, Netherlands.

different this painting is compared to the works Vincent is most noted for. While the expressionistic qualities of this painting are definitely present, there is an absence of color. This painting is also important because the subject matter of this work is that of the poor, the working class, laborers. However you would want to classify this group of people, it is a very unique subject matter for the time. Prior to the modern era, the people (not considering religious or mythological figures) who would most likely be presented in an art form, such as painting or sculpture, would be the leaders of a country, the leaders of the military, and the leaders of the church. The exception to that rule would be wealthy families. As we venture into the modern era, when artwork becomes more affordable, we begin to see middle- to upper-middle-class individuals being portrayed, such as with the works of the Impressionists (see chapter 23). Vincent's painting features the poor as the focal point of the work. This is a class of people he felt a connection with. Even in his *Self-Portrait with Straw Hat* (**fig 24.1**) he presents himself as a peasant. Self-portraits by other artists usually concentrate on their social standing, such as Diego Velázquez presenting himself as part of the court of King Philip IV, or are attempts to show their technical skill, as seen in the self-portraits of Artemisia Gentileschi and Jan van Eyck.

Vincent sends *The Potato Eaters* to his brother Theo who is living in Paris and is an art dealer of some renowned and asks him to sell the painting. Upon looking at the painting, Theo would have known that this was not a painting that would be easy to sell in Paris in the mid-1880s. During this period, Impressionism had finally caught on with the public. The most famous artists of the time were Monet, Renoir, Degas, and Cassatt. Impressionist works, as described in chapter 23, are bright and full of color and generally feature happy scenes of people at rest or at leisure.

Up until this time Vincent had been working in the Netherlands. It is easy to identify the work he produced there because it is dark, monochromatic, and has a heavy subject matter. Upon hearing of the Impressionists from his brother, he decides that it is time he moved to Paris, where he will reside for approximately the next two years, from 1886 to 1888.

What happens to Vincent's style while he is in Paris is remarkable! Comparing the *Interior of a Restaurant* (**fig 24.7**) with *The Potato Eaters*, it looks like a totally different painter created them. *Interior of a Restaurant* is much more in line with the Impressionist style, with its short, quick visible brush strokes. Although Vincent meets with the Impressionists and spends time with

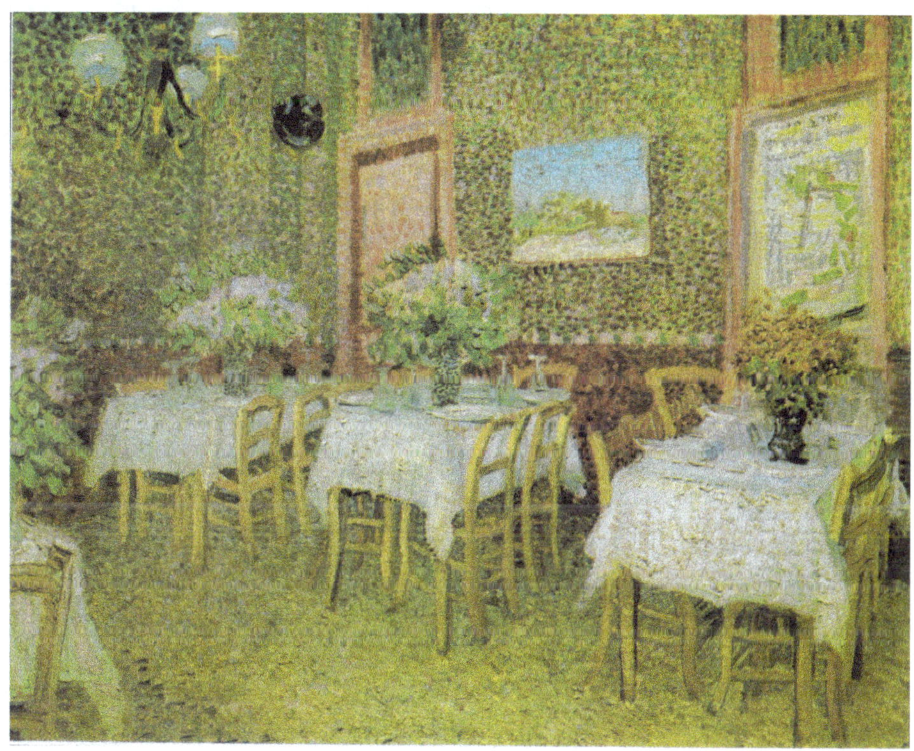

Figure 24.7: Vincent van Gogh, *Interior of a Restaurant*, 1887. Oil on Canvas, 45.5 cm × 56.5 cm, Kröller-Müller Museum, Netherlands.

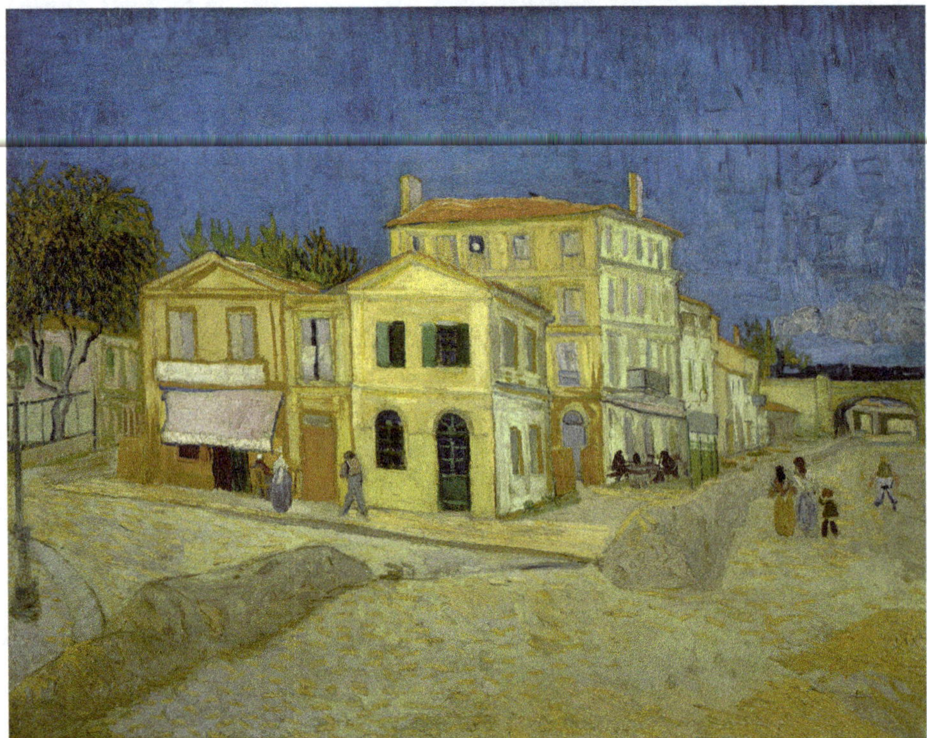

Figure 24.8: Vincent van Gogh, *The Yellow House*, 1888. Oil on Canvas, 28.3 in × 36 in, Van Gogh Museum, Amsterdam.

them, in the overall scope of art history he will be categorized as a Post-Impressionist. Vincent was not as concerned with the optical effects of light as the Impressionists were. Instead, Vincent was concerned with the expressive uses of color.

In 1888 Vincent decides that he has had enough of Paris and moves to the city of Arles, which is in the South of France. Here he moves into *The Yellow House* (**fig 24.8**), where he wants to establish an artist colony.[11] Vincent's friend, and fellow artist, Paul Gauguin becomes his roommate. Vincent wants Gauguin to lead the artist colony. You could not have picked a worse roommate than Gauguin. The two would constantly argue. Van Gogh scholar Patricia Craig states that this is because Gauguin was jealous of Vincent's talents.[12] Gauguin would stand over Vincent while he was painting and yell at him, "You're painting too fast!" Vincent would respond by yelling back, "You're looking too fast!"[13]

It is because of Gauguin that we have a narrative of the ear-cutting incident. It seems that earlier in the day Vincent and Gauguin had been fighting, and each goes storming off out of their apartment.

Later that night as Gauguin is walking down an alleyway, he hears someone following him. He turns and sees it is Vincent brandishing a razor. According to Gauguin, he states that "he stared Vincent down with a look and told him to go home."[14] Vincent turns and leaves, and allegedly upon returning to the Yellow House he severs part of his ear. According to Patricia Craig, this is where the story gets blown out of proportion. He did not cut his entire ear off, just the lower lobe.[15] Later that night Vincent goes to a brothel and hands a folded up handkerchief to a prostitute named Rachel. He tells her, "*Gardez cet objet très soigneusement*" (translated: "Guard this object carefully"), and then turns and leaves. Inside that handkerchief was the severed portion of his ear.[16]

What made Vincent van Gogh cut off his ear? Was it mental illness? Was it something else? Consider the different medical issues Vincent was facing. He had contracted syphilis and other venereal diseases from his frequent visits to brothels. It is now believed he had Meniere's disease, which is an inner ear disorder that causes severe headaches and vertigo. He had been diagnosed with epilepsy.[17] He had developed lead poisoning from putting paintbrushes into his mouth to hold them. He would sip turpentine, which has very addictive fumes, and was an absinthe drinker.

Vincent seeks help and admits himself to the asylum at St. Rémy, which is about 12 miles up the road from Arles. This is another common misnomer about van Gogh. People say that he was locked away, but this just not true. He admitted himself for care and could come and go as he pleased. His brother Theo was paying the bill and also rented the adjoining room so that Vincent could have a studio in which to paint.[18] The asylum at St. Rémy was originally a Catholic monastery, and today it serves as a popular tourist attraction. It looks very much like it did back in Vincent's time, as seen in his painting *Garden of the Hospital in Arles* (**fig 24.9**).

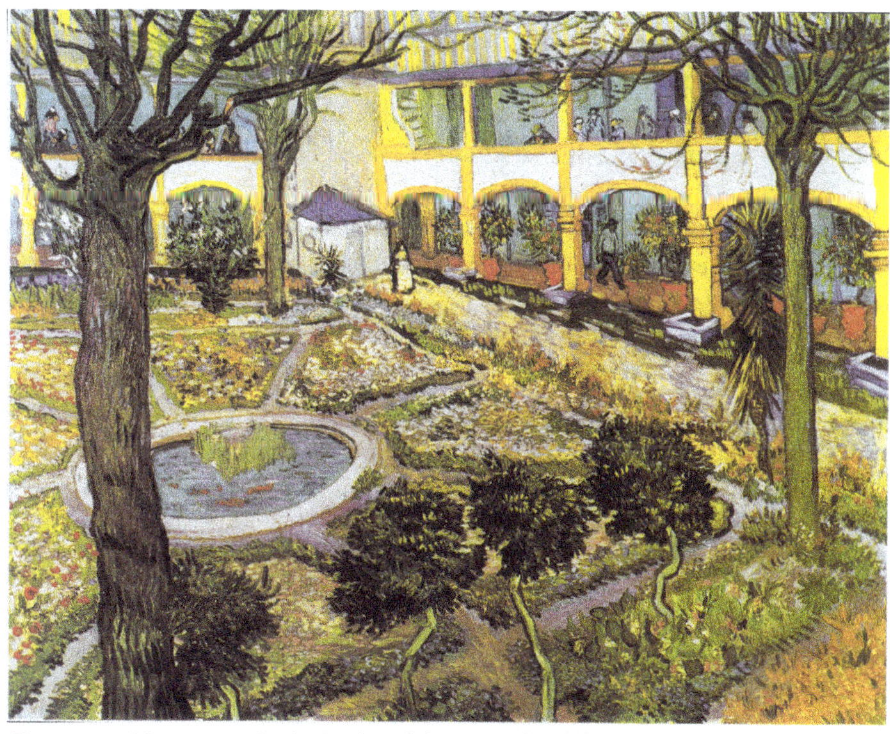

Figure 24.9: Vincent van Gogh, *Garden of the Hospital in Arles*, 1889. Oil on Canvas, 73 cm × 92 cm, Oskar Reinhart Museum, Winterthur, Switzerland.

It was during his time at St. Rémy that he began getting troubling news from his brother. Theo had fallen in love with and then married Johanna Bonger (**fig 24.10**). Theo and Johanna would have one child, who they named Vincent van Gogh. This is interesting in that it was not the first time someone in the immediate family had used this name. A year to the day before Vincent, the artist, was born, his mother, Anna-Cornelia, had had a stillborn son that was given the name of Vincent van Gogh. Vincent and his mother were never close. Perhaps Vincent was a remembrance of the child she lost. He longed for her affection, and one of the reasons he produced so many landscape paintings may have been because his mother was fond of those types of scenes.

Vincent left the asylum at St Rémy and moved to the town of Auvers-sur-Oise, just outside of Paris, where he spent the last few months of his life. He lived in the home of his friend Dr. Paul Gachet (**fig 24.5**), who would treat and look after him. Vincent commented about his doctor in a letter to his brother and sister-in-law stating, "I think that we must IN NO WAY count on Dr. Gachet. In the first place he is iller than I am."[19]

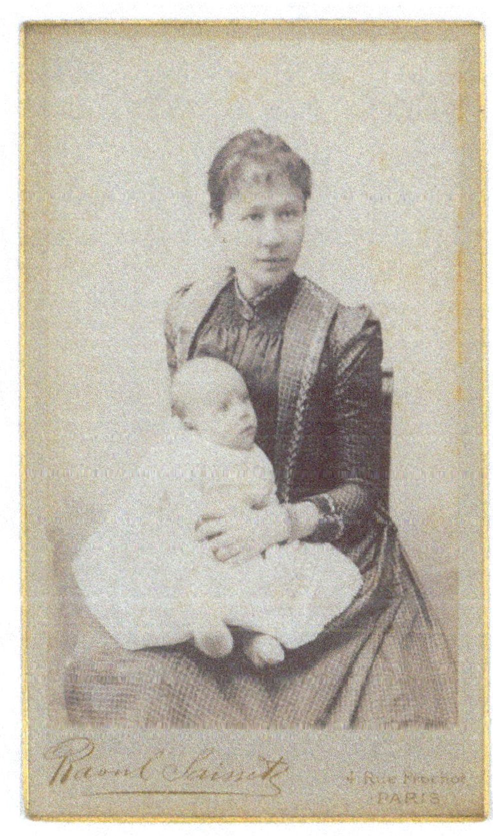

Figure 24.10: Johanna van Gogh (Theo's wife) and her son Vincent, 1890.

Vincent would live in Auvers-sur-Oise for only 70 days before committing suicide. The final set of paintings he would create included *Wheatfield with Crows* (see fig 4.10), which has been called his "suicide painting." The painting has an ominous feel to it. The sky is a rich purple, with crows flying off into the distance. Three pathways extend into the distance among the wheat fields, which appear to be blowing in an autumn wind. Viewers of this painting often describe it as sad, lonesome, and depressing. At the time that Vincent sends these three paintings off to his brother Theo, he also writes him a letter stating, "I almost think that these canvases will tell you what I cannot say in words."[20]

On July 27, 1890, Vincent van Gogh headed out with his painting supplies and a pistol, borrowed from a local innkeeper, which he said he was going to use to frighten away birds.[21] He shot himself in the heart, and missed. The bullet lodged inside his body. Theo was summoned from Paris the next day, and once he arrives the two brothers talk into the night. Vincent died in his brother's arms at 1:00 am on July 29, 1890, 30 hours after the self-inflicted gunshot. Vincent's suicide is nearly as popular as the ear-cutting incident. It is a somewhat romanticized, fitting end to an eccentric artist.

In 2012 Steven Naifeh and Gregory White Smith published *Van Gogh: A Life*. They raise many questions in regards to van Gogh's apparent suicide, such as what happened to the pistol, why did van Gogh not leave a note, why did he shoot himself in the chest and not the head, and why did the attending medical help conclude that van Gogh was shot at a distance rather than close up?[22] The authors also provide a *hypothetical reconstruction* of the events of that day, which centers on another individual who may have accidentally shot Vincent. Their reconstruction, based on extensive research, satisfies many of the unanswered questions left by Vincent's death.

Theo van Gogh will die six months later. It is Theo's wife, Johanna, who is owed a debt of gratitude, as she will be the one to compile a list of the artworks that Vincent created and document the letters written between the two brothers, publishing them in the early twentieth century.

Things to Consider:

His family·

Locations he lived and worked:

The time in which he painted:

His illnesses:

His death and legacy:

ENDNOTES

1. John Dorsey, "The van Gogh Legend," *Baltimore Sun*, October 25, 1998, http://articles.baltimoresun.com/1998-10-25/features/1998298006_1_gogh-red-vineyard-painting.
2. Francis Clines, "Van Gogh Sets Action Record: $39.9 million," March 31, 1987, *New York Times,* http://www.nytimes.com/1987/03/31/arts/van-gogh-sets-auction-record-39.9-million.html.
3. Rita Rief, "Van Gogh's 'Irises' Sells for $53.9 Million," *New York Times,* November 12, 1987, http://www.nytimes.com/1987/11/12/arts/van-gogh-s-irises-sells-for-53.9-million.html.
4. Suzanne Muchnic, "Van Gogh Painting Sells at Record $82.5 Million," *Los Angeles Times*, May 16, 1990. http://articles.latimes.com/1990-05-16/news/mn-262_1_van-gogh.
5. Letter to Theo van Gogh, dated Sunday, March 25, 1888, http://vangoghletters.org/vg/letters/let589/letter.html.
6. Simon Houpt, *Museum of the Missing* (New York: Sterling Publishing Company, 2006), 157.
7. Simon Houpt, *Museum of the Missing* (New York: Sterling Publishing Company, 2006), 73.
8. Cleve Wootson, "Two van Goghs Were Stolen 14 Years Ago," *Washington Post*, October 1, 2016, https://www.washingtonpost.com/news/worldviews/wp/2016/10/01/two-van-goghs-were-stolen-14-years-ago-last-week-they-were-found-in-a-drug-kingpins-safe/?utm_term=.6f6b908ff579.
9. Ingo F. Walther, ed., *Masterpieces of Western Art* (Köln, Germany: Taschen, 2002), 709.
10. "In Search of … Vincent van Gogh," accessed December 31, 2016, https://www.youtube.com/watch?v=mgVUFHHl84Q.
11. The Yellow House does not exist today. A bomb destroyed the home during World War II. The rest of the block looks exactly the same as it does in van Gogh's painting.
12. Personal interview, December 18, 2016, with Patricia Craig, a van Gogh scholar who was seen on the 2004 A&E Biography of Vincent van Gogh called *A Stroke of Genius*.
13. Personal interview, December 18, 2016, with Patricia Craig, a van Gogh scholar who was seen on the 2004 A&E Biography of Vincent van Gogh called *A Stroke of Genius*.
14. "In Search of … Vincent van Gogh," accessed December 31, 2016, https://www.youtube.com/watch?v=mgVUFHHl84Q.
15. Personal interview, December 18, 2016, with Patricia Craig, a van Gogh scholar who was seen on the 2004 A&E Biography of Vincent van Gogh called *A Stroke of Genius*.
16. "In Search of … Vincent van Gogh," accessed December 31, 2016, https://www.youtube.com/watch?v=mgVUFHHl84Q.
17. "In Search of … Vincent van Gogh," accessed December 31, 2016, https://www.youtube.com/watch?v=mgVUFHHl84Q.
18. *A&E Biography: Vincent van Gogh—A Stroke of Genius*, directed by Kathleen Callan (Los Angeles: Filmroos, Inc., 2004), DVD.
19. Letter to Theo and Johanna van Gogh, dated Saturday, May 24, 1890. http://vangoghletters.org/vg/letters/RM20/letter.html.
20. Mark Roskill, ed., *The Letters of Vincent van Gogh* (New York: Simon and Schuster, 2008), 338.
21. Steven Naifewh and Gregory White Smith, *Van Gogh: A Life* (New York: Random House, 2012), 873–876.
22. Steven Naifewh and Gregory White Smith, *Van Gogh: A Life* (New York: Random House, 2012), 867.

IMAGE CREDITS

- Fig. 24.1: Vincent van Gogh, "Self-Portrait with Straw Hat," https://commons.wikimedia.org/wiki/File:Van_Gogh_Self-Portrait_with_Straw_Hat_1887-Metropolitan.jpg. Copyright in the Public Domain.
- Fig. 24.2: Vincent van Gogh, "The Red Vineyard," https://commons.wikimedia.org/wiki/File:Red_vineyards.jpg. Copyright in the Public Domain.
- Fig. 24.3: Vincent van Gogh, "Sunflowers," https://commons.wikimedia.org/wiki/File:Vincent_Willem_van_Gogh_127.jpg. Copyright in the Public Domain.
- Fig. 24.4: Vincent van Gogh, "Irises," https://commons.wikimedia.org/wiki/File:Vincent_van_Gogh_-_Irises_(1889).jpg. Copyright in the Public Domain.
- Fig. 24.5: Vincent van Gogh, "Portrait of Dr. Gachet," https://commons.wikimedia.org/wiki/File:Portrait_of_Dr._Gachet.jpg. Copyright in the Public Domain.
- Fig. 24.6: Vincent van Gogh, "The Potato Eaters," https://commons.wikimedia.org/wiki/File:Vincent_van_Gogh_-_The_potato_eaters_-_Google_Art_Project.jpg. Copyright in the Public Domain.
- Fig. 24.7: Vincent van Gogh, "Interior of a Restaurant," https://commons.wikimedia.org/wiki/File:Van_Gogh_-_Interieur_eines_Restaurants.jpeg. Copyright in the Public Domain.

- Fig. 24.8: Vincent van Gogh, "The Yellow House," https://commons.wikimedia.org/wiki/File:Vincent_van_Gogh_-_The_yellow_house_(%60The_street%27)_-_Google_Art_Project.jpg. Copyright in the Public Domain.
- Fig. 24.9: Vincent van Gogh, "Garden of the Hospital in Arles," https://commons.wikimedia.org/wiki/File:Van_Gogh_-_Garten_des_Hospitals_in_Arles1.jpeg. Copyright in the Public Domain.
- Fig. 24.10: Raoul Saisset, "Johanna van Gogh and her son Vincent," https://commons.wikimedia.org/wiki/File:Jo_Bonger_and_son_Vincent_Willem_van_Gogh_1890.jpg. Copyright in the Public Domain.

*The numbers in parentheses indicate the chapter number where the term is found.

absolute symmetry A form of symmetrical balance where both sides of an artwork are exactly the same. (9)

abstract art Artwork where the objects are recognizable, but do not appear as they would in nature. (3)

action painting refers to specific paintings created by the Abstract Expressionist artists of the 1940s and 50s in which heightened physical/gestural movements were used. (7)

actual texture Texture that can be felt and physically experienced. (8)

additive process When two or more colors of light are mixed together to form a new color. (6) In sculpture, when objects are added upon until the desired form is achieved; includes the techniques of modeling, casting, and assemblage. (16)

afocal An artwork that lacks a specific focal point. (10)

amplified perspective Parts of objects are reduced or distorted, but still convey the illusion of three-dimensionality. (5)

analogous color scheme Colors that are next to one another on the color wheel. (6)

analytical line Type of line that is precise and controlled and based on mathematical principles. It can be easily recreated. (4)

arbitrary color Objects are represented in whatever color the artist decides. Also known as *subjective color*. (6)

Armory Show Held in New York in 1913. This was the first event that exhibited European modern art in America. (2)

Art Deco A design style during the 1920s and 1930s that was popular in both America and Europe. It is characterized by use of straight lines, 90-degree angles, and geometric shapes. (21)

Art Nouveau A design style popular during the early 1900s that is characterized by curvilinear line and organic shapes. (21)

Arts and Crafts movement Founded in England by William Morris during the nineteenth century. It is similar to the later design style of Art Nouveau because of its curvilinear line and organic shapes. The Arts and Crafts movement did not embrace modernism. (21)

asymmetrical balance The use of dissimilar objects on either side of a central axis in order to create a balanced composition. The objects must have equal visual weight or eye appeal. (9)

atmospheric perspective As objects recede into the distance, their contours become less distinct and begin to take on the color of the atmosphere. (5)

avant-garde Refers to modern artists whose works are considered to be both innovative and experimental. (23)

Bauhaus A school of art and design founded in Germany that was known for teaching an avant-garde approach to the arts rather than a traditional one. It was open from 1919 to 1933. (21)

bilateral symmetry A form of symmetrical balance where either side of an artwork is quite similar to one another, but not exact. (9)

Case Study House Project Home designs and models that were created to address the post–World War II housing shortage. The homes were designed so that they could be constructed quickly using easily gotten materials. None of these housing plans were ever mass-produced. (19)

chiaroscuro The term originates from the Italian words for "light" and "dark." It is a technique that artists use to create a seemingly three-dimensional figure or object through the gradual manipulation of value. (6)

classical line A line that is based on beauty and aesthetics, but also contains a mathematical element, such as ratios and symmetry, to the composition. (4)

coiling A technique used in the creation of ceramics where the clay is rolled into long ropelike strands and then the ends are connected and then layered one on top of the other. The sides are then smoothed. A common technique used by Native American Indians. (20)

collage Artwork created through the use of two-dimensional elements, such as newspaper, textiles, and photographs, that are then affixed to paper, wood, or canvas. (20).

complementary color scheme Colors that appear on opposite sides of the color wheel. A common example would be red and green, one cool color and one warm color. (6)

content The subject matter or narrative of an artwork. (3)

contrapposto In sculpture, where a figure is created using counterbalance, meaning that the hips and legs would be in a different position than the shoulders and head. This makes the sculpture look more life-like. Used during the Greek and Roman era and rediscovered by artists during the Italian Renaissance. (16) (22)

contour line Lines that indicate the edges of a figure or object. They also are used within the edges in order to create a sense of volume or mass. They help to create the illusion of three-dimensional space. (4)

cool colors Colors such as blue and green. These appear on one side of the color wheel, whereas warm colors appear on the opposite side. (6)

cross-hatching Lines that are set at an angle to one another. This technique is used for varying value in engravings and etchings. (4)

crystallographic balance All-over pattern. The same visual element is repeated throughout the surface of an artwork. A tessellation. (9)

curvilinear line Curved lines that are natural, organic, and flowing. Such lines are commonly found in nature. (4)

De Stijl An art style that emerged from Holland at the end of World War I. (21)

diagonal recession In one-point linear perspective, the situation where the vanishing point is *not* in the center of the artwork. (5)

emphasis by contrast When an element interrupts the overall pattern of the scene instead of continuing it. (10)

emphasis by isolation When a like element is set off by itself it garners more emphasis. (10)

emphasis by placement The person or object at the center of the composition is the most important. (10)

emphasis by scale The largest person or object tends to be the most important. (10)

en plein air Painting done in the open air, directly in front of the object being painted in order to capture perceptual/optical color. (6)

expressive line A very autographic line, as it conveys the artist's particular mood or feeling. (4)

figure Anything that can be felt, seen, or touched. Relates to two-dimensional art. (5)

focal point An area of emphasis in an artwork. (10)

form The purely visual aspects of an artwork. The way the formal elements are represented in an artwork. (3)

fresco (buon fresco) The technique of painting onto wet plaster. When the plaster dries the paint then becomes part of the wall. Used extensively during the Italian Renaissance. (15) (22)

fresco secco (fresco a secco) The technique of painting on already dried plaster. (15) (22)

frontal recession In one-point linear perspective, the situation where the vanishing point is in the middle of the artwork. (5)

frottage The technique of rubbing over a textured surface to transfer the textural qualities onto another surface, which creates visual texture. (8)

gesso A mixture of chalk and glue that is used as a priming agent on wood or canvas prior to painting. (15)

ground Short for *background*. Empty space. Relates to two-dimensional space. (5)

Happening The earliest form of performance art. (17)

hatching Lines spaced parallel to one another. Used in the creation of engravings and etchings. (4)

hieratic (hierarchical) scale A way of creating emphasis by enlarging a specific element in an artwork. (5) (10)

horizon line The line where the sky and land meet. This is an arbitrary line established by artists in the formulation of linear perspective. The line is continuous, extending past the borders of the artwork. (5)

hue Refers to the six colors that are created when white light is refracted through a prism. (6)

iconography The study of the meaning of images. (3)

imbalance When a work of art is not balanced we say that it is imbalanced. This is usually done on purpose to upset the viewer or play into their discomfort. (9)

impasto Thickly applied paint. (8)

implied line (psychic line) Lines that are invisible, but very powerful. These types of lines are "understood" and recognized and followed, although they do not physically exist. (4)

International Style A style of architecture seen in Europe during the 1920s and 1930s. It is characterized by the use of thin columns (called *pilotis*), free-floating façades, neutral colors, ribbon windows, lack of ornamentation, open floor plans, and rooftop gardens. (19)

kinetic art Art that can physically move. (7)

line of sight When individuals in an artwork are looking at a particular area or element it suggests to the viewer that this is where they should be looking as well. (4) (10)

linear perspective The most accurate way of representing the three-dimensional world on a two-dimensional surface. It is a mathematical formula where parallel lines converge on, or emerge from, a single point in the distance, the vanishing point. (5)

local color Objects that are represented in the color we know them to be. Also known as *objective color*. (6)

lost-wax casting method A technique used to create a hollow sculpture. It was first seen in the brass casting centers of Nigeria around 2500 BCE. (16)

mixed media Most commonly used to describe assemblage sculpture. Rather than listing several components of an artwork the artist can simply title the work as containing mixed media. (20)

mosaic An art medium where pieces of tile, stone, and/or glass are fitted together to form images or patterns. It's most popular usage was during the Roman Empire. (20)

multipoint perspective An artwork that utilizes three or more vanishing points. With this type of perspective, not all the vanishing points will be located on the horizon line. (5)

National Endowment for the Arts (NEA) The NEA was established by Congress in 1967. Its goal is to promote artwork in public spaces. (2)

negative space Empty space. Relates to three-dimensional space. (5)

nonobjective/nonrepresentational art Artwork where the subject matter is not recognizable. The artwork can only be defined or talked about through the formal elements. (3)

one-point linear perspective An artwork that is created using only one vanishing point. (5)

Optical Art (Op Art) A short-lived art movement from the mid-1960s where the illusion of movement was created through the manipulation of line, shape, and color. (7)

outline Lines that indicate the edges of a figure or object. They tend to be bold and stencil-like, creating a focus on two-dimensional space. (4)

overlapping Objects closer to the viewer hide parts of objects farther away. (5)

pattern A template or design motif where there is a noted repetition of visual elements. (8)

pendentives Curving wall sections placed between arches to support a dome. (18)

perceptual color Objects represented in the color they are at a particular moment in time. The Impressionists first demonstrated this theory. Also known as *optical color*. (6) (23)

photorealism a drawing or painting created in extreme detail where the image was originally derived from a photograph. (12)

Pointillism A technique created in the late 1800s where dots or points of pure color are placed next to one another (rather than mixing the two) to create a third color. (6)

positive space Anything that can be felt, seen, or touched. Relates to three-dimensional art. (5)

Prairie style A type of architectural style attributed to Frank Lloyd Wright where the home has strong horizontal elements. Frequently seen in the states of the Midwest. (19)

preliminary drawing (study) A work that allows the artist to experiment before putting something down in a more permanent media, such as paint. They might be sketches or complete full-scale drawings. (12)

primary colors The three colors from which all other colors are created: blue, yellow, and red. (6)

radial balance Artwork that radiates out from a central point. (9)

readymade Commonly manufactured items that are transformed into works of art, such as a shovel.

rectilinear line Straight lines. These are usually man-made and rarely found in nature. (4)

repetition Using the same element multiple times throughout a composition. (11)

representational art An artwork where the objects resemble those found in nature. (3)

Russian Constructivism An art style that emerged in Russia after the fall of the czarist monarchy. It is similar in appearance to the de Stijl and Art Deco styles. (21)

Salon Annual art exhibitions that showcased artworks from students who attended the École des Beaux-Arts. (2)

scale In the creation of space, objects closer to the viewer appear larger than those farther away. (5) Scale can also be used in determining relative sizes of either the artwork itself or the elements within the work. (11)

secondary colors Colors created when two primary colors are mixed together: orange, violet, and green. (6)

shade Color created when a hue is mixed with black. (6)

shell system Construction technique where one basic building material provides both the structural support as well as the outer covering for the building. (18)

site-specific Referring to sculptural installations and earthworks that are created by the artist knowing exactly where they are going to be placed. (16)

skeleton-and-skin system Construction technique where a building is constructed with a core framing device that supports its integrity. The frame is then covered or protected by another element, such as drywall, plaster, or glass. (19)

slab construction A technique used in the creation of ceramics where the clay is pounded out into a flat circular form and then the sides are brought upward usually to form a bowl or cup. (20)

streamlining A design style founded in America in the 1930s. The style revolves around curvilinear teardrop-shaped lines, which offer the least amount of air resistance. (21)

subtractive process When two or more colors of paint or pigment are mixed together, resulting in a new color. (6) In sculpture, the chipping, gouging, and hammering of an object until the desired form is achieved, carving. (16)

subversive texture A texture that undermines or subverts our thoughts and ideas about the object itself. The surface quality both attracts and repels at the same time. (8)

symmetrical balance A direct correspondence of like elements on either side of a central axis. (9)

tenebrism Dramatic illumination. (6)

tertiary colors Also known as *intermedicate colors*. Colors created when mixing a primary color with its neighboring secondary. (6)

throwing A technique used in the creation of ceramics where the clay is shaped by use of a potter's wheel. (20)

tint Color created when a hue is mixed with white. (6)

triadic color scheme Colors that are equally spaced throughout the color wheel. The two most common triadic color schemes are the primary colors and secondary colors. (6)

trompe l'oeil Translates "to fool the eye." It is the rendering of spatial qualities with incredible detail. (8)

two-point linear perspective An artwork that is created using two vanishing points. Here, objects can be seen at different angles rather than at the straight-on approach commonly seen in one-point perspective. (5)

tympanum A semicircular sculptural space positioned above doorways of medieval churches. (18)

unity An element within a composition that brings the entire work together. This might be a shape, a color, or an object. (11)

value A measurement of the lightness or darkness of a color or object. (6)

value contrast A comparison between colors or objects that contain different values. (6)

vanishing point In linear perspective, the point that all parallel lines appear to converge on or emerge from. It is an arbitrary point located on the horizon line. (5)

vertical location In two-dimensional art forms, the higher the object is placed the further recessed it is in space. (5)

visual texture An impression or suggestion of texture where none truly exists. (8)

warm colors An analogous color scheme using colors such as red and yellow. These appear on one side of the color wheel, whereas cool colors appear on the opposite side. (6)

warp Refers to the direction of threads used in the creation of textiles. These are the threads that are first positioned on the loom and are very taut. They run in a north/south direction and are the threads from which the textile should be hung/displayed by. (20)

wash Ink that has been diluted with water. (12)

weft Refers to the direction of threads used in the creation of textiles. These threads are shuttled in between the threads that are on the loom in an east-to-west direction. They have certain flexibility to them. (20)

CPSIA information can be obtained
at www.ICGtesting.com
Printed in the USA
LVHW061125210722
724004LV00004B/36

9 781634 879378